THE POLITICAL MEMOIRS OF AN INDIAN REVOLUTIONARY

Naina Singh Dhoot (1904-1989)

Naina Singh Dhoot in 1986

THE POLITICAL MEMOIRS OF AN INDIAN REVOLUTIONARY

Naina Singh Dhoot (1904-1989)

Introduction, Translation and Annotation by

SURINDER SINGH

MANOHAR
2005

First published 2005

ISBN 81-7304-633-6

Published by

Ajay Kumar Jain for
Manohar Publishers & Distributors
4753/23 Ansari Road, Daryaganj
New Delhi 110 002

Typeset at

Digigrafics
New Delhi 110 049

Printed at

Lordson Publishers Pvt. Ltd.
Delhi 110 007

Distributed in South Asia by

FOUNDATION BOOKS

4381/4, Ansari Road
Daryaganj, New Delhi 110 002
and its branches at Mumbai, Hyderabad,
Bangalore, Chennai, Kolkata

Contents

Preface 7

Introduction 13

1. Life in the Chenab Colony 63
2. Migration to Foreign Lands 86
3. The Soviet Connection 106
4. Underground in Colonial India 126
5. Involvement in Peasant Movements 149
6. Struggles of the Industrial Workers 188
7. Deoli, Okara and Amritsar 212
8. Partition and its Aftermath 236
9. Underground in Independent India 253
10. The Onward March 284

Appendix: From the Split to the Emergency 313

Bibliography 341

Index 349

Preface

In the annals of twentieth-century South Asia, the communists have played a role which has been larger than that warranted by their numbers. They exercised a tremendous influence on the content and course of the anti-imperialist struggle. Their vision went beyond the destruction of the colonial state. They uncovered the class contradictions in Indian society, brought the toiling masses – peasants and workers – to the centre of the contemporary political discourse and imparted a radical dimension to the national movement. They were instrumental in the passage of the anti-zamindari and pro-labour legislation. Displaying unprecedented sense of commitment and selfless spirit of sacrifice, they created political awakening among the lower most social layers. Yet, modern historians, by and large, have not done justice to their immense contribution. They have failed to appreciate the numerous constraints under which the communists were functioning during the colonial period. They have censured the communists for alleged sectarianism, ideological limitations, internal dissensions, dependence on the Comintern and inability to understand the character of Gandhian movements or the Congress itself. Obviously they have adjudged the communism of that phase with the yardstick of the 1970s and 1980s. Their analysis has often absorbed the colour of contemporary documentation, because colonial records betray a deep-rooted ideological bias against the communists, while the newspapers show little interest in their activities. The major communist parties, having refrained from producing authoritative versions of their growth, have failed to put the record straight. Therefore, it becomes imperative for us to seek the testimony of political participants themselves. The experiences of Naina Singh Dhoot (hereafter NSD), who remained in the thick of the communist movement for more than five decades (1936-89), assume vital relevance.

The significance of the present work can also be comprehended by a close examination of the circumstances prevailing in India today. The globalization of the Indian economy, which has been initiated by the Indian ruling elite since the 1990s under the dictates of the World Bank and the International Monetary Fund, has created serious problems for various sections of Indian society. Multinational companies have not only entered vital economic sectors like power generation, but have also penetrated the consumer goods industry. Public sector undertakings (including profit making units like the NALCO) are being privatized, even as their assets are undervalued and the proceeds diverted to meet fiscal deficit, rather than being ploughed into the infrastructure. Indigenous industries, unable to face competition from foreign capital, are closing down. Thousands of workers, failing to get relief from the new labour laws, are being pushed out of employment. The agricultural sector, thrown at the mercy of the World Trade Organization, has been dislocated. Owing to the withdrawal of subsidies and the failure of procurement agencies to lift fresh produce, debt-ridden farmers have been driven to suicide. Agricultural labourers, deprived of adequate employment and the meagre benefits of a shrinking Public Distribution System, have starved to death. The execution of mega power-projects has displaced thousands of tribals, without suitable rehabilitation. While the Indian state is spending enormous amounts on senseless militarization, it is withdrawing from essential social sectors like health and education.

The alarming rise of communal forces constitutes the greatest threat to the Indian republic. A movement built around the demand for a Ram temple at Ayodhya has catapulted the BJP to power at the centre and some states. Instead of pursuing a pro-people agenda of governance, it has consolidated the Hindu vote bank through anti-minority propaganda and anti-Pakistan war hysteria. It has systematically saffronized all areas of state activity, including the composition and functioning of professional academic bodies. RSS cadres with dubious academic credentials are being appointed as vice-chancellors of universities, directors of research institutes and governors of states. Communal riots, engineered by the Narendra Modi government in Gujarat, have deprived the Muslims of not only their lives and livelihood, but also their fundamental right of citizenship. It must be added that the communal elements among minority communities – Muslims, Christians and Sikhs – have also acquired strident postures, creating fresh problems in different parts of the country. In Punjab, the Shiromani Akali Dal government has wasted large amounts of public money on celebrating the tricentenary of the Khalsa and bicentenary of Ranjit Singh's coronation, with a view to consolidate its traditional vote bank among the Sikh peasantry and to camouflage the misdeeds of its corrupt administration under a glittering facade.

How can we emerge from this multidimensional crisis, which has been created by an indifferent state and a heartless market. The need of the hour is to develop a alternative socio-economic agenda, which is designed to provide basic amenities – health, housing, education, employment, social security and environmental protection – to the marginalized social groups. These issues have already been addressed by several social movements, which have been built for specific purposes by non-political components of the civil society. The mainstream communist parties, owing to their roots among the oppressed groups, could form a common platform with these organizations to achieve these goals. It is in this context that the experiences of NSD assume considerable significance. His political activities, spanning over a period of fifty years, were spread across the provinces of Bengal, Bihar, Uttar Pradesh and Punjab (including areas in Pakistan). He educated the urban proletariat of Calcutta (Kolkata) and Kanpur, besides leading major strikes at Jamshedpur and Amritsar. He organized powerful tenant movements in the Nili Bar, Una and the surrounding areas. Besides the construction workers of the Bhakra Dam site, he politicalized government employees, school teachers, college lecturers, paramedical staff, students and youth.

While going through the text of the memoirs, readers will do well to keep two points in mind. First, NSD was neither an armchair intellectual engaged in hair-splitting debates on

Marxian theory, nor an elected legislator excelling in scoring debating points against right wing political outfits. Nor was he a party bureaucrat, comfortably ensconced in a provincial party office, looking after party documents or editing party journals. Instead he was a grass-roots activist, who lived and worked among the toiling masses. For more than five decades, he remained in the thick of peasant struggles and working class movements. He suffered imprisonment in colonial jails or village internment, besides remaining underground for long periods. As a brilliant organizer, he played a pioneering role in building the cadre of the CPI and (after 1964) the CPM. Second, it must also be kept in mind that NSD did not receive any formal education. The only formal education that he acquired was Marxism–Leninism, which he studied (1933-6) at the University for the Toilers of the East in Moscow. Although Marxist literature was not available owing to colonial restrictions, yet he adopted self-education as a lifelong pursuit and endlessly learnt in the school of experience. During a long term of imprisonment in the Deoli Detention Camp, he preserved a meticulous record of lectures delivered by front ranking communists on various aspects of Marxism. In the post-independence period, he remained a regular subscriber of official organs of the CPI and the CPM. Because of his continuous intellectual growth, he emerged as a popular teacher of Marxism–Leninism, who attracted innumerable radical young men to his study circles. Thus, we can be certain that two factors in NSD's life – a struggle-based political activism and a lifelong pursuit of learning – have imparted a distinct character to his memoirs, which is not easily found elsewhere.

Readers are likely to be curious about the method employed in the preparation of this volume. In fact, the text passed through a number of stages before assuming the present form. To begin with, I recorded the personal experiences of NSD pertaining to the various phases of his long and eventful political career on audio cassettes. In the second stage, I listened to the recordings and prepared a typescript, translating the material from Punjabi into English. A perusal of this manuscript revealed several points that needed further elucidation. In the third stage, I made several trips to Dhoot Kalan village (Hoshiarpur district, Punjab) and stayed there for many days on each occasion. On the one hand, I secured NSD's approval of the translated version and, on the other, received clarifications on doubtful points and filled some of the gaps, with a view to achieve the maximum possible degree of objectivity and coherence in the presentation. Simultaneous with the above stages, I compared the memoirs with a wide range of secondary literature and primary sources including archival records, party documents, newspapers and interviews with the close associates of NSD. This part of the entire task has been presented in numerous explanatory notes at the end of every chapter, which are likely to benefit all categories of readers, particularly those who do not have easy access to specialized literature on the subject.

During the preparation of this volume, I was assisted by a number of individuals and institutions. I would like to place on record my gratitude to them.

This project was planned in consultation with Sukhdev S. Sohal (Amritsar) and Navtej Singh (Patiala). The constant guidance given by my senior colleagues, C.L. Datta and J.S. Dhanki, enabled me to delve into archival source materials. I received valuable support from Atlury Murali (Hyderabad) during the finalization of the manuscript. The public lectures of Randhir Singh, the veteran Marxist intellectual, filled me with fresh hopes. My dialogues with Harjeshwar Pal Singh on aspects of social theory were very fruitful. I received moral support from R.I. Malhotra, Kamlesh Mohan, Harjinder Singh Laltu, Ujjwal Kumar Singh, Ronki Ram, Supriya Varma, Ishwar Dayal Gaur and Bhupendra Yadav.

I benefited immensely from the seminal works of several scholars, whom I could not consult personally. They are Mridula Mukherjee, Bhagwan Josh, M. Mufakharul Islam, Gurharpal Singh and Vinay Bahl. Without this, it would not have been possible to place the political activities of NSD in their proper historical context.

I had long discussions with Joginder Singh, a veteran CPM activist and the librarian at the Department of Chemistry, Panjab

Universty, Chandigarh. Knowledgeable and articulate, he clarified numerous controversial issues regarding the growth of the communist movement in the Indian subcontinent.

The late Ishar Singh Sodhi, a senior CPM leader who had been actively involved in numerous peasant struggles, allowed me access to his personal collection of communist literature (including copies of the *Kirti Lehar*), which he had meticulously preserved in his humble one-room abode at the Punjab state headquarters of the CPM, Chandigarh.

Pratap Chand Dhoot, who remained intimately associated with NSD for more than fifty years, provided corroborative information on the subject of this study. Several active members of the CPM – Harbhajan Singh Ramdaspur, Beant Singh Mallewal, Gian Singh Moonak, Bachan Singh Mehatpur, Mohinder Singh Sangha, Kewal Kaloti and Nirmal Singh Ashant – who remained in close contact with NSD during some crucial phases of his political career, offered valuable inputs. Ranbir Singh Dhoot and Dalbir Singh Dhoot, NSD's sons (along with their families) extended warm hospitality during my visits to their village.

The staff members of several libraries assisted me in carrying out research in their respective institutions. These are the National Archives of India, New Delhi; the Nehru Memorial Museum & Library, New Delhi; Desh Bhagat Yadgar Hall, Jalandhar; office of the district committee of the CPM, Jalandhar; A.C. Joshi Library, Panjab University, Chandigarh; Dwarka Das Library, Chandigarh; the Institute of Development and Communication, Chandigarh; the Centre for Research in Rural and Industrial Development, Chandigarh; and Marxwadi Chetna Kendra, Baba Karam Singh Cheema Bhawan, headquarters of the Punjab state unit of the CPM, Chandigarh.

Needless to say, none of these individuals or institutions is responsible for the limitations of this volume.

SURINDER SINGH

Introduction

SOME CONTEXTUAL CONSIDERATIONS

With the consolidation of the British rule in India, the sub-continent was transformed into a colony in the true sense of the word. Its economy was integrated with the global capitalist order, in complete subordination to British colonial interests. All sections of Indian society, except the collaborators and beneficiaries of the empire, were affected. The new revenue policies led to the emergence of semi-feudal agrarian relations, where the position of the landed intermediaries was consolidated at the cost of the cultivators. Since the colonial state was primarily geared to the extraction of social surplus, the moneylenders acquired a dominant position in the agrarian economy.[1] The commercialization of agriculture increased the extent of differentiation among the peasantry, which became vulnerable to fluctuations in world agricultural prices. The unrestricted entry of machine-made goods on a massive scale led to the destruction of traditional handicrafts, while the Indian craftspersons lost access to the foreign markets. Factories and mines did offer alternative avenues of employment, but here the recruitment was controlled by contractors who exploited the illiterate workers in numerous ways. Widespread poverty was compounded by natural and man-made catastrophes like famines and epidemics. The growth of indigenous capitalist enterprises was inhibited by discriminatory tariff rules and administrative hurdles. Industrial development and technological innovations became dependent on foreign capital. The educated middle class was denied access to higher echelons of government jobs, which were monopolized by the racially arrogant colonial bureaucracy.

How did the suffering masses respond to this situation? In the nineteenth century, a number of tribes – the Santhals of Bengal, the Kols of Chhotanagpur, the Mundas of Ranchi, the Naikdas of Gujarat and the Kacha Nagas of Cachar – expressed their discontent in the form of violent rebellions. Several spontaneous and localized peasant uprisings occurred in many areas – indigo cultivators of Bengal, tenants of Pabna, farmers of Poona and Ahmadnagar and the Moplahs of Malabar – with the object of resisting their immediate oppressors and seeking the redressal of pressing economic grievances.[2] In the early part of the twentieth century, numerous young men and women, particularly those studying in colleges, adopted violent means to achieve freedom from colonial rule, giving rise to the trend of revolutionary terrorism. The bourgeois-dominated Congress mobilized large masses of common people around a broad anti-imperialist programme based on Gandhian non-violence. The communists, either acting independently or functioning within the organizational structure of the Congress, aimed at the destruction of imperialism and the building of powerful peasant and labour movements on class lines. Here we are primarily concerned with the last mentioned strand of the anti-imperialist struggle.

During the early 1920s a number of communist groups, inspired largely by the October Revolution, emerged in different parts of colonial India. Gradually assuming the common appellation of Workers and Peoples Party (WPP), these groups aimed at functioning within the Congress in a manner that it acquired a more radical orientation and mobilized the workers and peasants around their class demands. The WPPs had a strong presence in Bombay and Bengal, having organized powerful strikes of industrial workers in 1928. They developed fraternal relations with the Communist Party of Great Britain and benefited from the advice of M.N. Roy. Their members gained representation in the All India Congress Committee, provincial Congress committees and executive of the All India Trade Union Congress. Even the activists of the Communist Party of India, which was formally launched in Kanpur in 1925, but did not have any press or programme of its own, worked only through the provincial branches of the WPP.[3] Despite this fair amount of success, the WPPs decided (at the all-India conference held in 1928 and 1929) to evolve as a independent organization at the head of all revolutionary forces, terminating their alliance with the Congress which was characterized as counter-revolutionary. Before these aims could be realized, however, the WPPs were wiped out of existence.

The growth of the communist movement was obstructed because of state repression, as the imperialist government convicted prominent leaders under the Peshawar (1922-4), Kanpur (1924) and Meerut (1929-33) conspiracy cases. Over the next eight years (1934-42), the Communist Party of India and associated organizations suffered a complete ban under the Criminal Law Amendment Act of 1908. The entry of Marxist literature into the country from abroad was prohibited under the Sea Customs Act of 1878.[4] The communists themselves remained stuck in a sectarian groove from 1929 to 1935, seeking to bring the anti-imperialist struggle under the exclusive control of the CPI and, in the process, denounced the Congress as a bourgeois organization. It was only in 1935 that the CPI, having adopted the United Front line which was mooted at the seventh congress of the Comintern and which was elaborated in the Dutt–Bradley thesis, decided to join hands with the socialists and the Congress in the ongoing anti-imperialist upsurge.[5]

In Punjab, too, the October Revolution inspired several attempts at establishing communist and proto-communist centres. The *muhajirs*, who returned after studying at Tashkent and Moscow, were convicted in the Peshawar conspiracy case. After serving their sentences, some of them founded the Lahore centre as an affiliate of the CPI. In August 1922, Ghulam Husain (a teacher at the Edwards Mission College, Peshawar) began to publish the *Inquilab* from Lahore, with the active support of the Bolshevik centre at Kabul.[6] He also began to associate with the union of railway workers, while remaining in contact with M.N. Roy. In early 1926, a group of progressive young men studying in the colleges of Lahore, including Bhagat Singh, founded the Naujawan Bharat Sabha. They increased their knowledge through rigorous self-study, besides delivering lectures and publishing brief tracts on political issues for the youth of the country. Starting as revolutionary terrorists believing in direct action, they adopted the goal of a socialist revolution through mass action.[7] They collaborated with the Congress in anti-imperialist demonstrations, but developed a more meaningful relationship with the Kirtis.

The origin of the Kirti Kisan Party (KKP) can be traced to the strong anti-imperialist sentiment prevailing among Punjabi migrants, who had settled in the USA and South America. The Ghadar Party, after the failure of its first revolt (1915), began to disintegrate. At this stage, Rattan Singh and Santokh Singh made strenuous efforts to reconstruct the party around *Ghadar Di Goonj*, which was distributed to thousands of Punjabis scattered in different parts of the world. The two were deputed by the California branch of the party to attend the fourth congress of the Comintern, which was held in Moscow in the first week of November 1922. They played a crucial role in forging an alliance between the Ghadar Party and the Comintern, besides persuading the former to adopt Marxism as its ideology. They also sent a representative from the Kabul centre to the Shiromani Gurudwara Prabandhak Committee, with the suggestion of forming a Sanjhiwal Association on the lines of Tanzim and Sangathan, but which was to be recognized by the Soviet government. Rattan Singh travelled extensively in the Americas and motivated a large number of Ghadarites to study at the University for the Toilers of the East, Moscow.[8] Our understanding of this aspect of the Indian national movement – the revival of the Ghadar Party in its second incarnation, its conversion to Marxism and the nature of Marxist education in Moscow – has remained imperfect so far. Naina Singh Dhoot, who joined the Ghadar Party in Argentina at the instance of Rattan Singh and went to Moscow in 1933, provides detailed information on these little known aspects.

The communist movement in Punjab took a decisive step forward when Santokh Singh began to publish the *Kirti* in February 1926, with the financial support of the Ghadar Party. The paper propagated communist ideas in the Punjabi language (and later in Urdu as well) and simple idiom, avoiding technical Marxist jargon. Sohan Singh Josh, who wrote several articles and columns, took over as the editor of the *Kirti* after the death of Santokh Singh on 19 May 1927. The Kirti group was crystallized at meetings held in Hoshiarpur and Lyallpur in

October 1927. At a meeting held at Jallianwala Bagh on 12 April 1928, the group assumed the form of the Kirti Kisan Party which was, in fact, the Punjabi version of the Workers and Peoples Party. The programme of the KKP, as revealed in the successive issues of the *Kirti*, aimed at the annihilation of imperialism and capitalism, besides the elimination of landlordism and the establishment of small peasant holdings, paying a nominal rent.[9] Due to the dramatic fall in agricultural prices, following the Great Depression, the KKP was firmly entrenched in the central districts of Punjab. The KKP was further strengthened by the Moscow-trained Ghadarites and the establishment of contact with the Kabul centre of the Ghadar Party. Acting on the guidelines of the sixth congress of the Comintern, the KKP set itself apart from the Congress, which was perceived as a counter-revolutionary and bourgeois outfit. Its alienation from the Congress was reflected in its role at the annual session of the Congress and the third annual conference of the all-India WPP, both of which were held at Karachi at the end of March 1931. The growing influence of the KKP induced the provincial government to pass the Punjab Criminal Law (Amendment) Act in November 1932, which was strongly supported by the Unionist leader Sikandar Hayat Khan. On 10 September 1934, the KKP was declared illegal along with four other pro-communist organizations.[10]

With the assumption of office (July 1937) by a Congress ministry in the United Provinces, the Kirtis established a new communist centre at Meerut which was headed by Moscow-trained Harminder Singh Sodhi. This centre revived the publication of its weekly (under the title of the *Kirti Lehar*), received propaganda material from the National Front (the mouthpiece of the CPI headquarters at Bombay), organized communist study circles, deputed trade union activists to the industrial centres of Jamshedpur and Kanpur and established contacts with the Sikh units in the British Indian army. Meerut became the base for political operations that spread to Delhi, Dehra Dun, Lucknow, Benares, Kanpur, Bihar, Bengal and Bombay. Nearly sixty revolutionaries, belonging to different provinces, were associated with the Meerut centre.[11]

The agrarian scene in west Punjab was fundamentally altered

by the creation of canal colonies, which had opened over 7 million acres of virgin land. The colonial government, as a matter of policy, allotted these new plots to dominant sections of the rural and urban society, i.e. peasant proprietors, landed gentry and professional bourgeoisie.[12] At the same time, it deprived marginal farmers and landless poor, who were facing immense hardships in the densely populated central districts, of the opportunity of acquiring economically viable holdings in the newly-settled areas. Since the proportion of people earning their livelihood from agriculture in Punjab was 59 per cent as compared to 69 per cent in British India and the land : man ratio was favourable, there could hardly be any need for tenants in the canal colonies. In actual practice, however, there was a massive increase in the incidence of sharecropping tenancy in these areas. By the turn of the century, tenants came to occupy 53 per cent of cultivated area in the province and over the next twenty-five years another 4.3 million acres were brought under the sharecropping system.[13]

In an incisive analysis, M. Mufakharul Islam has identified the factors leading to this development. First, the size of new holdings was larger than could be cultivated with the limited resources of a single family. The grants of yeomen and capitalist farmers varied from 2 to 5 and 6 to 20 squares respectively, while the temporary lessees of the Nili Bar held 200 to 500 acres each. Second, the government policy debarred the landless rural population – agricultural labourers, subtenants and caste servitors – from acquiring land, for fear of reducing the supply of labour. Third, small proprietors from the central districts – 70 per cent of whom held less than 10 acres each – were attracted to larger holdings, where they could make optimum use of their family labour and means of production. Fourth, the crop yields were higher and more secure in the canal colonies. Fifth, agricultural operations involving canal irrigation and cotton cultivation were themselves labour intensive. Finally, the landlords preferred payment of rent in the form of produce because, having paid a part of the cost of production, they acquired a stake in the productivity of land. Since yields were increasing following the introduction of new varieties and agricultural prices were rising, a rent in produce meant an automatic increase in the share of the landlords.[14] Thus, the ground was laid for an intense conflict between the landlords and tenants.

These changes in agrarian relations were bound to have important political ramifications. On 7 March 1937, a number of peasant leaders held a meeting at Bradlaugh Hall, Lahore, and announced the formation of the Punjab Kisan Committee (PKC) which was to be affiliated to the All India Kisan Committee. They elected Baba Jwala Singh as president, B.P.L. Bedi as general secretary and Kartar Singh Gill as secretary. The first regular session of the PKC was held at Lyallpur in October 1937 under the chairmanship of Sajjad Zaheer. Of 500 delegates, 450 attended it and the number of participants varied between 15,000 and 20,000. The session elected Baba Kesar Singh as president, Baba Rur Singh as vice-president and Bhagat Singh Bilgha as general secretary for the coming year. Major demands of the PKC included cancellation of debts, assessment of land revenue on the basis of income tax, reduction in land revenue and water rates, abolition of feudal levies, tax exemption for uneconomic holdings and ownership rights for the actual tiller of the soil. The influence of the PKC spread rapidly and by the summer of 1938, 1,800 kisan committees had been set up in the province, while the total membership rose to 73,469. Identifying the most popular method of approaching the peasantry, Bhagwan Josh has noted that the PKC activists toured rural areas in groups of three to five and the local village level leaders, who had emerged as repositories of political ideas and political opinion during the Akali movement, organized the meetings in the face of hegemonic pressure of influential loyalist elements like *zaildars* and *lambardars*.[15] This understanding may be seen in comparison with the experience of Naina Singh Dhoot, who was deputed by the PKC to rebuild the muzara movement of the Nili Bar following the death of Baba Jwala Singh.

By mid-1938, intense peasant struggles were being waged in the districts of central Punjab. The long simmering sardar–muzara conflict erupted in the canal colonies with unprecedented fury. The muzaras organized strikes in the colony villages (*chaks*) in support of their demands, including the abolition of oppressive imposts, reduction in economic burdens and protection of their share in the produce. The *Kirti Lehar* regularly reported the violence inflicted on the muzaras during the harvest season by sardars and their hired goondas, who were invariably supported by the local police.[16] The weekly also carried detailed articles, written by the Moscow-trained Kirti leader Ram Singh Dutt, on the various aspects of peasant discontent and justification for the formation of the PKC. Such was the gravity of the problem that even a pro-moneylender newspaper, *The Tribune*,[17] took notice of a representation sent by the PKC to the state premier highlighting the unbearable oppression of tender holders on the muzaras of Dipalpur, Montgomery district, and sent a copy of the deed (*patta*) containing unreasonable terms, which the tender holders got executed from the muzaras, in violation of the terms declared by the government at Burewala mandi on 2 March 1938.

At this juncture, the pro-kulak Unionist government felt constrained to pay attention to the growing ferment in the rural areas, particularly the canal colonies. It admitted that the peasant movement had spread to the districts of Montgomery, Lyallpur and Amritsar, and it was threatening to spill over into Shaikhupura, Ferozepur and the princely states. In Lyallpur district, peasants from 40-50 villages agitated against the remodelling of water outlets (*mogas*) which culminated in the district level conference (11-12 July 1938) where a call was given for the boycott of canal water. In Montgomery district, muzaras in some villages ceased to work in protest against exactions of temporary lessees of government land, demanding the same concessions as had been granted to the tenants of the Nili Bar. In Amritsar district, kisan demonstrations were held to protest against a proposed increase of Rs. 4 lakh per annum in land revenue, reduction in canal outlets and such exactions as *malba*, *chowkidara*, *chahi* and local rates. In the princely state of Kalsia, peasants demanded that the land revenue be reduced to the scale prevailing in British India. The volunteers of the district kisan committees arrived in large numbers to picket the cattle fair at Chirik, which was a source of income for the government.[18]

The phenomenal intensification of the peasant movement in

Punjab during 1938 induced the colonial bureaucracy to undertake an in-depth study. It is important to examine the official perception, which was apparently formed by consolidating the inputs received from the local intelligence agencies. In its view, the ongoing agrarian agitation had been fomented by the PKC which was formed in March 1937, in pursuance of a decision of the All India Kisan Sabha arrived at the Faizpur session of the Congress. Based in Amritsar, it had branches in several districts and it claimed a membership of 75,000. Its aims corresponded with those laid down in the manifesto of the AIKS, i.e. complete freedom from economic exploitation and full economic power to peasants and workers. Its working committee represented all bodies with communist leanings, viz., the Congress Socialist Party, the Desh Bhagat Qaidi Parivar Sahayak Committee, the Riyasti Praja Mandal and the Institute of Agrarian Reforms, Ludhiana. There was increasing correspondence between the PKC and the kisan committees in central Punjab and the colony districts, indicating sound organization and coordination as well as recognition of the value of propaganda. The recognized paper of the movement was the *Kirti Lehar*, a revolutionary communist weekly published from Meerut in Urdu and Gurmukhi, which was funded by the American Ghadar Party.

Continuing in the same vein, the official report admitted that the agitators had some genuine agrarian grievances, but these had been placed along with some fraudulent demands to be exploited indiscriminately for economic, electioneering, sectarian, communal, socialist and communist reasons. The general effect of the movement was subversive. It was directed primarily to spread mass disaffection, rather than to secure redressal of grievances. Any change in the ministry was not likely to quell the agitation spearheaded by the kisan committees, since their support was drawn from over forty communists of the Sikh American Ghadar Party who had been trained in Moscow, ex-convicts of the 1914-15 conspiracy cases and disaffectd MLAs with little property or stake in the country. None of them had any honest political convictions, still less any belief in constitutional methods or the tenets of the Congress, though it suited them at present to use this organization to further immediate objects. Currently, the activists aimed at fuelling general discontent, distorting local grievances, exaggerating differences between landlords and tenants and vilifying the police as the instrument of a reactionary government. Impossible demands were made merely for the sake of bitterness which their inevitable rejection might be expected to engender. District kisan conference and local fairs were made the occasion for disseminating communist and revolutionary ideas. Further, there were strong anti-British feelings, coupled with opposition to war. The government hoped that the benefits to the peasantry of the agrarian policy of the Unionist Party may check the growing influence of the PKC, but the irresponsible nature of its leaders held out little hope of its activities becoming either useful or even reasonable.

The government admitted that the kisan committees of Ferozepur district and Kalsia state had succeeded in picketing the Chirik cattle fair, causing a loss of several thousand to the state. It also complained that the Ludhiana-based Institute of Agrarian Reforms had organized kisan schools to propagate socialism. The effort was characterized as a studied attempt to train rural communist propagandists, whose number was likely to increase in the course of the next few months.[19]

The perusal of this documentation, drawn from both official and non-official sources, confirms the existence of widespread agrarian discontent in central and western Punjab, besides the massive political mobilization of the peasantry – including small landholders and sharecroppers[20] – undertaken by the PKC during the premiership of Sikandar Hayat Khan. These developments have raised a wide array of historical issues to be explored by modern scholars. Bhagwan Josh and Master Hari Singh were the first to plough the field, which was abandoned soon after. Ian Talbot and Raghuvendra Tanwar have reconstructed the power-sharing arrangements forged by the provincial elites, drawing support from the landed gentry and religious establishments. The so-called Golden Laws were said to have strengthened the base of the Unionist Party as indicated by the large turnout of the peasantry in officially sponsored rallies. The quick decline of the party has been attributed to the unfavourable economic situation caused by the Second World

War and the revival of the Muslim League in Punjab.[21] This approach, having overlooked the agrarian discontent, offers only a partial analysis of a complex historical scenario. The PKC-led lower rung peasantry not only remained unimpressed by the Golden Laws, but also undermined the Unionist power structure through sustained militant struggles.

During the early 1930s, the ruinous impact of the Great Depression was apparent in the conditions of the Indian working class. As factories began to close down, capitalists resorted to wage cuts and retrenchment. With the closure of 50 per cent of cotton mills in Bombay, 61,000 workers were thrown out of employment. The jute mill industry dismissed 93,000 workers, reduced working hours from 54 to 45 per week and sealed 15 per cent of looms. Wages were reduced by 21 per cent in Bombay, 25 in Ahmedabad, 12.5 in Sholapur, 20 in Nagpur and 15 in Madras. Between 1930 and 1935 the number of unions doubled, the number of strikes remained the same and the number of workers involved increased by 14 per cent.[22] A three-month long strike (23 April 1934) involving 93,000 textile workers in Bombay became an exuse for the colonial government to suppress communist leadership all over the country. From the mid-1930s, a revival of international trade and increase in industrial production marked the beginning of a resurgence of the labour movement. The formation of Congress ministries (July 1937) in seven provinces raised the expectations of workers, regarding their outstanding demands. The trend was reinforced with the amalgamation of two bodies – the Red Trade Union Congress and the National Trade Union Federation – with the All India Trade Union Congress. From 1936 to 1939 the number of unions doubled, industrial disputes rose by 61 per cent and workers involved increased by 34 per cent. When the labour movement had thus advanced to a higher stage, Naina Singh Dhoot made his entry on the industrial scene.

This new phase of the labour movement was seen most clearly in Kanpur. The Mazdoor Sabha launched strikes in several textile units during July 1937, May and October 1939. The Pant ministry was forced to set up a Labour Enquiry Committee under the chairmanship of Rajendra Prasad, but the failure of mill owners to implement its recommendations prolonged the conflict. The influence of communists, who were led by R.D. Bharadwaj and S.S. Yusuf, increased tremendously as they succeeded in marginalizing the Congress Socialist Party in the Mazdoor Sabha. The agitation received consistent support from the district as well as the provincial Congress committees. The imperial bureaucracy as well as mill owners were unhappy with the Pant ministry for its failure to come down heavily against the communists.[23] The employers' association complained that red flags with communist symbols had replaced the Congress flags and class hatred was being preached openly at factory gates all over the city. It demanded that the government take active measures to check the spread of Marxist propaganda. The provincial government expressed a desire to improve the living standards of workers and refused to curb communism by coercive methods, 'even if one disliked communism as a school of thought'.[24] During several sojourns at Kanpur, Naina Singh Dhoot plunged into the ferment among industrial workers and acting in close cooperation with prominent leaders – R.D. Bhardawaj, S.S. Yusuf, Santosh Chand Kapoor and Arjun Arora – gave a militant edge to the labour movement.

Now we will turn our attention to the labour movement in Jamshedpur, where the Tata Iron and Steel Company had become a viable concern in 1927. In the 1920s a number of associated companies also went into production, e.g. Tata Foundry, Tinplate Company, Indian Steel and Wire Products Company and Agricultural Implements Company. The labour movement in this growing industrial township developed close relations with various nationalist groups during well defined successive phases. During 1920-4 it was dominated by the Swarajists, during 1924-8 by orthodox Gandhians and during 1928-37 by Subhas Chandra Bose, who encountered continuous challenges from non-Congress elements like the communists and Manick Homi.[25] During the early 1930s, the labour movement was rendered inactive as the Bose-led Jamshedpur Labour Association and the Homi-led Jamshedpur Labour Federation had been paralysed. Mangal Singh, a communist, made strenuous efforts to revive the movement with the help of Calcutta-based activists and the Kirtis. His externment from Jamshedpur in 1934 indicated that the Bihar government sought to prevent the communists from establishing a base in the city. From 1936 onwards, Prof. Abdul Bari, the Congress representative, began to organize the labour under a new body called the Tata Workers Union. In June 1938, the TISCO agreed to provide electricity in housing quarters in three years and to confer permanent status on temporary hands on the completion of one year of service. Since there could be no agreement on general production bonus and gratuity rules, labour unrest erupted in frequent demonstrations and strikes. The award of the Arbitration Board, consisting of Jawaharlal Nehru and Rajendra Prasad, failed to satisfy the workers and added to the discontent.[26] In mid-1939, strikes broke out in the Indian Steel and Wire Products as well as the Tata Foundry. On his arrival in Jamshedpur, Naina Singh Dhoot encountered an intense rivalry between the communists and socialists on the question of providing leadership to the striking workers.

Returning to the communist movement in Punjab, we encounter a schism between the KKP and the official group of the CPI, which appeared immediately after the release (November 1933) of Meerut prisoners and continued till 1952, despite numerous attempts to enforce unity from above.[27] The basis for this protracted conflict, according to a brilliant analysis by Gurharpal Singh, was located in the particularism of Ghadar–Kirti–Communism. This particularism was sustained by a cultural association with the egalitarian tradition of Sikhism, a militaristic orientation, a unique relationship with the Comintern, anti-intellectualism and an independent source of funds from the Ghadar Party. Its membership was constituted by three elements – veteran revolutionaries who had participated in the 1914-15 Ghadar uprising, Moscow-trained Ghadarites and small independent cultivators confined to the districts of Amritsar, Jalandhar, Hoshiarpur and Gurdaspur. They played a significant role in the movements spearheaded by the Punjab Riyasati Praja Mandal and the PKC. They supported the Satyapal-led progressive wing of the provincial Congress. Their primary membership in 1939-40 stood at 700. On the other hand, the Lahore centre or the official group could not assume the shape of a regional party, but remained a provincial outpost of the CPI. Its membership was confined to students, intellectuals and urban professionals. Its area of influence was limited to industrial labour and railway workmen in major cities. It supported the right wing of the provincial Congress that was led by Gopi Chand Bhargava.[28] In 1939-40 its membership stood at 80.

The unity between the KKP and the official group, which was forged (1941) at Deoli, has been rightly described as a 'shotgun marriage'. The CPI reconstituted the Provincial Committee more than once to accommodate the conflicting interests of the warring factions. But the differences continued to persist. Teja Singh Swatantra, the charismatic leader of the Ghadar-Kirtis, persisted in questioning the basic policies of the CPI on important political issues and revived his penchant for an armed uprising against the British rule, while hobnobbing with the German and Italian legations in Kabul. On behalf of the CPI, M. Gangadhar Adhikari (April 1944 and August 1945) and Ajoy Kumar Ghosh (April-November 1946) took several steps to make the Kirtis fall in line with the party's positions and thus strengthen the official group.[29] On 16 July 1947, the Swatantra-led Ghadar-Kirtis formed the short-lived Pakistan Communist Party and on 5-8 January 1948 established the Lal Communist Party which, after leading the muzara movement in the Patiala state, merged with the CPI in 1952. Though Naina Singh Dhoot was a Moscow-trained Ghadarite, he distanced himself from factional disputes. He was not only a member of the special committee formed at Deoli for the purpose of achieving unity, but also made earnest efforts to consolidate this unity after the CPI had been legalized. While remaining steadfast in his loyalty to the CPI, he maintained cordial social relations with the Kirtis.

The lifting of ban (23 July 1942) on the CPI did not signal the end of the party's troubles. The communists encountered numerous difficulties while approaching the people with their new policies, which were propagated through the newly launched fortnightly paper, *Jang-i-Azadi.* They opposed the Quit India movement and did not participate in anti-British agitations. They propagated the People's War thesis among the masses and supported the war efforts of the colonial state. They urged the youth to join the army in large numbers, farmers to grow more food and workers to produce more goods, without resorting to the drastic action of strikes. Having adopted the Adhikari Thesis at the first congress of the CPI (May 1943), they supported the demand for Pakistan as well as the Sikh homeland. They demanded the release of Congress leaders who had been imprisoned and emphasized communal harmony between Hindus and Muslims. They advocated unity between the Congress and the Muslim League, so as to forge a united national front. They even permitted some of their Muslim colleagues to join the Muslim League, with the object of bringing about a change in its political agenda. By pursuing these policies, the CPI not only distanced itself from the anti-imperialist movement, but also incurred the hostility of the Congress, the Congress Socialist Party and the Forward Bloc. Despite having secured a legal status, the membership of the CPI in Punjab increased by only 25 per cent, whereas the percentage in some other states was much higher – Kerala 243, Bengal 121 and Andhra Pradesh 54. However, it should be noted that the communists succeeded in reviving the strength of the PKC in rural areas because they took up the outstanding demands of the peasantry in the right earnest.[30] On the labour front, they succeeded in wresting control of many unions, which had earlier gone over to M.N. Roy's Indian Federation of Labour. It was in this context that the CPI assigned to Naina Singh Dhoot the task of leading the strikes of industrial workers at Okara and Amritsar during 1946-7, even as the balance of political forces was pointing towards partition.

In an extensive debate on the factors leading to the partition of the Indian subcontinent, modern scholarship has focused largely on the role of various political entities – the colonial state, the Congress and the Muslim League. It is only after the publication of a recent study by Tai Yong Tan and Gyanesh Kudaisya that attention has decisively shifted to the aftermath of partition, i.e. the rehabilitation of millions of displaced persons and the emergence of several unforeseen problems on both sides of the new boundaries. The sheer enormity of the task of resettlement was revealed by a few statistics. It has been estimated that 4.5 million Hindus and Sikhs were uprooted from their homes in West Punjab, while 5.5 million Muslims were torn from their traditional abodes and migrated to the other side. According to another estimate, property worth Rs. 1.5 billion was destroyed during the transfer of populations.[31] East Punjab had to start anew in the face of tremendous disabilities, because West Punjab retained 70 per cent of irrigated land, 55 per cent of population, 62 per cent of land area and 69 per cent of income of undivided Punjab. Hindu and Sikh landholders of West Punjab had abandoned 67 lakh acres of land out of which 43 lakh acres were irrigated, whereas the Muslims of East Punjab evacuated only 47 lakh acres of land out of which 13 lakh acres were irrigated. Given these shrinking resources, the government undertook the gigantic task of providing immediate assistance to thousands of refugees in relief camps, including land to migrant cultivators. Under the scheme of temporary allotments, each family was provided with a single plough unit, irrespective of the size of its previous holding. By 1949, Rs. 8.2 million in food subsidies and Rs. 11 million in loans for purchasing livestock had been distributed. Permanent allotments of land were made after determining the size of standard acres and evolving the procedure of graded cuts, so that by the end of 1949 the government had issued 250,000 allotment orders. The rehabilitation of mirgrant peasantry had important consequences – levelling down of large holdings, eradication of absentee landlordism, consolidation of holdings, reclamation of wastelands, massive increase in the number of tubewells and the creation of a new irrigational infrastructure.[32] This particular study, having based itself largely on official statistics, shows that the entire exercise undertaken to reconstruct the economy of East Punjab was a great success. However, it cannot be denied that this region reached a stage of economic prosperity only after paying a colossal human price in terms of large scale communal riots, widespread sexual violence against women, loot and plunder of movable property, dubious role of influential sections in collusion with the police, callousness and corruption of the state officials, etc. If these factors are overlooked or downplayed, the story of the aftermath of partition remains incomplete and unrealistic.[33]

After the retreat of British imperialism from the Indian subcontinent, the CPI was required to define its attitude to the Nehru government. At the outset, it extended active support to it, considering it essential for the gigantic task of national reconstruction which revolved around the integration of the princely states, suppression of communal strife and rehabilitation of refugees. This moderate line of loyal opposition, associated with P.C. Joshi, was attacked by a militant leftist faction led by B.T. Ranadive. Inspired by the Yugoslav communist ideologues like Zhdanov and the ongoing peasant movement in Telengana, this group called for an uncompromising struggle against the Nehru government. After the second CPI congress, which was held at Calcutta on 28 February 1948 (also attended by Naina Singh Dhoot), it was declared that the Indian bourgeoisie had aligned with the Anglo-American imperialist camp and, adopting the Telengana model, committed itself to bring about a People's Democratic Revolution after mobilizing the working class, the peasantry, petty bourgeoisie and intellectuals.[34] Having assumed the office of the general secretary of the party, B.T. Ranadive planned a massive strike and peasant uprising, coupled with guerrilla warfare and acts of sabotage. In a well coordinated retaliatory action, the Nehru government unleashed a wave of repression so that the CPI was banned in one state after the other. The communists were either jailed or forced to go underground, newspapers were suppressed and party offices were closed.

Ranadive's adventurism was challenged during a short-lived domination of Andhra based leaders, who rejected the urban bias of the People's Democratic Revolution and advocated adoption of the Chinese path.[35] In another shift (1951), the CPI postponed the pursuit of armed struggle and proposed the mobilization of anti-imperialist forces with the object of establishing people's democracy under the leadership of the CPI. While trying to fall in line with these strategic shifts, the provincial unit of the CPI in Punjab, already weakened by the defection of half of its membership to the Lal Communist Party, suffered from serious organizational problems, which were compounded by governmental repression. While several leaders had been locked up in jails, others were operating from their hideouts. Naina Singh Dhoot succeeded in evading arrest during this hazardous phase (1948-52) of his political career, when he went underground in the submontanous tract skirting the Bist Doab. Yet, he played a pioneering role in organizing the construction workers of the Bhakra Dam site and building the muzara movement of Una and, in the process, established units of the CPI for the first time.

For a period of seventeen years from the retreat of British imperialism to the split of 1964, Indian communism was plagued by perpetual internal dissensions over ideological issues. So intense were these differences that during the 1946-51 period as many as four divergent strategies were put forward, four general secretaries were appointed and two organizational purges were carried out. At the termination of an initial phase of adventurism, the CPI adopted its first ever programme at Calcutta in 1951. Rejecting both the Russian and Chinese paths, it advocated a specifically Indian revolutionary agenda. It described India as a semi-colonial country, with a government dominated by big landlords and reactionary bourgeoisie who were collaborating with British imperialism. The task of overthrowing the state was postponed, as the people were found unprepared.[36] The armed struggle in Telengana was withdrawn and preparations were made for participating in the 1952 general elections. However, the basic contentious issues – characterization of the Indian bourgeoisie, nature of the Indian state and the role of different social classes – divided Indian communism into Right, Left and Centre. The situation was confounded by the emergence of a pro-Congress trend in the CPI, which approved of the development of heavy industry in the public sector, economic cooperation with the Soviet Union and Nehru's foreign policy – all reinforced by the visits of Khrushchev and Chou En-lai. In fact, the fifth party congress at Amritsar (6-13 April 1958) proposed a peaceful transition to socialism through parliamentary means,[37] while the sixth congress at Vijayawada (7-16 April 1961) adopted a policy of struggle and unity *vis-à-vis* the Congress. The long-standing unresolved differences, intensified by the Sino-Soviet ideological dispute and the Indo-China war, induced the Right and Left factions to formalize their split into the CPI and the CPI (Marxist) or CPM.

Like the united CPI at the national level, the communist movement in Punjab was plagued by internal dissensions for a long time. Apart from the familiar ideological cleavages – Right, Left and Centre – there were some contentious problems that were specific to Punjab. It is true that the Lal Communist Party, which enjoyed the support of over half of the communist membership of the province, had returned to the parent fold in 1953. The event in itself did not galvanize the party factions into any unified conduct. The emergence of Harkishan Singh Surjeet at the helm of affairs, in place of the older urban leadership, enabled the Left to consolidate its position in the organizational structure.[38] But a determined Right, encouraged by active support from the CPI centre, continued to offer opposition. Fresh differences arose over the demands for the Punjabi suba, the regional formula, betterment levy and civil liberties. The Left was inclined towards the Shiromani Akali Dal, while the Right supported the Congress on these important issues. The repeated efforts made by Ajoy Kumar Ghosh to bridge the widening gulf did not materialize. Matters came to a head with the Sino-Indian border conflict and the arrest of the Left leaders. On 28 November 1962, the Right took charge of the provincial secretariat in a virtual coup. In early 1963, Teja Singh Swatantra, the charismatic leader of the Lal Communist Party who had been underground since 1948, emerged on the political stage and threw his weight behind the Right. On 20-21 May 1964, the Left retaliated by announcing its distinct identity. In separate conferences held in October and November 1964, the split was formalized in Punjab, a month before it was done at the national level. It has rightly been pointed out that the split restored the familiar dualism that had characterized long phases of Punjab communism – Ghadar Kirtis and Lahore Centre, Ghadar Kirtis and Official Group, CPI and LCP.[39]

In its new incarnation, the CPI viewed the Indian state as an organ of class rule of the nationalist bourgeoisie as a whole. The emergence of a bourgeois democratic state was an advance over the former imperialist bureaucratic rule. Indian capitalist growth, having proceeded along an independent path, had strengthened the economic base of nationalism. Only the big bourgeoisie, monopolist groups and feudal circles were the reactionary elements. Before embarking on the road to socialism, it was necessary to create a national democratic state through a national democratic front consisting of the working class, the peasantry including rich peasants and agricultural labourers, the intelligentsia and non-monopolist bourgeoisie. In this transitional stage, power would be jointly exercised by all classes to eliminate feudal, monopolist and imperial interests. Parliamentary democracy was to be strengthened as a forum for voicing the aspirations for peace, land reforms, working class rights and curbs on monopolies. But extra-parliamentary struggles were useful for changing parliamentary policies in favour of the masses. Contradictions were apparent in the Congress between the anti-people forces dominating the government and the party's mass base. A programmatic cooperation with the progressive leaders of this mass base was needed. The progressive measures initiated by Indira Gandhi – nationalization of private banks, abolition of privy purses for erstwhile princes and the Indo-Soviet Treaty of 1971 – were a step in the direction of the party's strategic goals.[40] As a logical culmination of this understanding, the CPI went on to support even the controversial emergency.

The programme of the CPM viewed the Indian state as being controlled by an alliance of the big bourgeoise and the big landlords. Capitalist development, while strengthening the monopolists, had enabled the penetration of foreign capital, increasing India's dependence on imperialist economic aid. The Indian revolution was at the agrarian stage, which was directed not only against the landlords and imperialists, but also against the Indian bourgeoisie. The immediate aim was to construct people's democracy, which would be a coalition of all democratic, anti-feudal and anti-capitalist forces. People's democracy was to be achieved by a people's democratic front, which would be constructed from below by organizing mass struggles of trade unions, peasants and other mass organizations. It was not possible to introduce fundamental structural changes in

Indian society by parliamentary means. Yet the formation of state governments through the electoral process strengthened the struggle of masses against the anti-people policies of the centre and solved a few of the local problems. Though the party was committed to a socialist transformation through a combination of parliamentary and extra-parliamentary forms of struggle, it warned the revolutionary forces to be prepared for the use of violence by the reactionary classes. It ruled out any alliance with the Congress which, despite subjective good intentions of some of its leaders, was dominated by reactionary elements. It did not believe that the Congress under Indira Gandhi reflected a leftward shift in the balance of social forces. At its ninth party congress held at Cochin in 1972, it declared that the so-called progressive measures – nationalization of banks and abolition of privy purses – were deceptive and hollow, designed only to serve the interests of the bourgeois-landlord state. It envisaged the Indian union as a federation based on democratic centralism, with all the states enjoying real autonomy and equal power.[41]

In 1969, the Communist Party of India (Marxist-Leninist), popularly known as the Naxalite movement, was formally launched under the leadership of Charu Majumdar. Its emergence may be traced to widespread agrarian discontent among the poor peasantry, a massive increase in the number of students in higher education and violent clashes between the peasants and police in the Naxalbari area of Siliguri subdivision (Darjeeling district, West Bengal). The Naxalites perceived India as a semi-feudal and semi-colonial country, the Indian state as fascist, the big bourgeoisie as comprador and the CPM as a revisionist party. They advocated the annihilation of class enemies through guerrilla warfare, so as to liberate rural areas from the clutches of landlords on the lines of the Chinese revolution. With the exodus of an estimated 17,850 Maoists from the CPM to the new outfit, the movement spread to such other states as Bihar, Orissa, Andhra Pradesh, Uttar Pradesh and Punjab. The movement was plagued by serious internal dissensions over aims and tactics, so that it splintered into scores of small fragments.[42] Since the heady days of 1969-72, the movement has undergone important transformations. Its appeal to urban intellectuals and reliance on urban middle class leaders has declined. It has taken root in specific regions of the countryside, where local leaders are drawn from the most oppressed groups such as tribals, landless labourers and poor peasants. In the 1980s, the movement was most vibrant in Bihar, Andhra Pradesh and the thickly forested regions of Madhya Pradesh, which has the highest percentage of tribals. In 1983, there were 35 to 40 Naxalite groups with nearly 35,000 members.[43]

During the late 1960s and the early 1970s, the Naxalite movement emerged and spread in Punjab. It offered new methods of achieving socialist reconstruction to the youth, particularly those studying in colleges and universities. After a brief initial phase of mass struggle, the Naxalites began to carry out annihilations in the districts of Jalandhar, Kapurthala and Sangrur. Their victims included landlords, factory owners, moneylenders, police informers, policemen and government officials. These activities were ruthlessly suppressed by the state machinery during the chief ministership of Prakash Singh Badal. Following the death of Charu Majumdar in 1972, the annihilation line was withdrawn and an agitational approach was adopted under the influence of the Nagi Reddy group, leading to the revival of the Punjab Students Union.[44] Even as the movement began to suffer from repeated fragmentation, the various emerging factions continued to employ this approach to organize popular struggles up to 1981. It must be noted that the CPM cadre of Punjab had a hard time grappling with the multi-dimensional challenge posed by Naxalism.

PERCEPTIONS OF THE PARTICIPANTS

In the following segment, we will analyse the writings of four veteran communist leaders – Gurcharan Singh Sahnsara, Bhagat Singh Bilgha, Chain Singh Chain and Sohan Singh Josh. There is a remarkable similarity in their social backgrounds and political careers. All of them belonged to the class of small peasantry, based in the central districts of colonial Punjab. Owing to general poverty and lack of resources, they received little formal education. They learnt the realities of life from the school of experience. They entered the political arena at a young age and played long innings. They fought against British imperialism, participated in peasant movements and served several terms in prison. They played a significant role in the emergence and growth of the communist movement in South Asia, and more so in undivided Punjab. They had strong reservations about the interpretations of the freedom struggle and communist movement, as reconstructed by the English-speaking university-based modern historians. They felt constrained to record their personal experiences of political life so as to meet the inadequacies of professional historiography pertaining to a momentous past. Since these writings (except the autobiography of Sohan Singh Josh) were produced in Punjabi, they remained inaccessible to a substantial number of interested readers. The following exercise, it is hoped, will familiarize a larger readership with the content of a distinct category of historical documentation. In addition, it is likely to complete the contextual backdrop, so essential for traversing the twentieth century through the political memoirs of Naina Singh Dhoot.

Gurcharan Singh Sahnsara's book *Oh Vi Din San* (Those Too were the Days) was published in 1973. Presented in the form of short stories, which are essentially autobiographical in character, the book illuminates some important dimensions of the communist movement in undivided Punjab. The author asserts that the KKP played a far greater role in the anti-imperialist struggle than was warranted by its small size. According to him, the party spread the message of the Congress deep into the villages of Punjab, propagated socialist ideas among the toiling masses of the province and led numerous struggles of peasants and workers against their oppressors. He treats his book as a small part of a future comprehensive study, which alone could recapitulate the tremendous contribution of the Kirtis. His narration is packed with suspense and sensation, while his language is spontaneous and colloquial. His rustic sense of humour is apparent even when he is describing dangerous enterprises, involving the fear of death.

Sahnsara's numerous journeys through the trans-Indus lands (in the guise of a Chachhi Pathan) enables him to provide a vivid description of the rugged terrain comprising mountains, ravines, valleys and passes, besides the routes and tracks that criss-crossed an inhospitable region. He lifts the veil from the secret network which had been established by the KKP, exploiting the anti-British sentiments of Afghan tribals, so as to send men and messages to the Soviet Union via Kabul and Transoxiana. He throws fresh light on the underground activities of the KKP, with reference to the publication of Marxist literature – the *Kirti,* the *Lal Dhandora* and the *Lal Jhanda* – by hoodwinking the British intelligence. He exposes the inhuman treatment of Indian revolutionaries in colonial jails at Amritsar, Lahore, Campbellpur and Attock. The prisons were overcrowded, accommodating more than double of their prescribed capacity. Not only was it hot and humid inside, but also there was no protection against wind and rain. Sometimes the detenus were taken from one place to another in cage-like rail coaches. At other times, they were driven like flocks of cattle over long distances, with their hands and feet chained, so that their flesh got torn and blood started flowing.[45] Several restrictions were imposed on the prisoners, which were devised by cruel daroghas like Gokul Chand who was conferred the title of Rai Sahib by the British. Special equipment was installed to inflict torture. Food was contaminated with sand, while medical facilities were absent. Newspapers and letters could be smuggled inside the prison only by paying bribes. The presence of Ghadarite stalwarts and revolutionaries like Bhagat Singh sustained the morale of the prisoners. Lectures on class struggle and socialist revolution, delivered by communists like Feroze Din Mansur, rejuvenated the sagging spirits of the inmates. Their only weapon was hunger strike, which was used as a last resort, to secure some measure of basic human dignity. They found some solace in meetings with relatives, which were arranged through the efforts of the Desh Bhagat Parivar Sahayak Committee.

Sahnsara's observations on the escape of Subhas Chandra Bose and related developments in Kabul deserve a closer examination. He asserts that the Kirtis supported Bose in his conflict with Gandhi and played a major role in his election as the Congress president (1939), yet they suspected Bose's commitment to the Left owing to his lack of faith in class struggle and support to a pro-Tata labour union at Jamshedpur. They assisted in his escape to Moscow on the condition that he would study the construction of socialism. Since he arrived in Punjab only after the departure of Ram Krishan and Achhar Singh Chhina for the Soviet Union, he was not welcomed by the Kirtis who were forced to choose Bhagat Ram Talwar – a raw communist – as his escort. The Kirtis' fears regarding Bose were confirmed when he ultimately left Moscow for Berlin. However, the Kirtis neutralized the impact of this betrayal by using their newly established contact with the fascists at Kabul. Talwar extracted strategic information from them which was passed on to the Russians. Simultaneously, the Kirtis misinformed the fascists about British power on the eastern coast, preventing a Japanese assault on that front. They also forewarned the Russians about a German plan of attacking Moscow from the south. In this manner, the Kirtis claimed to have changed the course of the Second World War by a clever manipulation of their contact with the fascists at Kabul.[46] It is another story that the German money extracted by Talwar, which was concealed at the Kirti hideout at Kot Saundha, fell into the hands of the police during the final raids.

Sahnsara expresses deep concern about the organizational aspects of the communist movement in Punjab. He would have us believe that the Kirtis were quite keen to be united with the so-called official group, but these efforts were scuttled by Sohan Singh Josh. He accuses the national CPI leadership of being partisan in its support to Josh, who had his eyes on the Ghadar funds. It was in pursuit of unity that the Kirtis sent Ram Krishan to Moscow with the necessary documents. For the same purpose, the Kirtis sought the assistance of Moscow-based Rattan Singh. Their communication with Moscow became difficult when the British removed Amanullah Khan from Kabul. The ground for unity between the KKP and the provincial unit of the CPI, which was forged at Deoli, was prepared by Teja Singh Swatantra who wrote persuasive letters to the Kirtis from Campbellpur jail. In fact, the Kirtis had formed joint committees even before receiving directions from Deoli.

It is not surprising that Sahnsara should have indentified the causes of the final police crackdown on the KKP. He observes that when the experienced Kirti leaders had been jailed, the new ones were too immature to comprehend the intricacies of underground political work and the counter operations by intelligence agents. Though Dulla Singh had been trained in Moscow, he failed to fulfil the crucial task of carrying cash and fell into the trap of a seemingly sympathetic CID inspector Hans Raj. More importantly, Sahnsara accuses Harbans Singh Karnana and Chain Singh Chain, who had been arrested from the Lahore headquarters of the KKP, of failing to bear even one police blow and of revealing all the secrets just like Harminder Singh Sodhi. This episode was followed by a series of raids and arrests,[47] which dealt a serious blow (1942) to the KKP.

Published in 1989 Bhagat Singh Bilgha's book, *Ghadar Lehar Dey Anfoley Varkey* (Unturned Pages of the Ghadar Movement) seeks to reconstruct the historical role of the Ghadar Party and the KKP from 1908 to 1952. In conformity with the title, the author presents the subject in nearly 125 short pieces of two to five pages each. Apart from relying on his own memory, he has utilized some other sources – newspapers, official reports and statements of contemporaries – without however making a specific mention. He begins by exposing the exploitative character of the colonial rule, which led to a severe crisis in the agrarian economy of Punjab, forcing small peasants to migrate to various Asian and African countries. Incensed by the discriminatory immigration laws and strong racial sentiments, the Punjabi migrants formed the Ghadar Party. It aimed at overthrowing the British rule in India by inciting the Indian soldiers to mutiny. The colonial government, however, laid its hands on the secrets of the proposed rebellion (1914-15) and crushed it by clamping five conspiracy cases. Yet the movement succeeded in establishing its branches in China, Malaysia, Singapore, the Philippines and Burma.

Bilgha, who served as the general secretary of the Argentine branch of the Ghadar Party, describes its activities in South and Central America from personal knowledge. He highlights the heroic exploits and tremendous sacrifices of the Ghadarites who suffered unspeakable atrocities, long-term imprisonment and death sentence. In this context, he quotes from the memoirs of Baba Jwala Singh describing the pitiable conditions prevailing in Montgomery jail. Bilgha alleges that Lala Lajpat Rai had misappropriated $3,500, which he had received from the headquarters of the Ghadar Party at San Francisco. The money, according to him, was earmarked for the legal defence of Bhai Parmanand and his associates, but Lala Lajpat Rai invested it first in the sugar industry of Cuba and later in constructing Lajpat Rai Bhawan at Lahore.[48]

Bilgha shows that the Ghadar movement did not perish as a result of imperialist repression. In fact, it emerged again (1926) in the incarnation of the KKP, which played a crucial role in Punjab during the second quarter of the twentieth century. The major difference was that it had decisively adopted the goal of socialist revolution on the principles of Marxism-Leninism. M.N. Roy had played a dubious role by advocating impractical views on the nature of Indian revolution, by sending wrong reports to the Comintern regarding the strength of Indian communists and by disapproving of all genuine revolutionaries who were opposed to his leadership. Due to Rattan Singh's ceaseless efforts, the Ghadar Party established independent contact with the Comintern and motivated the Ghadarites to study at the Eastern University, Moscow. The KKP led the militant struggles of muzaras in the Nili Bar, Gurdaspur, Kangra, Ferozepur and Kalsia. The party remained in the forefront of mass agitations, which were organized by the Punjab Kisan Committee, the Riyasati Praja Mandal and the State Peoples Conference. However, these important political activities of the KKP were not reported by the CPI to the Communist Party of Great Britain for onward transmission to the Comintern. The KKP fulfilled an outstanding need of the Punjabi youth by bringing out the weeklies – *Kirti* and *Kirti Lehar* – when there was a great dearth of Marxist literature, which was invariably confiscated by the colonial government. Contemporary scholars, who were surrounded by heaps of books on Marxism, have done great injustice by employing the critical standards of the 1980s to evaluate the writings of the early communists of Punjab.

It is true that the KKP disagreed with the Congress on such issues as the death sentence of Bhagat Singh and his associates, the Gandhi–Irwin Pact and rural indebtedness. Yet, it cooperated with the Congress when the United Front was formed to fight the menace of fascism. In 1937, the KKP participated in joint conferences held at Mahilpur, Garhdiwala, Sarhali and Cheema Kalan. In the 1938 elections to the Punjab Congress, the Kirtis won a majority of offices at the district and provincial levels. The progressive faction of the Congress, led by Dr Satyapal and supported by socialists and the Naujawan Bharat Sabha, came to the helm of affairs. The Congress programme acquired a radical character when 76 resolutions on pressing economic issues, prepared in accordance with a fortnightly plan, were sent from Jalandhar to the Congress headquarters at Allahabad. Alarmed at the turn of events, the central leadership of the Congress directed its Punjab body to abandon the economic agenda and to concentrate on spinning cotton yarn, wearing khadi and cleaning Harijan localities. In early 1939, the provincial Congress committee was dissolved and was replaced by an ad hoc committee under the right wing leader, Gopi Chand Bhargava.[49]

Bilgha explains the persistence of conflict between the KKP and the official (Josh) group of the CPI, despite the unity achieved at Deoli. After their release from Campbellpur and Gujarat jails, six communist leaders – Bilgha, Teja Singh Swatantra, Achhar Singh Chhina, Feroze Din Mansur, Fazl Ilahi Qurban and Karam Singh Maan – began to work among the people, explaining the CPI stance on the People's War and self-determination for minorities. On the other hand, Sohan Singh Josh and Iqbal Singh Hundal remained confined to the state secretariat of the party and failed to appreciate the revolutionary work done overground or contact comrades who were active underground. The official group, having little presence in Punjab, did not have the capacity to absorb the powerful organization of the KKP. Instead, it began to find fault with the functioning of the Kirtis and sent distorted reports of their activities to the central leadership of the CPI. It adopted an overbearing attitude towards the Kirtis and imposed humiliating conditions for their entry into the CPI.[50] The opposition of the KKP to the Adhikari thesis on the 'Right of Self Determination to the Minorities' proved to be the last straw on the camel's back. In January 1948, the KKP re-emerged as the Lal

Communsit Party, which led the muzara movement in PEPSU.

Chain Singh Chain joined the KKP in 1937 and became the secretary of the Jalandhar district committee in 1938. He served as a member of the KKP politburo from June 1940 to 26 February 1942 and as general secretary from 10 April to 31 December 1941. His personal knowledge as a member of the decision-making bodies of the organization, coupled with his access to the party documents, qualifies him to wield his pen with authority. His book entitled *Kirti Party Dooji Sansar Jang Samey* (Kirti Party During the Second World War) consists of two unequal parts. The first one constitutes a report submitted by the author to Dr G. Adhikari, with the object of familiarizing the CPI with the political activities of the KKP. The second and longer portion of the book seeks to answer the questions raised by Bhagwan Josh regarding the internal structure of the KKP, the differences between the KKP and the CPI, the failure to establish unity between the two organizations and the court martial of soldiers who mutinied under the Kirti influence.[51] While attempting this, Chain claims to have utilized such diverse source materials (besides the report in the first part) as circulars of the KKP, issues of the *Lal Jhanda*, written statements of nearly a hundred activists, official records available at the India Office Library (London) and the National Archives of India (New Delhi).

Chain's report to Adhikari is, in fact, a comprehensive response to an open letter dated 19 June 1943, which was circulated by the CPI politburo among the communists of Punjab. In a bid to dispel the ignorance of the national leadership of the CPI, Chain highlights the involvement of the KKP among peasants, industrial workers, youth, women and tribals. Efforts were made to educate the masses in Marxism by circulating such publications as the *Kirti* and the *Lal Jhanda*. Over a hundred study circles were secretly organized in villages, where selected participants were given lectures on the various aspects of Marxism. Seven district committees had their own equipment for printing the required material. Eight district committees had raised nearly 500 guerrillas who distributed newspapers and posters, wrote slogans on walls and acted as guards at secret meetings. The KKP launched a sustained campaign for the release of Deoli detenus. The unity between the KKP and the CPI materialized owing to the groundwork done by the Kirtis and not to instructions from Deoli. It was Teja Singh Swatantra, then imprisoned in Campbellpur jail, who convinced the Kirtis that the National Front was the real CPI. However, the Josh-led official group misinformed the national leadership of the CPI about the activities of the KKP, frustrating the emergence of a unified party.

Chain claims that a substantial part of the report was accepted (in a plenum held at Baghbanpura on 8-10 May 1944) by Adhikari who tried to amend the earlier mistakes committed by the CPI in dealing with the KKP.[52] However, according to Chain, unity could have been consolidated if Adhikari had reconstituted the Provincial Organizing Committee by including members of the existing body who had been active outside jail, rather than the recently released detenus of Campbellpur and Gujarat jails who were ignorant of the prevailing ground realities.

Divided into fifteen chapters, the second portion of Chain's book highlights the activities of the KKP over a period of twenty-five months (1940-2). As opposed to the Josh group, which was paralysed owing to the imperialist onslaught of June 1940, the work of the KKP was placed in the mould of a true communist organization. The leadership was provided by a secretariat consisting of Gurcharan Singh Sahnsara, Harbans Singh Karnana and Chain Singh Chain, besides a twenty-five member provincial committee. Acting on the principle of democratic centralization, the KKP maintained contact with the district committees through regular circulars and the district committees in turn sent monthly reports about the work done in their areas. The provincial committee established a small library to circulate relevant books among the district level leadership. Two thousand copies of the *Lal Jhanda*, printed secretly at Kot Saundha (Shaikhupura district), were distributed through a unique conveyer belt arrangement. Conferences were organized in support of Deoli hunger strikers and similar strikes were motivated in Montgomery and Campbellpur jails. Methods of underground work were perfected so as to evade arrest and befuddle the intelligence agencies.

The KKP organized mass struggles around agrarian issues. Following the election of office-bearers to the PKC on 23 March 1937, its units were formed in the central districts of the Province. Within a year, there were 1,800 primary kisan committees with a membership of 73,496. Peasants were mobilized for kisan morchas held at Amritsar, Lahore and Chirik (Kalsia state). In Jalandhar district, an agitation was launched for laying a canal in the Doaba region. The muzara movements in the Nili Bar and Kangra were intensified. The provincial conference of the PKC, held at Fatehgarh Kortana in Ferozepur district (21-23 September 1941), was a historic landmark.[53] Several women activists – Sushila Kumari, Shakuntala Sharda, Urmila, Sarla Sharma, Usha and Dhan Kaur – plunged into the political field. Cells were created in the north-western tribal areas, so that Kabul continued to serve as a conduit between the Punjab communists and the Soviet Union. With the publication of the *Kirti Lehar* from Meerut, anti-imperialist propaganda penetrated army units, resulting in mutinies in the Royal Indian Army Service Corps (Motor Transport), the Central Indian Horse (Risala No. 21) and 3/1 Punjab Regiment.

Chain joins issue with Sahnsara on various aspects of Bose's exit from Kabul. He asserts that the Kirtis did not charge Bose with national chauvinism, as they were fully aware of his political ideas. Talwar was chosen as an escort because of his knowledge of the topography and language of Afghanistan. Bose and Talwar could not be held responsible for the ultimate outcome of the episode. It was the failure of the Soviet ambassador to give a timely response to Bose that forced the latter to turn to the Germans. At that time, Moscow could not afford to offend Britain by inviting Bose in view of the impending fascist invasion. Bose visited the German embassy with the concurrence of Talwar. It was with the knowledge of the Soviet embassy that the Kirtis established contact with the German and Italian missions, which had been opened during the Bose episode. The KKP and the Forward Bloc, having entered into a formal agreement, sent Harminder Singh Sodhi and Shantimoy Ganguly to Kabul with the object of acquiring training in explosives from the Germans and Italians. Though the plan did not materialize, the Kirtis managed to secure funds and weapons from fascist sources, which were passed on either to their Afghan associates or the Soviets, retaining only a negligible part for themselves.[54]

The autobiography of Sohan Singh Josh (1898-1982) which was published in 1991, records his experiences as a participant in the anti-imperialist struggle as well as a prominent leader of the communist movement in Punjab. Born in a debt-ridden family of Chetanpura village (Amritsar district), he faced tremendous hardship during his childhood. Having passed Matriculation and F.A. examinations as a private candidate, he took up various jobs – an electrician at Hubli, a clerk in the censor office at Bombay, a soldier in the British Indian army and a school teacher at Majitha village. During the early 1920s, he plunged into the Akali movement for liberating gurdwaras from the control of mahants and participated in agitations for gurudwara Rakabganj and the keys of the Golden Temple. During his internment at Lyallpur, Montgomery and Multan, he observed the inhuman conditions – overcrowding, substandard food, hard labour, lack of privacy and basic amenities, snakes and scorpions, besides atrocities at the hands of darogha Gokul Chand. He was disillusioned with the Akalis as they were obscurantist in social outlook and short-sighted in political aims. After studying T. Sprading's book, *Liberty and the Great Libertarians*, he decided to join the larger struggle for India's independence. This book also served as a bridge for his passage to Marxism.[55]

Josh's initiation into Marxism began in early 1927 when he became the editor of the *Kirti*. He characterizes his writings as progressive and leftist but not Marxist because, at this stage, his ideas on the subject were half-baked. On 12 April 1928, he was appointed the general secretary of the newly formed KKP. At the same time, he founded the Naujawan Bharat Sabha in association with Bhagat Singh's group, with the purpose of mobilizing the youth. On 21 December 1928, he presided over the Calcutta session of the Workers and Peoples Party, which came down heavily against Gandhian trusteeship, the Nehru report and the reactionary leadership of the working class. In his view, the national movement underwent radicalization owing to the Chinese revolution, the Indian visit of Shapurji

Saklatwala and Nehru's participation in the Brussels conference (1927) of the Anti Imperialist League and his visit to the Soviet Union. Josh was one of the thirty-two communists who were tried in the famous Meerut Conspiracy Case, which implanted Marxism in the minds of the Indian masses.[56]

Since Josh was the undisputed leader of the official group of the CPI in Punjab, it is imperative to consider his complaint against the KKP. In his view, the Kirtis manifested political bankruptcy in failing to understand the significance of the Meerut Conspiracy Case and the great achievement of the accused in placing Marxism in the contemporary political discourse. The Kirtis did not contact those implicated, either during the trial or later in jail. They did not care to inquire about the well-being of the families of the Meerut prisoners. They did not welcome Josh and Abdul Majid when they were released (November 1933) after being incarcerated for almost five years. They ousted Bhag Singh Canadian from the Kirti management and replaced him by Santa Singh Gandiwind, who was not only illiterate, but also politically ignorant. The communist movement was in shambles, as both the KKP and the Naujawan Bharat Sabha had split into two factions each. There were serious differences in the KKP over the utilization of funds. The intelligence agencies had succeeded in planting their agent Parumal (sub-inspector Ghulam Muhammad) as the editor of the *Kirti* (Urdu) in place of Feroze Din Mansur.[57] The Kirtis had misguided the Moscow trainees into believing that the KKP was the Punjab unit of the CPI, whereas in reality the KKP did not represent the CPI. The Moscow trainees had fallen in line with the Kirtis in opposing the official unit of the CPI in Punjab. The Kirtis hoped that with the arrival of Moscow trainees and abundant Ghadar Party funds, they would be able to wipe out the official unit.

Continuing in the same vein, Josh alleges that the Kirtis were apprehensive about the success of his Anti Imperialist League and initiated several moves to liquidate the official unit of the CPI. The Kirtis wrongly accused Karam Singh Maan of being a CID agent, who was responsible for the arrest (June 1937) of Baba Gurmukh Singh. This episode forced the Josh group to align with the Gopi Chand Bhargava faction in the provincial Congress committee and, thus, endeavour to defeat the Dr Satyapal faction, which enjoyed the support of the KKP and the CSP. Sahnsara's claim of the KKP's efforts for unity was unreliable, because the KKP had made repeated requests to the Comintern for recognition as the genuine CPI. The Kirtis failed to understand that the KKP could not become affiliated to the Comintern over the head of the Communist Party of Great Britain. They wasted the funds of the Ghadar Party as well as the precious life of Ram Krishan B.A. National in this wild goose chase. They agreed to unite with the CPI only when they realized the strength of the CPI at Deoli and talked to leaders like S.V. Ghate, B.T. Ranadive, S.A. Dange and Z.A. Ahmad. Three Kirti leaders – Gurcharan Singh Sahnsara, Dalip Singh Jauhal and Bachan Singh Mehatpur – played a key role in keeping the two factions separate and creating the illusion that they could liquidate the official unit of the CPI in Punjab.[58]

In the remaining part of the autobiography, Josh narrates his political activities from 1937 to independence and partition. In the 1937 elections, he was elected on the CPI ticket from Tarn Taran, though four communists were elected on the Congress ticket. He was involved in a major peasant agitation (kisan morcha), launched from Lahore and Amritsar, against the Unionist government's proposal to increase the tax burdens. In June 1940, he was sent to the Deoli Detention Camp along with hundreds of communists who had launched an anti-recruitment campaign. He identifies three episodes of Deoli as important – the merger of the KKP with the CPI, the hunger strike and Jayaprakash Narayan's secret letter. According to him, Dange and Ranadive were responsible for giving formal shape to the line adopted by the CPI when Hitler invaded the Soviet Union. On his release, Josh revived the party office at Lahore and began to mobilize support for the war effort, in the face of slanderous opposition from the Congress, the CSP and the Akalis. He became the chief editor of a new Punjabi weekly, the *Jang-i-Azadi*, which propagated the changed position of the CPI on war. He attaches considerable importance to the first ever conference of the CPI at Bombay (May-June 1943) and the historic correspondence between Gandhi and P.C. Joshi on the policies and working of the CPI.

THE POLITICAL JOURNEY OF A REVOLUTIONARY

Naina Singh Dhoot was born in 1904 at Dhoot Kalan, a village in Hoshiarpur district of Punjab. During the colonial period, the village formed a part of the Bhunga pocket in the princely state of Kapurthala. Since the small ancestral landholding did not yield adequate returns, the family migrated to the Chenab Colony in west Punjab and settled as tenants on the extensive farms owned by big landlords. Though the immediate needs of the family were met, life became miserable due to the oppression of sardars. The young NSD, who did not receive any formal schooling, was deeply influenced by the widespread sardar-muzara conflict. Before he could come to terms with the inequities of the existing agrarian relations, his brothers and cousins died in the plague of 1917-18. In these distressing circumstances, his family returned to Dhoot Kalan. He lost his father when the family was reconciling itself to the conditions prevailing in central Punjab. Shattered by a series of tragic experiences, NSD did not see any future for himself in the village. Around 1924, he left his mother and sailed to Singapore.

In Singapore, NSD took up a few odd jobs to make a living. The importance of his short stay in Singapore lay in a chance encounter with the anti-imperialist movement, led by the USA based Ghadar Party. In fact, he found that the copies of the *Ghadar Di Goonj* (Echoes of the Revolution), containing intensely patriotic verses which highlighted the plight of Indians under the colonial rule and which were meant for circulation among Indians, were being passed on to the British intelligence agencies. Rising equal to the occasion, NSD put an end to this practice and ensured that issues of the weekly reached the Indian community. In this manner, he made his first personal contribution to the national movement. It must be admitted that, at this stage, his understanding of political issues was rudimentary. Nevertheless, he had taken a decisive step on a long path, which he was to traverse throughout his life.

After a brief sojourn in Singapore, NSD sailed to Argentina via Ceylon and France, which offered better employment opportunities to Indian migrants. He underwent a long ordeal to gain entry into this South American country because the

British government, unlike other states, did not stand surety for its own citizens. He became acutely aware of the unjust character of the colonial rule, which had been critiqued so effectively in the Ghadarite writings. He worked hard in the corn farms and railway companies, so as to make up for an earlier phase of inadequate employment. What was more important, he had long discussions with Rattan Singh and listened to the fiery speeches of Teja Singh Swatantra, the two Ghadarite stalwarts who toured settlements of Indian migrants in different parts of Argentina. Thus inspired and motivated, NSD enrolled himself as a front rank member of the Ghadar Party, committed to make supreme sacrifices for the organization. At the same time, he continued his political education by reading the successive issues of the *Ghadar Di Goonj*. As a result, his personality underwent a transformation, from a vague migrant labourer to a confident political being.

By the early 1930s, the Ghadar Party had discarded the creed of the gun and adopted the ideology of Marxism. Acting through Rattan Singh, it entered into an understanding with the Comintern. As a result of this alliance, the cadre of the Ghadar Party, then scattered in different parts of the world, was sent secretly to study Marxism-Leninism at the University for the Toilers of the East (Kutv) in Moscow. The Argentine branch of the Ghadar Party, with its headquarters at Rosario, chose NSD to join the second batch of such trainees. In 1933, the secret apparatus of the party enabled him to reach Moscow via Nazi Germany in a clandestine operation. He completed the stipulated one and a half year course in Marxism-Leninism. Since his teachers had given him excellent reports for his performance, he was selected to attend a one year advanced course in the subject. What was equally significant, he availed of the rare opportunity of attending the seventh congress (25 July–21 August 1935) of the Comintern. Here he was persuaded by Georgi Dimitrov, the general secretary of the Comintern, to extend his stay in Moscow in the larger interest of the working class of the world. Towards the close of 1936, he travelled through several countries – Czechoslovakia, Switzerland, France, Cuba and Ceylon – before entering India, after hoodwinking the British intelligence agencies.

The political activities of NSD in colonial India, spanning over a decade from 1936 to 1947, cannot be categorized into neat segments. Nevertheless, he appears to have divided his energies between two arenas – industrial and agrarian – in almost equal measure. Let us begin by considering the first one. He began his Indian mission in Calcutta after having long discussions with Muzaffar Ahmad, who provided valuable information on diverse aspects of the metropolis. He set up an eating place (*dhaba*) at the Haroganj crossing in Howrah, which served as a camouflage for his informal night school. He gave regular lessons in Marxism to young Bengali workers, who were keen to understand the dynamics of the Soviet socialist reconstruction. He enjoyed the rare advantage of explaining the process in simple Hindustani on the basis of his personal experience. He was forced to discontinue these classes within a year, when he learnt of an impending police crack-down. At the advice of Muzaffar Ahmad, he began to work openly among the working class in general and the employees of railway workshops in particular. He held public meetings, recruited sympathizers and collected funds. His work came to an end when, in the wake of his arrest, he was sentenced to a month long imprisonment in the Presidency Jail.

NSD's activities at Kanpur, where he stayed for short periods, were of a different kind. Since the trade union movement was at a more advanced stage, he assisted well established leaders – R.D. Bharadwaj, Santa Singh Yusuf and Santosh Chand Kapoor – in creating cells of the CPI in various unions, educating workers in the technique of organization and providing direction to their struggles. These activities helped NSD to understand the problems of the Indian working class in their local and ideological manifestations. This understanding further enabled him to assume a more challenging assignment at Jamshedpur.

In mid-1939, NSD was deputed by the Calcutta-based leadership of the CPI to Jamshedpur, so as to guide the striking workers of the Indian Steel and Wire Products, where the tragic death of the communist leader Hazara Singh had left an aftermath of demoralization. After making a careful analysis of the volatile situation, NSD gained entry into the strike committee and revived the agitation on scientific lines. While trying to block (10 August 1939) the entry of a train carrying new workers into the factory, he was injured in a brutal police lathi charge. The incident appeared as a major story in the *Kirti Lehar* of 20 August 1939. His skilful leadership at Jamshedpur went to a long way in isolating the management supported goondas, demonstrating the efficacy of Marxist technique of trade unionism and exposing the weakness of rival outfits – the Congress led by Prof. Abdul Bari, the CSP under Jayaprakash Narayan, the Forward Bloc headed by Subhas Chandra Bose and another body led by Manick Homi. He became instrumental in founding the first ever unit of the CPI in Jamshedpur, which was inaugurated by Mazaffar Ahmad. Rising above ideological considerations, NSD played a prominent role in inviting Bose to Jamshedpur and in organizing a workers' rally on the occasion. He appears to have been the first to suggest to Bose the means by which he could escape from India. His vivid testimony throws fresh light on the complexities of the labour movement in a premier industrial centre, the role played by many nationalist leaders in a veritable political battleground and the evolution of the communist movement in the country.

In Punjab, NSD got an opportunity to work on the industrial front only during the closing years of the colonial rule. In 1946, he was deputed by the Lahore office of the CPI to Okara where 2,000 workers of a textile mill had struck work and the government had arrested nearly seventy workers, including the CPI activists, who had been sent earlier from Lahore. On assuming charge of his assignment, he provided regular instructions to the strike leaders, so that the agitation was intensified. He participated in the final negotiations leading to the acceptance of demands of the workers, but not before isolating the pro-Congress local leadership. This success enabled him to play a prominent role in organizing a three-day session of the Provincial Trade Union Congress at Okara. Not long after, he was sent to Amritsar at the instance of Ajoy Kumar Ghosh, who served as the Provincial Organizer of the Punjab unit of the CPI from April to November 1946. Here, the task was more complicated, as there were two strikes going on simultaneously in the industrial pockets of Putlighar and Chheharta. NSD evolved a series of tactics which were applied in accordance with the demands of each situation, leading ultimately to an amicable settlement of the dispute. He paid particular attention, both at Okara and Amritsar, to bring the leading activists into the fold of the CPI.

With the installation of popular ministries in eleven states during the middle of 1937, high expectations were raised among the Indian masses. The peasantry looked forward to radical agrarian reforms specially because the Congress, in its election manifesto, had incorporated the agrarian programme of the All India Kisan Sabha which had been formulated at its Faizpur session (25-26 December 1936). It was in this context that NSD became involved in the struggles of the Indian peasantry. Supported by the working class leadership of Kanpur, he played a major role in organizing a huge march of peasants from Unnao to Lucknow, which culminated in a massive rally at a time when the Pant ministry was in office. His efforts resulted in imparting a decisive Marxist orientation to the demands of the peasantry, much to the embarrassment of the Congress leadership including Jawaharlal Nehru.

On his return to Punjab, NSD was provided with an opportunity to associate himself with the ongoing muzara movement in the Nili Bar. In mid-1938, he was deputed by the PKC to revive the agitation, which had suffered a setback owing to the accidental death of Baba Jwala Singh. Acting under the alias Sundar Singh, he established an office of the PKC in the grain market of Burewala and motivated the muzaras to set-up its branches in the villages of Arifwala, Chichawatni, Veharhi and Tulumba. On receiving specific complaints from the muzaras, he organized militant demonstrations in the concerned villages so as to secure a division of produce in the ratio of 50:50 and to restore the control of land to the muzaras wherever they had been forcibly evicted. The oppressive stranglehold of the sardars, who were invariably supported by the police and goondas, was broken. The provincial bureaucracy, in its fortnightly reports, admitted the widening sweep of the muzara movement under the leaders of the PKC, many of whom were identified as Moscow-trained Ghadarites. The Unionist government, which represented the class interests of big landlords, adopted repressive measures to crush the movement. During his subsequent internment in his native village, NSD continued to articulate the demands of the peasantry by exposing the insensitive feudal regime of the Kapurthala state.

That NSD maintained contact with the nationwide anti-imperialist struggle is indicated by the fact that he violated his internment (*nazrbandi*) and travelled all the way to Jabalpur to attend the Tripuri session (10 March 1939) of the Congress, where leftist elements rallied behind Bose to challenge Gandhi's bourgeois leadership. It is worth noting that the local police failed to notice his absence from the village for long periods.

NSD's involvement in the struggle of peasants and workers brought him into an inevitable conflict with the governments in power. He was often detained and, at other times, severe restrictions were imposed on his movements, so as to prevent him from initiating political activities. In 1937, while educating the workers of Calcutta, he was sentenced to a month long imprisonment in the Presidency Jail. In 1939, he was sentenced to jail in Jamshedpur for his role in a strike at the Indian Steel and Wire Products. His success in reviving the muzara movement in the Nili Bar incurred the wrath of the pro-British Unionist government, which was committed to uphold the class interests of big landlords. NSD was arrested (September 1938) and placed in solitary confinement in the notorious Lahore Fort. He was subjected to severe torture for two months by various CID inspectors, who interrogated him on the basis of a dossier, which had been prepared by the British intelligence agencies. Though the police treatment told severely on his health, he did not reveal a word about his stay in the Soviet Union or his ideological leanings. His family was also pressurized in a variety of dubious ways to extract vital information about his travels in foreign countries. Even after his release, he was placed under *nazrbandi* in his native village. It was another matter that he often violated governmental restrictions and, hoodwinking the police vigilance, continued to participate in the political activities.

NSD's incarceration in the Deoli Detention Camp (1940-1), along with nearly 260 anti-war radical elements, constituted an important phase in his chequered political career. His name figured at serial number 33 in the list of over a hundered security prisoners from Punjab. The jail offered him a rare opportunity of interacting with the prominent communists of the country including S.A. Dange, S.V. Ghate, B.T. Ranadive, Z.A. Ahmad, Sunil Mukherjee, Rahul Sankrityayan and Dhanwantri. Despite numerous restrictions, the detenus organized several collective activities. For NSD, the jail was an advanced school of learning, where knowledgeable and eloquent colleagues delivered lectures on various aspects of Marxism. Since the paucity of Marxist literature had been a serious handicap, he spent every ounce of his energy transcribing these lessons. His passion for acquiring knowledge, through a process of self-learning, is amply demonstrated by over a dozen neatly written notebooks bearing the seal of the jail superintendent. NSD took an active part in the three-week hunger strike, forcing the colonial government to confine the detenus in their respective provinces. He also played a leading role in forging unity between the CPI and the KKP. His personal experiences shed fresh light on the treatment of political prisoners in colonial jails and highlight their response to an oppressive state apparatus. The subject has aquired new significance with the publication of Ujjwal Kumar Singh's valuable study.

Some recent studies have shown that the muzara movement of Patiala reached a decivise phase during 1948-52 when the muzaras, led by the Lal Communist Party, refused to pay *batai* to the *biswedars* and adopted violent measures to resist eviction.[59] These writings have focused attention on the various dimensions – organizational, tactical and ideological – of the militant struggle. However, scholars have made only a passing reference to similar struggles which were launched around the same time in other parts of Punjab. The memoirs of NSD, by shedding light on the muzara movement of Una, have overcome this problem to a great extent. We often tend to forget that, in response to the countrywide crackdown on the communists in 1948, almost the entire provincial leadership went underground in the villages of Hoshiarpur district. Instead of going into political hibernation, it created a new party apparatus to suit the changed circumstances, which continued to function for over four years till the restrictions were revoked. NSD and a few associates established themselves in a hamlet near Bhakra and initiated political activities in the right earnest. They created cells in the villages of Una, mobilized the muzaras and built up a powerful anti-feudal movement, aimed at dismantling the worst froms of economic exploitation and social degradation. NSD and his comrades also carried out political propaganda among thousands of workers who were employed at the construction sites of the Bhakra–Nangal hydroelectric project. They organized secret meetings to create political awareness among the labourers and assisted in securing a better deal for them from greedy contractors. NSD organized these activities in such a manner that two parallel movements – Una and Bhakra – became complementary to each other. During this phase, he pioneered new methods of underground political work which the police failed to detect, despite constant vigilance and several raids at his hideouts. Little wonder, he came to enjoy an aura of invincibility in the submontanous tract of Punjab.

With the revocation of his warrants, NSD emerged on the political stage with renewed vigour. To begin with, he participated in the task of transforming an ad hoc party structure into an organization which could function under normal circumstances, unhindered by earlier inhibitions. As a member of the control commission on behalf of the state committee, he endeavoured to ensure discipline among members of the party. As a member of the district committee for Hoshiarpur, he worked to rebuild the party from below and particularly focused on bringing the local youth into its fold. In the process, he identified the reasons for the failure to establish a satisfactory base in certain areas and among certain classes. He played a prominent role in mobilizing peasants for a mass agitation against the betterment levy which had been imposed by the Kairon ministry. He sought to address the local problems by serving in the Panchayat Samiti of the Bhunga Block, even while the state government was not inclined to strengthen the democratic institutions in the rural areas. He organized the election campaigns of the CPI candidates from Sham Chaurasi and Mehna constituencies with limited financial resources and succeeded in neutralizing the terror unleashed by political gangsters.

NSD was deeply concerned about the growing dissensions

within the party, which ultimately led to the split of 1964. He joined the CPM because he was convinced that its programme conformed strictly to Marxist principles, as opposed to the right wing faction. Remaining steadfast in his commitment to the CPM till the end of his life, he devoted his energies on propagating the new party line among the people of the surrounding villages. In 1966, he guided a popular agitation of the rural poor against the state government's decision to sell the 55 acre Khiala Bulanda farm, which employed hundreds of landless labourers. After a short time, he witnessed the emergence of the Naxalite movement. He felt deeply distressed by the death of young Naxalites in police encounters. He made strenuous efforts, cycling from village to village, to bring these young men back into the fold of the CPM.

During the early 1970s, NSD devoted himself to creating class consciousness among the educated and salaried sections of society, viz., government employees, school teachers (both employed and unemployed), paramedical staff and lecturers of private colleges – all of whom were struggling for higher allowances and better service conditions. Due to his efforts, the control of several unions of different categories of employees, both at the district and state level, passed into the hands of leaders who owed allegiance to the CPM. He educated the union leaders on the theoretical aspects of trade unionism, besides providing guidelines on the day-to-day tactics that were employed during the agitational phases. In 1972, he assisted the lecturers of private colleges in organizing the longest strike in their history. It was due to his intervention that the CPM took up the cause of eighteen lecturers who had been dismissed from the DAV College, Hoshiarpur, by Chaudhuri Balbir Singh, president of the managing committee. He made repeated attempts to create a separate cell for college lecturers in the CPM. He played a leading role in organizing a massive general strike of government employees on 9 January 1974. In the same year, he assisted the Students Federation of India to lead a successful statewide agitation for concessional bus passes. He organized in Dhoot Kalan the annual conference of the Punjab Kisan Sabha, which concluded a day before the imposition of the emergency. His revolutionary spirit was not dampened by the authoritarian assault on democratic rights. He continued to organize study circles and special schools for young students at *Toteyan Wala Khooh* (Well of Parrots), his secret rendezvous, which was located in the ancestral farm of his in-laws at Jhawan village.

The political activities of NSD were spread across several countries and regions, besides spanning a period of six decades. Though he went abroad (1927) to earn money, he returned with the knowledge of Marxism-Leninism. He not only preserved this humble ideological stock with utmost care, but also continued to supplement it through rigorous self-study on the basis of Marxist literature, which was easily available in the wake of independence. Having travelled extensively in the different parts of the world – South-East Asia, Latin America, the Soviet Union, France, Germany, Cuba and Ceylon – he acquired the ability to mingle with diverse peoples. He moved with great ease from Calcutta to Kanpur and from Amritsar to Jamshedpur. He blended his mission of uplifting the downtrodden with the propagation of Marxism-Leninism. As a disciplined activist of the united CPI up to 1964 and thereafter of the CPM, he accepted numerous difficult assignments and completed them to the satisfaction of the party. He remained perpetually involved in leading the struggles of various sections of the society. He devoted his energies to consolidate democratic forces in the country, especially training the young communist cadres. While engaged in the single-minded pursuit of these objectives, he displayed a rare commitment and, in the process, made tremendous sacrifices. He has left behind a legacy which is a source of inspiration for the present and future generations of radical political activists. His contribution to building the communist movement in South Asia will always be acknowledged.

NOTES AND REFERENCES

1. According to the nationalist critique, the magnitude of land revenue was excessively high, uncertain and fluctuating owing to frequent revisions. The system was rigid and inflexible, offering no compensation for crop failure. It enabled the zamindars to

transfer the burden of tax increase to the actual tiller. It often led to mortgages and confiscation of land, besides distress sale of produce. It discouraged capital investment in land and agricultural improvement. Bipan Chandra, *The Rise and Growth of Economic Nationalism in India*, pp. 400-7.

2. The contradictions between the colonial state and various sections of Indian society, as reflected in sporadic plebeian outbursts, have been placed within the framework of a history from below. Sumit Sarkar, *Modern India: 1885-1947*, pp. 43-54.
3. The CPI was such an insignificant body that S.V. Ghate suggested in May 1928 that WPP should control it, completely reversing the perspective of the Comintern and M.N. Roy. Aditya Mukherjee, 'The Workers and Peasants Parties 1926-30: An Aspect of Communism in India', in *The Indian Left: Critical Appraisals*, ed. Bipan Chandra, p. 15.
4. The Communist International, the International Press Correspondence, the Labour Monthly or any printed matter issued by the General News Service of London, including their translations, reprints or other documents containing substantial reproductions from the above publications were banned from entering India. Home Department (Political), File No. 41/12/37.
5. The application of united national front tactics, especially after the Lucknow Pact, strengthened both the CPI and the CSP. Peasant movements were expanded, the All India Kisan Sabha was formed, the Congress adopted the Faizpur agrarian programme and labour organizations displayed considerable militancy in key industrial sectors. But the united national front collapsed owing to the communists' dissatisfaction with inadequate agrarian reforms and anti-labour policies in the Congress-ruled states, panic in the CSP over the growing communist influence in its ranks, the revival of the Congress right wing and corresponding marginalization of the left wing. For details, see Sanjay Seth, *Marxist Theory and Nationalist Politics: The Case of Colonial India*, pp. 157-87.
6. M.A. Persits, *Revolutionaries of India in Soviet Russia*, p. 222.
7. For a detailed analysis of the organization, objectives and methods of the Naujawan Bharat Sabha, see Bhagwan Josh, *Communist Movement in Punjab*, pp. 81-90; Kamlesh Mohan, *Militant Nationalism in the Punjab*, pp. 77-9.
8. For information on the revolutionary activities of Rattan Singh see David Petrie, *Communism in India*, p. 376; Sohan Singh Josh, *My Tryst with Secularism: An Autobiography*, p. 106; Bhagat Singh Bilgha, *Ghadar Lehar Dey Anfoley Varkey*, pp. 164-5.

9. Though the Kirtis did not offer a coherent and systematic programme, yet the following aims were laid down in the various issues of the *Kirti* – nationalization of the means of production, land to be taken away from landlords without compensation and distributed among cultivators, reduction of revenue and that too imposed on production, abolition of revenue on small holdings, increase in the wages of industrial workers who would work for only eight hours, panchayats elected by cultivators and rural workers to be entrusted with the authority to impose revenue, establishment of a Kirti or Bolshevik state. Bhagwan Josh, op. cit., pp. 94-5.
10. Besides the KKP, the other banned organizations were the Anti-Imperialist League and its branches, the Punjab Provincial Naujawan Bharat Sabha (Lahore) and its branches, the Amritsar District Kisan Sabha and the Punjab Kisan League. Subodh Roy, ed., *Communism in India: Unpublished Documents (1925-34),* p. 198.
11. Home Department (Political), File No. Secret-A/216-1940.
12. The colonization process enhanced the authority of the state over society, owing to its control of land and water. It perpetuated inequalities of the existing social structure. It induced a substantial movement of population towards West Punjab. The population of Punjab from 1891 to 1941 increased by 53.26 per cent, while that of Lyallpur district increased by a massive 2215 per cent. The average population density for the province was 47.6, while for Lyallpur it was 2540.0. Imran Ali, *The Punjab Under Imperialism,* pp. 10-11, 59-61. For migration to Chenab Canal Colony from the central and submontane districts of Punjab, see Himadri Banerjee, *Agrarian Society of the Punjab,* p. 28.
13. M. Mufakharul Islam, *Irrigation, Agriculture and the Raj: Punjab 1887-1947,* pp. 80-2.
14. Ibid., pp. 83-6, 93.
15. Bhagwan Josh, *Communist Movement in Punjab,* pp. 122-4; Master Hari Singh, *Punjab Peasant in Freedom Struggle,* vol. II, pp. 205-7.
16. *Kirti Lehar,* Meerut, 26 June 1938.
17. *The Tribune,* 28 June 1938.
18. Home Department (Political), File Nos. 18/6/38, 18/7/38 and 18/8/38.
19. Home Department (Political), File No. 18/9/38.
20. Sharecropping cultivation became so common that 79.3 per cent of cultivated land in Montgomery and 74.4 per cent in Multan was tilled by sharecroppers. The tender holder extracted such irregular

levies as *anna thaba, malba, khatta, jhajhari, pakhi* and *begar.* After meeting all exactions from one-half share and repaying some of the previous crop loans, a sharecropper was left with hardly one-fourth of his gross produce. Amit Kumar Gupta, *The Agrarian Drama: The Leftists and the Rural Poor,* p. 54.

21. For detailed discussions on these themes, see Ian Talbot, *Punjab and the Raj,* pp. 100-32, 142-74, 185-201; Raghuvendra Tanwar, *Politics of Sharing Power: The Punjab Unionist Party,* pp. 88-105, 109-26, 130-54.
22. Chaman Lal Revri, *The Indian Trade Union Movement: An Outline History,* pp. 175-8 ; Sunil Kumar Sen, *Working Class Movements in India,* p. 53.
23. Bhagwan Josh, *Struggle for Hegemony in India 1920-47: The Colonial State, the Left and the National Movement,* vol. II, pp. 236-43.
24. *The Tribune,* 9 July 1938.
25. Nirban Basu, 'National Upsurge and the Working Class Movement: A Study of the 1942 Movement in the TISCO Jamshedpur', *Proceedings of the Indian History Congress,* Calcutta, 1990, p. 612.
26. Abdul Bari, a Congress leader of Bihar, arrived in Jamshedpur in 1937 and assumed the leadership of the Tata Workers Union. TISCO did not recognize the TWU and supported Homi so as to weaken Bari. However, Bari won the confidence of workers by attacking both TISCO and the Congress. He organized several departmental strikes in protest against the bonus policies. However, a profit sharing scheme and a few welfare measures failed to satisfy the workers. The Congress leadership, at the instance of TISCO, advised Bari to exercise restraint. The Nehru–Prasad Award, emerging as a Congress memorandum on labour issues, poured cold water on the labour movement and sacrificed the prestige of Bari in order to save the Tata industry. Vinay Bahl, *The Making of the Indian Working Class: The Case of the Tata Iron and Steel Company,* pp. 350-5.
27. The leaders of the two rival communist groups justified their own position, while criticizing the other for various actions. For pro-Kirti and pro-official group positions, see Bhagat Singh Bilgha, *Ghadar Lehar Dey Anfoley Varkey,* pp. 193-7, 291-3; Sohan Singh Josh, *My Tryst with Secularism: An Autobiography,* pp. 200-7.
28. Gurharpal Singh, *Communism in Punjab: A Study of the Movement up to 1961,* pp. 47-57.
29. Ibid., pp. 85-101.
30. During the summer of 1942, the PKC organized forty conferences

in the villages of Ferozepur, Ludhiana, Jalandhar, Hoshiarpur, Gurdaspur and Amritsar. On 2-4 April 1943, the seventh session of the AIKS was held at Bhakna Kalan (Amritsar district). On 23-25 September 1943, the provincial kisan conference was held at Jandiala, Jalandhar district. During 1942-4, membership of the PKC increased from 56,000 to 1,36,811. Its demands included extension of irrigation facilities, moratorium on debts, end of profiteering in essential items, abolition of forcible eviction of tenants, reduction in rents, abolition of forced labour and illegal cesses, abolition of forcible collection of war funds, withdrawal of sugar cane control order in Jalandhar and collection of relief for victims of the Bengal famine. M.A. Rasul, *A History of the All India Kisan Sabha*, pp. 98-105; Ajeet Javed, *Left Politics in Punjab*, pp. 197-203.

31. Tai Yong Tan and Gyanesh Kudaisya, *The Aftermath of Partition in South Asia*, p. 98.
32. Ibid., pp. 128-37.
33. Creative writers, poets and artists, who experienced partition either personally or through others, have articulated with greater sensitivity and have captured the multidimensionality of human suffering more realistically than some of the conventional historians. S. Settar and Indira Baptista Gupta, eds., *Pangs of Partition*, vol. III, *The Human Dimension*, p. 12.
34. The strategy of People's Democratic Revolution has been elaborated in M.B. Rao, ed., *Documents of the History of the Communist Party of India*, vol. VII, 1948-50, pp. 75-8.
35. In a document entitled 'Report on Left Deviation Inside the CPI', prepared by the members of the Central Committee from Andhra, the PDR was attacked as adventurist, but a guerrilla warfare to fight the military onslaught of the Nehru government was advocated. This line was opposed by Ajoy Kumar Ghosh, S.A. Dange and S.V. Ghate in a report entitled 'A Note on the Present Situation in Our Party', which rejected both the Russian and Chinese paths and instead proposed an Indian revolutionary agenda, while admitting people's illusions about the Nehru government and the weakness of the CPI. For details, see M.B. Rao, op. cit., pp. 775-944, 945-1039.
36. For details regarding the programme, the tactical line and the state of policy of the CPI, see Mohit Sen, ed., *Documents of the History of the Communist Party of India,* vol. VIII, pp. 1-54.
37. Javeed Alam, 'Communist Politics in Search of Hegemony', in *Wages of Freedom: Fifty Years of the Indian Nation*, ed. Partha Chatterjee, pp. 199-203.

38. Born on 23 March 1916 in Bandala village, Jalandhar district, Harkishan Singh Surjeet received education up to matriculation. In 1930, he joined the Naujawan Bharat Sabha. He participated in the civil disobedience movement and in 1932 he was imprisoned for four years for seditious activities. On release from jail, he joined the CPI. In 1936, he co-founded the Punjab Kisan Sabha. He launched a journal, *Dukhi Duniya*, from Jalandhar to highlight socio-economic problems. In 1938, he moved to Saharanpur and revived the paper under the name of *Chingari*. In this year he was also elected secretary of the Punjab Kisan Sabha. During the Second World War, he was detained in Rajasthan along with other communists. In 1951 he was elected secretary of the state committee of the CPI. Joining the CPM after the 1964 split, he became a member of its politburo in 1967. In 1969, he was elected vice-president of the All India Kisan Sabha. A prolific writer, Surjeet has edited the party's Punjabi paper, *Lok Lehar*, besides publishing books on the political problems in Kashmir and Punjab. At present he is serving a second term as the general secretary of the CPM. Fauja Singh, *Eminent Freedom Fighters of Punjab*, pp. 122-3.
39. Gurharpal Singh, op. cit., p. 266.
40. Bhabani Sen Gupta, *CPI-M: Promises, Prospects, Problems*, pp. 46-7.
41. Ibid., pp. 33-44.
42. Prakash Karat, 'Naxalism Today: At an Ideological Dead End', *The Marxist*, vol. III, no. 1, January-March 1985, pp. 44-7.
43. These observations have been drawn from a succinct and insightful analysis contained in Achin Vanaik, *The Painful Transition: Bourgeois Democracy in India*, p. 185.
44. Paramjit S. Judge, 'The Naxalite Movement in Punjab', in *Social and Political Movements: Readings on Punjab*, eds. Harish K. Puri and Paramjit S. Judge, pp. 316-20.
45. Gurcharan Singh Sahnsara, *Oh Vi Din San*, pp. 18-28.
46. Ibid., pp. 85-108.
47. Ibid., pp. 183-92.
48. Bhagat Singh Bilgha, *Ghadar Lehar Dey Anfoley Varkey: Ghadar Party Te Kirti Party*, p. 114.
49. Ibid., pp. 221-2.
50. Ibid., pp. 290-3.
51. Chain Singh Chain, *Kirti Party: Dooji Sansar Jang Samey*, pp. 7-8.
52. Ibid., pp. 11-48.
53. Ibid., pp. 170-3.
54. Ibid., pp. 244-53.

55. Sohan Singh Josh, *My Tryst with Secularism: An Autobiography*, pp. 68-75.
56. Ibid., pp. 165-84.
57. Ibid., pp. 185-95.
58. Ibid., pp. 201-7.
59. Mridula Mukherjee, 'Communists and Peasants in Punjab: A Focus on the Muzara Movement in Patiala 1937-53', in *The Indian Left: Critical Appraisals*, ed. Bipan Chandra, pp. 408-11.

CHAPTER 1

Life in the Chenab Colony

If you board a bus from Hoshiarpur for Pathankot, you will pass through a terrain along the foothills of the Siwaliks, known as Sirwal.[1] The most outstanding feature of the landscape is the abundance of mango groves on both sides of the road. As the bus pushes northwards, it passes by several small places like Baghpur, Ghasipur Bhikowal, Hariana, Kangan and Bhunga. Another 10 minutes' drive brings you to a crossing locally known as Do Sarhka. If you disembark at this place, turn left and walk for a mile or so on a straight path, which makes a right angle with the Hoshiarpur–Pathankot road, you will reach my ancestral village, Dhoot Kalan.[2] I was born here in 1904 in the house of a farmer, Thakur Singh, who owned and tilled a small piece of land.

The pursuits of my father as an agriculturist were overshadowed by his activities as a devotee of his creed. Along with his two elder brothers Shiv Singh and Nagina Singh, he was instrumental in introducing the Sikh religion in our locality (*ilaqa*). He remained in constant touch with the Harmandir Sahib at Amritsar as well as another holy place at Kandhala Jattan, which was situated at a distance of 10 miles from our village.[3] The kind of orthodox Sikhism, as understood and practised by my father, was rather rare. He scrupulously followed the religious code of the Khalsa (*rehat*). He believed that it was the first and foremost duty of every Sikh to come to the aid of the weak and the poor, and that he should not covet anything which belonged to another. In this connection, I can recall an incident, which took place in the Chenab Canal Colony.

As a small child, I had taken a fancy to a calf which was unusually attractive. It was my constant companion wherever I went. One day I was walking along a water course (*sua*), which formed the boundary between our and the neighbour's field, and in all innocence, I cut off a few green stalks growing in the other field and fed them to the calf. My father, who was watching me, came up to me and gave me such a sound thrashing with a stick that I still remember it even though many years have since passed.

I vividly recall that while listening to recitations from the *Guru Granth Sahib* (*gurbani*), my father would sit with his face and head covered with a piece of cloth. He did this so as to prevent the senses from wandering and to enable his mind to concentrate. He was unduly fond of airing his views on various religious matters. If anyone entered into a dialogue with him on these issues, he became so engrossed in the discussion that he would forget all about the pressing agricultural operations which required his urgent attention. Such was his religious fervour that once, without informing anyone at home, he walked all the way to Hazoor Sahib (Nanded in Maharashtra) dressed as a pilgrim. When nothing was heard about him for over a year, the family had no alternative but to perform his last rites.

In spite of these peculiarities, my father had certain admirable traits. He was fearless, strong and courageous. At the same time, he was extremely conscious of his self-respect and was always willing to go to any length to see it vindicated. A full-blooded personality like that of my father's did not fail to influence those who came into contact with him. Though I inherited little from him materially, I imbibed several social and moral values from him, which enabled me to emerge as a fighter for just causes in my adult life.

Towards the close of the nineteenth century, agriculture in our area (*ilaqa*) was in a serious crisis. It had ceased to be profitable and farmers found it difficult to make both ends meet. For one thing, the landholdings in the entire Doaba had become so small as a result of repeated fragmentation that they were no longer economically viable.[4] A popular saying was that while looking for a suitable match for one's daughter, it was difficult to find a young man who owned even 2 acres of land.

Substantial areas of land had been rendered unfit for cultivation by the havoc unleashed by the seasonal torrents (*choes*).[5] Large tracts of agricultural land were covered by mango groves which did not bring any returns to the farmer. Moreover, standing crops were damaged by wild animals, who often descended from the thickly forested Siwaliks. Added to this was my father's charitable disposition. Whenever Sikh preachers came to our village, he went beyond his meagre resources to serve them.

In these circumstances, it was essential to supplement the family income. A trade route for pack animals, connecting the Siwaliks with Amritsar, passed through our village, Tanda and Sri Hargobindpur. Like other poor farmers of the region, my father transported merchandise on camels on this route. However, the crisis was too deep-rooted to be resolved by quick fix remedies. Soon it became evident that drastic decisions and measures were needed to neutralize the impact of adverse economic forces.

A large number of farmers of the Doaba region had migrated to foreign countries like Canada, the USA, Central America, Brazil, Argentina, Australia, the Philippines, Burma and Shanghai and many others were preparing to follow suit. Those who did not have the means or the inclination to leave their country moved to the Bar – the districts of Lyallpur, Montgomery, Multan and Sargodha – where agriculture was being developed by the British through a network of canals. As a matter of policy, land was allotted to pensioners who had retired from government service. But farmers who had shifted to the Bar as original settlers (*abadkars*) were given ownership (*milkiyat*) rights over one-fourth or one-half of the area settled by them. However, this was not possible in our case. Since our village formed a part of the princely state of Kapurthala, we could purchase land anywhere only with the permission of the Raja – a condition which in the eyes of my father was too humiliating.[6] Of course, we could and did settle there as tenants (*muzaras*). In fact, Inder Singh, the grandfather of Comrade Chanan Singh Dhoot, was the first man from our village to shift to the Bar. During one of his visits to our village, he met my father and described to him the favourable conditions in the Bar. He added that land and water were plenty and easily available. In fact, canal water was so abundant that one square (*murabba*, i.e. 27.7 acres) could be irrigated in four watches (*pehars*), leaving a considerable quantity of unused water.[7]

It was in these circumstances that my father took a momentous step. He migrated to the Bar along with his four sons. His only daughter had been married by then. The families of my two uncles, who were close to my father, also came with us. This development took place around the time I was born i.e. 1904. Initially, we acquired land as tenants in Chak 84, Lyallpur tehsil. For reasons which are not known to me, we moved after some time to Chak 40, Samundri tehsil.[8] After staying there for a year, we moved to the neighbouring village, Chak 39. Here the land originally belonged to a *sardar* named Subedar Sunder Singh who had no child of his own. He had adopted the son of a Chhimba who became the owner after the farmer's death. The new owner was a thorough gentleman and had deep affection for my father. Little wonder, we tilled the land belonging to him for a considerable period of time.

Life was tough during the early years of our stay in the Bar. My father who had associated himself with Teja Singh Samundri,[9] the famous leader of the Singh Sabha Movement, busied himself with religious activities. My eldest brother, Sadhu Singh, was for all practical purposes the breadwinner of the family. Besides tilling the soil, he did a number of odd jobs in order to supplement the household income. For a short time, he established himself as a confectioner (*halwai*) in Chak 40. He also carried water to the houses of Balmikis, a service for which he was paid in grain twice a year. Besides, he was responsible for the upbringing of his three brothers, who were too young to assist him. I, being the youngest, was only an infant if not a toddler. At that time we were forced to borrow money from some sardar in order to meet our household expenses.[10] When it became difficult to return the principal sum and the interest on it, my family sold some of our cattle to repay the debt.

With the passage of time, my other two brothers grew up into fine youngmen and began to participate in all agricultural activities. As the number of cattle in our possession increased, so did our capacity to work. Initially, the family tilled only one *murabba*, but later another one was acquired in view of our increased strength. Slowly, the family's financial position improved and we began to live in relative comfort.

The system which governed the relations between the muzaras and the sardar was known as crop sharing (*bhaoli*). It implied that the entire agricultural produce was to be shared by the two in the ratio of 50:50. All agricultural inputs had to be provided by the muzara, while water rates, land revenue and other government dues were borne by the sardar.[11] Yet the scales were tilted heavily against the muzara who was exploited by various agencies. For instance, he had to perform a number of odd jobs throughout the year for the sardar, for which he received no remuneration. The muzara could not refuse the frequent illegal demands of the village accountants (*patwaris*) who were often grasping, if not rapacious. It may be added here that all the sardars did not give their lands on *bhaoli*. Some of them gave it for cultivation on contract, while others did the work themselves with the help of agricultural labourers (*siris*), who were paid either in cash or kind.

Wheat, cotton, sugar cane and toriya were the main crops that were raised year after year. Each muzara possessed a large number of cattle, so that there was no shortage of manure. Crops were irrigated with water from the canal, which was brought to the villages through water courses (*suas*). Every village had one or two smaller water channels (*mogas*), which, in turn, received their supply of water from the former. The amount of water flowing through these water channels was often reduced due to silting.[12] To overcome the problem, the muzaras had to undertake manual desilting of the portions earmarked for them three or four times a year, when large mounds of silt accumulated at different places in the countryside.

I attended a school in Chak 40, which was run by Teja Singh Samundri. My father, however, was strongly opposed to the teaching of Urdu and English, the only languages taught in schools in those days. In his orthodox opinion, Urdu was the language of the Turks and English was that of the Europeans (*firangis*). He wanted me to study Punjabi, which was taught only by priests (*bhais*) in the gurdwaras. A person by the name of Balbir Singh, who was a teacher in the school in Chak 40, was on friendly terms with our family. My father approached him to teach me Punjabi. But Balbir Singh expressed his inability to do so, for teachers in those days knew only Urdu and English.[13] My brothers appealed to my father, 'He is the youngest of us all. Let him study Urdu and English. He might be able to get a government job. So far as the work on the farm is concerned, the three of us more than enough for it.' Because of his deep-seated aversion to Islam and Christianity, he refused to give up his obscurantist ideas, and withdrew me from school. As a result, I never received formal education in school. At home, I had little work to do as I was the youngest and the most pampered one (*ladla*). Therefore, I spent most of my time in various games and sports. As I grew older, I began to help my brothers in the fields.

My father's lack of interest in education was more than compensated by his obsession for sports. He was particularly fond of strenuous sports like wrestling, club wielding, rope pulling and putting the shot. He went to great lengths to see that his sons and nephews utilized their leisure in manly sports, in which other boys of the neighbourhood also participated. As a result of these activities, all of us grew to be tall, strong and well-built lads. Lal Singh, my second eldest brother, surpassed all of us in physical strength and became a good wrestler. Chatar Singh, the son of my uncle Shiv Singh, was almost seven feet tall and had earned a great reputation in the area as a powerful player of stick fighting (*gatka*). Harbans Singh, the son of my uncle Nagina Singh, also distinguished himself as a wrestler.

Once Harbans Singh was engaged in a series of wrestling bouts with Mahiya Singh, the son of a sardar of Chak 40. Each time Harbans Singh successfully pinned down his opponent, the latter would go to Amritsar to receive advanced training. Mahiya Singh, being the son of a sardar, was supported by ample resources. But Harbans Singh, being the son of a muzara, seemed to suffer from a lack of extra diet which was essential for him to wrestle. My father, who was held in high regard by his nephews, made it a prestige issue of the entire family. He approached Harbans Singh's mother and said, 'Do you want us to cut a sorry figure in the wrestling pit (*akhara*). Make sure that the boy is not faced with any shortage of milk or ghee.' My aunt (*tayi*) promised to do the needful and, as it turned out, Harbans Singh remained unbeaten. The incident had an impact in an unexpected quarter. The sons of the sardars, who often looked down upon the sons of muzaras, were forced to change their social attitude.

At that time my second eldest brother, Lal Singh got an opportunity to display his strength and skill acquired by him after sweating it out regularly in the recent past. It so happened that a wrestling match (*dangal*) was organized in the neighbourhood and Lal Singh sought the permission of our father in order to participate in it. They consulted Pal Singh of Sialkot, a well-known and experienced wrestler, who gave his approval. When the three of them – my father, Lal Singh and Pal Singh – left for the venue of the contest, they also carried me along on their shoulders.

Sammu, a renowned wrestler, had received an award of five *murabbas* of land from the British government for his extraordinary feats in the sport. He fielded Karma, a prominent disciple (*shagird*) of his, who was a goldsmith (*suniara*) by caste. The prize money was a mare, a turban and Rs 125. When Karma entered into the wrestling pit, nobody challenged him to a fight. Thereupon, Sammu suggested that the prize be handed over to Karma. Just then my father intervened and said, 'Please wait. Let me ask my son.' Lal Singh eagerly expressed his intention to fight, as he had come all the way just for that. Following quick consultations in our camp, Lal Singh was selected to fight against Karma instead of Pal Singh, who had a lighter physique.

My father conveyed the decision to the organizers of the match, who were themselves looking for someone to accept the challenge thrown by Sammu. This development came as a surprise to Sammu, who came over to us and began to judge Lal Singh with the eye of an expert. He turned to my father and said, 'Baba, your son is strong. There is no doubt about that. But he has no experience as compared to Karma, who is very cunning. If your son gets pinned down in his debut, he would be demoralized for ever. So let him first fight elsewhere and gain experience.' My father, a man of conviction, declared, 'I have given my word and I cannot go back on it. We must fight in any case.' There was much excitement among the large number of people, who had gathered there. The crowd demanded that Lal Singh should take a round of the *akhara*, clad in his wrestling costume (*kainch*) before the match. Obviously, they wanted to have a good look at the contender who had accepted Sammu's challenge. When Lal Singh walked around the arena in response to the popular demand, the crowd was visibly impressed by him as he was tall, handsome and powerfully built. It appeared as if nature had pasted layers of muscles at the appropriate places on his body. Instantaneously, he became the hero of the crowd that was eager to cheer him to victory. Many even laid bets in his favour.

When Lal Singh was about to enter the *akhara,* our uncle Nagina Singh (who had also been a wrestler in his youth) gave him last minute advice, 'Attack your adversary as soon as you shake hands with him.' Lal Singh did just that. The moment he shook hands with Karma, he pulled the latter towards him by the hand and pinned him down in the sand with such lightening speed that many of the spectators did not see what had happened. Shouts of joy rent the sky and drums (*dhol*) were beaten. As the victorious Lal Singh was escorted around the *akhara*, he was cheered by the crowd and money was showered on him by the admirers, whose appreciation and excitement knew no bounds. They vied with one another to pat him on the back and even to raise him up on their shoulders.

When the organizers came forward to give him the prize, Lal Singh said to our father, 'We are not professional wrestlers. We must give due honour to our opponents who are experienced sportsmen. Let the prize be given to Sammu. Let him tie the turban on his head and ride around the *akhara* on the new mare and declare that Lal Singh had achieved a victory over his own pupil, but the victor had handed over the prize to him as a token of our regard for him.' My father agreed to Lal Singh's suggestion. When Sammu learnt about it, he was immensely pleased, but was reluctant to accept the prize. My father told him that he had given his word, which was irrevocable. Sammu had no choice but to accept it.

The spirit of sportsmanship and sacrifice shown by our family was greatly appreciated by one and all. In fact, the entire episode became a popular topic of discussion in the neighbouring villages. In particular, the people of Chak 39 and 40 were extremely proud of the fact that Lal Singh was one of them.

A sardar by the name of Bhagat Singh owned land in Rusiyana, a nearby village. He was notorious for his cruel treatment of the muzaras. His *modus operandi* was simple. He would engage a muzara to till his land. As soon as the crops were ready for harvesting, he would have the muzara beaten and thrown out, so that the poor fellow was deprived of the fruit of his year-long labour, with no one to whom he could complain. The entire area was dominated by the sardars. If one of them faced any opposition from his muzaras, he could rely on the active support of the neighbouring sardars, who had common interests. In some cases, the concerned sardar would persuade the leader of the aggrieved party to join him at the liquor shop in Samundri, where everything would be forgotten over a long bout of drinking.

One unfortunate victim of Bhagat Singh's high-handedness was Rusli, a Balmiki,[14] who belonged to Teja Singh Samundri's ancestral village in Majha. When Rusli was unceremoniously evicted from the *murabbas*, he lashed out at his tormentor, 'Oh Sardar! You could treat us in this cruel manner because we are weak and helpless. But, if you treat the natives of Dhoot Kalan in the same way, they would deal with you in a befitting manner.'

Rusli's angry remark apparently pierced the sardar's heart like an arrow. He did not mention the episode to anyone, yet he accepted the challenge thrown by Rusli and began to devise various schemes to establish his power as the representative of a superior class. At last, he finalized a plan, which he began to put into practice with great patience. He developed friendship with my eldest brother Sadhu Singh and repeatedly promised him, with all professions of sincerity, that he intended to hand over his *murabbas* to him from then onwards. To strengthen this newly cultivated relationship with Sadhu Singh, he would buy one or half a bottle of liquor from Samundri everyday and offer it to Sadhu Singh. Having consumed the sardar's liquor,

Sadhu Singh agreed to the sardar's proposals regarding the cultivation of his holding. My father, however, rejected the idea and said, 'We are happy and contented here. People have got a lot of love and affection for us. There is no reason to shift to any other place.' The regular consumption of liquor at the cost of the sardar had made Sadhu Singh deaf to all sane advice. He was adamant on his resolve, 'Bapu! Why do you disagree with the proposal when you are not going to work at all. It is we who are going to till the land. We understand what is good and what is bad for us. So let us go ahead.' We decided to till two *murabbas* belonging to Bhagat Singh, notwithstanding my father's advice to the contrary.

Not long after, my father's fears proved to be well founded. We had sown sugar cane, cotton and fodder on the two *murabbas* acquired from Bhagat Singh. It was mid-May (*Jeth*) and the threshing of wheat was underway. On that particular day, it was our turn for water and Sadhu Singh was busy watering the fields. The sardar knew that my father would bring food for Sadhu Singh in the afternoon and decided that it was the right time to give shape to his nefarious designs. Having made all preparations, he arrived with his uncle and a gang of ten hirelings. Seeing my father he said, 'Oh Bhai! Do not dare to enter the *murabba*.' At this juncture, my father thought that the sardar was joking and did not pay much attention to his words. As he started walking, the sardar angrily shouted, 'Didn't I tell you not to step into the *murabba*.' As these words were spoken in anger, my father quickly assessed the situation and realized that the sardar had come with hostile intentions. He stopped and inquired coolly, 'What is the matter?' The sardar said, 'I gave the *murabbas* to Sadhu Singh and not to you.' My father still kept his cool and replied, 'Sadhu Singh is my son and there is no difference between him and me.' When my father moved to go ahead, the sardar stepped forward and brandished a thick bamboo stick (*dang*). My father, who was a skilful player of *gatka*, placed the food on the ground and prepared to defend himself against the impending attack. The sardar delivered the first blow, which was successfully blocked by my father, who did not attack in retaliation but only asked his adversary to come to his senses. When the sardar delivered the second blow, my father also swung his *dang*. It struck the sardar on his temple and he fell down on the ground. Thereupon, my father picked up the packet of food and walked away. Meanwhile the sardar stood up and along with his maternal uncle advanced towards my father who called out to Sadhu Singh. Sadhu Singh was busy with water channels at some distance. As soon as he heard Bapu's cry, he shouted back and ran towards him, carrying whatever he could lay his hands on – a curved stick (*khoonda*) and a mattock (*kahi*). By that time the two attackers had caught up with Bapu, who again placed the packet of food on the ground. Since the wheat had been harvested, the fields were absolutely clear. Whenever the two adversaries swung their *dangs*, Bapu cleverly dodged them so that most of their blows went abegging. On the other hand, he succeeded in hitting both of them twice or thrice. Consequently, they turned back thoroughly demoralized.

The sardar and his uncle began to prepare themselves for the second and final phase of their assault. They signalled to the group of hired goondas, who had been waiting all this time, at a place where wheat was being threshed, to rush to their aid. In their frustration after the first encounter, they declared, 'Now we are not going to spare them (Bapu and Sadhu Singh) even if we are forced to spend the entire income from our five *murabbas*.' Meanwhile, Sadhu Singh joined Bapu who said, 'Didn't I tell you not to take the *murabbas* from these people. Now, see with your own eyes what they have done to us. Anyhow, whatever was to happen has happened. Now you must remain close by my side. Do not worry, for we are not going to be overpowered by them.'

The dozen assailants, led by the sardar, took the offensive and engaged Bapu and Sadhu Singh in an unequal combat. They were armed with sharp-edged weapons like axe (*ghadali*) and hatchet (*takuya*). Fighting commenced and went on for a long time. Though Bapu and Sadhu Singh were clearly outnumbered, they did not lose hope. In fact, they defended themselves with great vigour and skill. As the fight continued, Bapu was struck by the *takuya* on his shoulder. When Sadhu Singh was ready to strike with his *khoonda*, a powerfully built Mahton youth came from behind, caught hold of the *khoonda* and pulled it down with great force. Sadhu Singh fell flat on the ground and was immediately surrounded and attacked by the sardar's men.

At this critical moment, Bapu showed his indomitable courage. He roared and charged at the adversaries like a lion and exhorted Sadhu Singh to get up and fight boldly. Sadhu Singh who possessed a strong physique, got up from the ground, picked up the *kahi* and swung it at the sardar. Though his intention was to strike only with the wooden and blunt edge of his tool, yet in the heat of the moment, he managed to strike the sardar's head with the sharp edge. The blow felled the sardar and he lay prostrate on the ground – a spectacle which proved to be a turning point in the clash. The hired goondas fled. Bapu threw away his *dang*, caught the sardar's maternal uncle by the hair and overpowered him by the sheer strength of his arms. On his part, Sadhu Singh ran after the fleeing Mahton, and struck him with the back of his *kahi*, so that he fell down.

When Bapu saw the three men lying on the ground, he delivered the final blows. He said to Bhaiya, 'Look here, son. Tired and wounded as we are, we may not be able to fight with them again. We must see to it that they are not able to resume the fight.' They began to shower blows on the sardar and his accomplices till they were unable to retaliate. Soon, they were effectively immobilized, as not a single part of their bodies remained free from injuries. They were in a truly bad shape. Their clothes were torn and blood was oozing from every part. In fact, it was not possible to recognize them.

Bapu and Sadhu Singh slowly retraced their steps towards our house in Chak 39, which was more than four *murabbas* away. While their injuries were fresh and warm, they did not feel much pain. But when they crossed a water course (*sua*) the water of which was knee-deep, their wounds were drenched and pain became unbearable, especially in their lower limbs. Unable to walk fast because of their injuries and fatigue, they reached home after sunset. As soon as their condition became known to the members of the household, there was a great commotion which awakened me from sleep. I was shocked to see Bapu and Sadhu Singh splattered with blood all over. The news of the clash spread like wild fire to the neighbouring villages. Our cousins, who lived in Chak 40, and a number of well-wishers of the family rushed to our house. Soon there were around forty or fifty persons, each carrying a weapon – sticks, swords, axes, daggers and spears. Needless to say, the sardar's high-handedness had incensed them and they were thirsting for revenge.

Meanwhile, the news of the fight reached Teja Singh Samundri. Since he knew Bapu from close quarters, he was convinced, even before inquiring into the details of the incident, that the attack was totally unjustified and called for strong condemnation. He called on his close friend Ujagar Singh, who belonged to the same village, and asked him to put saddle on his mare, so that they were able to meet Bapu at the earliest. Before leaving, Teja Singh Samundri collected a bottle of brandy which, he thought, might be needed in case the condition of the injured so demanded. Riding at a fast pace, they reached our house and found that a large group of men had gathered there. Sensing the mood of the crowd, Samundri realized that there would be much bloodshed if these people were allowed to go to Rusiyana. But before making any move, he gave a peg of brandy each to Bapu and Sadhu Singh. Then he said to Bapu, 'Bhai ! You must prevent these boys from going to Bhagat Singh's village, otherwise there will be tragic consequences.' Bapu called the leading members of the group, including his nephews Chatar Singh and Basant Singh (the father of the martyr Comrade Chanan Singh Dhoot) and said, 'Look here, boys! You need not go to Rusiyana, because we have already done what you intend to do now. It would be better if you take us to the hospital at Samundri.'

Incidentally, the doctor incharge of the hospital at Samundri was a religious-minded person and, as such, a close friend of Bapu. He was a frequent visitor to our house. Whenever Bapu went to Samundri, he would call on the doctor and the two would remain engaged in a long discussion on religious matters. Whenever the doctor was in need of milk, Bapu (who was extremely fond of raising cows) sent one to his place. Seeing my father's condition, the doctor was shocked and said, 'Bhai ! How did you manage to involve yourself in this dirty business.' Bapu replied, 'Whatever was to happen has happened. We could do nothing to prevent it.' He attended to the injuries of Bapu and Sadhu Singh with utmost care. He cleaned the wounds, applied ointments and tied the bandages with his own hands. Similarly, the injured in Bhagat Singh's camp, including his maternal uncle and the Mahton, received appropriate medical treatment.

Meanwhile, all the sardars of the area rallied round to support Bhagat Singh, while a large number of muzaras came to stand behind our family. For the first time in my life I saw a polarization of this kind – the exploiting class of the rich and powerful landlords on the one side and the exploited class of the poor and weak tenants on the other. Rusli, who had frequently been victimized by Bhagat Singh's tyranny, could not remain unaffected by this bloody incident. In fact, he came out strongly in favour of those whom he had referred to as 'Dhootan-wale' during the course of his arguments with the sardar in question. He sent one of his seven sons, who was the eldest and the strongest, along with a buffalo to our house. On his part, Rusli went to Samundri and joined the ranks of those who wanted to see the guilty sardar humbled in public.

The most important question before the gathering at Samundri was – What steps should be taken to diffuse the explosive situation? Bapu declared, 'Whatever was to happen has happened. Now, we are not going to the court, for we do not intend to enter into any litigation. The sardar himself gave his *murabbas* to us. We must cultivate them for a year and then we would relinquish them and go to some other place.' Hearing this, Bhagat Singh lamented before the mediators, 'Give us any punishment you like. But for God's sake, please get my *murabbas* released from their control. They were only two and they thrashed us like anything. Had they been more in number, they would have killed the entire population of our village.' Bapu stood his ground and said emphatically, 'We would till the *murabbas* for one year. We are not going to leave them in any case or by any means. If we have committed any indiscretion, let the sardar complain. It is he who has been high-handed. In spite of this, we are willing to cultivate his *murabbas* for the rest of the year.' The sardar pleaded, 'If you allow my *murabbas* to remain with them, I would understand that you want us to be killed.' There were endless arguments and counter arguments, but no solution in sight.

Seeing that Bapu would not be swayed, Teja Singh Samundri and Ujagar Singh pressurized him and said, 'We promise to get you already sown *murabbas* as well as compensation for your crop, if you agree to release Bhagat Singh's *murabbas* from your control.' Bapu finally relented under pressure and said, 'If you insist on your plea, I am willing to abide by your decision. But let me tell you that the sardar is the kind of man whose *murabbas* should not be released. His treatment of the muzaras has been such that he should be taught an unforgettable lesson.' To mollify Bapu, Teja Singh Samundri said, 'He (Bhagat Singh) has learnt enough of a lesson. There is nothing more which he ought to learn. The people of this area universally condemn his conduct and heap curses on him.'

Eventually, we agreed to release Bhagat Singh's *murabbas* with immediate effect. In return, we were given two *murabbas* in Chak 35 on which crops had already been sown. Besides, we were granted a cash compensation of Rs. 1,000. In the circumstances, it was an honourable agreement, which could be brought about only by a spirit of accommodation on both sides. It was the prudence of Teja Singh Samundri that extinguished the fire of conflict, diffused a potentially dangerous situation and hammered out a settlement acceptable to the two conflicting parties. We cultivated the new *murabbas* for a year and then returned to Chak 39 to till the land which we had earlier tilled.

With the outbreak of the First World War, recruitment for the Indian army began on a large scale. The sardars, who acted as agents of the British government, used their influence in the rural areas to send the young sons of the muzaras for recruitment.[15] In return for this service, the sardars received awards from the British government in the form of commendation certificates, titles, etc. An attempt was made to induct my brothers into the army, but Bapu was strongly opposed to the idea. He stated that he would, under no circumstance, allow his children to be taken away. The sardars offered all kinds of allurements,[16] but did not succeed in the face of Bapu's firm opposition.

Around 1918, when the First World War was drawing to a close, the dreadful epidemic of plague swept the plains of Punjab and took a heavy toll of human life in Chak 39, Chak 40 and the neighbouring villages. In fact, deaths occurred in such quick succession that the dead bodies could not be removed for disposal. Sometimes four or five bodies were found being burnt at the same time in the cremation ground. The contagion created so much fear in the countryside that people fled from their homes in the villages and sought shelter in their cultivated fields. The first member of our family who succumbed to the disease was Harbans Singh, the son of my father's elder brother Nagina Singh. He was followed by Sadhu Singh, my eldest brother. I was also infected by the disease. But I survived, probably on account of the medicines which were administered to me. Then Santa Singh, the son of my elder uncle Shiv Singh, and my brother Khem Singh also died. For a while there was some respite from death and we all believed that my brother Lal Singh would survive. But it was not to be. The plague took away all my three brothers. The elder son of my uncle, whose younger brother had also died, visited us and asked us not to be disheartened, for these tragedies were willed by nature and we were helpless. Unfortunately he, who had come to offer all possible help in the difficult circumstances, also fell a victim to the epidemic.[17]

Within a period of fifteen days, we had lost seven or eight members of our family. The series of tragic deaths caused a sadness, the intensity of which could only be felt, but not described. Bapu, who was extremely religious, was a fatalist to the core. He believed that children were a gift of God, they were God's possession and He could take them back as and when He so willed. He did not wail or weep, though he allowed those who came to mourn the deaths of his sons and nephews. He immersed himself in the *gurbani* and did everything within his means to help my mother bear the great loss. I became the sole recipient of their love and affection, care and attention, which I had earlier shared with my brothers when they were alive.

The epidemic adversely affected all aspects of our life in the Chenab Canal Colony. Before the plague, my family owned a large number of cattle and our agricultural activities were quite extensive. I was too young at the time, having just entered my teens. I could neither handle the plough nor cut the fodder. All I could do was to lead the cattle to the grazing ground or feed them at home. Add to this, the sorrow and gloom which had engulfed our family. After the plague, our survival became difficult in that harsh environment. In this state, we sent letters to our kith and kin in our native village and informed them of our plight. My sister and her husband, who belonged to a village called Rarha, came to our rescue. Acting on their advice, Bapu sold off some of our cattle, and taking the remaining ones with him, left for Rarha along with our visitors.

Bapu returned to the Bar after a long time. In his absence, our turn came to utilize the canal water. We were entitled to it only after a neighbouring farmer had done so. This farmer had in his employment a man named Bhagtu (a Chuhra by caste),[18] who had close relations with my family. He often visited us after working for his master. Whenever he came, my mother would offer him milk or some dairy product, a gesture which he never failed to appreciate. When it was time to water our fields, I asked Bhagtu to help us engage a man for the purpose. He replied that there was no need to arrange for one when he was there. He offered to do the job and said that it was a question of only one night. He, however, asked me to accompany him.

The two of us reached the fields at the appropriate time. The procedure followed in the Bar was simple – water was 'cut' either at sunrise or sunset. For instance, if a farmer received his supply at sunrise, it continued till sunset and vice versa. When we were about to make the cut, the neighbouring sardar who had already received his share of water, decided that he wanted more water. There were two reasons for this. First, I was only a young lad and was not in a position to assert my family's right. Second, it was the month of October-November (*Katta*) and sowing was in progress. The sardar thought that if he got the supply for another two hours, he would have a sufficient quantity of water. With this in mind, he challenged us to make the cut. Bhagtu interceded on my behalf and said to the sardar who was his employer, 'On sardar! Have some sense. These people have lost almost all the members of their family due to plague. His father has gone to his native village along with the cattle. This boy is too young and he is doing you no harm. So do not be high-handed.' The appeal, however, fell on deaf ears for the sardar refused to give up his evil intentions. Bhagtu could not tolerate this injustice and asked me to go ahead and make the cut. When I proceeded to do so, the sardar advanced towards me, flourishing his *dang*. Bhagtu moved swiftly and overpowered the sardar, lifted him off the ground and threw him into the water. Bhagtu then dealt a severe blow to the sardar with his *dang*. When the sardar saw his own servant fighting for my family's right, he had no alternative but to leave the scene in a huff.

Thereafter, we began to water the fields. Bhagtu feared that the sardar would return with his men to avenge himself. Pre-empting such a possibility, he decided to get his friends from Chak 35. He asked me to lie still in a uncultivated patch (*van*) which stood in the midst of a sugar cane field. After having assured himself about my safety, he went away and returned with about a dozen young and strong Balmiki men. Bhagtu and his friends watered the fields the whole night. At daybreak Bhagtu said to me, 'My relation with that sardar is severed for ever, for he will not allow me to come near him any more. From now onwards, I belong to you. Go home and tell the whole story to your mother. Let her prepare meals for all of us who have gathered here.' I went to my house and narrated the incident. Hearing this, my mother called in a neighbouring woman to help her prepare the food, including a lot of *ghee-shakar*. I carried the food to Bhagtu and his friends. Once they had eaten, they left. There was no sign of the erring sardar who had unjustly tried to deprive us of our legitimate right.

In the meanwhile, Bapu returned to the Bar after visiting our ancestral village. Someone made him familiar with the dispute over water, which had taken place during his absence. On hearing the unpleasant details of the incident, he flew into a terrible rage. He was tending the cattle at that time. He left the task unfinished, picked up his *dang*, found the errant sardar and dealt him several blows with his stick. The sardar was taken aback by this sudden but determined attack and ran away in order to save himself from further punishment. Seeing this, a large number of people gathered there and cursed the sardar for his high-handedness and also condemned the attitude of other sardars, to whom I had earlier reported the matter, but who failed to warn the wrong doer.

There was no reasonable justification to extend our stay in the Bar. Therefore, we decided to return to Dhoot Kalan, our ancestral village. We gathered our harvest and disposed off some of our cattle in one way or the other. The entire family of one of my uncles (Shiv Singh) had been wiped out by the epidemic. In other words, the very lamp (*chiragh*) of his family was extinguished. But a part of the family of the other uncle (Nagina Singh) had survived and now it returned along with us. I and my cousin Amar Singh packed our household goods, loaded them in bullock-carts and left the land of the Bar, where we had tilled the soil for a long time.

After having settled down, we began work on our ancestral land, which was being cultivated by some kin. However we had not been receiving anything from them for carrying on cultivation on our land. The agricultural practices current in this part of Punjab were entirely different from those in the Bar. For one thing, the plots (*khattis*) were smaller measuring between 10 *marlas* and 2 *kanals*. In fact, the working space was so limited that it became difficult to turn the pair of bullocks while ploughing. Second, canal water, which was the life blood of the farmer in the Bar, was not available here.

Bapu breathed his last in 1924. I was the sole surviving male member of our family. At this time, I was about twenty years of age. My mother and I found ourselves struggling for equanimity in the ocean of grief. I was lonely and confused. The future loomed like an endless dark tunnel.

During those days, the Akali movement dominated the political stage of Punjab. It had gathered a lot of strength, with morchas being organized at Jaito and Pheruman. Contingents (*jathas*) of Akali activists toured all over Punjab. One such *jatha* visited our village. We extended a warm and enthusiastic welcome to the members of the *jatha*. It organized a number of religious congregations (*diwans*) which included singing of hymns (*shabad kirtan*) from the Sikh scripture and lectures.

The *jatha* left a deep impact on the minds of the people.[19] Bachan Singh Saini and Udham Singh Goka, both of whom belonged to the village, joined the *jatha*. A large number of the people marched to Pur Heeran, where the *jatha* had organized the next phase of its programme.

NOTES AND REFERENCES

1. Bordering on Jalandhar, Sirwal formed a long strip of land between 3 and 8 miles in width. It constituted the most fertile part of Hoshiarpur district, as it received the fertilizing matter flowing down from the highlands. Water was found at a depth of 12 to 15 feet. *District Gazetteer, Hoshiarpur*, 1904, p. 3.
2. The village was included in the Bhunga taluqa, one of the detached pieces of territory, which constituted the princely state of Kapurthala. Having an area of 24 square miles, Bhunga was annexed to Kapurthala in 1822 by Raja Fateh Singh. Lying at the foot of the Siwaliks and irrigated by the *chos*, the Bhunga pocket was exceedingly fertile. *District Gazetteer, Kapurthala State*, 1904, pp. 1-2.
3. For a study of the foundation, architecture, history and ceremonial practices of Harmandir Sahib, see Harbans Singh, ed., *The Encyclopaedia of Sikhism*, vol. II, pp. 239-48.
4. In 1927, a special study on the subdivision of landholdings, showed that 22.5 per cent of cultivators (owners or tenants) of Punjab tilled 1 acre or less and 33 per cent cultivated between 1 and 5 acres. In Hoshiarpur district, nearly one-third of cultivators tilled 2.5 acres or less. Board of Economic Enquiry, Punjab, *The Size and Distribution of Cultivators Holdings in Punjab*, 1928, p. 15.
5. Seasonal torrents or *chos*, which rise in the Siwaliks and spread like a network in the plains, constituted the principal feature of the submontane tract. In an earlier period, the silt washed down from the Siwaliks contributed to the formation of the alluvial plain, but owing to the deforestation of the hills the *chos* have destroyed the fertility of the soil. Remaining dry in rainless months, they become raging torrents after heavy rains. While entering the plains they flowed in well-defined channels, but gradually widened their way and broke into several branches before spreading over the surface and burying all cultivation under infertile sand. The area covered by torrent beds increased from

72 square miles in 1852 to 147 square miles in 1896. *Imperial Gazetteer of India, Provincial Series, Punjab,* vol. I, p. 393.

6. The inhabitants of Kapurthala State suffered from severe disabilities even in the mid-1930s. Fresh settlements of 1921 and 1931 had doubled the land revenue rates, as compared to the British districts of Jalandhar and Hoshiarpur. In addition, the peasants had to pay various cesses that amounted to over Rs. 14 per Rs. 100 of land revenue. They were incensed by a shorter unit of land measurement, as an acre comprised 239 marlas as compared to 211 in Jalandhar district. Master Hari Singh, *Punjab Peasant in Freedom Struggle,* vol. 11, p. 214.
7. The development of the Chenab Colony was largest of the nine canal projects. Having an allotted area of over 2 million acres, it covered the southern section of the Rachna Doab. The main canal and its three great networks were colonized during 1892-1905, while extensions were carried out in the second and third decades of the twentieth century. Imran Ali, *The Punjab Under Imperialism,* p.18.
8. Samundri was a tehsil in the newly created Lyallpur district. Spread over 1,309 square miles, it had 495 villages. In 1906, its population stood at 266,277 and the revenues amounted to Rs. 6.7 lakh. Its soil generally was a fine loam. It was wholly irrigated by the Chenab, except a few scattered plots in the Ravi lowlands which depended on wells. *Imperial Gazetteer of India, Provincial Series, Punjab,* vol. II, p. 220.
9. Teja Singh Samundri was born in 1881 in village Rai Ka Burj, Amritsar district. His father retired as risaldar major from the Indian army and migrated to Samundri, where he had received five *murabbas* in Chak 140 on the Gugera branch. Teja Singh, after serving in the army for 3 years, immersed himself in socio-religious activities. He was instrumental in opening schools in Rai Ka Burj, Sarhali and Lyallpur. He provided financial assistance to two newspapers, viz., the *Akali* and the *Akali Te Pardesi.* In the early 1920s, he held important positions in the Shiromani Gurdwara Prabandhak Committee, the Shiromani Akali Dal and the All India Congress Committee. As a front ranking leader of the gurudwara reform movement, he played a prominent role in the morchas held at Guru Ka Bagh and Jaito. Piar Singh, *Teja Singh Samundri,* pp. 9-25.
10. Besides extravagant expenditure on social ceremonies, indebtedness was caused by the smallness of holdings, insecurity of agricultural conditions, general improvidence, recurring loss of cattle

due to disease or drought. Since these factors were not dominant in the colonies owing to greater agricultural security, the burden of debt was less as compared to other parts of Punjab. Malcolm Darling, *The Punjab Peasant in Prosperity and Debt*, pp. 126-30.

11. Under this sharecropping (*batai*) system, the landowners paid a certain part of the cost of production, e.g. payment to village menials, government dues, water rates, and seeds. But the proportion of produce appropriated by them varied from one-fourth to one-half or even higher. M. Mufakharul Islam, *Irrigation, Agriculture and the Raj: Punjab 1887-1947*, p. 82.
12. Water rate (*abiana*), charged from the actual user, was doubled between the late nineteenth century and the mid-1920s. It was fixed on the basis of area irrigated and not volume, though a higher rate was charged in crops requiring a larger number of waterings. In the case of the lower Chenab Canal it was 128 annas per acre for sugar cane, 68 annas for cotton and wheat and 48 annas for gram. Islam, op. cit., pp. 125-7.
13. Primary education did not spread in the rural areas because of a popular notion that it prejudiced the rural scholar against his ancestral occupation and made him unfit for agriculture. In 1886 zamindari schools, which required half-time attendance and were closed during harvest, were opened. Since they did not find favour with the agricultural classes, they were replaced by rural schools from 1908 onwards. The new curriculum, which excluded Persian and included the Indian system of account keeping, was adopted progressively by all primary schools in villages. *Report on the Progress of Education in Punjab, 1901-2*, p. 18; *Administration Report of the Punjab and Its Dependencies, 1907-8*, p. 48.
14. Balmikis were regarded as a sect of Chuhras, the group of scavenger castes. They worshipped Lal Beg or Bala Shah, who has been identified with Balmiki, the author of the *Ramayana*. For details, see H.A. Rose, *A Glossary of the Tribes and Castes of the Punjab and North West Frontier Province*, vol. III, pp. 20-3.
15. Since the British government treated Punjab as a major recruiting ground, the number of infantry divisions recruited from the province increased from 28 in 1862 to 57 in 1914. At the outbreak of the First World War, there were 100,000 Punjabis in the army, but during the war another 380,000 were added. In each district there was a League of Recruiting Board, consisting of bureaucrats and influential non-officials. Each territorial unit – tahsil, zail and village – was informed about the number of recruits it was

expected to provide. Bhagwan Josh, *Communist Movement in the Punjab*, pp. 18-25.

16. The greatest allurement to potential recruits was the prospect, after retiring from the army, of securing a land grant. Military grantees were allotted plots, varying from 25 to 55 acres, in the four larger colonies, viz., Chenab, Jhelum, Lower Bari Doab and Nili Bar. In the Nili Bar, military pensioners were allotted 75,000 acres and another 25,000 were allocated to them from the civilian quota. Imran Ali, *Punjab Under Imperialsim*, pp. 113-14.
17. In Punjab, the plague was more severe than in any other part of India. During the 1898-1918 period plague claimed 2,992,166 lives which accounted for 30 per cent of the total for the entire country. In the order of severity, the death rate for 1906-7, 1903-4, 1904-5 and 1914-15 was 27.28, 16.93, 16.73 and 10.62 respectively. The outbreak of 1917-18 was below average intensity. It claimed 105, 459 lives, i.e. a death rate of 4.36 per mile. Major Norman F. White, *Twenty Years of the Plague in India, with Special Reference to the Outbreak of 1917-18*, pp. 3-4.
18. Chuhras were numerically and economically important but socially regarded as lowest of the low. They were comparatively few on the frontier, but were most numerous in the Lahore and Amritsar divisions, where they performed hard agricultural labour. They were also engaged in scavenging houses and streets, working and carrying manure to the fields, and making winnowing pans, thatch, ropes, etc. Denzil Ibbetson, *Punjab Castes*, p. 293.
19. The movement aimed at securing exclusive control over nearly 200 important religious places through the promulgation of the Sikh Gurdwaras and Shrines Act. Over a period of five years, nearly 30,000 men and women were imprisoned, 400 lost their lives and 2,000 were wounded. While the leadership was provided by middle-class Sikh nationalists, the Sikh peasantry formed the backbone of the movement. Further, 66 per cent of volunteers belonged to the Jat Sikh peasantry, the majority of them hailing from the districts of Lyallpur, Shaikhupura, Amritsar, Jalandhar and Hoshiarpur. Mohinder Singh, *The Akali Movement*, pp. 137-43.

CHAPTER 2

Migration to Foreign Lands

My decision to go abroad in search of employment did not involve any painstaking planning and preparation, but it was a sudden development. I had gone to Rarha to visit my sister's husband, who had unbounded affection for me. One evening, during my stay, the village headman (*lambardar*) appeared outside the house and began to hurl abuses at my brother-in-law's relatives.[1] Since he was using a filthy language without any restraint, it was clear that he was totally drunk. Probably, because of this no one in the house retaliated. I was, however, incensed by this outburst. It was certain that the *lambardar* would not stop unless made to do so. I picked up a *dang* and dealt him a number of quick and telling blows, so that he fell flat on the ground. He was so badly injured that his brothers had to carry him away.

My brother-in-law feared that the *lambardar*, who had contacts with the police and other civil officers at the various levels of administration, would not only have me arrested, but would also implicate me in false cases. He became extremely worried about my safety and well-being, particularly in view of the fact that I was the lone surviving member of his wife's family. He gave me Rs. 100 and asked me to leave forthwith for Singapore and join my cousin Jwala Singh Dhoot (the son of my uncle Nagina Singh), who had gone there earlier.

It was under these circumstances that I left the country in 1927, without even informing my mother. In those days, it was easy to reach Singapore, as one had only to go to Calcutta and board a ship bound for Singapore, and no passport was required.[2] On reaching the city, I found widespread unemployment. I met my cousin Jwala Singh Dhoot and sought his help in getting a job. I managed to get several jobs, one after the other, but the salary was only $ 10, which was too meagre to make a decent living. In the absence of a better alternative, I was forced to accept these low paid jobs. I had made arrangements to stay in the main gurdwara along with two companions, Teja Singh of village Munda (Amritsar district, near Goindwal) and another person whose name I cannot recall but who belonged to village Kathu Nangal in the same district. We became good friends. Being young and independent, we developed a fondness for eating and drinking. Since we were physically strong and courageous, we did not hesitate to chastise anyone who dared to be high-handed and unjust. On account of this kind of lifestyle, we acquainted with a sizeable number of Punjabis, including a man named Ujagar Singh. He belonged to Mangeki, a village near Kartarpur in Jalandhar district. He had been actively involved in the Akali movement. As he was proficient in singing hymns (*shabads*), he moved into the gurdwara and became friendly with us.

One day, Ujagar Singh told us that the priest (*bhai*) of the gurdwara received the literature of the Ghadar Party from the USA and passed it on to the British intelligence.[3] At that time, we did not know anything about the Ghadar Party or its literature. Ujagar Singh explained to us in detail the aims and objectives, ideology and methods of the Ghadar Party, as also the content of its literature. The idealism of our youth could not tolerate the unpatriotic conduct of the *bhai*,[4] who had already become unpopular with the Sikh community because of his somewhat loose morals. The three of us discussed the matter among ourselves and decided that such a man had no right to hold the position of a *bhai*.

We drew up a plan to oust the *bhai* from his post. We bought half a bottle of liquor and a dish of chicken curry. Around 9 O'clock at night, we entered the *bhai's* room and placed both these things in front of him. Apparently shocked at our audacity, he protested, 'What are you doing? You must know that this is a gurdwara.' We replied, 'Bhai ji ! Please do not get agitated. We know that you drink, but we believe that there is no harm in doing so. The congregation (*sangat*) is sleeping. If you take a few pegs and go to bed, nobody will know any thing about it.' We succeeded in luring him into the trap we had laid for him. When he had helped himself to liquor and meat, we fell upon him, caught hold of his beard and pulled him out into the courtyard. Teja Singh began to beat him with a shoe. Hearing the commotion, the *sangat* was roused and collected around the *bhai*. Everyone was shocked to learn that the *bhai* had been caught red-handed indulging in evil deeds within the premises of the gurdwara. Incensed by the *bhai's* behaviour, they proceeded to thrash him. In fact, they vied with one another in giving him blow after blow. They said, 'Didn't we say that the man possessed loose morals. Now, he has been thoroughly exposed.' Others said, 'All of you felt that the conduct of these boys was improper. Now it has been proved that the criticism was unfair, as the credit for exposing the corrupt *bhai* goes to them.'

Though the *sangat* expelled the *bhai*, yet our task remained unfinished. We could not ignore the fact that the *bhai* was hand in glove with the British intelligence, the local chief of which was a man who belonged to Amritsar. We feared that the latter would mobilize the natives of that district and, with their active support, would make an all-out effort to reinstate the *bhai*. We began to make feverish preparations for a clash, which appeared to be inevitable. First of all, we asked the *sangat* to lock the gurdwara doors from inside. Then we came out of the building and contacted everyone who was known to us and informed them of what had transpired and sought their help in consolidating our gain. Our efforts bore fruit as a considerable number of people offered their support. In this context, I must mention the name of one Dalip Singh, who belonged to Bhagwanpur, a village near Bholath, in the princely state of Kapurthala.

The following day being a Sunday, a large gathering was expected at the gurdwara. We asked Ujagar Singh, who possessed a sweet voice and great skill in playing on the harmonium, to lead the prayers. As people began to arrive, we found that the congregation was broadly divided into two groups. Those who supported our cause belonged to Doaba and Malwa, and those who were opposed to us belonged to Amritsar and had openly received the support of the police in mobilizing themselves.

Since majority of the people had the ouster of the *bhai* uppermost in their minds, the situation in the gurdwara was extremely tense, if not explosive. Both groups had come prepared for a clash, as they were armed with swords and sticks. However, a section of the congregation was interested only in the customary prayers and not in anything else. This group assertively said, 'Please start the *bhog* ceremony for which we have come. Let other things come afterwards.' Thus, a clash was averted for the time being. Ujagar Singh completed the *bhog* ceremony, sang a few hymns and recited the final prayer. His performance, which was impressive as well as flawless, succeeded in casting a spell on the *sangat*. As a consequence, a number of our opponents decided to abandon the cause of the *bhai*, who was simply no match for Ujagar Singh. As our opponents were reduced to a miniscule minority, they were forced to fall in line with the rest of the congregation, which recognized Ujagar Singh as the successor of the *bhai* who had been ousted unceremoniously. The tension was diffused and a number of people congratulated us for exposing the undesirable activities of the former *bhai* and thus restoring the sanctity of the holy place.

Four days after this incident, another interesting development took place. Ujagar Singh came to our room, when we were asleep. He awakened us and asked us to come to his room. Ujagar Singh opened a huge packet which he had received that day, while we watched in suspense. To our pleasant surprise, the packet contained a large number of copies of the *Ghadar Di Goonj*.[5] Ujagar Singh picked up a copy and started reading aloud, especially the poetry contained therein. The verses were intensely patriotic, with a strong revolutionary flavour. Each one was more fiery than the other and had a spontaneous impact on our young minds. Filled with enthusiasm, we distributed the copies to our friends the next morning. As soon as they read the contents, they too were spellbound by the contents. It appeared as if a new spirit had been injected into them.[6] Once again the people praised us, for they realized that because of the former *bhai* they had been deprived of the opportunity of making themselves familiar with the revolutionary activities of the Ghadar Party.

My cousin and I were not satisfied with the employment

opportunities available in Singapore. We therefore decided to leave Singapore for some other country, so as to make a decent living. Jwala Singh Dhoot had secured a passport for Mexico and I followed suit. While we were in the midst of making preparations to leave, Radha Singh, another cousin of mine, arrived in Singapore after spending seventeen years in America. He was a friendly and affectionate person. As soon as he learnt that two men from Dhoot Kalan were in Singapore, he sent us a message. We met him and discussed in detail our future plans. We availed ourselves of the opportunity of benefiting from Radha Singh's experience. He advised us against going to Mexico, on the grounds that it was extremely difficult, if not impossible, to reach the capital city for one had to cross a vast tract of dry land where the natives often preyed on the life and belongings of travellers. The journey through this dangerous tract was possible if a close friend offered to give a lift to the migrants in his car. Thus Mexico was ruled out. After examining various possibilities, Radha Singh suggested that we should sail to Argentina. Understandably, we agreed with him.

I had another friend who was also very keen to accompany us. His name too was Jwala Singh and he belonged to Sidhwan Manjhaki (a village near Shankar in Jalandhar district). In order to distinguish him from my cousin, Jwala Singh Dhoot, I will henceforth refer to him as simply Jwala Singh. Since we had very little money, we began to augment our meagre resources by various means. At this juncture, a man who belonged to village Bir (near Shankar in Jalandhar district) arrived from America. I requested him to loan Rs. 500 to Jwala Singh, who already had Rs. 700. Jwala Singh Dhoot and I also had some money. Finally, the three of us left Singapore and sailed for Colombo. After getting our passports stamped from the consulate of Argentina in Colombo, we left for France from where we were to sail for Argentina. In France, we checked our funds and discovered to out dismay that we had sea-fare only for two, with £3 to spare. In this predicament, Jwala Singh Dhoot suggested to me, 'The two of us should make use of our funds to reach Argentina, while Jwala Singh stays back. Afterwards, we will send him the money as early as our sources permit, so that he can also join us.' I mulled over the proposal and replied, 'There is no doubt that we will call Jwala Singh sometime after we reach Argentina. But we are related to each other. If we leave him here to wait, he is quite likely to doubt our commitment to his cause. Therefore, it will be fair and just if the two of you go, while I remain here to wait.' My cousin understood my point of view and said, 'I have served in the army. I have a considerable experience of staying at unknown places and meeting unknown people. On the other hand, you do not possess this experience. Therefore, I think that I will have no problem staying here. The two of you should go ahead.' We accepted this suggestion and divided the remaining £3 between us. Jwala Singh Dhoot entered into a contract with a French bank and succeeded in making arrangements for his daily expenses.

After sailing for seventeen days, we reached Brazil. From there we sailed for Buenos Aires, the capital of Argentina, on a German ship named *Monto Sermente*. As soon as we reached our destination, all the passengers disembarked. But the two of us were not allowed to do so. Agitated, we complained to the Captain, who explained, 'The consuls of various countries have stood guarantee for their respective citizens, but your (British) consul has failed to do so. Therefore, you will be sent back.' Taken aback by this revelation, we resigned ourselves to our fate.[7] In those days, the ships followed a standard practice. As soon as a ship was unloaded, it had to leave the harbour and was anchored in deeper waters. Accordingly, our ship moved about 1 km into the sea, where it was supposed to remain for eighteen days.

Needless to say, we were not prepared for this shock. We could never imagine that our efforts will result in a miserable failure. In fact, I was so desperate that I resolved to get down there or even end my life by jumping into the sea. More importantly, for the first time, I was filled with unbounded anger against the British who were responsible for our plight. Since the Germans, too, were anti-British, the crew exploited our sentiments to their advantage, while cultivating cordial social relations with us. In particular, the Captain was sympathetic towards our cause and assured us that he would not carry us along with him but would drop us at some convenient place.

Meanwhile, I remembered that I had the address of a man named Ralla, who originally hailed from Shrinh (a village near Nakodar in Jalandhar district) but had permanently settled in Argentina. He owned more than 200 qualras (approximately over 1,000 acres) of land in partnership with Inder, a native of Rurkha (a village on Goraya-Jandiala road in Jalandhar district). I handed over the address to the Captain and requested him to contact Ralla on the wireless. Incidentally, Ralla's brother, Amar Singh, was expected to arrive from India. As soon as he received the message, Ralla assumed that it had something to do with his brother. Though the distance between his farm and Buenos Aires was the same as that between Dhoot Kalan and New Delhi, yet he took the trouble of coming all the way. We met him and introduced ourselves. I gave a pound (the only one I had) to Jwala Singh and asked him to buy three mugs of beer. The three of us sat down and looked at one another. Since both of them hailed from neighbouring villages, I thought Jwala Singh stood a better chance of getting help from our guest. I asked my partner to initiate the talk. Jwala Singh narrated our tale, but Ralla was not impressed. Apparently, he lacked the ability to communicate with others. Therefore, I assumed the responsibility of pleading our case. In spite of the fact that I made a judicious use of wit and wisdom, Ralla was reluctant to help us. However, it did not take us long to understand why he was disinclined. On two previous occasions, he had helped batches of immigrants from Amritsar district, but they had failed to reciprocate the kindness of their benefactor. It was no wonder that Ralla had resolved against extending any help to migrants from Punjab. I did not lose heart and put forth a number of arguments to win Ralla's favour. I asserted that all fingers of a hand were not similar, that only he could save us from the jaws of death, and that if he helped us, we would prove that his opinion of Punjabi migrants was wrong. Eventually, Ralla relented and took pity on us. He promised to make all the arrangements necessary for our release, a process which would take a week. After finalizing the plan for our release in the presence of the Captain, Ralla left the ship.

After Ralla's departure, we were assailed by many doubts. The biggest question was – what would we do if Ralla did not keep his promise. We realized that we should not rely solely on Ralla and began to examine other options. Our first hope hinged on the German boys who cooked and served food in the ship. They promised to give us life jackets and to escort us to safety, in case we decided to jump into the sea and swim to the coastline. The alternative depended on the Captain, who had offered to take us to Brazil or Uruguay from where we could enter Argentina by the land route. After weighing the relative chances of success of the two plans, I said to Jwala Singh, 'I am in favour of swimming to the shore along with one of the German boys, because no one will ever suspect anything as the entire area is crowded with so many ships and boats.'

However, Jawala Singh did not accept the alternative as he did not want to be swallowed by the fish. I argued, 'Do you think that we are alive. We are already as good as dead, for the British government has left no means for us to survive.' Jwala Singh remained adamant. When I saw that my arguments had failed to convince him, I lost my patience. In my desperation I decided to leave him sleeping and go it alone. In the end, however, better sense prevailed and we decided to wait for a week before pursuing any other alternative.

Seven days passed, but there was no news of Ralla. Jwala Singh said in despair, 'We are in a foreign land. Who helps whom?' Consoling him I said, 'Ralla must have been held up by some small and insignificant technicality, which usually crops up in these matters. We should have patience and wait for another one or two days.' The following day at noon, the Captain asked his peon if there was any visitor. He answered that a man with a cap on his head had come. Unable to control our excitement, we rushed to the cabin. We found to our joy that the visitor was none other than Ralla. He had brought the legal documents which were essential for our entry into Argentina. In these documents he had affirmed that he was responsible for us in all respects and that he possessed the financial resources to take care of us. We were overwhelmed by the efforts made by a total stranger to secure our release. In fact, our benefactor had stood as a saviour in our struggle against death, for the British government had virtually pushed us on the road to destruction. We did not have words to express our feelings and emotions. The Captain also rejoiced at our success and arranged a lavish party in which fish, meat, eggs and large pegs of liquor were served. After thanking the Captain and his men for their invaluable moral support, we took our leave of them.

In Buenos Aires, Ralla first took us to a restaurant and treated us to a lavish meal. Then he turned his attention to our clothes. Having expressed his dissatisfaction, he led us to a shop which sold readymade garments. He spent an amount of Rs. 1,000 on purchasing clothes for us, which were tailored in accordance with the fashion of that country. Then we went sightseeing in the city, with Ralla as our host, escort and guide. We were deeply impressed by what we saw in Buenos Aires, which was undoubtedly the most beautiful, well-maintained and cleanest city in the South America.[8] Later, we left for Ralla's farm, which was situated near the small town of Rasifa.

On reaching his farm, Ralla said, 'Listen to me carefully. From today onwards, I will not talk to you for fifteen days and you will not talk to me during this period. Here you will find everything you need – eggs, pork, mutton, wine and beer. Eat and drink as much as you can. Take complete rest and get rid of your fatigue. The only work you have to do is cooking. Choose your own methods, for I will not interfere at all. I will appear only when it is time to eat. If you cook well you will get the credit and if you do not, the discredit, too, will be yours. In short, you are the complete masters of the show.' During the next fifteen days, we followed Ralla's instructions in letter and spirit, giving him no cause for complaint. We made ourselves at home and performed various chores like tending the cattle and collecting the milk. We looked into every minute detail, so that nothing was wasted or remained unfinished. The way in which we managed the household left a deep and favourable impression on Ralla's mind.

At the end of the fifteen-day period, Ralla hosted a lavish tea party. Satisfied with our performance, he said, 'Now you are in a position to go wherever you like and do whatever you like.' We sought his advice about various employment opportunities. He explained, 'If you ask me, the most profitable season here is that of corn harvesting. In fact, the work brings so much income that a large number of people, holding well-paid white-collar jobs in the cities, are seen plucking corn cobs in the fields. The task, however, is slightly difficult because the weather is a bit cold.' We informed him that we were used to this kind of work as we had done it back home. Ralla agreed with us, 'The work will be advantageous to you in two respects. First, you will be able to earn a handsome amount in a short time and second, you will get an opportunity to learn the native language.' As there were two weeks before the corn harvesting season, we worked for Ralla during this period and he offered to pay for our labour. But we refused to accept any wages from him. Nevertheless, he bought a few things for us such as a chocket (*sua*), a collar (*patta*) to be worn around the neck and a bag (*bora*) made of leather. These, we soon discovered, were absolutely essential for us during the harvest season.

Maize was cultivated in Argentina in the same way as potatoes in Punjab.[9] The crop was sown in *ohris*, which were 1½ feet apart. As the plants grew, soil was raised on both sides. When the corn cobs ripened and began to hang, they were ready to be plucked, an operation which was performed manually while standing. We began our work with great enthusiasm. I found that I could pluck 150 to 175 maunds of corn cobs everyday, which brought me an income of 55 to 70 peso (1 peso was equal to Rs. 1.25). At the end of the harvest season, the landlord organized a grand feast. The workers were not only given their wages, but were also served liquor and meat. The feast appeared to be somewhat similar to the celebrations held in Punjab, where *marunda* was prepared and *fakka* was distributed following the harvesting of wheat.

In all this we had not forgotten Jwala Singh Dhoot, whom we had left behind in France. We had to send him some money so that he could join us at the earliest. But the question was whom to approach for such a large sum of money. We did not have the courage to seek Ralla's help as he had already done a lot for us. Yet, he had promised that whenever Jwala Singh Dhoot arrived, he would help him in securing an entry into Argentina. I consulted Jwala Singh and went to Rosario to meet Parsan Singh, the brother of Matta Singh (both were uncles of Chanan Singh Dhoot and had been in Argentina even while I was in

India). I succeeded in borrowing £32 from him and sent the money to Jwala Singh Dhoot. We began to wait for his arrival with the hope that we would go to another suitable place after he joined us.

Just as our work in the maize farms was nearing completion, we had a visitor. He was Rattan Singh of Raipur Dabba (a village near Phillaur in Jalandhar district). A prominent leader of the Ghadar Party and a full-time worker, Rattan Singh was constantly travelling and mobilizing support for the anti-British movement. During the course of his campaigns, he had visited Europe, Canada, the USA, Panama and Argentina.[10] His visit was a pleasant surprise and we welcomed him warmly. He talked about the political situation in India and the international developments that had a bearing on it. We felt as if we were listening to a divine messenger who had descended straight from the other world. He described the injustice suffered by Indians under British imperialism. Since we had been its recent victims, Rattan Singh had no difficulty in creating a rapport with us. Our conversation turned to the Ghadar Party and its activities. We narrated to him the Singapore episode involving the *Gadhar Di Goonj*. Hearing this, he praised our courage, daring and enterprise. He told us that he would ensure that we received the leaflet regularly.

When Rattan Singh prepared to leave, we thought it fit to give him some money. We approached Ralla for a loan of $100 and explained to him the noble work being done by Rattan Singh for the freedom of our motherland. Ralla readily handed over the money, but Rattan Singh refused to accept it. We prevailed upon him, 'It has been very kind of you to have travelled all the way to visit us. We are honoured by your presence. Kindly accept this small amount as a token of our support to our national cause. We have come here recently and we have been able to manage only an insignificant amount. With the passage of time, we will be able to earn more and save more. Then, we will be in a position to contribute in a more substantial way.' Reluctant to accept the money he said, 'You are still newcomers in this foreign land. You are yet to establish yourself firmly. At this stage, you should confine yourself to reading the Ghadar literature, while trying to understand our national problems.' Realizing that we were sincere in our resolve, he accepted the money and left.[11]

By the end of the harvest season we had earned around $6,000 to $7,000. We decided to pay back Ralla some amount that he had spent on us. We said to him, 'You have been very kind to us. You have not only saved our lives, but you have also supported us during a very difficult phase of our existence. In fact, we do not have the words to express our sense of gratitude. As we are leaving this place in a day or two, kindly accept a small amount of money as a token of our indebtedness to you. We will pay the balance as soon as we are in a position to do so.' Ralla refused to accept any money from us. Overwhelmed by emotion, he said, 'I often think about the two of you. Now, I realize that if I had not tried to secure your release from the ship, I would have committed a great blunder. You have proved by your conduct that the five fingers of a hand are not alike. I have complete faith in the truth contained in the saying. In no case can I ignore the sincerity, devotion and honesty demonstrated by you while managing my household, which you treated as your own. So, the very question of accepting anything from you does not arise.' We argued, 'You have spent a lot of money on us, such as on travelling to and from Buenos Aires twice and preparing the essential legal documents for our entry. Besides the money, you had to devote invaluable time in these efforts at the cost of your work on the farm, which must have suffered in your absence. We cannot forget what you done for us as long as we live.' Ralla protested saying, 'Listen to me. I am all alone here. I have no family, no brother or sister, no son or daughter. The choice before me is simple and clear. Either I accept the money offered by you or I cherish the affection, which has developed between us. So far as money is concerned, I have enough of it. I am more than satisfied with what I have. By no means shall I accept anything from you.' Several people tried to persuade Ralla, but he remained unmoved. After much discussion, he agreed to accept $100 from each of us, but with the clear understanding that he was accepting it so as not to hurt our sentiments. When we bade farewell, he said, 'I have spent a memorable time with you. I pray for our relationship to continue in the time to come. I would have loved to have you here with me for a longer period. As it is, you must keep in touch with me. Write to me as and when you feel like.' Thereafter we parted.

We went to the city of Rosario, which was second only to Buenos Aires in size.[12] Here we met Parsan Singh, the uncle of Comrade Chanan Singh Dhoot. We asked him to suggest any work we could do to earn our livelihood. He informed us about several jobs, but they were somewhat arduous. Acting on his advice, I accepted one such job. Around this time, Jwala Singh was alienated from me at the instigation of certain Punjabis. In fact, he had fallen into bad company and within no time had squandered all his money. He tried to borrow money but no one was willing to lend. In a foreign country nobody helps a stranger in trouble. After having failed in his efforts, he retraced his steps and approached me. He apologized for his conduct and I took pity on him and offered him $30. Repentence was writ large on his face when he said, 'I would prefer staying in your company rather than accepting money from you.'

Parsan Singh had a friend by the name of Lal Singh, who belonged to Nagajja (a village near Kartarpur in Jalandhar district). Parsan Singh asked the latter to help me find a suitable job. We met Lal Singh near the *qualaries* and submitted our applications for employment. At that point, however, there was no suitable work for us. We wandered aimlessly and came across a native landlord who guessed that we were in search of work.[13] When he disclosed that he needed people to work on his farm, we expressed our willingness to work for him. We drove down to his farm. I was appointed to look after the bungalow, while my partner was assigned the task of milking the cows. The landlord provided us free boarding and lodging, in addition to a daily allowance of $3. Considering the fact that we were unemployed, it was not a bad bargain. It was certainly better than living on one's savings. In no time, we were able to get jobs in the nearby town. Without informing the landlord, we left the farm with our belongings. Unfortunately, we met the landlord and his wife on the way. They wanted to know where we were going. Trying to feign innocence, we declared that we were going to meet some friends. The landlord exclaimed, 'No, no. I cannot believe you. I am sure that you will not come back.' We assured him that we would certainly resume our work at his farm. Unable to stop us, he made us promise that we would return and drove away.

We were employed in a British company, the Pacific Railway.[14] The entire workforce was divided into gangs called *qualaries*. The majority of workers were natives. They were employed on a permanent basis and were involved in trade union activities. On the other hand, the Punjabis constituted the temporary workforce. Though they were in a minority, they dominated a *qualary* called 'Balantey' which was put into operation whenever a train derailed or a defect surfaced. At that time, the economy was facing a crisis because of global depression.[15] Because of widespread unemployment, there was tension among labour. Time and again, the Punjabi workers demonstrated their loyalty to the British employers by breaking the strike. For this reason, they were paid 40 paise more than the natives. The natives, at least on one occasion, clashed violently with the Punjabi strike-breakers who were tied hand and foot and given a severe beating.

At this juncture, it is important to mention Jwala Singh Dhoot. After he left France, difficult days lay ahead of him. He travelled through British Guyana, Dutch Guyana and French Guyana and ultimately reached Trinidad. Hindustanis had been brought to these islands to develop the lands. The working conditions were appalling as the land was unproductive and poverty was rampant. Jwala Singh Dhoot got married, but felt unsettled and insecure in life. He wrote to me regularly and kept me informed about his misadventures. Concerned about his welfare, I sent $20 to him on one occasion. When he wrote to me that the amount was inadequate, I sent him another $100. Thus, over a period of time I had sent him $150. I realized that these small amounts would not improve his situation. Therefore, I persuaded him to join me. Jwala Singh Dhoot heeded my advice and left for Brazil from where he entered Argentina. He joined me when I was working in the Pacific Railway.

Around this time, a significant event took place. We were visited by Teja Singh Swatantra and Bujha Singh on behalf of the Ghadar Party. They visited a number of places in Argentina and explained to the Punjabi workers the aims, organization and methods of the party. Swatantra had earlier been sent to Turkey for military training. Before he could complete the course, he was recalled and was sent on a mission to organize units of the Ghadar Party in countries like Panama, Brazil and Argentina. A persuasive orator, Swatantra was friendly and affectionate.[16] Since we were politically naive, his lectures had a deep impact on us. Besides, our sufferings in the recent past had prepared a fertile ground for our political orientation. As a result of Swatantra's efforts, a wing of the Ghadar Party was set-up in the *qualaries* for the first time. We began to receive the literature of the party, particularly the *Ghadar di Goonj*. In this manner, we came under the influence of the Ghadar ideology. Its avowed aim of ousting the British from India was to be achieved through the cult of the bomb. We were given to understand that we would be trained in making explosives before being sent to India to spread terrorism against the alien rulers. As such, the methods adopted by the Ghadar Party were quite similar to those which had already been employed by the Babbar Akalis.[17] It should be pointed out that Marxism had no place in the Ghadar ideology at this stage. This became evident from the fact that whenever the word 'Red Army' appeared in the Ghadar literature, which often referred to developments in the Soviet Union, we assumed that it was so called because its soldiers were clad in red. We did not understand the political connotation of the word. Even an Italian captain, who was fairly intelligent and read a number of newspapers, could not enlighten us on the matter and correct our misconceptions.

Punjabi workers began to join the ranks of the Ghadar Party. They were divided into different categories depending upon the nature of support they could extend. My name was included in the list of front rank members, who had declared their intention to sacrifice their body, mind and wealth (*tan*, *man* and *dhan*) for the party. There were others whose circumstances permitted them to sacrifice either one or two of these three things, and as such, their names were entered in separate lists.[18]

Teja Singh Swatantra was instrumental in inviting Ajit Singh, the well-known freedom fighter and uncle of Shahid-i-Azam Bhagat Singh. From Germany, Ajit Singh went to Brazil and then to Argentina where he addressed numerous meetings at different places. However, he failed to make an impact on his audiences. Possessing neither energy nor enthusiasm, he appeared to be a spent force. He did not adhere to any political ideology worth the name. Moreover, he could not secure the support of any existing political organization.[19] Little wonder that he failed to establish rapport with Indian workers in Argentina.

NOTES AND REFERENCES

1. As headman of the village, a *lambardar* acted on behalf of the landowners, tenants and other residents in their relations with the state. His most important function was collecting land revenue and depositing it in the treasury, receiving 4 per cent of the total demand as his remuneration. J.M. Douie, *Punjab Settlement Manual*, p. 61.
2. The island of Singapore is separated from the Malaya peninsula by the Johore Strait. It has an area of 217 square miles. Developed as a British colony since 1819, its free port handled voluminous trade with Europe, America and the East. Local industries included rubber, tin, oil, timber, engineering, foundry, motor coaches and ship chandlers. After the First World War, the British established a huge naval and air base. In 1931, Indians numbered 600,000 or 14 per cent of population, which included Chinese and Malays. Kenneth Scott Latourette, *A Short History of the Far East*, pp. 339-44. For details on the historical evolution of the Indian community in Malaya, see Usha Mahajani, *The Role of Indian Minorities in Burma and Malaya*, pp. 95-138.
3. Alarmed at the sudden outbreak of a revolt (15 February 1915) by 800 Singapore based men of the 5th Light Infantry, the imperial government armed itself with fresh powers so as to establish military censorship on the mail passing through Singapore and to examine or intern suspects who otherwise could not have been touched. T.R. Sareen, *Indian Revolutionary Movement Abroad*, pp. 107-11; compare with Bhagat Singh Bilgha, *Ghadar Lehar Dey Anfoley Varkey*, pp. 84-6.

4. This person, normally well versed in the Sikh scriptures, was employed by the gurdwara management to conduct the religious services and lead the prayers.
5. Each copy was a collection of poetry, containing selections from Ghadarite periodical literature, viz., *Ghadar, Hindustan Ghadar* and *Yugantar.* Appearing in a series of seven parts, nearly 25,000 copies were dispatched from San Francisco for free distribution. Recently, a comprehensive volume has been published, which contains the entire available corpus of this poetry. Kesar Singh Kesar, ed., *Ghadar Lehar Di Kavita*, compiled by Kesar Singh Navalkar, Patiala: Punjabi University, 1995.
6. This poetry highlighted the economic exploitation of the Indian masses under British imperialism, exposed the plight of Indian migrants in foreign lands, condemned the collaborative role of feudal elements in Indian society, invoked the radical historical traditions, paid glorious tributes to anti-British martyrs, glorified the sentiment of sacrifice, asserted the unity of various religious communities and advocated the establishment of socialism after the ouster of alien rulers. The poets used simple indigenous idiom, easily understood by the illiterate Punjabi villager. Kesar Singh Kesar, op. cit., pp. 21-53.
7. Compare with the restrictions imposed in 1908 by the Canadian government on Asian immigrants, i.e. possession of at least $200 on arrival and travelling only by a continuous passage. Hugh Johnston, *The Voyage of the Komagata Maru: The Sikh Challenge to Canada's Colour Bar*, pp. 4-5.
8. The city was so named owing to its healthy climate. Situated near the head of the Rio de la Plata, it was the capital of Argentina as well as the largest city in the southern hemisphere. A terminal port on the east coast of South America, its harbour was frequented by vessels of all nations. The introduction of refrigeration in around 1880 enabled it to become the greatest meat exporting port in the world by the early twentieth century. The construction of railways coupled with the expanding cultivation of wheat, maize and linseed made the city a leading grain exporting centre.
9. The maize belt was restricted to Santa Fe, south-eastern Cordoba and north-western Buenos Aires. South of this belt, frost was a limiting factor, while in the west in Cordoba, maize gave way to wheat with a decrease in rainfall. In the pre-war years, maize exceeded wheat in yield, the former averaging 8.5 million and the

later 6 million metric tons in 1938-40. E.W. Shanahan, *South America: An Economic and Regional Geography with an Historical Chapter*, pp. 180-1.

10. Born in 1879 at village Raipur Dabba (Nawanshahr tahsil, Jalandhar district), Rattan Singh left the army as he could not support his family on the meagre salary. After living in China and Canada, he arrived (1913) in San Francisco. He joined the Ghadar Party and rose to be its president. In 1919, he came into contact with the communists. In 1923, he attended the fourth congress of the Comintern and second congress of the Red International of Labour Unions. Besides activating the Ghadar Party in Europe, Asia and America, he sent volunteers to Moscow for studying Marxism. In 1931, he replaced Nehru on the executive of the League Against Imperialism. In 1941, he was arrested in France, only to be released later. He died in France in September 1943. David Petrie, *Communism in India*, p. 376. Also see Sohan Singh Josh, op. cit., p. 106; Bhagat Singh Bilgha, op. cit., pp. 164-5.
11. Since the inception of the Ghadar Party, the speeches of leaders were followed by collection of funds from the audience. A major part of the fund was donated by prominent members from their meagre personal resources. In Punjab, money was collected through some dacoities. Harish K. Puri, *Ghadar Movement*, p. 64; Gurcharan Singh Sahnsara, *Ghadar Party Da Itihas*, vol. 1, pp. 186-7.
12. Situated 186 miles north-west of Buenos Aires, Rosario was a river port on the west bank of the Parana. The city was laid out with chessboard regularity, with wide streets and spacious parks. Its industries included sugar refining, flour milling, brewing, manufacture of bricks, leather, furniture and various kinds of food. Accessible to ocean going steamers of 26 feet draught, the city served as a shipping port for a large part of Argentina.
13. Individual immigrants, who desired small acreage, had little scope in Argentina. The system of landholding was unbalanced, with only 5 per cent of population being landowners. Most of the land was in the possession of large owners, whose ranches were spread over 10 square miles or more. They were willing to sell only 500 acres or more, to the disadvantage of the humble immigrant. Fred A. Carlson, *Geography of Latin America*, pp. 171-2.
14. Argentina was well provided with railways, particularly the humid Pampa region which had 70 per cent of lines. Owing to a nearly level surface, construction was easy and maintenance cost low.

Built by British companies, the railways had a mixture of gauges. In 1948, the railways were taken over by the government. H. Robinson, *Latin America*, p. 401.

15. As the Great Depression swept across the world, the economy of Argentina, like other Latin American countries, collapsed as its international trade depended heavily on a few primary products whose prices went into a free fall. Farmers dependent on the market, particularly the export market, were ruined unless they could fall back on subsistence production. Eric Hobsbawm, *Age of Extremes: The Short Twentieth Century*, pp. 91-2.
16. Teja Singh Swatantra (1901-73) graduated from Khalsa College, Amritsar, and held a Master's degree in Punjabi from Punjab University, Lahore. He joined the national movement as a lieutenant of Saifuddin Kitchlew. A member of the first SGPC, he took an active part in the Akali morchas. In 1924-9, he lived in Turkey and graduated from the Military Staff College. In 1929-31, he travelled extensively in North and South America, organizing the Ghadar Party. In 1931-4, he studied Marxism at the University for Toilers of the East, Moscow. On returning to India, he remained underground till his arrest on 16 January 1936. From 1936 to 1942, he was confined in Campbellpur jail. During detention, he was elected unopposed to the Punjab legislative assembly. In 1944-7, he served as the secretary of the provincial committee of the CPI. He also served as the general secretary of the Lal Communist Party. He remained underground from 1948 to 1963. After the 1964 split, he sided with the CPI. Closely associated with the Punjab Kisan Sabha, he was elected to the Lok Sabha in 1971 from the Sangrur constituency. Fauja Singh, *Eminent Freedom Fighters of Punjab*, pp. 235-7.
17. Apparently a revival of the Ghadar of 1915, the Babbar Akali movement swept the districts of Jalandhar, Hoshiarpur and Kapurthala from 1921 to 1924. The movement was manned largely by the Sikh peasantry with small holdings. The activists carried out a fiery anti-British propaganda through their mouthpiece the *Babbar Akali Doaba*. Besides organizing daring docoities, the members murdered village headmen, zaildars, safed posh and police informers. For organization, ideology and methods, see Kamlesh Mohan, *Militant Nationalism in the Punjab*, pp. 41-77.
18. During the first phase of the Ghadar movement, the organizational structure remained informal and spontaneous. With the publication of its weekly, the Punjab immigrants formed autonomous branches, which had minimal formal contact with each other.

Membership, being open to all Indians, was regarded as fellowship and comradeship. Decision-making was diffused and the assumption of roles spontaneous. The absence of formalism was compensated by a spirit of sacrifice. Harish K. Puri, *Ghadar Movement*, pp. 126-45.

19. Born in 1881 in Khatkar Kalan (Jalandhar district), Ajit Singh graduated from DAV College, Lahore. He discontinued the study of law at Bareilly and joined the national movement. During 1907 and 1908, he campaigned against the anti-farmer policies of the Punjab government. He was deported along with Lala Lajpat Rai to Mandalay in Burma. In 1909, he fled to Persia where he launched a paper to advocate India's independence. The following year he went to Rome, where he taught Persian in a college. At the outbreak of the War, he left for Brazil. From 1914 to 1932, he lived in Rio de Janeiro and established contacts with the Ghadarites of the USA and South America. Shifting to Europe in 1932, he formed the Friends of India Society and the Azad Hind Fauj. His passionate anti-British speeches were broadcast over Rome radio. He was imprisoned by the allied forces following the defeat of Mussolini. Pardaman Singh and Joginder Singh Dhanki, eds., *Buried Alive: Autobiography, Speeches and Writings of an Indian Revolutionary – Sardar Ajit Singh*, pp. 1-15.

CHAPTER 3

The Soviet Connection

Around this time, the revolution broke out in China. Communist International (hereafter Comintern) appointed a commission to visit China with the purpose of extending support to the revolutionary movement and providing guidance to the Chinese Communist Party. The continent of Asia was represented in that delegation by M.N. Roy,[1] who betrayed the communist movement by revealing all the secrets to Chiang Kai Shek. The latter, having come to know of the plans of the Comintern, succeeded in delivering a severe blow to the communist movement. When the Comintern learnt about M.N. Roy's abominable conduct, he was expelled from the organization.[2] As a consequence, relations between this body and India were severed. The Comintern made an attempt to revive relations by establishing contact with the Ghadar Party with the help of the Communist Party of the USA. This contact was established through Rattan Singh, a frequent visitor to Russia. Acting under the direct supervision of the Comintern, he took over the charge of the secret apparatus, which selected the newly created cadre of the Ghadar Party, scattered in the USA, Canada, Central America, Brazil, Argentina, New Zealand, Africa and even India. These Ghadarites were to be secretly sent to Moscow to study Marxim-Leninism at the University for the Toilers of the East (Kutv), which was patronized by the Comintern and supported by the Bolshevik Party. The first batch of students included men like Teja Singh Swatantra, Bujha Singh, Achhar Singh Chhina, Bhagat Singh Bilgha, Iqbal Singh, Lal Singh and Chanan Singh. In this manner, the Ghadar Party was given a Marxist orientation. The Ghadarites abandoned the ideology of terrorism based on individual action and adopted the path of socialist revolution to be brought about by the mass movement of peasants and workers.

The headquarters of the Ghadar Party in Argentina was located at Rosario, from where the activities of smaller centres, like Tukuman and the *qualaries,* were monitored and guided.[3] A meeting was held at Tukuman which was attended, among others, by Kartar Singh Shrinh, Bachan Singh Gholia and Milkha Singh. It was decided that the second batch of students (including me) bound for Moscow should start making the necessary preparations, like making provision for money, as they could be asked to leave any time. After a few days, the wife of our captain at the *qualaries* handed over a telegram addressed to me. Since the message was in the native language, she translated it for me. In response to the message, I decided to go to the appointed place from where I was expected to collect a sum of Rs. 2,000 which was collected from Punjabi workers for the activities of the Ghadar Paty. In Argentina, there were special goods trains which transported calves meant for slaughter and human consumption. Since these trains were faster than the mail trains, I decided to board one such train. Finding an unoccupied compartment, I entered it and saw that there was another man in the compartment. I looked at him carefully and realized that he was a vagabond who earned his livelihood by committing petty crimes. Such people are called *lavera* in the native language. The train had barely crossed two stations when he brandished a large knife called *cachew* and asked me to hand over whatever I had. I acted quickly but with caution. I pulled out my pistol and aimed it at him. It may be added here that all types of weapons were freely available in Argentina and everyone carried a firearm for self-defence. In this particular exigency, the pistol proved its positive worth. As I placed my finger on the trigger, my adversary lost his wits and looked helpless, not knowing what to do. With all the authority I could command, I forced him to drop his knife, take off his clothes and sit in a corner. It was past midnight when I reached my destination. Before I got off, I warned the man against repeating such acts. He begged to be forgiven and went away. On my part, I collected the money and returned.

Meanwhile, Jwala Singh Dhoot learnt about my plans of leaving for the Soviet Union. He expressed an earnest desire to accompany me. But I was disinclined for a number of reasons. Since he had not received any formal or informal political education, he was not committed to the party's cause. The other reason was purely financial. Whatever amount I could spare, after spending on my own necessities, I had sent to him. As yet, I had not sent any money home. Of course, the Ghadar Party had sent a paltry sum to my mother through the agency of the Desh Bhagat Pariwar Sahayak Committee in Amritsar.[4] I said to Jwala Singh Dhoot, 'A lot of money has been spent in bringing you to this country. Now you should stick to the place and work hard so that you are in a position to send some money to your home.' But the bond of affection between us was too strong to be weakened by any amount of logical reasoning. Since he had led a miserable life while staying away from me, Jwala Singh Dhoot had become attached to me. In fact, he was willing to pay any price to be able to accompany me. In these circumstances, it become impossible for me to persuade him to give up his resolve. Having decided to take him along with me, I had to overcome two hurdles, viz., securing the approval of the party to his inclusion in our batch and arranging a passport for him. Fortunately for him, I managed to succeed on both the fronts.

Soon, it was time for us to leave Argentina. Accompanied by Jwala Singh Dhoot, I reached Buenos Aires. Here, we bought some clothes for ourselves and then boarded the ship bound for Germany. Our batch comprised of nine members. As soon as we reached Germany, we were joined by another man named Shiv Singh, who had come all the way from Fiji. Interestingly, all the ten members of the group belonged to Doaba.[5] They had inherited extremely small plots of land, which were inadequate to meet their basic necessities. Many of them had mortgaged their land and borrowed money to pay for their fare to foreign countries. Besides earning money, they availed themselves of the opportunity to acquire general knowledge, nurture political ideas and widen their outlook. The following is a list of the students who constituted the second batch of trainees, sent by the Ghadar Party to Moscow.

No.	*Name*	*Village*	*District*
1.	Kartar Singh	Shrinh	Jalandhar
2.	Milkha Singh	Atta	Jalandhar
3.	Pakhar Singh	Not known	Jalandhar
4.	Jwala Singh	Bilgha	Jalandhar
5.	Raja Singh	Sabdullahpur	Hoshiarpur
6.	Raja Singh	Kharodi	Hoshiarpur
7.	Jwala Singh Dhoot	Dhoot Kalan	Kapurthala State
8.	Naina Singh Dhoot	Dhoot Kalan	Kapurthala State
9.	Shiv Singh	Mahiya Patti	Hoshiarpur
10.	Banta Singh	Bhularai	Kapurthala State

When the ship reached the port, we saw Rattan Singh. Since we had been given strict instructions to keep away from him, we just followed him. Apparently, he had been assigned the task of acting as our guide and escort. We were led to a hotel in Berlin, where arrangements had been made for our boarding and lodging. We stayed here for a few weeks. Rattan Singh gave all of us notebooks and pencils and advised us to learn reading and writing. This came to us as a surprise. One of the men jokingly asked, 'Bhai! Do you want to make village accountants (*patwaris*) of us.' Though Rattan Singh tried his best to impress upon us the need to acquire education, yet we failed to perceive the relation between education and our ultimate aim. At this stage, we hardly possessed any general knowledge or general awareness. In our ignorance, we believed that our fight would involve individual acts of terrorism against the British in India. We did not know the real meaning of a number of commonly used words such as capitalism, class struggle and revolution. Of course, I had seen the manner in which workers were treated by their employers in Argentina. I was reminded, time and again, of the strained relations between the sardars and muzaras in the Chenab Canal Colony. I could not reconcile myself to these injustices, yet I did not know the means by which things could be changed for the better.

Hitler had come to power just before 1933. There was political turmoil in Germany. Every night we were visited by young German communists, who never failed to bring fruit for us. They not only tried to make our stay comfortable as well as interesting, but also made us familiar with the political environment prevailing in Germany. We were shocked to learn that Hitler had unleashed a reign of terror against the communists and all those who subscribed to progressive ideas. The localities inhabited by these political groups were surrounded by soldiers who murdered the innocent and unarmed residents in cold blood. Often the dead bodies were cut into small pieces, packed into boxes and sent to their surviving relatives. Day after day, we heard blood-curdling stories of the large scale and indescribable atrocities committed by Hitler's fascist regime.[6] However, we failed to grasp the significance of this conflict between the communists and the Nazis because of our limited understanding of political, social and economic issues.

Our next aim was to secure an entry into a Soviet ship. This was successfully achieved with the help of German communists, who were members of the secret apparatus of the Comintern. The operation was carried out with such intelligence and secrecy that even we were taken by surprise. Once on board, we were hidden in a cell. In accordance with the standard practice, a boat of the German Immigration Department escorted our ship into the sea. As soon as our ship had crossed the territorial waters, the boat returned, whereupon, we were allowed to come out of hiding and had to report to the captain. The captain extended a warm welcome to us and arranged a sumptuous meal for us. Throughout the voyage, we were shown utmost kindness, warmth and courtesy. The thought that we were absolutely free from any danger, made us feel relaxed. We were optimistic about our visit to the Soviet Union.

On reaching the port of Leningrad, we got down from the ship. We were received by some people, who had been assigned the task of doing so. We got an opportunity to go around the city and we got a glimpse of the country we were visiting for the first time.[7] We felt that we were in a world of the rich where everyone, without any exception, was well fed and well clothed. The people wore trousers, overcoats and hats of the same kind and looked alike to a remarkable degree. During the course of this observation, our minds went back to our own country where every man was so different from the other. In any Indian market place, one could easily see the contrast between the people dressed in finery and those who could not afford even a loin-cloth. While sharing the experiences of our first day in the Soviet Union, we were surprised not to find anyone who could justifiably be described as poor. In our ignorance, we concluded that such unfortunate people lived only in some remote corner of the city. We were assailed by numerous doubts but we could not find answers to them as we did not know the language. Shiv Singh and Pakhar Singh (a matriculate), who knew a smattering of English, gave us some information after seeking clarifications from our Soviet escorts.

After staying in Leningrad for a few days, we travelled to Moscow by train. We found that the Comintern had made all arrangements for us in advance.[8] Officers of the Kutv University brought us to the campus, where we were allotted quarters. A careful attempt had been made to segregate us from other batches, including the Punjabis who were studying there. The first to visit us were Soviet professors who were conversant in Punjabi, Hindi and Urdu, and they informed us about the task lying ahead of us. A few days later Teja Singh Swatantra came to meet us and encouraged us, 'You must avail yourself of this opportunity by putting in your best efforts.' Another visitor was Rattan Singh who spoke in a similar vein. He assured us, 'If you put your heart and soul into your studies, you will become intelligent and wise. One day, you will go back to our country and assume the political leadership in your hands.' We were surprised to hear this as we could not imagine how this could ever happen.

After having spent a few days in trying to adapt to the new circumstances, we were shifted to our section. Since the Comintern was working for a number of different countries, students from each country were organized in a section of their own.[9] Each section had its own managing committee and faculty. The most outstanding feature of the functioning of a section was discipline, which was maintained at every cost and by every means. In particular, the system of bringing in new batches of students, making arrangements for their stay and education, and sending them after completion of their courses, was worked out extremely efficiently. Another feature of the working of a section was its secrecy. Students were given strict instructions to keep their identity a closely guarded secret. Each one was given a new name, which was used for all practical purposes. They were warned against disclosing their nationality, birthplace or name, lest the unkown inquirer should be an intelligence agent. Every section comprised of a number of batches, each one of which had joined at a different point of time. An earlier batch in our section, which had completed the stipulated course of one and one-half years, was segregated from us. The purpose was to push the batch through the first phase of its education-cum-training before sending it away. The authorities decided to teach a new batch, only when the previous one had been sent off.

The administrative affairs of a section were managed by an incharge who was elected by the students. He was assisted by a committee of students, one of whom was chosen as the secretary. This committee acted in coordination with the Comintern whose representatives were always present at its meetings. In our case, two Russians named Mazud and Mills, performed this function. They kept the Comintern informed about the multifarious activities of our section. The first secretary of our section was Iqbal Singh, the second was Teja Singh Swatantra and I was the third.

At our section we met a number of members of the previous batch like Teja Singh Swatantra, Bujha Singh, Achhar Singh Chhina, Bhagat Singh Bilgha and Harbans Singh. We were overjoyed to meet our fellow countrymen, since we could talk freely and that too in our own language. We felt that we were no longer strangers lost in an unknown land. Moreover, we had begun to understand the new environment in which we were placed. Preparing ourselves mentally to assume the role of students, we became confident about the future. However, at times we were caught on the wrong foot as revealed by the following incident. Mazud was married to an English lady. Experience had taught us to regard everything English as worthy of contempt. In one of the meetings of our section, the conduct of 'Biro' was the subject of a heated discussion. In our ignorance, we passionately asserted, 'This Biro has been responsible for all our problems. We have escaped from her with great difficulty and now you have allowed this bitch to sit in our midst.' Everyone burst out laughing, as it was explained, 'Biro was the name of the committee and not the poor English lady.' It was clear that we had a long way to go before we could aspire to play a useful role in the political life of our country.

The arrangements for our stay were perfect. We were lodged in comfortable rooms, which were properly furnished with a bed, a table, a chair, etc. Classes were held at some distance from our residential quarters. These too were adequately furnished. Our batch of ten students was taught separately, in accordance with the practice evolved in the past. Extracurricular activities formed a regular part of our schedule. We were often taken to theatre and cinema. Excursions were also organized at fixed intervals. We participated in public functions to commemorate the October Revolution and May Day. On such occasions, we were expected to join the workers of one or the other factory, to be able to participate in the grand processions.

Our syllabus had been formulated on scientific lines. Initially, we studied the development of nature, including the creation of our planet after its separation from the sun, the beginning of life on earth, the emergence of different species in the plant and animal kingdoms, and finally, the evolution of man. The other subject was geography which covered the topographical details of a given region, its natural resources and climate, agricultural and industrial production, economic position and political structure, and its military and strategic importance.

The development of society and political economy of the world were closely interconnected subjects. Society was analysed on the basis of formation of classes and not tribes, castes or religious groups. All stages of human history – slavery, feudalism and capitalism – witnessed a conflict between two classes. Of course, there were no classes in the earliest stage known as primitive communism. During this period, men acquired things collectively, distributed or stored them collectively, and defended themselves collectively. As means of production changed with the application of science and technology, classes emerged.[10] For instance, the earliest man hunted in groups with the help of extremely crude weapons. As soon as he learnt the use of bows and arrows, he acquired the capacity to hunt on his own. Now he began to assert his right over his possessions and acquisitions, and denied any claim of the others over them. As a consequence, some people were able to acquire more than the others, creating inequalities in the society or classes, which were perpetually in a state of conflict. In short, the mode of production prevailing at a given point of time determined the structure of society as well as the nature of the state. Any change in the former was necessarily followed by a change in the latter. It follows that society was not static. It was constantly changing in order to evolve from one stage to the other. However, religion did not accept the principle of change. Karl Marx was the first philosopher to visualize a classless society, which would emerge in the wake of the successful socialist revolution by peasants and workers.

We also studied the history of revolutionary movements which had emerged in different regions of the world. The concluding part included an in depth study of the Bolshevik Party.[11] Moreover, we were taught the geographical situation, historical development, economic position, strategic importance and the current problems of our own country.

The medium of instruction was Punjabi. If a teacher delivered a lecture in English, it was simultaneously translated into Punjabi.[12] Two or three of our teachers were extraordinarily intelligent, particularly Professor Dyakov. A great orator in Punjabi, he was extremely proficient in teaching political philosophy, geography and history. When he was unable to produce a Punjabi equivalent of anything, he drew its exact figure on the blackboard. Though, he was honest, sincere and sober, he was somewhat eccentric in his habits and manners. For instance, he would often dip his fingers into the inkpot and put his inky fingers into his ears or nose. Sometimes, he would fall backwards while giving a lecture in the classroom.[13]

The methods of teaching designed for us were extremely effective. The programme had been formulated with great care. Realizing that mere theoretical knowledge was not enough, it was supplemented by practical training. Every effort was made to ensure that theory and practice went hand in hand. For instance, when we were lectured on the organization, working and achievements of the Bolshevik Party, we were taken to the museum where the instructor showed us paintings of the revolutionaries at work. Similarly, short trips were arranged to agricultural farms and factories. Such experiences not only removed all doubts and misconceptions which assailed us in the classroom, but also went a long way in strengthening our understanding of historical phenomena and social reality.

Former activists of the Bolshevik Party were invited to deliver special lectures. On the basis of their personal experiences, they focused on the methods, techniques and strategies, which were essential to carry out revolutionary struggles, particularly secret work. They informed us about the ways and means adopted by the enemy forces to undermine the revolutionary movements. They discussed the ways in which political workers could survive even in the most adverse circumstances, particularly in jails. Military training constituted an integral part of our education. An army officer lectured us for an hour everyday on various aspects of military science. Towards the end of our course, we were taken to the military areas where we stayed for nearly a month. Here, we were given practical training in the use of various weapons and battle tactics. Each one of us took turns to act as a commander and assigned a specific task like destroying an enemy installation with the help of a contingent of soldiers, arms, maps, etc.

From the foregoing discussion, it became evident that our training programme was systematic as well as comprehensive. Though, we started from a scratch, we made steady but sure progress. Once we found ourselves on the road to advancement, we took rapid strides, never to look back. In the main, we studied three aspects of human life, viz., political, economic and philosophical. After having mastered the fundamentals of each subject, we moved on gradually to grasp the details of each. The knowledge acquired in the classroom was supplemented by practical experience gained through personal observation outside it. Now we were equipped, both intellectually and physically, to take part in active politics.

The completion of our studies coincided with the seventh and the last congress of the Comintern, which was held in

Moscow from 25 July to 21 August 1935. I had the privilege of being sent as a representative along with Sardara Singh Sikandar.[14] Georgi Dimitrov, secretary of the Comintern, presented the main thesis covering a variety of methods to counter the threat of fascism. The second thesis, presented by the Chinese representative Wang Ming, highlighted the problems of countries suffering under the yoke of colonialism. A thesis on war was prepared by Ercoli Togliati, the Italian delegate. An experienced representative from Germany, Wilhelm Pieck, read a paper on the communist movement. Manuilski, the Russian representative, discussed the development of socialism. Though the delegates representing the communist parties of various countries presented a large number of papers on a variety of topics, the above-mentioned themes drew maximum attention, in particular the one which focused on the struggle against fascism.[15] Besides deliberating on the papers, the congress reviewed the performance and problems of the communist parties in different parts of the world.

After having completed the stipulated course of one and a half years, we sought permission to leave for India. But this was not to be. The Comintern had selected three of us – Kartar Singh Shrinh, Sardara Singh Sikandar and I – for an advanced one year course. We protested, 'We have acquired the knowledge of the theoretical aspects of class struggle. Time has come when we must be allowed to put it to practical use by taking an active part in the working class movements.' Our request, however, was turned down by the body entrusted with the task of looking after us, on the ground that the decision had already been taken by the Comintern and that it was not empowered to review it. On our request, a meeting with Georgi Dimitrov was arranged.[16] We presented our case to Dimitrov. He gave us a patient hearing and then explained, 'We have examined your report in detail. We have found that you have made a tremendous amount of progress ever since you arrived here. We are of the view that if you are given an opportunity to undergo another phase of advanced training, you will prove to be a success in the field. Our aim in inviting you here was to educate you in the theory and practice of Marxism, so that when you return to your own country, you are able to play an effective role in the struggle against colonialism, in the movements of peasants and workers, and in disseminating the ideals of communism. Moreover, let me bring it to your notice that the decision concerning you was taken by the executive committee of the Comintern. As you have studied the working of the party organization, you know that this decision cannot be altered by the secretary. On my behalf, I would request you to avail yourself of the opportunity which awaits you with open arms.'

Dimitrov's explanation had its desired impact on us. Though disappointed, we gave up the idea of returning to India. We took pride in the fact that only three of us had been chosen by the Comintern for advanced training. While recognizing our past performance, the august body had great expectations from us, and we were duty bound to make every possible effort to come up to those expectations. Therefore, with renewed vigour and enthusiasm we attended our classes. We were taught the same subjects, which we had studied earlier, but in greater detail. Special emphasis was laid on the study of intricacies of political economy and Marxism-Leninism.

After we had stayed in the Soviet Union for another year and a half, time came for us to leave for India. We learnt that one or two, who had returned in the recent past, had shown their weakness by revealing a number of secrets to the British intelligence department. The main culprit was Karam Singh Dhuleta, who belonged to a village near Goraya (Jalandhar district). The CID came to know about the route followed by us while travelling from Argentina to Moscow, and also the route from Moscow to India via Bombay and Madras. The Comintern had been advised not to send the trained cadre into India through these points. The only alternative through which we could enter the country was Calcutta.

At the end of 1936 I left the Soviet Union. Though I accompanied Gallick, a British parliamentarian who belonged to the Communist Party, yet I had been instructed to avoid any conversation with him and only to follow him quietly. From Moscow we went to Minsk, the last Russian city, and onwards to Warsaw. We travelled through Czechoslavakia and Switzerland, and arrived in Paris, after bypassing Germany. I contacted a Paris-based German communist who was incharge of the secret apparatus of the Comintern and discussed with him the avenues open to me. On his advice, I approached the consulate of the USA to secure a visa for Manila, the capital of Philippines. However, my request was rejected. I met the German a second time and reported the unfavourable development. After a detailed discussion, we reached the conclusion that the Americans had become suspicious about my bonafides. We decided that I should go to Cuba. The distance between France and Cuba was almost the same as that between France and India. I had no difficulty in this regard. Sailing from France, I reached Santiago. Disembarking at this port, I travelled to Havana, the capital of Cuba. I found it to be a large and beautiful city.[17] In fact, it could compete with Buenos Aires in its size and beauty. I stayed there for a few months. One day, I wandered through one of the less frequented areas in a corner of the city. This was a settlement exclusively for the Americans. When I had gone far into the interior a sentry in uniform appeared and asked me whether I did not know that the entry of blacks in that locality was prohibited. I responded that I did not know the language, and left.

During the course of my wanderings in the city, I came across a travel agent. When he learnt that I was planning to go to India, he offered his services and informed me that a British ship was to leave for India shortly. I replied, 'I have no doubt that you will enable me to board the ship. But I have a problem. When I was lying on my sickbed, a theft took place and I lost everything including my passport. Now, I must acquire a new passport. And I must make some arrangement for the money I will need.' The agent was eager to help me because he knew that he would get a commission for his services. He asked me to sit in his car and drove me to the British Council and talked to the concerned officer on my behalf, 'This gentleman intends to sail for India, but his passport has been lost in a theft. Therefore, he needs a new one as early as possible, for the ship is due to leave very soon.' The officer listened to him patiently and replied, 'Come day after tomorrow at 10 O'clock and collect the passport.' The agent was pleased at his success and dropped me back to my hotel. Before leaving, he assured me that he would pick me up and drive me to the British Council. I spent another day in visiting the different parts of the city like any tourist. A day later, the agent appeared at the appointed time and we drove to the British Council, from where I collected my new passport.

My problems were not over as yet. For, now I had two passports. I had reached Cuba on the strength of the old passport. Since I had arrived here only as a visitor, it had been deposited with the immigration authorities along with a sum of $200. I knew that I would get it as soon as I left the shores of this country. The old passport was the source of my worries because the Comintern had sent a large number of men to different parts of the world on this very passport.[18] As a result, it had been stamped numerous times over the years by the immigration departments of various countries. It could easily rouse the suspicions of the inspecting authorities, particularly the British, regarding my identity. It was absolutely essential for me to procure and destroy it.

I thought of a plan to get out of this quagmire. I checked out of my hotel on the day I was supposed to board the ship and checked into another hotel. In all probability, the travel agent would have come to pick me up, but I did not want to meet him because I could not have, in any case, boarded the British ship on account of the reasons given above. In the meantime, I learnt that a French ship was due to leave for France. I reserved a berth in the second class and boarded the ship. As soon as the vessel left the port, the officers of the immigration department, who were following us in their boat, handed over my old passport along with a $200 to the captain. The latter returned these to me. At the first opportunity, I threw my old passport into the sea. In a similar manner, I disposed off two valuable possessions, viz., a cap and a Parkers' fountain pen. The Comintern had issued strict instructions to the effect that I should not have any printed material, stationary or even a pencil on my person. I had been instructed to pose as a complete illiterate in case of any inquiry.[19] It was with a heavy heart that I parted with my beautiful pen, to which I had become emotionally attached.

When I sailed from Havana, the authorities had stamped my

old passport, which I had thrown into the sea. My new passport did not have this particular stamp on it. As such, it suffered from a major defect. I knew that I would be in serious trouble if the French immigration officers noticed this omission. I began to think of ways and means of overcoming this problem. At last, I hit upon a plan. When our ship (after completing a voyage of thirteen days) was nearing the French port of Bardeaux,[20] from where I was to take a taxi for Paris, I decided to change my appearance. I began with a good shave and paid more attention to my bath than was my habit. I put on the best set of clothes I had including a suit, a tie and a pair of shoes. I looked at myself in the mirror and felt reassured. I came down from the board in order to secure clearance from the immigration department. I joined the queue meant for passengers who had travelled by first class. Seeing them standing with their passports open in their hands, I followed suit. When I reached the counter, I was asked to disclose my identity. I answered briefly, 'A British subject.' The concerned officer looked at me. He could not have imagined that a well-dressed person like me would possess incomplete documents. Without waiting for a moment, he stamped my passport. The trick had worked. My passport was now complete in all respects. I had nothing to worry in this connection.

I hired a taxi and reached Paris. Once again, I met the same old German communist. He was quite pessimistic about my future plans and he lamented, 'Things have turned out badly for us. I cannot think of any route which is safe for you. I am helpless. Rather, you should come out with a proposal.' I replied, 'Have no worries. Let me go directly to India and that too on my real name.' The German agreed readily. I sailed to Colombo on a Japanese ship. The immigration office cleared all the passengers. But I was detained, as they did not return my passport. When I requested them to hand over my passport, they explained that they were waiting for an officer who had to check it before clearing it. I realized that these people had succeeded in establishing my identity and the purpose of my return. Apparently, the British intelligence had circulated a blacklist to a number of ports from where dangerous people like me could enter India. Since my passport bore my real name, which was included in the blacklist, the immigration officials had informed the intelligence department.

After some time, two men in civil dress appeared on the scene. Though they tried to conceal their identity, yet I realized that they were intelligence agents. Returning my passport, the officers of the immigration department said, 'We are sorry for this delay. But we were helpless, because the officer who was supposed to examine it was not available immediately.' However, I was not deceived, as I knew that they only wanted to gain time so that the CID personnel could arrive and take the case in their hands. The question arose: what prevented them from arresting me, if they knew who I was. The only plausible answer was that they knew that if I were allowed to move freely, I would definitely try to establish contact with political workers in India. Therefore, they intended to use me as a link between the intelligence agency and the rest of our cadre, all of whom could be arrested after some time in a major crackdown.

NOTES AND REFERENCES

1. M.N. Roy (1887-1954) was born in village Arbela, 24 Parganas district. He had little education beyond school. Between 1905 and 1915 he lived in Calcutta. He was involved in the Howrah Conspiracy Case and came in contact with the Yugantar group of revolutionaries. In 1915 he left for the USA and later founded the Communist Party of Mexico. He lived in the Soviet Union between 1919 and 1928. As a member of the presidium and secretariat of the Comintern, he was given the charge of organizing communist movements in Asia. Sibnarayan Ray, ed., *Selected Works of M.N. Roy*, vol. 11, pp. 9ff.
2. Roy's expulsion could not be sufficiently explained by his actions in China or the alleged misappropriation of funds. His downfall was related to the power struggle within the CPSU and to his penchant for voicing dissent at a time when Stalin was determined to establish absolute authority both within the CPSU and the Comintern. Roy's views on India placed him inadvertently in the camp of Bukharin and other opponents of Stalin within the CPSU. John Patrick Haithcox, *Communism and Nationalism in India:*

M.N. Roy and the Comintern Policy, p. 134. Also see, Samaren Roy, *M.N. Roy: A Political Biography*, p. 85.

3. In mid-1920s, the Argentina branch of the Ghadar Party, with its headquarters at Rosario, became quite active. It distributed the literature of the Ghadar Party and the Kirti Kisan Party and published two special Argentine editions of the former. It sponsored lecture tours for Indian immigrants by Rattan Singh, Teja Singh Swatantra and Ajit Singh. It organized ten-day camps in the northern jungles, where Swatantra provided military training. It arranged the passage of Ghadarites who travelled to Moscow for studying Marxism. It thwarted the attempts made by the British to destroy the Rosario centre of the party. Bhagat Singh Bilgha, op. cit., pp. 163-8.
4. This body was formed at the second annual conference of the Central Sikh League, which was held in October 1920 at Bradlaugh Hall, Lahore. The moving force behind it was the famous Ghadarite Baba Wasakha Singh, who served as its president till 1956. Its office was housed in a rented room in Mochi Bazar, near Ram Das Sarai, Amritsar. It was funded by villages, but also received donations from abroad. Its aim was to provide financial aid to the families of freedom fighters who were serving prison sentences, to establish contact between the families and detenus, to fight legal battles on their behalf and create public opinion for their release. Interview with Bachan Singh Mehatpur who was closely associated with this body. Bikram Singh Ghuman, *Ghadri Baba Wasakha Singh*, pp. 117-31; Jaswant Singh Jas, *Baba Wasakha Singh: Jeevani*, pp. 153-5.
5. The term may be used for an area lying between any two rivers. Generally, it was used to denote the territory lying between the Beas and Sutlej, comprising the districts of Jalandhar and Hoshiarpur, besides the state of Kapurthala.
6. Since a Dutch communist Marinus van der Lubbe was held responsible for setting fire to the Reichstag on 27 February 1933, this single act became an excuse for Hitler to imagine a communist conspiracy of launching a civil war and to order cruel repression of six million German communists including social democrats, trade unionists and left wing intellectuals. Truckloads of Nazi storm troopers roared through cities all over Germany, arresting communists in the middle of the night, dragging them out of bed and taking them to SA barracks where they were savagely beaten. The victims were often shot and thrown into a river or dumped by the roadside. The terror was unparalleled in states under Nazi

control. In Prussia alone 25,000 persons were arrested by April 1933. Communist newspapers and meetings were banned, communist deputies were debarred from taking seat and party assets were confiscated. Allan Bullock, *Hitler: A Study in Tyranny*, p. 274; James Pool, *Hitler and His Secret Partners*, pp. 34-40; Jan Kershaw, *Hitler 1889-1936: Hubris*, p. 460.

7. Formerly the capital of Russia as St. Petersburg from 1712 to 1918, Leningrad was situated on both banks of the mouth of river Neva. After Moscow, it was the largest cultural and industrial centre of the USSR. It was an important railway junction and maritime port. Its industry was dominated by mechanical engineering and metal working, including shipbuilding and precision instruments. After the October Revolution, large power stations were built in and around the city. It combined stately buildings with planned squares, wide avenues, straight streets, parks and gardens. In 1939, it had an area of 113.5 square miles and a population of 3,191,304.
8. Also known as the Comintern or the Third International, it was a international organization that existed from 1919 to 1943. It was founded on Lenin's initiative in response to requirements of the revolutionary workers' movement during the first stage of the general cirisis of capitalism. For details see, A.M. Prokhorov, ed., *Great Soviet Encyclopaedia*, vol. 12, p. 236.
9. Students from India, China, Japan, Persia and Turkey formed only a small part of the total. Majority of them were from eastern and southern provinces of the Soviet Union. Instead of training professional revolutionaries, the university aimed to train future political and economic leaders of the more primitive areas of the Soviet Union. A.G. Freeman, 'Russia's University of Oriental Communism', *Soviet Russia Pictorial*, New York, 1923, in Muzaffar Ahmad, *Myself and the Communist Party of India*, p. 70.
10. According to Marx's theory of history, which goes by the name of historical materialism, history could be best understood through an examination of material conditions of society, rather than studying only the prevailing ideas. The most important factors were the economic level of development in a given society, changes in the mode of production and exchange, the various class divisions, and the extent and nature of class struggle. Kelly Boyd, ed., *Encyclopaedia of Historians and Historical Writing*, vol. II, p. 771; G.A. Cohen, *Karl Marx's Theory of History: A Defence*, p. 22.
11. In 1903, the more radical and larger of the two factions of the

Russian Social Democratic Labour Party emerged as the Bolsheviks under the leadership of V.I. Lenin. The split was formalized in 1912 when the Bolsheviks acquired a separate central committee. In 1918, it assumed the name of the Communist Party (Bolshevik), which continued till 1952. Since then it has been known as the Communist Party of the Soviet Union (CPSU).

12. The trainees, who were proficient both in English and Punjabi, acted as interpreters. Such students first attended their own classes in the English medium and then joined the Punjabi medium sections, where they translated the lectures from English to Punjabi. Bhagat Singh Bilgha, op. cit., p. 169.
13. Dyakov was quite popular with the students, because of his ability to communicate in Punjabi. He looked like a Kashmiri in physical appearance and treated the students with warmth and affection. He often said to them, 'I am your teacher only inside the class room. But outside, you are my teachers.' Bhagat Singh Bilgha, op. cit., p. 169.
14. The Congress was attended by 513 delegates, who represented 65 communist parties and other international organizations affiliated to the Comintern. A.I. Sobolev et al., *Outline History of the Comintern*, Moscow, 1971, p. 371.
15. For a detailed account of the proceedings of the congress and a critical appraisal of the resultant resolutions, see E.H. Carr, *Twilight of the Comintern*, pp. 403-27.
16. Georgi Mikhailovich Dimitrov (1882–1949) rose from the ranks of trade unions to enter the central committee of the Bulgarian Communist Party in 1909. A prominent leader of the Revolutionary Trade Union Federation from 1905 to 1923, he organized the activities of the Bulgarian proletariat. As deputy in parliament from 1913 to 1923, he denounced Bulgarian expansion in the Balkans and Bulgaria's involvement in the First World War. In 1923, he led a anti-fascist armed unprising. He emigrated from Bulgaria, where he was sentenced to death in absentia. His spirited self-defence in the Leipzig trial (1933) made him a international hero. Having been granted the Soviet citizenship, he lived in the USSR from 1934 to 1945. He served as the general secretary of the Comintern from 1935 to 1943 and a deputy of the Supreme Soviet from 1937 to 1945. Returning to Bulgaria in 1945, he became the general secretary of the Bulgarian Communist Party and directed the construction of socialism in the country. A.M. Prokhorov, ed., *Great Soviet Encyclopaedia*, vol. VIII, p. 262.
17. Havana, the capital of Cuba, was one of the most progressive

tropical cities in the new world. Owing to its location on one of the finest harbours, it became commercially and militarily important from colonial times. Since a major part of Cuba's imports and exports passed through Havana, it has emerged as a world shipping centre. Its salubrious climate, picturesque location and gay entertainment have made it a mecca for tourists. It was well provided with hotels, restaurants, bars, casinos, race tracks, beaches, parks and drives.

18. The Moscow trainees followed a variety of routes to enter India. Some succeeded in their aim by travelling across the Hindukush and Chitral mountains. Prithvi Singh Azad gained entry via Italy and Pondicherry, Harjap Singh via China and Bhagat Singh Bilgha via Germany, Paris and Colombo. Gurmukh Singh, Iqbal Singh Hundal and Teja Singh Swatantra followed the Kenya route. Bhagat Singh Bilgha, op. cit., pp. 170-2.
19. One of the most successful tricks for hoodwinking the immigration authorities and intelligence network was to disguise as illiterate Punjabi artisans, who frequently travelled between Bombay and Kenya, wearing crumpled clothes and carrying tools in their bags. Bhagat Singh Bilgha, op. cit., p. 173.
20. Situated on the southwestern coast and on the west bank of the Garonne, Bordeaux was one of the largest ports of France. Its port was 8 miles long, with an average width of 550 yards. It had large marshalling yards and two wet docks, with railways serving both banks of the river. The city traded chiefly with the USA, Argentina, Great Britain, Spain and Portugal.

CHAPTER 4

Underground in Colonial India

According to Hindu mythology, India and Ceylon were connected by a bridge, constructed by lord Rama with the help of the monkey-god Hanuman and his tribe. I crossed the distance by boat in two hours. I found that the CID of Madras province was waiting for my arrival. The two Ceylonese intelligence men, who had travelled in the same boat, talked to their counterparts in Madras, handed their charge over to them and returned. As soon as I reached the railway station, I saw that the CID of Madras city was waiting for me. It took over the task of keeping a watch over my movements from those who had performed it for a short time on behalf of the province. I stayed in Madras for two or three days, during which I was closely watched by the CID. Thereafter, I boarded a train for Nagpur. As soon as the train crossed into the confines of the Central Provinces, the CID of this particular state replaced the men who had followed me all the way from Madras.

By the time, the train reached Nagpur, it had become quite dark.[1] I stepped out of the railway station and began to look for a place where I could spend the night. On making an inquiry, I learnt that there was an inn (*dharamshala*) [2] where I could get a room. As I was busy in making myself comfortable, a man appeared at the door. I recognized him instantaneously. He was one of the two CID men who had been following me. In a feeble attempt to conceal his identity, he had removed his cap. He informed me that whoever stayed at the *dharamshala* was required to give his name and address. I told him that I was tired after a long journey and that he should come the next morning. Acting smart, he said, 'We are not the police. This is just a routine matter. The CID is very....' Irritated by his behaviour, I cut him short and blurted out, 'The CID does not have horns on its head. Only the cap is not there.' As soon as I said this, I realized my mistake. I should have acted with more caution while dealing with these people. For, once I had made known that his identity was not hidden from me, he could have acted against me. Anyhow, I regained my composure and gave him the correct details about myself. I spent the night in the *dharamshala* without any further trouble.

The next morning, I made inquiries about a gurdwara and learnt that there was one on the railway road. I reached the place and met the priest (*bhai*) and told him, 'I have come from abroad. Sometime back, I suffered from an illness. At the advice of the doctor, I was forced to cut my hair. Originally, I belong to a Sikh family. I will not dare to return home until I grow my beard and hair. I request you to permit me to stay in the gurdwara till then.' Impressed by my story and convinced that I was a religious-minded person, the *bhai* allotted me a room on the first floor. In this manner, I started staying in the gurdwara. Often I wandered through the large city, which was a leading centre of the textile industry.

The intelligence men kept a round-the-clock vigil on the gurdwara. One day, the *bhai* said to me, 'I fail to understand as to why these white-clothed people move about on the four sides of the building, sticking out their necks all the time like cranes (*bagulas*).' I feigned ignorance and replied, 'Well, I cannot guess. I am a complete stranger to this city. You have been living here for a long time. You should know better than I do.' Though the *bhai* did not suspect me, I realized that I had to give the slip to the CID before it was too late. Accordingly, I devised a plan to achieve this aim.[3] I had read in the newspaper that a Calcutta-bound train left Nagpur at 4 p.m. I also noticed that the back wall of my room had a window, which opened out into a colony of labourers. An hour before the departure of the train, I lowered my suitcase out of the window and jumped down. Picking up my suitcase, I went directly to the railway station, purchased a ticket for Calcutta and boarded the train.

When I reached Calcutta, I headed for the main gurdwara,

which was located in Bhiwanipur. As I was walking down the road, I was accosted by the police who wanted to check my suitcase. I could not believe that they had already received the information about my arrival. I was not prepared for anything like this. Earlier, I had felt elated at my success in having dodged the intelligence agents at Nagpur. Now I was depressed at the possible failure of my mission, even before it had taken off. Somehow I controlled my thoughts, held the key of the suitcase in my hand and said, 'I have nothing to hide. You can open it for examination.' However, they insisted that I should open it. I did as I was directed. They looked at it cursorily and said apologetically, 'Please excuse us. It is our duty to detect the possession of weapons and narcotics, brought into this city in a clandestine manner. We regret the inconvenience caused to you. We are helpless.' I said, 'It does not matter at all. You must satisfy yourself.' Needless to say, I was greatly relieved at the favourable outcome of this unexpected encounter with the police. I picked up my suitcase and moved on.

Inder Singh, a jhinwar by caste, belonged to the district of Hoshiarpur in Punjab. He was the *bhai* of the gurdwara. On my request, he allotted me a room next to his. I spent my time either resting in my room or wandering through the city. Interestingly, a man named Dharam Vir, who belonged to Goa, visited Inder Singh everyday and they exchanged views on a variety of subjects. There was a door connecting the *bhai's* room and mine, which remained open most of the time. I would lie down quietly on the cot, with my back turned towards them and overhear their discussion without ever participating in it. For a week, I followed their conversation very closely and analysed it at the end of each day. I reached the conclusion that Dharam Vir was a communist, while Inder Singh was in the process of being converted into one. The former took an authoritative stance on every subject of discussion, while the latter usually accepted these views without expressing any doubts. They often referred to Muzaffar Ahmad, Somnath Lahiri and other leading communists, who were active in India. While I was studying in the Soviet Union, I had often heard these names since the Comintern maintained contact with the revolutionary movements in different parts of the world.

After having spent a number of days in Calcutta, I decided to establish contact with the Indian communists with the assistance of Dharam Vir. Though I had often exchanged greetings with him, I had never talked to him at length. One day, I left the gurdwara while Inder Singh and Dharam Vir were engaged in their discussion and went in the direction which Dharam Vir usually followed. After passing two crossings, I saw him following me at some distance. I slowed down and appeared in his path. The following conversation took place between the two of us.

NSD : Babuji, how do you do?
DV : I am quite well. What are you doing?
NSD : Nothing in particular. Come let us sit over a cup of tea.
DV : No, thank you.
NSD : Babuji, come on. Do not disappoint me.
DV : Let it be as you wish.

We located a wayside tea stall and sat facing each other. I ordered two cups of tea and some snacks. I renewed my conversation with him.

NSD : What do you do?
DV : I am a communist.
NSD : What do the communists do?
DV : Communists are engaged in educating and organizing workers and labourers. I work in the trade union of dock workers.
NSD : What is the numerical strength of communists in Calcutta?
DV : Our party is quite strong, but it is underground.[4]
NSD : Are you a member of the party?
DV : Yes, I am.

I asked him a number of questions in a innocent tone. When I felt that I had won his confidence, I briefly acquainted him with my past. I told him that I was also a communist and had returned from the Soviet Union after receiving training in Marxism. I expressed my desire to work actively for the party and requested him to arrange a meeting with Muzaffar Ahmad.[5] Though this disclosure came as a pleasant surprise to him, he said that it would be difficult to arrange the meeting. When I persisted in my request, he promised to make an attempt. Before we parted, I warned him to keep our meeting a closely guarded secret.

Dharam Vir talked about me to Dr Ranen Sen, a member of the central committee of the Communist Party of India.[6] Sen conveyed the message to Muzaffar Ahmad, who agreed to meet me at his residence on a particular date and time. I covered the distance to Muzaffar Ahmad's house in a number of stages. First, I accompanied Dharam Vir to a restaurant. From there, Dr Ranen Sen escorted me to a man who was not known to me. This man introduced me to yet another man, who led me into a narrow lane, where Muzaffar Ahmad lived in a room at the top (*chaubara*) of a small house. As I made my entry, I saw him sitting on the floor and busy writing something. He was surrounded by books, which were scattered all over the place. He asked the man, who had acted as my guide, to bring a cup of tea for me. He did as he was told and went away. I gave a brief introduction about myself and sought his advice about the future. He began to highlight the contribution being made by the Punjabis in strengthening the party.[7] In this context, he named a number of people – Nand Singh (the proprietor of a restaurant), Hazara Singh Akali (a transporter), Gainda Singh (a driver) and Balwant Singh Pardesi – who had established contacts with the Punjabis migrating to Calcutta and collected funds for the party. Muzaffar Ahmad said to me, 'A man as healthy and stout as you are should not remain idle in Calcutta. You must do some work.' I replied that I was willing to follow his advice in the matter. He said, 'I am of the opinion that you should set up a restaurant (*dhaba*) in the Howrah district, an area dominated by workers and labourers. On the one hand, you will be able to make a decent living and, on the other, you will get the opportunity to establish contact with the working class. Moreover, your business will camouflage your activities, because you are not likely to fall into the trap of the CID.' I felt that the advice was practicable and decided to work on it at the earliest. Before taking my leave of him, I said, 'Kindly let me know if I can perform any service right now.' Muzaffar Ahmad replied that he needed money for the publication of a newspaper called *Saathi* which he was bringing out in Hindi. I gave him whatever money I had and promised to collect more funds from my friends among the Punjabis in the near future. He expressed his happiness at this gesture. Thereafter, I took leave of him.

Acting on Muzaffar Ahmad's advice, I went to Howrah and made a survey of the area. I decided in favour of a road crossing (*chaurasta*) called Haroganj, where there were already three restaurants. I rented a premises and began to collect the materials needed for the venture. Meanwhile I remembered one Ujagar Singh who belonged to Kandhala (a village in Hoshiarpur district). He owned a small tea stall, where he boiled tea in a small saucepan, his most prized possession. He was also an opium addict. I met him and said, 'Look here, Ujagar Singh. You are pressed under the burden of running this tiny shop. Why not close down your shop and join me in a bigger enterprise. The only thing I will require from you is to just sit at the counter. You will spend your time in comfort and ease. You will no longer have to worry about managing your tea stall all by yourself.' Ujagar Singh jumped at the idea of working in partnership with me. I also employed a few cooks and serving boys to perform a variety of tasks in the restaurant (*dhaba*), which went into business soon after. Fortunately, the enterprise was an instant success. A large number of people started taking their meals at our joint. We gave preferential treatment to Bengalis in terms of liberal servings of rice and curry. It was no wonder that about twelve kilograms of meat and a huge quantity of rice was consumed everyday. In a short time, we overshadowed the other restaurants in the neighbourhood.

When I was confident that the business was firmly established, I decided to concentrate on political activities. Having observed the working class of Calcutta from close quarters, I had become familiar with their economic problems, intellectual level and political orientation. On the basis of my understanding of the situation, I chalked out a programme to educate lay workers as well as those who were actively involved in trade union activities. The business hours of the *dhaba* did not extend beyond 11.00 p.m. The men who came to attend the meetings were ushered in through the back door and served unsold food as well as tea. Following the guidelines given by Muzaffar Ahmad, I concentrated on teaching the fundamentals of Marxism and the principles of party organization. I also offered advice on the problems faced by the workers in their respective professions. Excerpts from communist literature, which I regularly bought from the market, were read and explained to them. On their part, the workers read *Saathi,* the newspaper published by Muzaffar Ahmad.

The number of workers attending the study circles increased with each passing day. There were two reasons for this. First, my first-hand experience of the Soviet Union had a tremendous impact on the minds of young men. They asked me innumerable questions about the changes brought about in the society and economy of the Soviet Union in the wake of the revolution. They listened to my answers with rapt attention. They went home, full of enthusiasm, and told their friends, 'You must accompany us tomorrow. For, we will introduce you to someone who has witnessed the impact of the socialist revolution in Russia with his own eyes.' The other reason was that because of my consistent efforts and single-minded devotion, I had acquired the capacity to explain the principles of Marxism in a simple manner. It was the sheer simplicity of my style which made me acceptable, and even popular, among the workers. As far as possible, I avoided the use of high sounding technical terms found in Marxist terminology. Though the majority of workers were Bengali-speaking, yet language was never a problem. I could communicate with ease in Hindustani, which they understood without any difficulty.

I endeavoured to induct a large number of workers within the scope of my activities. I came into contact with workers belonging to different linguistic, religious and ethnic groups. Among them was Comrade Ismail (at present a MP or a MLA) who was a close associate of mine. A majority of the workers were employed in jute factories, hosiery units, dockyards and railway workshops.[8] The militant among them were singled out for special attention. I knew that a party was organized like a machine. Some of its parts were extremely important, others were not. But all were absolutely essential for the smooth functioning of the machine. As such, I welcomed all categories of workers – the militant, the active, the passive and the casual. While my work continued to expand without any obstacle, my *dhaba* became a meeting ground for communists, both actual and potential. By my single-handed efforts, I managed to link an increasing number of them with the party. I have no doubt that if circumstances had permitted the continuance of my business, I would have succeeded in making an extremely significant contribution to the strengthening of the trade union movement as well as the foundations of the communist party in Howrah district.

In spite of this encouraging development, there remained a cause for worry. This was the constant threat to my activities from the CID. As soon as I had arrived in Calcutta, I met by sheer coincidence two brothers, Inder Singh and Ujagar Singh, who belonged to Manakrai (a village near Adampur in Jalandhar district). They were extremely affectionate towards me and I had stayed with them for a while. One day I invited Ujagar Singh to drinks and said to him in complete confidence, 'Nobody except the CID knows that I am in India. But the CID does not know that I am in Calcutta. You must keep my presence in the city a secret, otherwise I will be in serious trouble.' Having comprehended the gravity of the matter, he promised to abide by my instructions.

At this juncture, the scenario of my story shifts to Punjab. One day, my mother and Jwala Singh Dhoot's mother went to Pindori Nijjaran. While they were returning, they felt thirsty, as the summer was unusually hot. When they reached a village called Dhugga, which was situated near Riyaran, they stopped to quench their thirst at the house of a lady by the name of Mahon (who was the sister-in-law of Ujagar Singh's brother). Incidentally Ujagar Singh, who was on a visit to Punjab at that time, was in the house. Mahon said to my mother and aunt, 'You must be very tired after having travelled a long distance in the sweltering heat. You must rest on these cots, in the shade of the courtyard. You have covered a major part of your journey and only a short distance is left. You can proceed after the sun goes down.' The two accepted the invitation. Soon after, they were engaged in a lively conversation, which revolved around their sons, Jwala Singh Dhoot and myself. Ujagar Singh overheard their conversation and became inquisitive about them. As soon as Mahon went inside the house, he inquired about the visitors. When she told him about them, he wanted to meet them. After exchanging the usual greetings, he gave them whatever information he had about me, perhaps out of sympathy. At the same time, he impressed upon them the need to keep this information a closely guarded secret. Enriched in this manner, the ladies returned to our village, Dhoot Kalan. In spite of Ujagar Singh's strict instructions, they failed to keep the matter secret. They revealed my whereabouts to my sister's son Beant Singh and others. Soon everyone in our village and the surrounding area knew that I was in Calcutta.

When I had succeeded in giving the slip to the CID officers at Nagpur, they felt like a hunter who had lost his prey after having entrapped it. The CID made frantic efforts to nab me. It conducted inquiries and searches in our village, Dhoot Kalan, and even Bhunga. However, it failed to get any clue about my whereabouts. Immediately after Ujagar Singh's visit to Punjab, the CID received information about me. Renewing its efforts to entrap me, it focused on Calcutta. After putting together the different pieces, it concluded that I was hiding in Howrah district. By sheer coincidence, the task of apprehending me was assigned to a CID inspector, who took his meals regularly at my restaurant. It was quite natural for him to seek my help in getting some clue about the man in question. One day, he invited me to a feast of whiskey and fowl. At first, I laughed at his suggestion, 'I cannot really believe that a person working in your profession will ever be willing to spend money from his own pocket.' He repeated his invitation but I was not convinced and said in a lighter vein, 'You come here twice a day for your meals and on each occasion you are able to get two ladles of curry free of cost. How can you hold a feast for me.' Thus forced on the defensive, the inspector, in order to prove the genuineness of his invitation, offered me money to buy liquor and fowl. I accepted the money and began to prepare myself mentally for the crucial meeting, which was to be held that very evening.

I bought a bottle of whiskey and asked the servant to cook the fowl. When the inspector arrived, we sat down in the privacy of a room at the back of the restaurant. After a couple of drinks, I said, 'It seems that there is something which is bothering you.' He replied, 'You are right. A man, who originally belongs to Punjab, has come from abroad and has settled in this area. According to our information, he is very dangerous. So far, I have not been able to spot him. Since you are a Punjabi, you can certainly help me in searching for him. In case, an officer who is senior to me, is able to catch him, then I will be ruined. And you know that I am a householder with a family and children to support. This is the hour of trial for me. You must help me in this task and I will give you all possible support.' Assuming an angry posture, I said, 'Do you agree with me that I have been proved right. Have you not acted like an illegitimate one. You have been coming here regularly for such a long time and even then you have failed to talk to me about this insignificant matter. I am surprised at your attitude.' Explaining his position he said, 'I did not talk to you earlier because I did not realize the seriousness of the matter. But now, as I have told you, my future is at stake.' Posing as a close confidant, I offered him a solution, 'One thing is quite clear from the case. If the man is really residing in this area, he is most likely to avoid a place which is frequented by a CID inspector. In these circumstances, the best course of action for you is to stop coming to this place for at least a week. During this period, I will be able to locate the man for you.' The inspector saw no difficulty in accepting my proposal and he left.

The following day I locked the door of the restaurant and went to meet two young men of Bir (a village in Jalandhar district) who had earlier expressed a desire to purchase my restaurant. I said to them, 'I have received an urgent telegram from home. I must rush back to my village immediately. I do not know whether or not I will to able to return. Therefore, you can go ahead with the purchase of the enterprise.' They wanted to know the price and I told them that I would be satisfied if I got what I had invested in the venture. However, they paid me more than that. Thereafter, I had to reach a settlement with my business partner Ujagar Singh. Fortunately this turned out to be an easy task. I invited him to a feast and over drinks I said, 'Look here, Ujagar Singh. Our business has been a success. We have outclassed a number of restaurants in the neighbourhood. Since we have acquired the necessary experience, we should go in for a bigger enterprise. In fact, I have already started looking for a new premises. Meanwhile, there are people who have their eyes on buying this restaurant.' Thus, I succeeded in winning the confidence of Ujagar Singh, who had no objection to my proposal of selling the restaurant. I gave him a sum of Rs. 50 and said, 'Keep this little amount with you. You may need it in the near future.' Ujagar Singh expressed his pleasure at this gesture. Soon after, I prepared the legal documents for the transfer of ownership of the premises and secured the signature of Ujagar Singh on the papers. I packed the few clothes I had and left for Bhiwanipur. The next day I learnt that the place had been raided and the new owners had been arrested.

Having been forced to close down the business, which I ran successfully for a little less than a year, I came to Bhiwanipur, an area dominated by Punjabis, all of whom were on friendly terms with me. Here, I met Hazara Singh Akali (the transporter) and Nand Singh (the proprietor of a restaurant). They had great affection for me. When they came to know about my recent experience, they reassured me and promised to make suitable arrangements for me. I began to live with Hazara Singh Akali and often ate at Nand Singh's restaurant. Around this time, I met Muzaffar Ahmad and informed him of the circumstances under which I was forced to close down my business and discontinue my political activities. He said, 'You need not feel disheartened at this temporary setback. From now onwards, you should start working more openly among the workers. The ministry in Bengal is headed by Fazl-ul-Haq.[9] Even if you are arrested, they will detain you in jail for ten to twenty days. But the government of Bengal will not deport you to Punjab even if the latter demanded it.' Acting on his advice, I renewed my activities. In particular, I worked in the railway workshops along with Comrade Nripen Chakravarty. On the one hand, I collected funds for the party and, on the other, recruited an ever-increasing number of sympathizers for it. I began to discuss political issues in public places, without making an attempt to conceal my ideological leanings.

This new style of working did not fail to attract the attention of intelligence agencies. One day I was asleep in Hazara Singh's house when a police party led by an inspector raided the premises and arrested me. They began investigations at all the places with which I was associated. They had information that I had been staying at the main gurdwara on Harrison Road and I was taken there. They searched my suitcase which was still lying there, but failed to find any incriminating evidence in it. The inspector asked me my educational qualifications and I answered, 'I am totally illiterate. I do not even understand the alphabet.' Thereupon, the inspector turned towards the manager of the gurdwara and angrily said, 'What for are you being paid by the government? He is a very dangerous man. There is a commotion in the whole country because of his presence. We have laid our hands on him after a Herculean effort. It is strange that you were unable to perceive the truth about him, even though he had been staying with you for a long time.' The manager pleaded, 'Believe me, sir, I do not know anything about the man. We did allot a room to him. He used to enter the room quietly, lie down in it quietly and go out of it quietly. He never carried anything – books, newspapers or pamphlets – which could indicate that he was a political worker. His behaviour did not rouse any suspicion because he was gentle in his speech, manners and actions. I could not understand him at all.' However, the manager's explanation failed to convince the inspector who threatened him, 'Now we will spare you for the time being, but we will deal with you in the appropriate manner, when we summon you to the office.'

The police party took me to the CID office for further interrogation. On the way, I thought about the villainy of the manager who was on the regular payroll of the CID. I realized that something had to be done to expose him. On the way, I saw three Sikhs coming from the opposite direction, I requested the policemen to allow me to talk to them. Acting quickly, I approached the men and recounted the episode involving the manager. I said, 'You must haul him up in front of the congregation and ask him whether or not he was mixed up with the CID. Before he gives the answer make sure that he takes an oath of truth in the presence of the *Guru Granth Sahib.* But if he denies his involvement, tell him that you will bring him face to face with a person who knew everything about his secret activities.' The men assured me that they would do everything to expose the manager.

At the office of the CID, I saw the same old inspector who used to frequent my restaurant. He rushed forward and embraced me. I enquired after him. Saying that his condition was good as well as bad, he elaborated, 'I came regularly to your restaurant for quite a long time, but failed to detect that you are a political worker.' I protested innocently, 'You people are mistaken even now, for I have nothing to do with politics.' But the inspector insisted that he was right, 'I have seen all the documents concerning you, which form a considerable bundle of files. I am thoroughly convinced that you are deeply involved in political activities. It is only now that I know the type of person you really are. Nevertheless, I am happy that you were able to evade arrest for a long time and did not allow yourself to fall into the net of the rival officer. For, in that case, I would have suffered a lot.' The inspector was so pleased with me that he invited me for a cup of tea. However, I politely declined.

The police produced me before a magistrate, a European officer. In response to his fresh order, they interrogated me again. But they failed to extract any information from me. They asked me if I had returned from the Soviet Union. Denying it outright, I said that I had come directly from Cuba, where my passport was issued. I was sent to the presidency jail, where I remained for a month. Here, too, I could not be restrained from delivering lectures on Marxism to the prisoners, who often gathered around me out of curiosity. My release could be attributed to two factors. First, party activists as well as my friends among the Punjabis pressurized the police to secure my release. Second, the police itself failed to frame a chargesheet against me, for it did not possess any evidence or record of my activities. After being released from jail, I resumed my work in the railway workshops along with Comrade Nripen Chakravarty.

Let us see what was the fate of the manager of the gurdwara. The three Sikhs, who had met me on the way, did as they had promised. They met Inder Singh, the *bhai* of the gurdwara, and told him whatever they had learnt from me about the manager. The news of the episode spread like wild fire among the Punjabis, who were greatly agitated. The next day being a Sunday, they thronged the gurdwara in large numbers, so that the congregation was unusually big. There was much excitement in the air. At the end of the prayer service, the manager was forced to appear before the congregation. The charges against him were read out and he was asked to confess his guilt. As first, he made a feeble attempt to prove his innocence. But soon, he realized that it was prudent to admit that he had been in the pay of the CID. The management of the gurdwara made a correct estimate of the popular discontent against the manager, who was immediately dismissed from his post. It was natural for the members of the congregation to be curious about the man who had been instrumental in exposing the manager. They were surprised to learn that a communist had saved their religious institution from the corrupt practices of the manager.

Around this time, a session of the All India Trade Union Congress was due to be held in Delhi. I met Muzaffar Ahmad and asked him whether or not I should attend the session. He had a positive attitude in this regard, 'You must participate in the session, for it will provide you with an opportunity to meet your friends in Punjab.' He also gave me a letter of recommendation for Ajoy Kumer Ghosh (a member of the central committee as well as the politburo of the Communist Party of India) who was the main organizer of the session. I arrived in Delhi in January 1938 and actively participated in the proceedings of the conference. Delegates presented reports on the condition of workers employed in the railways, mines, textile industry, etc. They reviewed the past, identified current problems and suggested lines of action for the future. They placed a number of demands before the government relating to minimum wages, inflation, allowances, unemployment, security of service, housing, etc. All these were contained in several resolutions, which were passed after being thoroughly discussed.[10] I used the opportunity to familiarize myself with various aspects of the trade union movement in the country.

I also had a meeting with Karam Singh Dhoot, one of the founders of the Ghadar Party. He was popularly known as Karam Singh 'Khoondewala' because he had served as a guard at the office of the Ghadar Party in San Francisco. He carried a curved stick (*khoonda*), which he did not hesitate to use. He was in Moscow in 1926-7 and had returned to India before I reached the Soviet Union. He remained interned (*nazrband*) in Punjab for a long time. He had resumed the publication of the *Kirti Lehar* from Meerut, after it had ceased to be published from Punjab.[11]

At the end of the conference, I left for my ancestral village, Dhoot Kalan. In those days, facilities of transport were quite unsatisfactory. The roads were unmetalled and the buses were run by private operators. Since I had decided to meet only a few people in the village, I got down at Bhan Singh Di Khui, from where a narrow path led to my village. At this stage, I was enjoying extremely good health. The wholesome effect of living in the temperate climate of western countries had not eroded as yet. I was dressed like a native of the Majha area (*majhail*). I wore a long Bengali style *kurta*, an equally long *chadar* covering my lower limbs, a white turban with one end sticking out proudly and the other end falling down below my neck, a neat *safa* hanging down from my shoulders and reaching up to my knees. I also carried a huge staff, the upper end of which touched my ear. Dressed like this, it was not surprising that Jagat Singh, Bishan Singh and Inder Singh failed to recognize me. They took me for a *sardar* who had come from the canal colonies (*Bar*) to meet Jagat Singh, who had also lived in that region. When I informed them that I had come to meet them, they began to walk with me towards the village. Bishan Singh and Inder Singh were ahead while Jagat Singh was walking besides me. After crossing two fields, we reached a mango grove. I stopped here and asked Jagat Singh if he was still unable to recognize me. He looked at me carefully but failed to recognize me. When I told him my name, he embraced me spontaneously, expressing his surprise and joy at the same time. We sat down in the grove and I told him, 'Listen carefully. I am not going to enter the village right now. Do not tell anyone about my arrival, except Radha Singh. Ask him to bring some food for me. I will wait for him in the neighbouring sugar cane field.'

When Radha Singh (my cousin who had met me in Singapore) received the message, he was anxious to meet me. He got the meals prepared in a short time. Carrying the packet of food, he hurried towards the field where I was waiting for him. Seeing Radha Singh in that area, a few people became suspicious and one of them by the name of Shiv Singh began to follow him. I saw Shiv Singh hide behind a row of jamun trees. However without bothering about his objectionable behaviour, I met Radha Singh. I told him that I was going to Chichowal, a neighbouring village, where he should send Jagat Singh, Chanan Singh Dhoot and Santokh Singh to meet me. Radha Singh promised to convey the message and left. As I was leaving the village, I realized that I was being followed by Shiv Singh. I stopped and asked him to come closer. In a stern voice, I said, 'I have recognized you and you have also recognized me. The relations between us had always been friendly and cordial. Be sure that you do not tell anyone about my presence. For, if you do, it will be very bad on your part.' He replied nervously, 'No, no. I will not talk to anyone. You need not worry at all.'

I reached Chichowal and waited in a mango grove for Chanan Singh Dhoot, Santokh Singh (both of whom were active members of the Communist Party of India) and Jagat Singh. We talked well into the night and decided that I should sleep there. The next day Santokh Singh would escort me to Shahbazpur on my may to Rarha. We soon parted and I went to Radha Singh's house. Everyone, including Radha Singh's wife Gurbachan Kaur, knew that I had come and were curious to see me. They were staring at me through the crevices of door and windows. I overheard remarks like, 'He has grown so strong, stout and tough.' A message was sent to my mother, informing her that I would come home at night and she should leave the door open. I reached my parental home at the appointed hour and met my mother and aunt, the mother of Jwala Singh Dhoot. We discussed personal and family matters for a long time. Though I conducted myself with equanimity, the two women were overwhelmed. I consoled them as much as I could. Before leaving the house, I gave some money to my mother.

Early next morning Santokh Singh came to the mango grove. We passed through such villages as Kandhali and Khakhan and proceeded to Shahbazpur, from where Santokh Singh turned back. I resumed my trek, passed the Bein and the bridge, and reached the village of Bhoorpur. Next, I crossed the Dhusi, an embankment raised to protect agricultural land from the floods of river waters. It was quite dark when I reached Rarha, the village where my sister had been married. As soon as my arrival became known, the house was engulfed in a wave of excitement. The members of the family extended a very warm welcome to me and organized a feast in my honour. In accordance with their wishes, I gave them a detailed account of my adventures in foreign lands. My sister's brother-in-law said to me, 'You have been moving about here and there in the midst of so much risk. If you need any help in terms of money, do not hesitate to tell us.' I told him that I did not need anything and only wanted to meet my near and dear ones. Following my instructions, they had made arrangement for my stay in the enclosure for cattle (*haveli*) instead of the house.

Early next morning, Beant Singh, my sister's son accompanied me to Dhilwan from where we boarded a train for Amritsar. On reaching the city, I collected my suitcase from the office of the Desh Bhagat Pariwar Sahayak Committee. I had sent it from Calcutta with the help of a source. It contained some warm clothes, which could be worn only in the cold countries of the West. Since I did not need them, I asked Beant Singh to take the suitcase to his house. I left for Harse Chhina village, where I spent a night with Achhar Singh Chhina,[12] whom I had met in Moscow.

Thereafter, I came to Cheema, a village near Nurmahal in Jalandhar district. I stayed here as also at Bilgha for a considerable period of time. I began to work in active collaboration with Bujha Singh, Baba Karam Singh Dhoot and Bhagat

Singh Bilgha.[13] The residential quarters in the neighbouring villages were so organized that we were able to carry out our activities without any fear of exposing ourselves to public view. In most cases, single houses were located near wells. Wherever houses were grouped in clusters within a village, we confined ourselves to the wells, where food could be brought from the village without rousing any suspicion. Having made Cheema (the ancestral village of Comrade Bhola Singh) the centre of our activities, we organized study circles in such villages as Cheema (big and small), Danduwal, Bilgha, Uppal, Jandiala, Chak Maidas, Sidhwan, Sariala, Barha Pind and Dosanjh Kalan. These meetings were attended by enthusiastic young boys. We taught them the basic essentials of Marxism and explained to them the problems faced by the Indian peasants and workers, who were suffering at the hands of feudalism, capitalism and colonialism. Two young lads, Gurcharan Singh Randhawa and Chain Singh Chain, who had just left the school after passing their matriculation, evinced a keen interest in the new ideology.[14] We also organized a number of meetings in the villages around Tanda such as Litran, Dehriwal, Babak and Jajha in Hoshiarpur district. Due to our efforts, a number of people were drawn into the cadre of the party. A significant achievement was the conversion of Master Hari Singh, a Congressite-Akali, to communism.

While these activities were under way, I found time to visit Bachan Singh of Tarkhanvad, a village near Moga. When I entered the hamlet, I inquired about him from some people who were sitting in a small group. However they were unable to give me any information about him. They said that there was one Bachan Singh, but he was not the man I was looking for. I said, 'I am talking about Bachna, who used to graze cattle.' Immediately they replied in chorus, 'Oh, now we understand that you mean Bachna who has come from abroad, one who belongs to such and such family.' I said, 'Yes, he is the man.' A boy led me to Bachan Singh's house, who was overjoyed to see me. While he engaged himself in performing the duties of a host, I said, 'Nobody knows anything about you in the village. Why have you not organized a meeting?' He answered, 'Somehow it could not be worked out, so far.' The two of us went to the neighbouring village of Daudhar where we met Gainda Singh, with whom I had formed an intimate friendship in Calcutta. On our return to Bachan Singh's village, we organized a meeting which was well attended. Gainda Singh and I addressed it. Besides other things, we highlighted the fact that Bachan Singh was a patriot who had studied Marxism at Moscow and had returned to his country to fight for the cause of peasants and workers. We exhorted them to look to him for guidance in political matters. This information came as a pleasant surprise to the people and they began to take pride in the fact that a patriot like Bachan Singh, who had made great sacrifices, was one of them.

During the course of my stay in Punjab, I succeeded in achieving three aims. First, I joined hands with a number of leading communists in sowing the seeds of Marxism in the countryside. I endeavoured to strengthen the roots of the CPI by bringing several young men into its fold. Second, I established personal contacts with a large number of communists who were actively engaged in political work. Third, I also made myself familiar with the nature, strength and imperfections of communist movement in Punjab. I found that the communists were mainly divided into two groups, viz., the Kirti group and the Josh group, the latter being aligned with the CPI.[15] My social relations were confined mainly to the Kirti group. I made a humble effort to unite the two groups. The Comintern had issued repeated instructions to the communist parties of various countries that they should make earnest efforts to assimilate smaller communist groups into the larger movement.

NOTES AND REFERENCES

1. Originally the capital of Bhonsalas, Nagpur was the capital of the Central Provinces. A leading industrial and commercial centre, its population increased from 84,441 in 1872 to 127,734 in 1901. It had two major textile mills, twelve cotton ginning factories and numerous cotton weaving units employing 5,000 persons. The city had offices of provincial departments, three central jails, agricultural and engineering institutes, normal schools for training

teachers, schools and colleges run by Christian institutions, and a military cantonment at Sitalbadi. *The Imperial Gazetteer of India*, vol. XVIII, pp. 318-21.

2. Found in almost all cities and towns, a *dharamshala* was a traditional inn, which was normally managed by the local religious institutions or charitable trusts. It provided temporary accommodation to pilgrims and travellers, charging little or no money.
3. In view of a strict vigil on the Colombo route, the Moscow trainees adopted a variety of tactics to hoodwink the CID. While travelling northwards via Nagpur on a train, Bhagat Singh Bilgha was closely shadowed by the CID. He exchanged his rail ticket with a co-passenger, threw away his fake passport after tearing it and disembarked at a obscure station, thus giving the slip to the CID agents. Bhagat Singh Bilgha, op. cit., p. 172.
4. The great depression resulted in the closure of mills, reduction in wages and dismissal of workers. In 1933, labour unrest was widespread and there were nearly 40 strikes. Communist activity revived following the release of convicts in the Meerut conspiracy case. The CPI joined hands with the Royists to organize (23 April 1934) a massive general strike in Bombay textile industry, in which 90,000 workers participated. Similar strikes were organized in Sholapur, Nagpur, Kanpur and Delhi. Alarmed at the turn of events, the government banned (23 July 1934) the CPI and associated organizations under the Criminal Law Amendment Act of 1908. Bhagwan Josh, *Struggle for Hegemony in India*, vol. II, pp. 104-6; Sunil Kumar Sen, *Working Class Movements in India*, pp. 52-3.
5. Muzaffar Ahmad was born in 1893 in a impoverished peasant family in south Bengal. He attended school at Noakhli and later joined Bangabashi College in Calcutta, but left his studies after he failed the intermediate examination. Besides taking a keen interest in Bengali literature, he participated in the non-cooperation and Khilafat movements. After embracing Marxism, he became active in the WPP and edited its journal, *Ganvani*. He was imprisoned under the Kanpur and Meerut conspiracy cases. He remained in jail or village internment till 1936, when he returned to Calcutta to resume work in peasant organizations and trade unions. Overstreet and Windmiller, op. cit., p. 556.
6. Ranen Sen was a trade unionist of Bengal, who had been active in Calcutta since his student days. After joining the CPI in 1930, he served on its central committee from 1930 to 1948. He was also secretary of the Bengal Provincial Trade Union Congress and vice-

president of the AITUC. Most of his time was devoted to working for the AITUC and the trade union sub-committee of the CPI. Overstreet and Windmiller, op. cit., pp. 572-3.

7. The communists of Calcutta did some organizational work among members of the Sikh community. In his memoirs, Muzaffar Ahmad was unable to provide an account of these Punjabi comrades owing to various reasons, but promised to do so at a later date. Muzaffar Ahmad, *Myself and the Communist Party of India*, p. xii.
8. In the 1930s the working class of Calcutta – millhands, railwaymen, scavengers, carters, transport and dock workers – showed cross-professional solidarity and agitational politics. The trade union movement was controlled by the CPI and other leftist groups, where leaders like Muzaffar Ahmad, Somnath Lahiri, Abdul Hamid and Ranen Sen rose to prominence. Their success was attributed to the efforts of early communists to declass themselves from their petty bhadralok background and dissemination of communist ideology through propaganda literature and populist campaigns. Suranjan Das, 'The Politics of Agitation: Calcutta 1912-1947', in Sukanta Chaudhury, ed., *Calcutta, the Living City*, vol. 11, pp. 22-3.
9. Abul Kasim Fazlul Haq (1873-1962) played a dominant role in Bengal politics for three decades before the partition. Though he was active in the Muslim League, yet he remained associated with the Congress. He contested the 1937 elections under the banner of his newly established Krishak Praja Party and formed a coalition ministry with the Muslim League, which lasted till 1941. During his tenure, a commission was appointed to examine the land revenue system. Severe restrictions were imposed on zamindars' powers to enhance rents and recover arrears. Restrictions were also imposed on moneylending. The Calcutta Municipal Act was amended to increase the representation of Muslims and Scheduled Castes. S.P. Sen, *Dictionary of National Biography*, vol. 11, pp. 135-8; Parshotam Mehra, *A Dictionary of Modern Indian History*, p. 286.
10. The All India Trade Union Congress had suffered two major splits in 1929 and 1931, as three groups – communists, moderates and Royists – formed separate bodies. The revival of labour movement in the mid-1930s and the emergence of a broad left united front created conditions for unity. Accepting the proposals of V.V. Giri, the Delhi session of the AITUC paved the way for the return of Joshi-led National Federation of Trade Unions to the fold of the AITUC. This development was a momentous event in the history

of the Indian trade Union movement. Chaman Lal Revri, *The Indian Trade Union Movement*, p. 237; Kiran Saxena, *Trade Union Movement and the National Movement*, pp. 153-61.

11. Karam Singh Dhoot was arrested in 1930 at Kabul, while returning from Moscow. In spite of being tortured in the Lahore Fort, he did not disclose any information to the imperial government. From 1930 to 1937, he suffered imprisonment without trial under Regulation III of 1818. He rose to be the president of the Punjab Riyasti Praja Mandal. During the Second World War, he was imprisoned at Deoli and Gujarat along with other communists. Bhagat Singh Bilgha, op. cit., p. 170.
12. Achhar Singh Chhina (1889-1981) migrated to the USA in 1921 and enrolled in the University of California, but worked for the Ghadar Party. In 1932, he went to Moscow and studied at the University of the Toilers of the East. He returned to India in 1936, only to be interned in his village. He was implicated in the Fattewal murder case in 1938, but evaded arrest by escaping to Jamshedpur. He made arrangements, in collaboration with Bhagat Ram Talwar, for the escape of Bose from Peshawar to Kabul. He went to Moscow in 1940 to seek clarifications on the 'Imperialist War' and the position of the Kirti Kisan Party *vis-ā-vis* the CPI. While returning through the Hindukush, he was arrested at Gilgit and imprisoned in Campbellpur jail till 1 May 1942. He served as president of the Punjab Kisan Sabha from 1942 to 1949 and was a member of the Punjab legislative assembly from 1952 to 1962. Fauja Singh, *Eminent Freedom Fighters of Punjab*, pp. 59-60; Bhagat Singh Bilgha, op. cit., pp. 278-80; Gurharpal Singh, op. cit., p. 34.
13. Bhagat Singh Bilgha was born in 1907 in village Bilgha, Jalandhar district. He migrated to Argentina, where he served as secretary of the Ghadar Party unit during the late 1920s. He studied Marxism–Leninism at the Eastern University in 1931-2. He was imprisoned during the Second World War. He remained aligned with left faction in the communist movement of Punjab, i.e. with the Lal Communist Party and after 1964 with the CPI(M). He was the moving force behind the establishment of the Desh Bhagat Yadgar Hall, Jalandhar, a memorial in honour of Ghadarites. He has written a book on the communist movement in Punjab, focusing on the Ghadar Party and the Kirti Kisan Party, covering the 1908-52 period.
14. Chain Singh Chain joined the Kirti Kisan Party in 1936 and became its general secretary in 1941. He also served as secretary of the Punjab Kisan Sabha from 1936 to 1940. He was imprisoned during

the Second World War. He was the secretary of the short-lived Lal Communist Party. Following the split of 1964, he joined the CPI and served as secretary of its Jalandhar district committee. He has authored a book on the role of the Kirti Kisan Party during the Second World War.

15. For critical insights into the respective characteristics of the two strands in Punjab communism, see Gurharpal Singh, op. cit., pp. 47-57.

CHAPTER 5

Involvement in Peasant Movements

From Punjab, I went to Kanpur, which was a leading industrial centre of the country. Here I shared a room with R.D. Bhardwaj, a member of the central committee of the CPI. A hard working man, he remained busy writing articles, which appeared in English newspapers like the *Peoples' Democratic Front.* Our room was the nerve centre of the political activities of the working class in Kanpur. It was here that we received instructions from the central office of the party in Calcutta and it was from here that we issued guidelines to the working class of the province in general and Kanpur in particular. We worked in close cooperation, discussed all policy matters and evolved strategies essential for protecting the interests of the working class. Besides a perfect understanding on various political issues, Bhardwaj and I shared many things in common. He had unbounded affection for me, which I reciprocated in full measure.

In Kanpur, I worked openly and on a full-time basis. However, the nature of my activities was different from those which I had undertaken in Calcutta. For, the trade union movement was more developed in Kanpur than in the area where I had worked in Calcutta.[1] Though I was only a part of the collective leadership, my suggestions were often accepted at the meetings. My understanding of Marxism-Leninism as well as my ability to make a correct analysis of a situation enabled me to play an effective role. During this period, I came into contact with Santa Singh Yusuf,[2] president of the trade unions of Kanpur, and Santosh Chand Kapur, secretary of this large body. We endeavoured to set-up cells of the party in the various workers' unions. An increasing number of workers were brought into the fold of the trade union movement and we educated them in the methods and techniques of running the organization. At the same time, we re-educated the existing cadre. We guided workers whenever they struck work, by addressing them at their meetings.

As we were engaged in these activities, we learnt from the newspapers that Bishamber Dyal Tripathi was planning to lead a mammoth procession of 100,000 muzaras from Unnao to the provincial assembly at Lucknow to protest against landlordism.[3] In response to my request, a meeting of the Kanpur district committee of the CPI was convened at which I proposed that we should participate in the grand march. The proposal, however, was rejected on the grounds that we had not been invited by the organizers. I argued, 'We are revolutionaries. The unity of kisan and mazdoor is absolutely essential for the achievement of our ultimate aim. The Unnao march has provided us an opportunity to register this unity.' Despite my arguments, the proposal could not be carried through. In the end, I made a request that I should be allowed to participate as an individual. None of the members had any objection to this. Armed with the flags and banners of the party and accompanied by a few unemployed workers, I boarded the train to Unnao. We reached Unnao late at night and met the organizers of the rally and handed over the letter of introduction from the secretary of the Kanpur district committee of the CPI addressed to Tripathi. I was told that I would be able to meet Tripathi the next morning.

As I waited for daybreak, I noticed the preparations being made by the volunteers for the next day's programme. A number of young men were busy writing slogans such as 'Raja Ram Chandra ki Jai', 'Dharti Mata ki Jai', 'Mahatma Gandhi ki Jai', on 200 to 250 yards of a thin red cloth (*halwan*). I was infuriated as well as surprised at their ignorance because these slogans failed to highlight the problems of the peasantry. Therefore, they were not only irrelevant but also ridiculous. Unable to contain my feelings, I asked the young men to assemble at one place, as I intended to address them. Discontinuing the various tasks assigned to them, they sat in a semi circle in front of me. I delivered a short but powerful speech, in which I highlighted the exploitation of the peasantry at the hands of three classes, viz., the landlords, the money-lenders and British imperialists. I explained to them that the landlords extracted a major part of the agricultural surplus, leaving the peasants with barely any means of subsistence. They were often compelled to do forced labour (*begar*). They were evicted in an arbitrary manner and their womenfolk often became the victims of the landlords' lust. They were suppressed in innumerable ways by the landlords with the connivance of the police and hired goondas. I concluded by arguing that they must demand the abolition of *zamindari* without compensation and the right of ownership of land for the muzaras.

My arguments had an immediate impact on the young men, who declared in chorus, 'You have come at a very opportune moment. We were proceeding in the wrong direction. You have done a great service to our cause by showing us the right path.' Thereafter, they began to prepare the banners again. In the changed circumstances, I had no difficulty in persuading them to adopt new slogans such as 'Abolish Zamindari System', 'Down with Moneylenders', and 'Death to British Imperialism'. I found that a considerable length of *halwan* remained to be used. I feared that if the youngmen failed to finish the entire quantity of cloth before daybreak, the organizers including Tripathi and some Congressmen might ask them to write meaningless slogans. Therefore I asked the volunteers to proceed with their work at the maximum possible speed. At my insistence, a few demands of our party were also painted on the banners. One of these concerned the recognition of the CPI as a lawful body and another related to the publication of a report of a commission which had been set up to inquire into the condition of industrial workers in Kanpur.[4] On my own part, I made a large flag which carried the emblem of the CPI.

A little before sunrise it was found that not a single inch of *halwan* was left unused. Having successfully accomplished the task of preparing the banners, the volunteers were satisfied. Though they were tired after having worked the whole night, yet they were brimming with the spirit of militant enthusiasm. I said to them, 'It is quite possible for Tripathi and other leaders to object to our slogans. They might protest when I stand with my flag along with your tricolour while you sing patriotic songs. What will you do in such a eventuality?' They assured me that they would not allow any one to remove my flag. In this manner, I succeeded in winning over the young men. After sunrise they met their leader, Tripathi. While handing over the letter brought by me from Kanpur, they explained with excitement, 'This Sardarji is a very intelligent man. He has made us understand many aspects of the condition of the peasantry. He has been instrumental in inventing many meaningful slogans. We are greatly indebted to him.' When Tripathi saw the banners, he exclaimed, 'The sardar has imparted his colour as soon as he has arrived.' He was appreciative of the work done by the volunteers, particularly preparing the banners under my supervision. Understandably, he did not approve of some of the slogans. But sensing the mood of the young men, who had expressed a preference for my ideas, he thought it prudent to remain silent.

Soon, the participants began to arrive at the spot, which was the starting point of the march. The first item on the agenda was the singing of the national song under the national flag. While they hoisted the tricolour, I stood besides it with the CPI flag. As I had anticipated, the Congressmen demanded the removal of the CPI flag. I stood firm on my ground and asserted, 'The tricolour stands for our fight against the British, the princes and other feudal elements, while the red flag symbolizes the struggle of the kisans and mazdoors against an exploitative capitalist system. Therefore, there is no contradiction between the two flags. In fact, they are complementary to each other. As such, both of them are essential.' Hearing this, Tripathi, who had already made up his mind on the issue, asked everyone to leave the matter at rest. He said to me, 'Sardarji. Kindly take your place with your flag.' While the national song was being sung, a volunteer stood on the right with the tricolour and I stood on the left with the red flag.[5]

The number of participants swelled to 10,000. A majority of them were peasants, whose poverty was clearly visible. They were ill-clad and had brought no extra clothing. They were ill-fed and had brought nothing to eat except parched gram, which had been tied in a piece of cloth slung over their shoulders. When they felt hungry, they ate a few handfuls, drank water and continued their march. As the procession left the town and passed through the suburbs, several groups of peasants from the neighbouring villages joined the procession. Before we had traversed only a few miles, the khadi-clad Congressmen slipped away one by one. When Tripathi saw this undignified conduct on the part of these deserters, he said to me, 'Sardarji ! If you assume the responsibility of leading this procession up to Lucknow, I will be able to reach the capital in advance in order to make arrangements for the rally.' I replied, 'I have come only to serve you. I am willing to perform whichever task is assigned to me. I am prepared to lead the march, provided you instruct the young men to follow me. I will be able to shoulder this responsibility only if the leading participants actively cooperate with me.' Endorsing my suggestion, Tripathi summoned the young men and told them to march under my leadership. They readily accepted the new arrangement and promised to extend their wholehearted support to me. In fact, this was what they desired.

Soon after, Tripathi drove away in his car. As soon as his vehicle was out of sight, we stopped the procession (*julus*) to enlighten the marchers about our problems, aims and tactics. This continued for nearly two hours during which a number of speakers came forward to address the peasants. The workers who had accompanied me from Kanpur were experienced trade unionists and had been actively involved in a number of strikes. Since they could speak Hindi in the local dialect, I invited them to address the gathering. They focused on the current problems of the peasantry, came down heavily on the various forces responsible for the plight of the rural masses, stressed the need to establish fraternal relations with industrial workers and declared their intention to continue their fight for social justice until the outstanding demands were met. Further, they warned the peasants against the indefensible conduct and unsympathetic designs of the Congressmen, who had failed to make a common cause with them. They exhorted the peasants to ignore the deserters, while remaining steadfast in their commitment to the cause. These speeches had a tremendous impact on the peasants who demonstrated their newly acquired inspiration by raising slogans. As we resumed the march, we evolved a particular schedule: after covering a distance of every 5 miles, we stopped in order to refresh ourselves, while the speakers took the rostrum. As we proceeded in this manner, numerous contingents of peasants merged with the *julus* at successive intervals along the route. By the time we reached Lucknow, the number of marchers swelled to 100,000. Since we had made an excessive use of our vocal chords while making speeches and raising slogans, our throats became choked and voices became hoarse.

While we were on our way to Lucknow, I sent a fellow worker to Kanpur with an urgent message for the district committee of the CPI. I informed my comrades that the *julus* was very large and its leadership was securely in our hands and they should join us in full strength so that we could consolidate our position. In response to my message, a number of active party workers joined us. As they were fully trained for the kind of activity in which we were engaged, their arrival was greeted by the peasants with great enthusiasm. In a similar message to the Lucknow district committee of the CPI, I conveyed the information that we were leading a procession of peasants with the aim of holding a mammoth rally at the provincial assembly and that they should prepare themselves to join us in maximum numbers. In this manner, the Lucknow unit of our party was also activated.

We reached Lucknow on Sunday evening and found a large open space where the marchers settled down to rest. Since it had been decided to spend the night at that very spot, they became busy in making whatever arrangements they could afford in the circumstances. A meeting was called to work out the details of the next day's programme which was attended by Tripathi's followers as well as by my comrades who had come all the way from Kanpur. I proposed that Tripathi should be chosen to preside over the rally because he had his roots in the region from which the demonstrators were drawn and, as such, he was in a position to make a realistic analysis of the problems faced by them. I had already convinced the young men about the necessity of preventing anyone other than Tripathi from acting as the chairman of the proceedings. I had done my best to ensure that they remained steadfast in their resolve. On their part, they had assured me that they would support this move by all means.

Tripathi appeared at night only to inform us that he had completed all the arrangements for the rally and that he had made Acharya Kriplani its chairman.[6] We were taken aback by this news and strongly objected to the nomination of Kriplani for the exalted office. Tripathi tried his best to bring us round to his point of view. We argued, 'If Kriplani is allowed to act as the chairman, the very purpose of the demonstration, from the beginning to the end, will be defeated.' Finding himself in a tight corner, Tripathi continued, 'It will not be appropriate for me to assume the chairmanship at this stage. I have myself conferred this honour on Kriplani. If I deprive him of it, he will definitely feel hurt.' In an attempt to find a solution to this tricky situation we assured Tripathi, 'You need not feel embarrassed at this change in the chairmanship, for we will ourselves meet Kriplani in order to make him understand our position.' This suggestion was rejected by Tripathi, who assumed the responsibility of apprising Kriplani about his (Tripathi's) limitations. Having acquired an initial advantage, we began to consolidate our gain. On our demand, Tripathi agreed to have a large number of leaflets printed for free distribution at the rally. The leaflets would highlight our demands, such as the recognition of the CPI as a legal body, the publication of the report of a commission which had inquired into the condition of industrial workers in Kanpur and the solution to the problems of the peasantry as visualized by us. Besides, we gave in writing a detailed explanation of our demands to Tripathi, who agreed to include them in his presidential address at the rally the next day.

The next morning we were joined by our Lucknow-based comrades. We began to make preparations for the demonstration to be held in front of the provincial assembly. The procession, composed of innumerable peasants, was formed in a orderly manner. Duties were assigned to the leading volunteers. At the appointed time, the procession marched towards the assembly. Every thing proceeded in accordance with the plan chalked out by us. The Congress ministry of the United Provinces, headed by Govind Ballabh Pant, tried its best to thwart the rally.[7] In the first instance, it refused to give permission for holding the meeting in front of the assembly. Instead, it allotted an alternative site at the Aminuddaulah Park, which was at a considerable distance from the place where we had encamped for the night. Undaunted by this rebuff, we decided to go ahead as planned and continued to march towards the assembly. Holding the CPI flag, I led the procession along with a volunteer who carried the tricolour. I warned him repeatedly to hold the flag tightly, because the Congressites were likely to snatch it at the first opportunity. He assured me that he would not let it go even if he had to sacrifice his life in the effort.

When we reached our destination, the peasants sat down on the ground. The Congress government made a determined attempt to create confusion in our ranks. A number of Congress leaders, one after the other, appealed to the demonstrators through loudspeakers to leave for an alternative site, the Aminuddaulah Park. They claimed that all the facilities including microphones and drinking water were available at the site. The last to exhort the marchers was the chief minister himself. These implorations, however, failed to have any impact on the peasants who refused to move. Reposing their faith in me, they looked towards me for direction. In spite of its best efforts, the government failed to persuade the peasants to shift to another place. In response to these efforts, we requested that we should be given an opportunity to use loudspeakers. The request was turned down forthwith. The peasants became restless. The atmosphere was charged with tension. Sensing trouble and pre-empting any untoward incident, I moved quickly among the demonstrators and gestured to them to remain seated in protest against the uncooperative attitude of the Congress government, particularly its refusal to allow us the use of loudspeakers. Following my instructions, my fellow comrades spread out among the peasants and told them to squat in a disciplined manner, ignoring the machinations of the authorities. Our efforts produced the desired result as the peasants demonstrated their firm resolve to abide by our instructions.

Once order had been restored, the Congressmen made another attempt to achieve their aim. They contacted my comrades – Santosh Chand Kapur, Santa Singh Yusuf and Arjun Arora – and requested them to persuade me to lead the peasants to Aminuddaulah Park. As I had anticipated, they expressed their inability to do so: 'The man is not under our influence. He is his own master.' Convinced that we would not budge from our position, they resorted to another trick: Jawaharlal Nehru arrived on the scene. Cutting through the crowd with great energy and determination, he approached the volunteer who was holding the tricolour and swiftly snatched the flag and made his way to the spot where the other Congress leaders were standing. I taunted the flag bearer, 'Did not I warn you about this possibility. This is exactly what I had feared.' This provocation was enough to make him spring into action. He charged forward menacingly towards Nehru, caught up with him and retrieved the tricolour from him. As he returned to take his place beside me, he was given a standing ovation by the gathering. The incident was a signal for the peasants to raise a volley of angry slogans. Caught unawares, Nehru stood crestfallen with one hand on his forehead. Dazed and insulted, he joined the other worthies of the Congress who were mute spectators to the public humiliation of one of their foremost leaders.

In view of the deafening slogans raised by the peasants, it became impossible for the government to resist our immediate demands. It reversed its earlier stance and allowed us to use the public address system. Bishamber Dyal Tripathi ascended the rostrum amidst thunderous applause. A barrister-at-law from England, he was a socialist who held progressive ideas. He delivered a powerful, impassioned and hard-hitting speech, drawing the attention of the government towards the plight of the peasants as well as industrial workers. He launched a scathing attack on the feudal lords, moneylenders and mill-owners. He systematically enumerated the demands of the working class. More importantly, he touched on the nature, objectives and tactics of communism. While praising the role played by the communists in the Indian subcontinent, he made a strong plea for granting legal status to the CPI. In fact, it would not be an exaggeration to state that none of the party's comrades would have succeeded in presenting our demands more effectively than Tripathi. At the end of the speech, a number of resolutions were passed, each pertaining to a particular demand. Then, Govind Ballabh Pant, the chief minister, explained the position of his government *vis-à-vis* these resolutions. While accepting the genuineness of the demands, he gave a solemn assurance that his government would look into them. He added that they would be implemented in consultation with Tripathi and other leaders of the peasants.[8] At the end of the rally, the mammoth gathering raised fiery and militant slogans. The peasants began to leave the venue in order to return to their native villages.

I was surrounded by a number of leading participants who insisted that I should accompany them to Unnao. They promised that they would make appropriate arrangements for my stay. Though I was touched by their gesture, I excused myself on the grounds that I had to report at Kanpur. However, I promised that I would maintain contact with them and would visit them at the first opportunity.

The newspapers carried front page stories about the peasants' march and rally. They reported that though the Congressmen and socialists claimed that they had organized the demonstration, the task had been accomplished by the communists. It was stated that the communists controlled the march like an experienced and efficient general who led his soldiers on the battlefield in a disciplined and orderly manner. The *Pioneer* and *Tej*, for example, published photographs of the peasants. In the latter, I was seen carrying a communist flag. I returned to Kanpur, where a meeting of the district committee of the party was held. It was attended, among others, by R.D. Bhardwaj. I presented a detailed report of the recent happenings at Unnao and Lucknow. The members, who had read about them in the newspapers, admitted that my proposal regarding the peasants' demonstrations had proved to be correct, while they had made a mistake in having opposed it. Other party leaders, including P.C. Joshi (the general secretary of CPI), appreciatively justified the role played by me in organizing the *julus* and in highlighting the outstanding demands of our party.

I stayed in Kanpur for two or three months before returning to Punjab. I used this opportunity to make myself familiar with the political situation in general and the position of the left in particular. As it always happened before the formation of a single full-fledged political party, there existed a number of groups, some of which did not have any well-thought-out programme. It was little wonder that, at this stage, individual sentiment was strong. This explained the emergence of three leftist groups, viz., the CPI, the Kirti group whose secretary was Ram Singh Dutt and the socialists who were led by Mushi Ahmad Din, Mubarak Sagar, Tika Ram Sukhan, Kulbir Singh and Kultar Singh (the latter two were brothers of Shahid-i-Azam Bhagat Singh). In accordance with the instructions issued by the Comintern, efforts had been made to bring the Kirti group into the fold of the CPI. However, these efforts did not bear fruit because of a number of differences between the two. These differences were not political, rather they were organizational in character. Moreover, they were confined only to the leadership. As far as I was concerned, I had friendly relations with political activists who had returned from abroad. I often attended their meetings.

Baba Jwala Singh, a veteran of the Ghadar Party, was the first president of the Punjab Kisan Sabha, a mass organization of peasants. He had been leading a muzara movement in the Nili Bar, which embraced the districts of Multan and Montgomery. The movement had acquired a lot of strength and momentum. Unfortunately, Baba Jwala Singh died in a bus accident near Okara on 7 May 1938.[9] At this juncture, the Punjab Kisan Sabha was faced with the problem of nominating a successor to Baba Jwala Singh in the Nili Bar. A meeting was convened by Kartar Singh Gill, secretary of the Kisan Sabha, and was attended, among others, by Dr Bhag Singh and Baba Kesar Singh. I was also present. The names of several persons, who could carry on Baba Jwala Singh's unfinished task, were considered. A majority of members proposed the name of Baba Kesar Singh. However, the latter expressed his unwillingness to accept the responsibility, 'You have always placed such responsibilities on the shoulders of old men. Why not select a younger man for the job.' There was a heated discussion and a number of names were proposed, only to be rejected by others. I observed that no one was willing to assume the responsibility of leading the muzara movement in the Nili Bar. I intervened and said, 'My contention is that the work started by Baba Jwala Singh should in no case be allowed to discontinue. I am willing to go to the Nili Bar in order to ensure the continuance of the movement. But this would be only a stopgap arrangement. In this way, you will get sufficient time to find a suitable person to take the place of Baba Jwala Singh.' My proposal was accepted without any opposition. Kartar Singh Gill gave me a letter of introduction addressed to Baba Jalwant Singh, who had been asked to render all possible help to me during my stay in the Nili Bar.[10] This man was a commission agent (*arhti*) who ran a small business in partnership with one Atma Singh at Boorewala. He had been providing money, provisions and lodging to the workers who were engaged in organizing the muzaras under the leadership of Baba Jwala Singh. At that time his premises had served as the office of the Punjab Kisan Sabha.

During the summer of 1938, I travelled to Boorewala by bus. At the bus stop, I met Harbans Singh (a native of village Budhala in Jalandhar district) who had also returned from Moscow. He had been deputed by the Kisan Sabha to lead the muzara movement in the Nili Bar in the wake of Baba Jwala Singh's death. But Baba Jalwant Singh had advised him to go back as the task ahead was extremely formidable and required the services of a sagacious man. He had given Rs. 5 each to Harbans Singh and his companion, so that they could return home. Though the prospects of my stay appeared to be discouraging, I said to Harbans Singh, 'Let us meet Baba Jalwant Singh. If he advises me to return, we will travel together.' We met Baba Jalwant Singh and I handed over the letter of introduction from Kartar Singh Gill. Baba Jalwant Singh read the letter and looked at me from head to foot. After having looked closely at my rustic attire, he said, 'I know from personal experience that the political work in the Nili Bar is a difficult proposition. Only a man who is educated, intelligent and wise can perform the task with some hope of success. I doubt if you can fill the berth. Therefore, the best thing for you to do is to have your meals and go back at the earliest.' I replied, 'You are right, Baba ji. Since we have never been in this area before, we would like to see it and we will return tomorrow.' He agreed and said, 'You can stay here for the night. You will find cots and beddings inside.' I thanked him and went into the town accompanied by Harbans Singh and his companion.

The three of us sat down and talked. I told him what I had on my mind. 'Look here, Harbans Singh. We have returned from Moscow after having received education and training in Marxism. A lot of money has been spent on us by the working class of the world. The Comintern has prepared us for a particular purpose. Do we need the help and advice of others. No, we do not. This is not what Marxism teaches us. We should jump into the field on our own strength, for we are quite familiar with the methods of political work. Tomorrow, we will visit the colony villages (*chaks*), interact with the muzaras, understand their problems and form kisan committees. Let them bring more educated activists as and when they feel like. But we are not going to turn our back on this. It does not behove us to go back without going into the field.' The two of them gave me a patient hearing and were convinced by my arguments. We returned to Baba Jalwant Singh's quarters to spend the night.

The next morning the three of us (Harban Singh's companion was a matriculate and his name was also Harbans Singh) undertook a study tour of the villages located around Boorewala. We spent an entire week moving from one *chak* to another, familiarizing ourselves with the problems faced by the muzaras.[11] First, we tried to ensure that each and every village had a kisan committee. Where such bodies had been established by Baba Jwala Singh, we revived and activated them. New kisan committees were set up where none existed earlier. The procedure adopted was quite simple. The muzaras were asked to meet at a particular place and they formed a kisan committee comprising five to ten members. One of them was chosen as the secretary who convened regular meetings, where day-to-day problems of the peasants were discussed, strategies for action were evolved and funds were collected. In some cases, small farmers who had more in common with the muzaras than with the big landlords also became members of these bodies. We were able to raise a fund of Rs. 500 through voluntary contributions made by the peasants. Out of this amount, I gave Rs. 100 to Harbans Singh's companion and asked him to rent a house in the grain market (*mandi*) area which would serve as our central office. The task was performed in a satisfactory manner by him. A red flag was hoisted on the top of the building so that it was easily visible from a distance.

Having done this preliminary groundwork, we decided to hold a mass meeting of peasants in front of the new office on Sunday. Verbal invitations to this effect were sent to as many *chaks* as possible. At this stage, I went to meet Baba Jalwant Singh who could not believe his eyes when he saw me.

BJS : Are you still here?
NSD : Yes, I am.
BJS : What have you been doing?
NSD : At present, we are making arrangements to hold a mass meeting of peasants. We have decided to offer its chairmanship to you.
BJS : Where do you intend to hold the meeting?
NSD : In front of our office.
BJS : Where is it located?
NSD : In the mandi.
BJS : Who has set-up the office?
NSD : We have done it.
BJS : But you never told me anything about it earlier.
NSD : How could we tell you anything unless and until we had actually done something.

When he heard about the work we had done in the *chaks*, he was very happy. On the appointed day, he came to the venue and saw that about 500 muzaras had gathered there from the neighbouring *chaks*. I began the proceedings by delivering a short speech, enumerating the problems faced by them, highlighting the significance of setting up kisan committees in all the *chaks* and explaining the form their struggle would assume in the time to come. My speech was followed by the recitation of a few poems imbued with revolutionary ideas. In his presidential address, Baba Jalwant Singh congratulated us on our recent achievements which had revived the muzara movement, and exhorted the peasants to put their heart and soul into the struggle. At the end, I appealed to the peasants to contribute to our fund. We collected over Rs. 500 and handed over a sum of Rs. 1,000 to Baba Jalwant Singh, requesting him to keep the money in his safe custody from which we would borrow as and when required.

Within no time our office became the nerve centre of the muzara movement, which continued to spread in all directions. Our activities extended to the *chaks* situated in and around Boorewala, Arifwala, Chichawatni, Veharhi and Talumba.[12] Peasants from these areas visited us regularly with their problems and complaints. Their economic condition was relatively better than that of the peasants of the United Provinces, who not only suffered from a greater degree of exploitation but were also culturally backward. In fact, their condition was no better than semi-serfs. Peasants, in this part of the Indian subcontinent, had tremendous fighting capacity but it could be channellized only through proper mobilization, organization and education. The most pressing problem facing them was related to the division of agricultural produce.[13] They demanded that it should be divided between the landlord and tenant in the ratio of 50:50, but the landlords had resorted to various tricks to increase their share. They managed to extract 14 sers for every maund on petty grounds. On the other hand, the muzaras sought the application of the principal of *banney uttey adh-o-adh* in letter and spirit. This meant that the division should be affected on the spot where the crop was harvested. Earlier, the landlords forced the peasants to deposit their share of the produce at their doorstep. This meant transporting a large quantity of grain over a considerable distance from the field to the sardar's premises. This amounted to forced labour (*begar*).

Besides an unfair and arbitrary division of agricultural produce, the landlords often forcibly evicted their muzaras with the help of hired goondas and the police.[14] We fought this particular menace in the following manner. Whenever we received a complaint of this nature, we led the volunteers of the kisan sabha to the *chak* in question. We hoisted the red flag in the midst of the fields and stationed a drummer (*dholi*) near the flag. Young muzaras as well as our volunteers armed with *dangs* guarded the field on all the four sides. While the drummer beat the drum and the peasants raised slogans, the evicted muzaras entered the field with a pair of bullocks and started ploughing. This collective action instilled fear in the high-handed landlord who did not dare to challenge us. In several cases, we succeeded in restoring the control of *murabbas* to the muzaras. Everyone in the region realized the growing strength of our movement.

One day a group of muzaras came to our office from Talumba. They tilled the *murrabbas* owned by Sardar Ujjal Singh. They requested us to visit their *chak*. We refused as we were concentrating on the struggle in Boorey Mandi, Arifwala and Channu. But the muzaras implored us to spare our time for them, as their problem demanded urgent attention. They informed us that the sardars had launched a malicious campaign against us and had spread the word that we had mis-appropriated the funds collected from the muzaras. Hearing this, we accepted their invitation and fixed a particular date for our visit. On the appointed day, we reached Talumba by rail.[15] A large number of muzaras, including their womenfolk, came to receive us. On seeing us, they were filled with joy. They accorded a warm welcome to us. Though they had only rudimentary knowledge of political matters, yet they raised such slogans as 'Abolish Jagirdari System', and 'Inquilab Zindabad'. They brought us almost in a procession to their *chak*. We worked out a course of action and organized meetings in a number of *chaks*. We adopted a variety of methods to educate and inspire the muzaras. After addressing them, I asked Karam Singh Safari (who belonged to village Cheema in Jalandhar district) to recite revolutionary verses. Then Baba Karam Singh (from Bilgha village in the Jalandhar district) engaged the peasants in an informal discussion.

One day, we were marching, with flags in our hands, through the *chak* where Sardar Ujjal Singh had his *murabbas*. Trying to demoralize and ridicule us, the manager (*munshi*) of this sardar asked, 'Who are these people. What does this flag indicate?' I replied, 'Sardar ji ! This flag symbolizes the fight of the peasants and workers against the feudal and capitalist elements. We will explain it to you in detail when we hold a meeting here tomorrow.' Taken aback he said, 'You mean at this very spot.' I replied, 'Yes, at this very spot.' In an overbearing tone, he said, 'No, no. Your meeting cannot be held here.' I asserted, 'We never shift from the venue which has been once decided.' Having thrown this challenge, we marched on.

We drew up the programme for the next day. Particular attention was paid to overcoming obstructions, if any, raised by the sardar's goondas. Four *jathas* consisting of 500 men each were scheduled to converge at a particular place from four different directions. At the same time, we prepared a group of strong young men who were skilled in the use of the *dang*. They were instructed to retaliate with full force if attacked by the goondas. The next day our demonstration proceeded as planned. Our *jatha* of about 500 men was the first to reach the venue. We had not settled down, when the second *jatha* appeared from the opposite direction, shouting slogans. Soon after, the other two *jathas* also arrived, raising the number of demonstrators to over 2,000. They marched in a procession through Sardar Ujjal Singh's *chak*. Our aim was to enable his muzaras to emerge out of their houses and join the processionists without being intimidated by the landlord or his men. Having achieved our purpose, we led the procession to the venue, which had been decided a day before. As anticipated, the sardar had arranged to prevent us from holding the meeting. Chairs had been placed under a shisham tree (*tahli*) and several hired goondas had taken their position around the venue. When they saw our numbers as well as our determination, they were demoralized. We requested the sardar's men to pick up the chairs, failing which we threatened to remove them ourselves. A young Muslim muzara (*musalli*) shouted, 'Take the chairs away immediately. For, if you force us to remove them, then you would be doing it at your own peril. You must be familiar with our ways.' The threat had an immediate impact, as the sardar's men picked up the chairs without even looking in our direction. They seemed to have realized that we would go to any extent to have our way.

The meeting commenced and several speeches were delivered, each one interspersed with anti-landlord slogans. When I took my turn at the pulpit, I castigated the sardars for patronizing goondas with a view to suppressing the muzaras. Other speakers, who represented the various kisan committees of the area, highlighted the problems and demands of the muzaras. They succeeded in casting a spell over the peasants, who responded by raising full-throated slogans. Such was the impact of the demonstration that even the sardar's *munshi* was swayed. As soon as the meeting came to an end, he humbly approached us and offered to provide drinking water and tea. I said, 'You need not take the trouble, for the entire congregation is eager to bear this burden. But for your part, you must take a warning: do not try to come into any conflict with the muzaras, thinking that they are weak, physically and numerically. You have had a glimpse of our strength. We are in a position to bring many more men in the field, if and when the need arises. In that case, the position of your sardar would become precarious.' The *munshi* said with folded hands, 'To me, you appear to be a good man. You have delivered a meaningful speech. Your demands are genuine. As far as I am concerned, I am not the owner of the land. I am only a servant of my master. You need not prepare yourself for any further action in these parts.'

The next morning we convened a meeting of a group of selected muzaras, who possessed leadership qualities. I explained to them, 'We came in response to you invitation. We have set-up kisan committees and have brought you into contact with the neighbouring kisan committees. We have advised the muzaras of the region to seek your guidance in their day-to-day problems. We have also asked them to bring more and more volunteers into the fold of the movement. Now you are strong enough to stop the sardars from engineering forcible evictions. If you are unable to do so on your own, you must inform us immediately. We will come to your aid, equipped with the full strength of our resources.' The muzaras expressed their sense of gratitude to us, for having visited them at a time when they were placed in difficult circumstances. They also collected some funds for the Kisan Sabha.

In this way, the muzara movement spread to the *chaks* neighbouring the *murabbas* of Sardar Ujjal Singh, while it had already taken root in the *chaks* of Boorewala, Arifwala, Chichawatni, Veharhi and Channu. The writ of the landlords ceased to run in these areas. In fact, they found themselves at the receiving end in their conflict with the muzaras. In an attempt to recover their position, they informed the police about our activities.[16] On its own, the police had failed to identify the political activist who was responsible for transforming the dormant grievances of the muzaras into a militant movement, which had assumed wide ramifications and that, too, in the absence of Baba Jwala Singh. The police decided to apprehend this man, who had not become visible to them so far.

In July 1938, we organized a conference of the muzaras at Veharhi. I had sent a message to the central office of the Punjab Kisan Sabha at Amritsar to send a few good orators for the occasion. Since they did not send anyone, our own leading activists had to fill the berth. It may be mentioned here that I was operating in the Nili Bar, under a false name. I was known to one and all as Sunder Singh. In spite of this, the police suspected that I was the man who had created a ferment in the region. As soon as the conference ended and the people began to leave, the police pounced on me. Immediately there was a commotion. The people rushed angrily from all directions and surrounded the police to secure my release. In a flash, I recalled the Fattewal episode (13 March 1938) in which a few people were killed, and Achhar Singh Chhina and Joginder Singh Chhina were falsely implicated.[17] I realized that the unfortunate incident might repeat itself as the policemen were outnumbered by the demonstrators, who were in an extremely aggressive mood. I tried to ensure that their passion did not get the better of them and lead them to violence.

While I was being taken to the police station of Veharhi, the muzaras followed us in a procession. As soon as I entered the building, they surrounded it and raised slogans, demanding my release and condemning the police. So much din was raised outside that I could hear the thanedar with great difficulty when he said, 'Sardar ji, ask these people to disperse, otherwise I will be constrained to act in my own way'. I said, 'What can you do. You have no resources, not even a telephone. The police station (*thana*) has been besieged by the people. If I give them the signal, they will raze this building to the ground, in which case you will perish along with your colleagues. Do not act rashly. I do not want the demonstrators to indulge in violence. However, I do not want to give an opportunity to the government to crush our movement, which has reached a crucial phase. Now, do as I say. Tell the people that I have been arrested by the CID, that you are helpless in the matter and that legal proceedings will take over the case. Therefore, they should disperse.' Having realized the gravity of the situation, the thanedar lost his nerve and insisted that I should address the demonstrators. I saw that the thanedar did not have the courage to face the people in an emotionally surcharged atmosphere. Since my aim, at the moment, was to prevent any untoward incident, I went to the courtyard and addressed the muzaras, 'Friends! I have been placed under arrest. I will be taken to Lahore to be produced before senior officers of the police. Then they will lock me up in the Lahore Fort, where I will be subjected to interrogation. You need not worry about me because I will come to no harm. Very soon, I will be replaced by another comrade of ours, who will lead you through your struggle. Therefore, I request you to peacefully return to your *chaks*.' They bade me farewell and walked away reluctantly, cursing the police for depriving them of a dearly loved friend.

As soon as the people left, I was put in a motor van and taken to Lahore. I was produced before a senior British police officer, probably the Inspector General. He was informed that I was the man who had been leading the muzara movement under an alias. Speaking in English, the officer ordered his subordinates to take me to the Fort and treat me in an appropriate manner. They brought me to the Fort. We crossed three or four iron gates before we reached a cell where I was locked up in solitary confinement. The cell was dark, dingy and stuffy. Food was passed to me in a plate which was slipped under the door. There was no bathroom and the call of nature had to be attended to inside the cell.[18] A single sentry was posted outside the cell, but he was never on duty. I left the cell only when I had to be interrogated. On the first day of my confinement, I was summoned by the warder. I went into his room and as I sat down on a chair, he delivered a sharp blow on my back. A wave of anger rose inside me and I picked up the chair and hurled it at him. The warder ducked and escaped unhurt. After this, he did not approach me again. Nor did he disclose to any one the treatment he had received from me.

The interrogation at the Fort followed a set procedure. Every week a new inspector took over the charge of my interrogation, after studying the documents relating to it. Sampuran Singh, a Sikh, was senior to these inspectors and was the overall in charge of the interrogation. For two weeks, I was subjected to intensive questioning. They used physical torture but failed to extract any information from me. At the end of two weeks, a Muslim inspector was assigned my case. He said to me, 'Tell me if the information contained in these big bundles (*pands*) is true or not.' Apparently, the police had received from the intelligence agencies much information about me, including my stay in the USSR and my involvement in political activities in different parts of the country. But I surmised that they wanted to extract a confession from me. I answered, 'I do not know the contents of these papers. How can I say whether they are true or not.' Hearing this, he opened a bundle of papers and began to read them. I explained, 'There were two factions of workers in Argentina. The one which was opposed to me prepared these false reports and passed them on to the intelligence men in order to create problems for me. The truth is that I am totally illiterate. I have nothing to do with politics, and I have no connection whatsoever with the reports in your possession.' The inspector gave me a patient hearing and said, 'Be sure about the truth of your statement. You have denied everything in my presence. But if you admit your involvement in these activities in the presence of one of the inspectors who succeeds me, I will surely lose my job.' Assuring him I said, 'I will never do such a thing. You need not worry on that account. I gave this statement to the two inspectors who preceded you and I have given exactly the same to you.' He added, 'I have dealt with you in a sympathetic and graceful manner. Now it is your duty to help me.' Surprised by what he said, I asked, 'Imprisoned as I am in the Fort, what sort of help do you expect from me?' He offered a long explanation, 'There are two factions in the police. Each one of them wants to take the credit for extracting a confessional statement from you.' I intervened, 'But this is your internal matter. How am I concerned with it?' He asserted, 'Yes, you are very much concerned with it. If you give some information to others, which you have withheld from me, they would succeed whereas I would fail.' I assured him once again, sticking to my earlier stance. At the end, he asked, 'If you have spoken the truth, should I tie up this bundle.' I answered, 'Yes, please do so.'

The inspector visited me regularly for a whole week. He gave a detailed account of the procedure followed in the Fort, including the various forms of torture, to extract confessional statements from suspects. He made all efforts to ensure that I remained steadfast in my views and did not breakdown under torture or any other form of pressure. I gave whatever assurance I could. I was aware that some of our workers like Karam Singh Dhuleta had succumbed to pressure and had passed on vital information about the political activists trained in the Soviet Union. I assessed these facts in the light of repeated instructions given to me by the inspector, and stood as firm as ever. The inspector often engaged me in informal conversation and asked me a number of questions about the life of people in England, France, the Soviet Union, etc. While denying knowledge about the Soviet Union, I stated that I had been to France on my way to Argentina, but I did not divulge any information about my involvement in political work. At the end of the week the inspector visited me and said, 'I have treated you with kindness. Now you must maintain my honour (*izzat*).'

A new inspector assumed the charge of my interrogation. His first sentence to me was 'Listen carefully. You are a Sikh and I am a Pathan. Soon there will be a contest (*muqabla*) between the two of us.' Understandably, I was shocked by this foolish statement. In normal circumstances, I would not have retaliated in terms of religious identities. But the inspector had provoked me to retort, 'If you happen to be a Pathan, then I am surely a Sikh. And you should know the stuff of which a Sikh is made.' This short verbal duel was overheard by the warder, who himself had learnt a bitter lesson on the day of my arrival to the Fort. He rushed to his seniors and informed them about this happening. Showing prudence, the higher authorities recalled the Pathan and sent a Sikh inspector instead. In response to the wishes of the new inspector, I narrated whatever had transpired between his predecessor and me. He regularly visited me for a week, used kind words as well as physical torture and went away. Another two or three inspectors followed suit.

Then came still another inspector, who happened to be a Sikh. He said, 'Listen to me, Sardara. I will not harm you. But tell me, what will you do if an English officer were to pass in front of your door. Will you keep on sitting quietly.' I could not understand the logic behind this question and answered, 'I cannot say what I would do in such a situation.' The inspector made an offer, 'We will allow you to go if you put your signature on a plain paper.' I replied, 'For one thing, I cannot sign my name as I cannot read or write. But even if I could, I would not do so as who knows what you would write on the paper afterwards.' Having failed to persuade me to fall in line, he led me to the slaughter house of the Fort, which was designed to strike terror in the hearts of even the bravest. There was a well in a corner and a tree in another. A number of large ugly rocks splattered with blood were placed one above the other. Many human skulls and bones were scattered all over the place. A few large knives and axes were also covered with blood. To add to this, two fierce looking men were standing in a corner. The inspector said to me, 'I am a government servant. I am bound to obey the orders passed by the higher authorities. Today is the last day of your life. Now you are taking your last few breaths. You can eat whatever you feel like. You can also meet any person you want to. But only for the last time. These two men are waiting for a signal from me. They will despatch you to the other world in no time.'[19] I replied, 'If this is the fate which is in store for me, then I welcome it. Please do not delay giving them orders for my execution.' My indifferent attitude compelled the inspector to say, 'Take him away. He is not the one to be scared. Such people have already been subjected to a lot of battering.' Having failed in his aim, the inspector brought me back to my cell.

In the evening, Sampuran Singh, an officer senior to these inspectors came to see me and said, 'I had not given them the instructions to put an end to your life, otherwise these people would have done their job.' I replied, 'I am thankful to you for this act of kindness. But it would have made no difference to me even it they had done their job.' Sampuran Singh ordered one of the sentries to bring some grapes and asked me to eat them. I said, 'Sardar ji, I will only eat the food worth six paise to which I am entitled. I will not eat these grapes at any cost.' Though Sampuran Singh tried his best to persuade me, I stood firm. Having failed in his aim, he went away. The warder said to me, 'Sardara! You should have eaten the grapes. Why were you so adamant?' I said, 'What for? I do not need to eat them. I have eaten a lot of grapes in the past. But now there is no such desire in me.'

The last inspector to interrogate me was Banta Singh, a resident of Jandu Singha village in Jalandhar district. His attitude towards me was entirely different from that of his colleagues. He said, 'It is very strange that I did not know it earlier. But you are our own man. Niranjan Singh, the bus owner (who was related to me) of your village, is a great friend of mine. I am also known to Radha Singh, besides a number of others who belong to your village.' Without showing any enthusiasm or emotion, I said, 'It is a good thing that you know these people. But the reality of the situation is that jats are like roots of a grass (*khabal diyan tirhan*). Turn them in any manner, you will find them invariably connected with another of its kind. This phenomenon is attributable to the typical nature of jat relationships. Moreover you yourself belong to that area. It is, therefore, quite likely for you to know me through your relatives and friends.' Offering me barfi and grapes Banta Singh said, 'Had I known earlier that you are here, I would have made better arrangements for your meals.' I remained silent because I was not going to be entrapped by these blandishments. I had doubts about Banta Singh's real intentions. I knew that he was trying to win me over by posing as a well wisher and sympathiser who had come to my rescue. It was clear that he would try to extract information about my activities in the past. I, therefore, refused to eat the sweetmeats or fruits. Undeterred by my indifference, Banta Singh persisted in his mission. He kept on probing me again and again in order to get the information required by the police, but to no avail. Finally, he said that he had heard that Radha Singh had arranged my marriage in Garhdiwala. I replied that I was not aware of Radha Singh's plans, as I was virtually cut off from my village. Banta Singh insisted that his information was correct. I responded, 'You may be knowing about it. As far as I am concerned, I know nothing about this.'

Since I did not provide any clue to my interrogators, they resorted to another tactic. One day the warder was not around. When he appeared after two or three days, I asked him, 'Where were you all this time?' He gave evasive replies. I said, 'You are not speaking the truth. You had gone to bring one of my relatives who is now in your custody.' Though he denied it, I was certain that they had brought my nephew Beant Singh (the son of my sister) from Rarha, for I had overheard a conversation between the inspector and the warder. The next part of my story is based on what was related to me by Beant Singh, who was then eighteen years old.

During the course of my imprisonment in the Lahore Fort, inspector Banta Singh and constable Ujagar Singh went to my ancestral home and informed my family that they had come to take my mother and nephew to Lahore, as I had requested a meeting with them. My mother and nephew went along with them. My mother, however, could not reach Lahore and was asked to return from Jandu Singha (the native village of inspector Banta Singh). Beant Singh was brought to Lahore, where he was placed under the care of Banta Singh's wife. The lad was taken to the Fort for seventeen days but not once was he permitted to meet me. It must be added here that during my last visit to Rarha, I had explained my situation to my relatives, 'In view of my political activities, all of us will have to go through difficult times. The police will interrogate you to extract information about me. But you must tell them that I had left the country twelve years ago and since then you have not heard anything about me.' Fortunately, Beant Singh strictly followed my instructions and the investigators failed to extract any information from him.

The intelligence officers tried to win over Beant Singh, an immature village lad, by being kind and courteous. The CID inspectors touched his feet when they learnt that he was my nephew. This gesture perhaps reflected the high esteem in which freedom fighters were held by the masses. Realizing that this strategy had failed, they brought a number of young girls to entertain him. They cracked jokes, played cards and provided lively company. Often he was offered liquor, which he refused. They employed every possible device to seduce my nephew. However, all their efforts came to naught.

At the end of seventeen days, the jail authorities brought Beant Singh to my cell and made him sit on a chair outside, flanked by Banta Singh on one side and another inspector on the other. The window of my cell was opened and seeing Beant Singh, I exclaimed, 'Oh ! You have grown so much in the last twelve years, I could not recognize you.' My nephew took the hint from my words and continued a stick to his original statement. Subsequently we were not permitted to converse freely. Whenever I tried to do so, the two inspectors would interrupt in accordance with their predetermined plan. The only thing which Beant Singh was able to catch was my feeble complaint, 'I have not been able to sleep these days.' Acting swiftly, the inspectors closed the window of my cell and marched off with Beant Singh.[20]

That evening, Banta Singh took Beant Singh to the famous red-light district of Lahore and told him to enjoy himself. Overwhelmed with revulsion, Beant Singh declared, 'I have no need for any such thing. None in our family has indulged in these games.' At last, the CID realized that it would be futile to detain Beant Singh any longer. So he was permitted to leave. He left for Amritsar and immediately contacted the office of the Desh Bhagat Pariwar Sahayak Committee. He narrated all that he had seen and experienced, including my battered physical condition after repeated bouts of torture.[21]

The period of my confinement at the Lahore Fort, which had

been fixed for two months, came to an end. The concerned authorities contacted my relatives to inform them that I would be released on a particular date and that they should be there to receive me. The police repeatedly asked me as to where I would go after being released from jail, but I did not give any definite answer. I said, 'When you open the door, I will follow the direction in which my mind takes me.' As soon as I was released, I went to the bus stop and was informed by Banta Singh that I had been externed from Punjab. I was ordered to leave the province within (18 October 1938) twenty-four hours.[22] While I was deciding where to go, I saw my mother and my nephew, Beant Singh. I told them that I had been externed from Punjab and would go to Delhi and that they should return to the village. Since I was a native of Kapurthala state, there was no restriction on my going to Dhoot Kalan. But I was not keen to go there because living there would have been as good as externment. At this stage, my mother intervened and implored me to accompany her. There was no one in the world whom she could fall back for emotional support. Overpowered by such feelings, she started crying. Moved by her tears, I decided to go to the village with her, because I knew that I could leave the place as and when I so desired.

In these circumstances, I returned to my ancestral village. Banta Singh had been entrusted with the task of ensuring that the order regarding my externment was duly executed. He escorted us till Bhunga, reported at the police station and informed them about my arrival. Before returning, he visited my village. Soon after, I was made *nazrband* in the village and had to cope with a number of restrictions. I was not allowed to stand or talk among any five persons. People of the village would visit me and ask me endless questions about my stay in foreign lands, the kind of work I had been doing and the amount of money I had earned over the years. None of them was aware of my activities in the Nili Bar, though my nephew had informed them about my confinement at the Lahore Fort. In the meantime, the CPI heard that I had been working among the muzaras in the Nili Bar under the alias Sunder Singh and that I had been arrested after having organized a conference at

Veharhi. The Punjab Kisan Sabha sent its activists to the Nili Bar to take my place. The muzara movement, which had made substantial gains in the recent past, continued to gain strength.

When I studied the situation prevailing in the village, I observed that the people, due to their illiteracy and ignorance, always lived in fear of the police and bureaucracy. Chanan Singh Dhoot, Santokh Singh Dhoot and Master Hari Singh were involved in political work at a higher level. However, no attention had been paid to creating political consciousness in the village itself. On my return to the village, I thought that something ought to be done in this regard. I made arrangements for teaching Punjabi to young boys. They were encouraged to memorize poems inspired by nationalist and revolutionary ideas, which I had selected myself. They were also trained in the art of public speaking. I lectured them on political matters and encouraged them to ask questions, so as to deepen their understanding. Using maps, I taught them the geography of the world and described the major historical developments in the various countries. This was followed by lectures on Marxism-Leninism. I also highlighted the changes, which had been brought about in the Soviet society in the wake of the October Revolution, with particular reference to the working of collective farms and the position of nationalities. I exposed the exploitative character of British imperialism and suggested ways to mobilize the Indian masses against it. Among the young men who attended these lectures were Pratap Chand Dhoot, Rawal Singh, Swarn Singh Kirti and Bachan Singh. With the passage of time, many of them began to work independently among the people.

Now I would turn my attention to a deep-rooted tradition of our village. Since the cultivation of opium was permitted in the princely state of Kapurthala, a number of villagers took advantage of this provision.[23] After raising the crop, they selected the best poppy husk (*dodas*) for themselves and sold off the remaining quantity. This practice had given rise to a permanent group of addicts (*amlis*). They would assemble in a mango grove near the gurdwara, which was located almost in the centre of the village. They brought their shallow bowls and consumed the intoxicating beverage made out of *dodas*. There was no doubt that they always had a nice time. A number of non-addicts also converged under the shade of the huge trees so as to spend their hours of leisure, during the long summer afternoons. I also began to spend time with these people because I wanted to awaken them from their decades-old slumber and make them scientifically understand their socio-economic problems. I went there everyday and answered their questions about my visit to foreign lands and the momentous transformation taking place in the Soviet Union. In this way, I set in motion the process of politicizing my fellow villagers.

Further, whenever a comrade visited me, I would take him to the grove. I would introduce the guest to the people who assembled there and urged them to ask questions from the visiting activist. Once Bachan Singh Tarkhanvad, who was with me in Argentina and Moscow, paid a visit to our village. I took him to the mango grove, where nearly a score of *amlis* were present. After I had introduced the visitor, the villagers asked him numerous questions and extracted their answers from him. As we were leaving the place, Bachan Singh Tarkhanvad (who was mentally exhausted) said to me, 'I thought the *amlis* of your village would be no different from the ones we have at my place. But I am surprised to find that they are quite advanced in their political consciousness and general awareness.' I explained, 'This is because of the long discussions in which they participate with much enthusiasm. After you leave the village, I am sure that they will ask me questions on those issues which have been touched upon by you and which require further elaboration.' Besides, the *amlis* approached me for clarification whenever any doubt appeared in their minds during their conversations among themselves or with any other person. They felt satisfied only when they had listened to my views on a particular subject. In this manner, the village gossip club was transformed into a school of political education. It must be added here that, apart from the *amlis*, a number of toiling farmers also regularly attended these meetings, initially to rest their weary limbs after hours of ploughing the fields. Even the women began to encourage their growing sons to attend these meetings, because they felt that the youngsters would definitely learn something and would return home better informed than before.

I focused the energies of this school in another direction. I organized public meetings (*jalsas*) in the neighbouring villages and prepared the young lads for the same. When we entered any one of these villages the boys would carry the flag of the CPI and make public announcements, inviting the villagers to assemble at a predetermined place. During the course of the *jalsa*, the boys recited revolutionary poems, which were followed by my own speech. The depth of the newly acquired political consciousness could be gauged from the fact that when a conference of the Riyasati Praja Mandal was held (Februray 1939) at Ludhiana – where Baba Karam Singh Dhoot was secretary of the reception committee and Jawaharlal Nehru was chairman of the proceedings – a large *jatha* of young men of Dhoot Kalan went all the way on foot to participate in the conference.[24] On other occasions, some of these people courted arrest and suffered varying terms in jail. It could be claimed, without any exaggeration, that the inhabitants of our village had become politicalized to a considerable extent.

One year the monsoons failed and the area was in the throes of a severe famine. The entire kharif (*sauni*) crop was destroyed. Acting on my suggestion, the villagers sent a petition to the maharaja of Kapurthala. In response to the petition, the maharaja dispatched his *wazir* to our village to make an on the spot study of the loss. All the inhabitants of the village collected at the mango grove. Kabul Singh, the *zaildar* and my uncle, the *lambardar*, both of whom were quite cunning, led the villagers in welcoming the high ranking dignitary. When the proceedings of the assembly commenced, the reader of the *wazir* read the contents of the petition. The *zaildar* stood up to speak and said little apart from showering praises on the maharaja and his regime. The *lambardar*, who did not wish to be left behind, surpassed the *zaildar* in flattering the royalty. The people listened helplessly because, in accordance with their old habit, they were terror stricken at the very mention of the maharaja's name or that of his representative. I was sitting alone nearby under a peepal tree because I had been restrained, by an official order, from standing in a assembly of five or more persons. I observed that nobody was coming forward to speak the truth, so I stood up and sought permission to make my submission. The *wazir* accepted my request and asked me to come closer. The *zaildar* intervened to inform the *wazir* that I had been forbidden by an order to stand among five persons. Rejecting the *zaildar's* objection, the *wazir* said, 'It is we who have passed that order. Let him come here and have his say.'

Stepping forward I said, 'The prevailing state of affairs in the area has been placed before you by the *zaildar* and *lambardar*. My only request is that you should take a look at the fields in all the four directions from here – east and west, north and south. If you find that the crop is standing even in a small pocket, you may increase the land revenue (*muamala*). But if you find that the entire crop has perished, then please have pity on these poor farmers.' Having said this, I turned to the gathering and asked, 'Do you agree with what I have said.' All the villagers raised their hands and supported me with one voice. The *wazir* asked the *zaildar* to explain the contradiction between his statement and mine. Trying to extricate himself from an extremely embarrassing situation, the *zaildar* said, 'Hazoor! We are salt-eaters (*namak khwars*) of the sarkar. We can do nothing except praise it.' The *lambardar*, too, followed suit. Hearing this, the *wazir* lost his temper and criticized the conduct of the two in extremely strong words. He declared, 'It is a must that the voice of the people (*praja*) reaches us. We have appointed you to important positions so that you communicate the sentiments of the *praja* to us. We have not appointed you to go against the interests of the *praja*.'[25] This dramatic turn of events had a tremendous impact on the people. They came to believe that the only person who had the courage to stand up for them was me. Subsequently, I utilized the support of these people to isolate the *zaildar* and *lambardar*. The influence of the reactionary forces was considerably weakened, while that of the progressive elements continued to increase. Since I regularly visited the twenty-four villages of the Bhunga pocket, the people of these villages became attached to me.

At that time a conflict between Gandhi and Subhas Chandra Bose had assumed much importance on the national stage. The next session of the Congress was to be held at Jabalpur. In this connection, Dasaundha Singh Dhada,[26] an old comrade, came to our village and invited me to participate in the Jabalpur session. I was initially reluctant because I was *nazrband* in the village. Dhada, however, insisted and put forward several arguments to convince me, 'A number of crucial issues are likely to come up for discussion at Jabalpur. The participation of wise and committed political activists like you is essential. We are sure to derive a lot of benefit from the exercise.' At last, I agreed to travel to Jabalpur even if it meant violating my *nazrbandi*, thinking that the worst possible scenario would be that the police would arrest me. I picked up my bicycle and went to all those villages where I had set-up centres (*addas*) of political activity and gave instructions to my sympathizers, 'In case the police comes to inquire about me, tell them that I was very much here a few minutes ago and that I had just left the place.'

Thereafter I left my village and remained away for nearly a month (March-April 1939). At Jabalpur, I met a number of my old associates and had detailed discussions with them on outstanding political issues. We unanimously decided to support Netaji in this conflict with Gandhi.[27] After attending the session, I left for Calcutta to meet my old comrades, friends and sympathizers. During this visit, I met such people as Muzaffar Ahmad, Abdul Halim, Nand Singh (the owner of a restaurant), Hazara Singh Akali (who often gave me shelter), Balwant Singh Pardesi, Mani Singh and Inder Singh Kirti. When I returned to Dhoot Kalan, the policemen who had been assigned the task of keeping a watch over my movements, wanted to know as to where I had been during the last so many weeks. I replied innocently, 'I was very much here and in these very villages.' They said, 'You are right, because you are always on the move and nobody can say anything definite about your whereabouts.'

In spite of my internment (*nazrbandi*), I not only worked in the twenty-four villages of Bhunga, but also extended the scope of my activities beyond. Once three of us from our village – Chanan Singh Dhoot, Santokh Singh and I – resolved to meet Bhagat Singh Bilgha at his native village, Bilgha. We decided to walk from Dhoot Kalan to Kathar and to board a train from there to Nurmahal. We walked through the country-side and reached a small town (*qasba*) called Nanda Chaur.

Here we were intercepted by the police who asked us many pointed questions. Since I had been placed under the restrictions of *nazrbandi*, I had to conceal my identity with the help of some instant trick. Assuming an air of confidence I said, 'Look here. Elections to the District Boards are going to be held soon. We are on official duty, for which purpose we are going to Lahore. If we are not able to reach in time, then you will be held responsible. So think of the consequences of your action.' The policemen were alarmed and allowed us to proceed. Though we had succeeded in giving the slip to the police, we still had to be on our guard. I convinced my companions that we must leave the main road and walk along the less frequented side routes, lest the police should have second thoughts and start in our pursuit. On reaching our destination, we met Bhagat Singh Bilgha and narrated the story of our adventurous journey.

Thus I did not permit my *nazrbandi* to confine my activities to the twenty-four villages of the Bhunga pocket. I attended the meetings of our comrades, which were held outside the Kapurthala state. Moreover I did not hesitate to overstep my restriction in order to slip out of Punjab and participated in important political developments, which were taking place in other provinces.

NOTES AND REFERENCES

1. Encouraged by the presence of a popular government under the Congress, a wave of strikes occurred in the textile mills of Kanpur during July-September 1937 and May-June 1938. Though the CPI and CSP were united in the Mazdoor Sabha, the communists managed to marginalize the socialists during the struggle. For a critical analysis, see Bhagwan Josh, *Struggle for Hegemony in India*, vol. 11, pp. 236-7.
2. Born in 1911, Santa Singh Yusuf was actively involved in the trade union movements in Delhi, Bombay, Ahmedabad and Kanpur. His main centre of activity was UP, in which he was a member of the Congress committee for seven years. He spent seventeen years in fourteen different jails. Embracing Marxism in 1930, he held high offices in the AITUC. He served on the central committee of the CPI from 1948 to 1950. Overstreet and Windmiller, *Communism in India,* p. 575.

3. Having sensed the popular mood in the state, the agrarian programme sub-committee of the Congress met under the chairmanship of P.D. Tandon. It proposed a complete review of relations between landlords and tenants, immediate relief to the peasantry, suspension of all cases relating to arrears of rent and ejectment till an adequate tenancy legislation was passed. These proposals had been accepted by the Congress members of the UP legislature. *The Pioneer*, 27 and 28 July 1937.
4. Mounting pressure of the agitating textile workers forced the Pant ministry to appoint a labour enquiry committee comprising of Rajendra Prasad, S.K. Rudra and B. Shiva Rao, to report, with effect from 30 August 1937, on the condition of labourers employed in Kanpur factories. Though the committee was required to submit its report in two months, it did not touch the basic question of wages even after six months of proceedings. Bhagwan Josh, *Struggle for Hegemony in India*, vol. 11, pp. 238-9.
5. The All India Kisan Sabha had also adopted (28 October 1937, Calcutta) the red flag carrying the crossed sickle and hammer in white as its official banner. The red flag caused annoyance to many who perceived it as foreign and anti-national, while others viewed it as a symbol of violence. Swami Sahjanand, president of the Comilla session (11-14 May 1938) of the AIKS, asserted that whereas the tricolour was a symbol of nationalism, the red flag was one of international solidarity and aspirations of the exploited and oppressed. M.A. Rasul, *A History of the All India Kisan Sabha*, pp. 31-2.
6. Born in 1881 at Hyderabad (Sind), J.B. Kriplani started his career as a teacher at Muzaffar College, Bihar. He taught for two years (1919-20) at Banaras Hindu University. From 1920 to 1927, he served as the principal of Gujarat Vidyapeeth, which had been founded by Gandhi. While working for the Gandhi Ashram, he steadily built his position in the Congress, serving as its general secretary from 1934 to 1945. Verinder Grover, ed., *J.B. Kriplani: Political Thinkers of Modern India*, pp. 637-8.
7. During the election campaign of 1937, the Congress committed itself to a moratorium on debts, a drastic reduction in rent and abolition of zamindari. On assuming office, the Congress failed to restructure the existing land revenue system, as the dominant right wing in the Pant ministry considered the agenda as too drastic. Pant advocated harmony between zamindars and tenants. Nehru was no longer concerned with the lot of tenants. A resolution calling for the abolition of zamindari, introduced at a

political conference in December 1937, was dropped at the instance of the president of the provincial Congress committee himself. B.R. Tomlinson, *The Indian National Congress and the Raj,* pp. 94-5.

8. A rally of peasants, held on the opening day (29 July 1937) of the assembly session, was a pointer that the Congress was no longer in favour of any agitation by the peasants and that Pant was unhappy at the growing political consciousness among the peasantry. Mahendra Partap, 'The Ideological Contradiction of Peasants Movement in U.P. (1936-1947)', *Proceedings of the Indian History Congress,* 54th Session, Mysore, 1993, p. 620.
9. Baba Jwala Singh (1866-1938) was born in village Thathiyan, Amritsar district. Little is known about his early life. In 1905, he left India in search of better economic prospects and travelled to China, Panama and Mexico. He reached California in 1908, where he purchased some land and began farming along with Baba Wasakha Singh. He toured the Pacific Coast with other revolutionaries and was one of the founders of the Ghadar Party. In 1914, he sailed for India and was arrested on his arrival at Calcutta. Convicted in the First Lahore Conspiracy Case, he remained imprisoned for eighteen years (1915–33), six of which were spent in the notorious Andaman Jail. After his release he plunged into the peasant movement while working for the *Kirti.* Undeterred by a year long imprisonment in 1935, he continued to spearhead the agitation of the muzaras in the Nili Bar. On 7 May 1938 he died in a accident while he was on his way to attend a conference of the All India Kisan Sabha; S.P. Sen, ed., *Dictionary of National Biography,* vol. 11, pp. 233-4.
10. An owner of seven *murabbas* of land, Baba Jalwant Singh provided food to 500 Akalis who were on their way to the Jaito morcha. As a retribution for this act, the government confiscated his land. He refused to recover his possessions by seeking pardon. Instead, he established himself as a commission agent in the mandi of Arifwala. His shop became the nerve centre of the muzara movement in the Nili Bar. After partition, he became a full-time activist and sold communist literature in Ludhiana, riding on his bicycle. Bhagat Singh Bilgha, op. cit., p. 238.
11. A newspaper report referred to these three activists, while describing that the Punjab Kisan Committee had sent a special delegation consisting of Ram Singh Majitha, Harbans Singh and three other comrades to the Nili Bar, with a view to get the grievances of tenants redressed. *The Tribune,* 18 June 1938.

12. The year 1938 saw active agrarian agitations, which spread to the districts of Multan, Montgomery, Lyallpur, Lahore and Amritsar. For related details, see Bhagwan Josh, *Communist Movement in Punjab*, pp. 130-40.
13. These problems may be compared with a charter of demands drawn up by the striking muzaras of several *chaks* in Okara tahsil – to stop a kharcha of 2.5 ser per man, to reduce chara shalgham from 8 to 3.5 per kanal, to stop Rs. 6 as the rate of chari, to stop a rate of Rs. 4 per kanal for senji and moth, to implement the government rate of Rs. 3.5 for each chara, the muzara to pay only half of the water charges, the landlord to pay the malba, sharing of harvest in the ratio of 50:50, recovery of loans from gross produce after exempting fodder for cattle, not to carry out cultivation in the name of the khud kasht. *Kirti Lehar*, Meerut, 26 June 1938.
14. In Chak 174-UR (Veharhi thana, Multan district), license holder Ram Chand led a bus carrying 50 hired goondas, beat up women and children, broke open locks of houses and looted everything including cash and grain, while the tenants were busy guarding mounds of grain in the fields. In Chak 195-3L, license holder Thakur Das and his munshi Ghanoo Ram, supported by the police and goondas, assaulted the tenants and carried away the grain. The incident was reported to the chief minister via a telegram. *Kirti Lehar*, Meerut, 26 June 1938.
15. Talumba, a town in Kabirwala tahsil, Multan district was situated 2 miles from the modern left bank of the Ravi and 51 miles north-east of Multan city. A place of great antiquity, it was a centre of local date trade and production of stamped floor cloths. *Imperial Gazetteer of India, Provincial Series, Punjab*, vol. 11, p. 244.
16. According to official reports, the muzara agitation was fomented by the Punjab Kisan Committee, which had branches in several districts and boasted a membership of 75,000. Its working committee represented all bodies with communist leanings – the Congress Socialist Party, the Desh Bhagat Qaidi Parivar Sahayak Committee, the Riyasti Praja Mandal, the Radical League and the Institute of Agrarian Reforms, Ludhiana. It drew strength from 40 Moscow-trained Ghadarites, ex-convicts of 1914-15 conspiracy cases and disaffected MLAs with little property or stake in the country. It carried out propaganda through the *Kirti Lehar*, district kisan conferences and local fairs. It exploited economic grievances for electioneering, sectarian, communal, socialist and communist

purposes and above all for fomenting mass disaffection. Its growing influence was not restricted by the agrarian reforms of the Punjab government. Home Department, (Political), File No. 18.9.38.

17. On 13 March 1938 a political meeting was organized in Fattewal village (Amritsar district), which was to be addressed by Gopi Chand Bhargava, Sohan Singh Josh and Begum Fatima. The goondas of Mir Maqbool, the local landlord and parliamentary secretary of the Unionist ministry, disrupted the meeting and destroyed the stage. Achhar Singh Chhina and his associates arrived on the scene and held the proposed meeting, despite the impending threat. After Chhina had left for Amritsar, goondas attacked the people who were dispersing. When the people retaliated, two attackers were killed, after being pushed down from a roof. The police booked a number of people for indulging in violence. A murder case was registered against Joginder Singh Chhina, while Achhar Singh Chhina was falsely implicated. The former managed to get away with one year imprisonment. The latter was declared an absconder, having escaped to Jamshedpur. Bhagat Singh Bilgha, op. cit., pp. 225-9. The trial of the accused received wide coverage in the press. *The Tribune*, 1, 2, 7, 8, 12, 14, 22, 24, 25 and 28 June 1938.
18. For first-hand accounts of the conditions prevailing in various jails of Punjab – Lahore, Attock, Lyallpur, Montgomery and Multan – with reference to the inhuman treatment of political prisoners, see Gurcharan Singh Sahnsara, *Oah Vi Din San* pp. 8-52; Sohan Singh Josh, *My Tryst with Secularism: An Autobiography*, pp. 45-57.
19. Apart from physical torture, the detenus in the Lahore Fort were subjected to psychological pressure to weaken their resistance against interrogation, for example, by not allowing them to sleep for weeks while the questioning took place. S.S. Caveeshar, *The Lahore Fort Torture Camp*, Lahore, 1946, quoted in Ujjwal Kumar Singh, *Political Prisoners in India*, p. 190.
20. While confirming this account of his three weeks' detention at Lahore, Beant Singh insisted that, while leaving the cell after his last meeting, he heard Naina Singh Dhoot give out a loud cry as if he was being given an electric shock. Interview with Beant Singh at Dhoot Kalan, 29 September 1997.
21. The mother and nephew of Naina Singh Dhoot, who had a meeting with him at the Lahore Fort, stated that his health had deteriorated owing to bad food and high blood pressure. *Kirti Lehar*, Meerut, 18 September 1938.

22. In a application addressed to the chief secretary of the Punjab government, Naina Singh Dhoot complained that he had not been paid any allowance since his externment on 18 October 1938, despite Nawab Daultana's statement in the assembly that all persons externed in 1938 would be given an allowance of Rs. 32 per month and Re. 1.6 annas for food. *Kirti Lehar*, Meerut, 7 May 1939.
23. Before this period, the manufacture of opium was prohibited in Kapurthala. The state was permitted to procure 15 chests of Bengal opium under certain conditions. In 1924, it demanded, along with other princely states, the right to cultivate poppy and manufacture of opium, as the restriction undermined its internal sovereignty and adversely affected its economic interests. Anju Arora, *The Princely States, British Paramountcy and Internal Administration 1858-1948: A Case Study of the Kapurthala State*, pp. 107-10.
24. The Punjab Riyasti Praja Mandal, which was under the effective control of the communists, hosted the session in an environment of peasant struggles. The police and bureaucracy, with the collaboration of loyalist elements, tried to forestall the arrival of *jathas* from the various princely states. The conference passed two resolutions demanding responsible government and restoration of civil liberties. Ramesh Walia, *Praja Mandal Movement in East Punjab States*, pp. 150-1.
25. Compare with a detailed study of the land revenue system of the Kapurthala state, with reference to the three successive revenue settlements, functioning of revenue officers, provisions of relief measures and causes of agrarian discontent. Anju Arora, op. cit., pp. 205-30.
26. Dasondha Singh Dhada was born on 28 July 1900 at Dhada Kalan, Garhshankar tahsil, Hoshiarpur district. Being literate, he opted for the profession of a contractor. He migrated to the USA and joined the Ghadar Party in 1925. He travelled to Japan, Korea, Mongolia and Tibet to widen the base of the party. On returning to India, he was detained under Regulation III of 1918. From 1929 onwards, he suffered several prison sentences in the jails at Gujranwala, Gujarat, Ferozepur and Montgomery. In 1940, he was arrested for violating his internment and was detained till 11 September 1945. Fauja Singh, ed., *Who's Who: Punjab's Freedom Fighters*, vol. I, pp. 331-2.
27. The Tripuri session of the Congress (10 March 1939) was held when Subhas Chandra Bose had challenged Gandhian policies.

He disapproved of non-violence and differed on such vital issues as landlordism, princely order, capitalism and industrial growth. He appealed to the leftist groups to pool all their resources for democratizing the Congress and reorganizing it on the broadest anti-imperialist basis. Despite the opposition of right wing stalwarts and even Nehru, Bose defeated P. Sitaramiyya by 1580 to 1375 votes. M.N. Das, *A Centenary History of the Indian National Congress*, vol. III, pp. 250-5.

CHAPTER 6

Struggles of the Industrial Workers

While involved in political activities in Calcutta, I learnt that Chanan Singh Dhoot and Santokh Singh (both whom belonged to Dhoot Kalan) had become members of the CPI and were engaged in political work in the area. Though I had met them earlier, yet I came into close contact with them during the course of my internment (*nazrbandi*) in the village. Differences persisted between the provincial unit of the CPI and the Kirti group, preventing their merger into a single large organization. Despite the sincere efforts of several comrades, unity remained elusive. There were several obstacles in the way of this unity. While I was grappling with this issue, Ram Singh Dutt (who belonged to a village in Gurdaspur district), the secretary of the Kirti Kisan Party, came to our village and delivered an important message to me. In order to understand the significance of this message, it is essential to refer to the supreme sacrifice made by Comrade Hazara Singh, in his fight for the working class in Jamshedpur.

Comrade Hazara Singh belonged to Bhalarhi, a village near Santokhgarh in Una tahsil, Hoshiarpur district. After being convicted in the Ooty bank dacoity case, he was deported to the Andaman Islands.[1] During the course of his detention, he came into contact with a large number of freedom fighters such as Baba Gurmukh Singh, Dhanvantri and Bengali revolutionaries who had been convicted in the Chittagong case. They were educated, intelligent and energetic. They had acquired a considerable proficiency in the theory and practice of Marxism, which they explained and interpreted to their fellow prisoners. Regular classes on the subject were held in the prison. A number of Ghadarites, including Sohan Singh Bhakna, Kesar Singh, Wasakha Singh and Arurh Singh, benefited immensely from these lessons. In this way, a number of young men including Comrade Hazara Singh were initiated into the new ideology. A hunger strike in the Andamans and a simultaneous agitation on the mainland were organized to secure the release of these prisoners or their transfer to India. The struggle was a success, as the British government brought these men to India.

When Comrade Hazara Singh was released, he was fired with the spirit to fight for the cause of the working class. He chose the steel city of Jamshedpur as the arena of his political activities. As is well known, the industrial empire created by the house of Tatas was the largest of its kind in Asia and Africa.[2] The writ of the owners, who patronized goondas in a big way, ran in every part of Jamshedpur as the authority of the government and the rule of law did not exist. It may be added that the kind of intimidation (*goonda-gardi*) seen in Jamshedpur, had not been reported from any other part of the world. Since the Indian National Congress was agitating to oust the alien rulers, it made several abortive attempts to gain a foothold among the workers of Jamshedpur. For instance, a rally slated to be addressed by Jawaharlal Nehru (1927-8) was disrupted by goondas, who had been paid Rs. 10,000 by the owners. Nehru could not communicate with the workers at all. Subhas Chandra Bose, who made a similar attempt, met with the same fate.

The CPI, with its base at Calcutta and with Muzaffar Ahmad as its leader, was eager to set-up its cells among the workers of Jamshedpur. It also aimed to organize trade unions with the purpose of strengthening the party. In spite of the fact that a number of experienced workers, including Somnath Lahiri and Abdul Halim, were entrusted with the task of achieving these goals,[3] no progress could be made because of the violent opposition of goondas. The murder of Comrade Hazara Singh has to be viewed in this context. He was crushed to death on 3 July 1939 by a automobile while he was playing a leading role in a strike of the Indian Wire Products Company which was owned by Baldev Singh,[4] the son of Inder Singh.

Coming back to Ram Singh Dutt, who had delivered an

urgent message to me, informed that a letter had been sent from Calcutta, which contained a directive for me to leave immediately for Jamshedpur. I asked, 'What is happening there that requires my presence.' He explained, 'A strike has been going on there for some time in one of the industrial units. Comrade Hazara Singh has laid down his life while fighting for the cause of the workers. Our party intends to send someone to take his place, so that the struggle does not wither away. The party has been looking for someone who is physically strong, politically wise, well versed in Marxist ideology and, above all, experienced in leading the struggles of the working class. Taking all these qualifications into consideration, the choice has fallen on you.' In deference to the decision of the party, I prepared to leave and asked my mother to prepare food, as I had to leave for a new destination. My mother said, 'You have been made *nazrband* in the village. How can you go anywhere.' I replied, 'These are the well known ways of the capitalists. They will continue to make us *nazrband*. On our part, we will continue to break these restrictions. It is a long-drawn-out struggle. It will continue till we are able to achieve our ultimate goal.' Being a simple rustic woman, she was unable to understand the significance of the struggle I was talking about. We ate the food and left for Tanda where we parted to go our separate ways.

I boarded a train to Meerut where I met Baba Karam Singh Dhoot, Mubarak Sagar and Harminder Singh Sodhi, who was a Moscow trainee. They informed me about the recent developments on the workers' front at Jamshedpur. Though they claimed that a strike had been going on under the banner of the CPI, yet they did not have any evidence to substantiate their claims. Soon after, I went to Calcutta and met Muzaffar Ahmad who instructed me to go to Jamshedpur with the mission of continuing the work started by Comrade Hazara Singh.[5] He assured me that he would send all possible help to me from Calcutta, which I would need during the course of my activities in Jamshedpur.

On reaching Jamshedpur, I observed that the murder of Comrade Hazara Singh had transformed the industrial town into a political battleground as a number of organizations had converged on the scene. The Congress Socialist Party was the first to jump into the fray when their leaders – Jayaprakash Narayan, Kishori Lal, Basawan Singh and Yogendra Shukla (who was popularly known as the 'Tiger of Bihar') – arrived in Jamshedpur.[6] Ajmer Singh and Amrit Kaur, followers of Gandhi who belonged to Pothohar region, made their presence felt because of their wisdom and sagacity. The Indian National Congress was represented by a staunch communist-baiter, Professor Abdul Bari. Manick Homi, a tout of the British, led a workers' orgnization of his own. But the union of the workers of the wire products factory had been squarely in the hands of Comrade Hazara Singh and Comrade Chandrika Singh. After the former's death, the socialists managed to assume control of the strike, which had been going on in this unit. Further, they left no stone unturned to gain political mileage out of Comrade Hazara Singh's supreme sacrifice. The leading newspapers repeatedly referred to the late trade union leader as a socialist. I was shocked to see that the various political outfits did not hesitate to claim as their own the sacrifices and achievements of people who neither belonged to their rank and file nor adhered to their political creed.[7]

As soon as the socialists heard about the arrival of a man all the way from Punjab, they adopted a variety of tricks to ensure my exit from Jamshedpur. They started a false propaganda against me among the workers. My difficulties were compounded by the fact that there was no one who could give me a true and unbiased account of the ongoing workers' strike in the wire products factory. I made repeated attempts to locate such a person, but to no avail. Finally, I met a man who belonged to the ranks of the socialists and who appeared sympathetic to my problem. I asked him if he knew of any associate of the late Comrade Hazara Singh. He informed me that there was a man named Chandrika Singh, a Bihari, who had returned from Kale Pani. I began to search for Chandrika Singh and eventually succeeded in locating him. Much to my disappointment, I found that he was entirely under the influence of the socialists and was afraid to talk to me. I realized that if I wanted information from him I would have to talk to him in a solitary place where no one would recognize him. I invited him to a restaurant at a particular time. He accepted my invitation and appeared at the appointed hour. A friendly conversation began between us as we started sipping tea. Gradually, Chandrika Singh overcame his self-imposed inhibitions and gave me the much needed information about the strike. He told me that the leadership of the workers was in the hands of the socialists, who were led by Jayaprakash Narayan.[8] They were supported by a follower of Gandhi named Jamiat Singh who was anti-labour at heart.

I discovered the root cause of the workers' unrest, which had been analysed in successive issues of the *Kirti Lehar.* I learnt that the trouble began in the Indian Steel and Wire Products almost six months ago, when five labour leaders were dismissed. Fearing that they may be treated in a similar manner, the workers resorted to agitation. The owners set-up an enquiry committee to look into the grievances of the workers. However, this move was aimed at diverting the attention of the workers, who unwillingly walked into the owners' trap. In their complaint before the committee, the workers stated that the temperature in the Hot Mill was extremely suffocating and a normal person could not stand there even for 15 minutes, whereas 500 workers had to toil for 8 hours in the terrible heat which had affected their health. Besides, the wages were so low that the workers could not even meet the basic needs of their families. A worker who was earning nearly Rs. 10 for the owner was getting only 8 annas. Out of the blood sucked from the bodies of the poor workers, the owners had made a massive donation of Rs. 1.5 lakh to the Sikh National College, Lahore. In the process, they were able to project themselves as front rank philanthropists, who had a deep concern for spreading education among the people. In reality, their hypocricy was reflected in the miserable living conditions of their workers, who resided in dark and dingy hovels, which were located in narrow and filthy lanes. The owners had never thought of making any arrangement for educating the children of their own workers.

Meanwhile, the owners had presented a distorted picture of the company finances before the enquiry committee. Neither did they increase the wages, nor did they reinstate the dismissed employees. The enquiry committee failed to publish its report, even though more than three months had passed since the completion of its work. In fact, the harassment of workers had intensified. They were frequently transferred from one department to the other so that they could not forge a spirit of comradeship among themselves. The German foremen of the Hot Mill treated the workers like dumb driven animals. The restrictions were maximum in the Machine Shop, where workers had to forego a part of their daily wages even if they went to the toilet. Not only this, the workers were often beaten and abused.[9]

I realized that the best course for me was to visit the place where the workers assembled for picketing, to participate in their agitation, to educate them by organizing study circles and to establish a rapport with them. This was how I began my mission among the workers of Jamshedpur. A study of the situation, revealed that about 2,000 workers were on strike, which had been going on for many weeks since 3 July 1939. Their demands included an increase in wages and bonus, besides improvement in housing and management. Day after day, I went along with the picketing parties. I sat with them, conversed with them and remained with them even at night. Besides learning about their difficulties, I explained many things to them. In course of time, I successfully established a bond of understanding with the workers, particularly the Punjabis who were more militant than the others. They were convinced that I was their only genuine sympathizer, who shared their difficulties and sorrows in equal measure. Their primary concern was how to counter the threat of the goondas. They believed that if they were able to frustrate these hired goons, they would be able to achieve their cherished goal. On my part, I tried to ensure that my name appeared among the leadership of the workers, as this would play a decisive role in the success of my mission. I asked the workers to propose my name for inclusion in the strike committee. This was easily achieved as the Punjabi and Bihari workers were strongly in my favour.

Soon a meeting of the strike committee was held. Its secretary was Abani Sen and the chairman was Desa Singh, the president of wire products workers' union, who was under my influence. During the course of the discussions, some members suggested expansion of the strike committee so that more workers could be brought into its fold. However, I was of the view that the primary task before us was to break the socialists' monopoly on influence. At the third meeting, I argued in favour of setting up a small sub-committee which would lead the strike, take stock of the situation on a daily basis, issue the necessary instructions and, if need be, convene a meeting of the larger strike committee. My proposal was carried through without any opposition. Consequently, all the socialists, except Jayaprakash Narayan, were weeded out. More significantly, the majority was now with me.

We began to guide the strike, which had become prolonged. The workers found it difficult to make both ends meet.[10] Things became extremely difficult for workers from the Central Provinces, especially the women of Chhattisgarh who lived in abject poverty. I raised the issue of collecting funds for the starving workers in the committee meetings, but everybody expressed helplessness in the matter. Therefore I decided to take the initiative and activated my personal contacts and began to collect money with a view to provide meals to those in distress. On 10 August 1939, I visited the tin plate factory, where I enjoyed some influence among the Punjabi workers. While I was standing at their gate, I received a message that the capitalists had loaded a train with workers and raw material with the intention of sending these into the factory, where the strike was going on. As expected, the picketing party stopped the train and prevented it from proceeding. The workers immediately sent a messenger, who related to me a brief account of the dramatic happening. Asking me to reach the scene as quickly as possible, he lent me his bicycle while he followed on foot. It may be mentioned that the local administration had clamped Section 144 within a radius of one mile around the wire products company for the last two months. More than five persons were forbidden from meeting at a place or from carrying weapons.

I rushed to the scene and assumed control of the situation. I asked the workers to form rows of three on the railway track up to a distance of a hundred yards. Women workers were directed to sit at the end. I met the guard as well as the signalman. They argued that the train could not move unless a hundred yards of track was cleared in front. We convinced them about our firm resolve to sit on the track and succeeded in winning their sympathy. Thus, the entry of the train was effectively blocked. The entire administrative machinery of Jamshedpur had been geared to meet the situation which had become increasingly tense. The Deputy Commissioner, the Superintendent of Police and the Area Commander of the army were present at the scene, along with a large number of uniformed men. At this point, representatives of the management and the administration made an attempt to negotiate with us. They asked us to allow the train to steam into the factory. We declared that we would let the train move only after physically checking that it was not carrying any workers or raw material. However, they refused to let us carry out the search and we did not allow the train to move. The negotiations having ended in a stalemate, the authorities resorted to police action. The British police officers ordered lathi charge many times, with short intervals between them. We received many injuries. I received a blow on my forehead which began to bleed profusely.[11] Since we were full of fighting spirit, we did not bother about the pain and suffering. At one stage, the police attempted to handcuff the workers and tied thick ropes around their waists to remove them forcibly. However strong resistance of the workers did not permit the move to succeed.

As a result of the repeated police attack, the workers were mercilessly beaten. Since they did not retaliate in any manner, the confrontation became one-sided. Seeing the utter helplessness of the workers, I asked them to use umbrellas and stones against the lathi wielding policemen. Yogendra Shukla (a Bihari socialist popularly called the 'Tiger of Bihar'),[12] stood atop an elevated place and shouted to the workers to bring swords, daggers and lathis from home. I realized that if the workers actually obeyed Shukla's ill-conceived plan, they would suffer heavy casualties in an armed confrontation with the police who were equipped with automatic and semi-automatic weapons. Pre-empting such a situation, I rushed to the spot and spoke to the workers at the pitch of my voice, exhorting them to remain steadfast where they were as we had to fight on the strength of our organization and not with the help of weapons. My impassioned appeal had the desired effect. The workers, who were going back to bring weapons, returned and ultimately none of them went away. The refusal of the workers to obey Shukla's command had a dramatic consequence. The socialists were exposed. The superficiality of their understanding and the limitations of their tactics were laid bare. Now they were a demoralized lot.

The lathi charge was ordered eight times. Before the eighth time, the authorities decided to arrest us. By this time, the workers of the adjoining iron and steel factory had also converged on the scene. The police arrested about seventy active workers including Chandrika Singh, Basawan Singh, Yogendra Shukla, Desa Singh, Abani Sen, Lalit Prasad Singh, Siya Ram, Mohinder Singh, Sarwan Singh and me along with four women. We were led away from the train. The lathi charge was ordered for the eighth time. Since there was no leader to inspire the workers, we feared that they would succumb to pressure and the authorities would succeed in clearing the track. I spoke to two army men, who were guarding us, 'Look here ! You too are our brothers. Our interests are identical. This is a fight of the poor for their bread. Therefore, you must help us.' They said, 'We cannot let all of you go. That is out of the question. But if one of you were to run away, it would not matter much. We would say that the man had run away by sheer force.' By this time, the authorities had evicted the workers from the rail track and the engine blew the horn, indicating that the train was about to steam into the factory. At that point, I broke away from the group of arrested persons and raced towards the track. With lightning speed, I jumped before the engine, took out the red flag hidden in my shirt and started raising slogans. As a spontaneous response, the workers rushed in from every direction and filled the track like a flood. The workers of the Tata Iron and Steel Company, who were mere spectators, also rushed to the spot. We succeeded in stopping the train.[13] The district administration officials adopted a polite posture and requested us to allow the train to enter the plant. We were adamant that the train would be allowed to move only after we had searched it. Finally, the two sides arrived at a settlement – the train was to be driven back to the station and the leaders of the strike were to be arrested.

As I have pointed out earlier, about seventy activists were arrested. We were detained in the jail of Jamshedpur for a month. Taking advantage of my absence from the scene, Professor Abdul Bari of the Congress launched a false propaganda against our party.[14] He boasted that the strike would have been successful if the workers had fought under his banner and that he would have ensured the reinstatement of all the workers to their respective jobs.

While in the prison, I found that the socialists were not knowledgeable about matters relating to the struggle of the working class. I could claim that I was the only person among them who was well versed in Marxism, having acquired sufficient mastery over its theoretical aspects as well as its practical application. This advantage enabled me to establish study circles in jail, where I began to educate the workers. In fact, these classes were held in a regular and disciplined manner. Responding to my efforts, some workers evinced a special interest in their lessons and even became members of the CPI.

After being released from jail, I found that the workers were imbued with a fighting spirit and were ready to go on strike again. However, I sounded a note of caution, 'Strike is not something which you can resort to as and when you feel like. This weapon is meant to be wielded only in special circumstances. Unless these circumstances are created, we cannot go on strike. We have to wait for those conditions to emerge, before we decide to strike work. Otherwise, we would be defeated. Right now the time is ripe to close you ranks and unite yourself. Overcome your weaknesses and identify the limitations of the leadership. When we are fully prepared, we can go on strike again.'

By this time, all the striking workers had been reinstated to their jobs except seven, despite the tall claims of Abdul Bari. These workers recognized me as the leader of the strike. Studying the situation after my release from jail, I began to understand the motive behind Bari's propaganda. I knew that whenever capital was victorious in any struggle, it gave no concessions to the workers. It is true, it might give some minor concession when we force it to lie prostrate in the dust and strangle its neck with our heels in such a manner that its tongue and eyes bulge out. Since, in our case, it had not been reduced to this sorry state, I did not expect to get any benefit from it. I perceived that Bari's propaganda was only a desperate attempt to acquire leadership of the workers. I said to these seven workers, 'I permit you to go to Bari. Ask him to lead you and get you reinstated as per his claims.' Some of them were happy at the prospect of getting their jobs back. But others, who were my supporters, did not agree to the proposal and, in fact, two or three of them even started crying. I assured them, 'We are revolutionaries. We have our own tactics, which are aimed at revolution. Please do not be plagued by worries and doubts. I am not pushing you on the wrong path. My guidance will prove beneficial to our movement. So, go ahead without any hesitation.' Ultimately, they approached Bari, who was surprised to see them. When he learnt that I had sent them to him, he could not believe his ears. The pro-Congress workers convinced him about the truth. Henceforth I sent every worker, who came to me with a problem, to Bari. As a result of this strategy, Bari's fraud was thoroughly exposed for he was not in a position to help any worker, much less get anyone reinstated. Ultimately, Bari failed to establish his foothold in the wire products company.[15]

There was another factory at Jamshedpur, the Tata Foundry. Owned by a capitalist named Sri Ram, it employed about 6,000 workers. During October-November 1939 there was a strike in this factory also. Half the workers – who hailed from Bihar, UP and Punjab – were in favour of the agitation and were led by Abdul Bari. The other half, comprising the Adivasis (tribals) of Chhotanagpur, acted as strike-breakers. These Adivasis were led by Manick Homi, an agent of the British in the trade union movement, who had succeeded in weakening the agitation.[16] When Bari's followers failed to contend with Homi's strike-breakers, they decided to approach the communists because they had learnt about our recent contribution to the workers' movement. They approached me and sought guidance and assistance. I explained to them, 'Your strike has reached a critical stage. Your leadership has failed to direct your agitation in the appropriate manner.' They replied, 'Our leaders have been doing only what they are capable of. But it is our earnest desire that you should come to our aid.' I promised to attend their next meeting, which was held that very evening. They had placed two chairs in the front, one for Bari and the other for me. When Bari arrived for the meeting, he was greatly irritated to see two chairs. In his speech, Bari cirticised me in such strong words that he did not spare any weapon in his verbal armoury. In fact, he had nothing else to say. While referring to me, he said that some goondas had come from Punjab with the purpose of misguiding the workers and creating disturbance in the area. The workers, who were close to me, did not approve of Bari's outburst, but I signalled to them to remain clam.

When Bari was going towards his car after his speech, the workers asked me to address the meeting. Seeing a small hillock nearby, I said, 'Let Prof. Abdul Bari, our great leader, go to the top of the hillock and declare that we would do our utmost to bring the strike to a successful end and that we would leave no stone unturned to stop goondaism.' The workers rushed to Bari and conveyed my message. Bari retraced his steps and asked me whether the message was correct. When I replied in the affirmative, he lost his nerve. On my suggestion, the workers forced him to declare that we would picket the next day. Finding himself in a tight corner, he made the declaration. Before leaving, he turned to me and aired his inner feelings, 'I shall come tomorrow at 2.00 p.m. to see the number of dead bodies that would be lying here.' I countered, 'Professor Sahib! Rest assured. There will be no bloodshed. There will be no dead body either. With the strength of our organization, we will not permit any goonda to come anywhere near the scene of picketing at the factory. When you come tomorrow in the afternoon, you will see for yourself the positive results of our strategy.' Bari responded, 'In that case, I shall be very happy.' Thereafter, he left.

In the evening, I convened a meeting of the sympathizers of our party. I issued guidelines regarding the manner in which the crucial demonstration was to be organized. Those who were physically strong were given special instructions to come fully prepared to counteract any assault on us. We sent a clear challenge to Homi's goondas, 'Tomorrow, picketing will be done by the communists. You must think twice before you come to disrupt it.' The Adivasi workers in our camp were dispatched to the residential quarters (*bastis*) of the Adivasis with the message, 'Do not disrupt our picketing tomorrow. If you persist in your nefarious activities, you will have to face dire consequences.' The threat had the desired effect. The slogans raised by our workers, who were present in full strength (about 1500), rent the sky. None of Homi's strike-breakers dared to come near our demonstration and, in fact, they could not even think of disrupting it. At 2.00 p.m., we held a rally which was a great success. In accordance with his word, Bari also arrived. In my speech, I turned the tables on Bari, highlighting the shortcomings of his tactics. In the process, I avenged myself for his unfair criticism of me. Thoroughly demoralized, Bari spoke a few vague sentences and left. The occasion signalled the political demise of Bari.[17] The influence of the communists was established in the Tata Iron and Steel Company, the tin plate factory and among the middle-class of Jamshedpur.

One of the major problems facing the workers of Jamshedpur was the presence of a large number of professional goondas. Whenever there was a strike, the goondas intimidated and terrorized the workers. They would demolish the temporary sheds erected by the workers to take shelter during picketing. They would enter the *bastis* of the workers inebriated, burn their houses and molest their womenfolk. I realized that the goondas had to be demoralized if the workers' movement was to be strengthened. For this purpose, I trained a number of men who were physically strong. I gave them various types of instructions so that they were able to offer resistance to the goondas. This group included men like Makhan Singh, Teja Singh, Desa Singh and Sarwan Singh, all of whom had played a militant role in the recent strike. I warned them not to carry any weapons, not even a bamboo staff. They were to depend solely on their physical strength. They were asked not to beat their opponents. Instead they were instructed to immobilize the goondas by holding them tightly by the waist or by squeezing their neck or by gripping a knee and raising it up in the air. I personally searched the men to ensure that they did not carry any weapons on their person. I assigned specialized tasks to each one of them. For example, some were only to hold the goondas in a iron-like grip, others were to twist their necks and still others were to keep a watch around, lest more goondas should come to the rescue of the gangsters. One day a car packed with goondas arrived to intimidate the striking workers. Our men rushed to the scene and put our plans into action with lightning speed. Before the goondas could realize the gravity of the situation, they were pinned down and made to lick the dust. After subjecting them to this humiliation, we allowed them to run away. The news of the incident spread like wild fire in all directions. Our opponents alleged that the communists had indulged in violence. We feigned ignorance, declaring that it was in all probability a clash between two rival groups of goondas. But nobody was willing to believe us. The incident had far-reaching consequences. The goondas were demoralized, while the workers' morale was boosted.

During my stay in Jamshedpur, an important development took place. The local unit of the Forward Bloc, comprising numerous small political groups, was planning a massive rally with their leader, Subhas Chandra Bose, as the main speaker. Though the Forward Bloc enjoyed some influence among the middle-class of Jamshedpur, yet it had no support base among the working class.[18] The purpose of Netaji's visit, therefore, was to fill this critical lacuna of his party. The local unit of the Forward Bloc convened a meeting to discuss the arrangements for the proposed rally. They had invited the communists to this preparatory meeting. Since I was running fever at that time, I called a meeting of our workers to discuss our response to the invitation. It was decided that I would attend the meeting if I recovered. In case my fever did not subside, we would send our representatives who would take guidelines from me. The next day, my fever subsided and I led the group of communists to the meeting convened by the Forward Bloc. During the deliberations, we placed our proposals but refrained from assuming a dominant role. The president of the local unit of the Forward Bloc was nominated chairman of the reception committee. Dinak Babu, a representative of the Anusilan Party (a semi-terrorist group),[19] was appointed secretary. We did not accept any formal position, 'We are mere workers, we have no money. We will contribute by mobilizing the largest contingent of workers for the rally. But you must take the responsibility to prepare the flags, banners and mottos.'

Unfortunately, some groups headed straight to the press from this meeting. They spread misinformation that some people had created a disturbance at the meeting which, therefore, ended without any decision being taken. When I read this report in the newspaper the next day, I met the newly appointed chairman of the reception committee and informed him that we would have to leave for Calcutta immediately. When he asked me to explain the reason, I said, 'If Netaji were to read the report of our meeting in the newspaper, he is sure to cancel his visit. Remember, the goondas of Jamshedpur did not permit Netaji's rallies to be held on earlier occasions as well.' My argument appealed to the chairman, who decided that I should accompany him to Calcutta the same evening. When I informed him that I had no money to pay for my fare, he willingly agreed to meet all the expenses. In the evening, we boarded a train for Calcutta. On reaching the city early next morning, I thought of Niranjan Singh Talib who had social relations with rich transporters. As a member of the Forward Bloc, he was a close lieutenant of Netaji.[20] Besides, he published a paper, the *Desh Darpan*. He was known to me, for I had lived in Calcutta in an earlier phase of my life. In fact, he had a considerable regard for me. As such, I decided to call on him immediately. On reaching his house I called out his name. He recognized me and exclaimed, 'Comrade ! How have you come at this hour ?' As soon as he opened the door, I asked him to get ready and come along with us to meet Netaji. Talib put on whatever clothes were available and invited us to sit in a car, which had been made ready in the meantime.

We drove through the streets of Calcutta and reached Netaji's house at 5.30 a.m. When we knocked at the door, Netaji was about to brush his teeth. As Talib announced himself, Netaji ushered us inside and asked a servant to bring betel leaf (*pan*) for us. When I told Talib that I did not chew betel leaf, he replied, 'It is immaterial. You may take it and throw it away. Offering *pan* is only a formal custom among Bengalis.' Soon Netaji joined us and we were served tea. Talib asked us to discuss the matter. We explained the situation prevailing in Jamshedpur, apart from highlighting the purpose of our visit, 'We have made elaborate arrangements for the rally. We apprehended that you would not come after reading the misleading reports in a section of the press. That would have greatly demoralized us. Therefore, we decided to travel all the way and consult you in the matter.' On hearing our story, Netaji replied, 'You adopted the right course in coming here and giving a true picture of the situation. For, I had decided to cancel my visit to Jamshedpur after going through the newspaper reports.' The president of the reception committee clearly informed Netaji that I was the one who was very keen to come to Calcutta and meet him personally, so that the rally would be a success. We requested him to come to Jamshedpur without any fear or hesitation and assured him that we would give him such a welcome as had not been given to anyone in the past. Netaji was immensely pleased to hear these words.

Introducing me to Netaji, Talib informed him that I was a communist and that I was deeply involved in the trade union movement in Jamshedpur. Hearing this, Netaji took me to another room and said in confidence, 'My position here is like someone who is *nazrband.* I want to get out of this place. Could you help me ?' I replied, 'My party has sent me to Jamshedpur. I have to remain there till such time that the party does not direct me to go to some other place. Right now, I can only say that if you contact the communists of Punjab like Achhar Singh Chhina and Ram Krishan they may be in a position to help you.' This hint was enough for Netaji. Since his escape from India was a separate issue, there was no need for me to go into it at this stage.[21] We returned to Jamshedpur and busied ourselves in making preparations for Netaji's visit.

When Netaji arrived in Jamshedpur, he was received with unprecedented enthusiasm. A long procession was taken out which converged in a massive rally. At this point, a meeting of workers was held at which several conditions were imposed on Netaji (*a*) he was not to accept hospitality from the factory owner, Sri Ram. (*b*) he was not to visit the Bengali Club, (*c*) he was not to attend meetings or functions organized by any reactionary organization, and (*d*) he was to highlight in his speech the supreme sacrifice made by Comrade Hazara Singh. During the course of his address, Netaji outlined the programme of the Forward Bloc and made a frontal attack on the Congress, the capitalists and the goondas who had not permitted his meetings to be held in the past. However, Netaji violated all the four conditions of the workers. He not only called on Sri Ram and paid a visit to the Bengali Club, but also attended a meeting convened by Jaipal Singh, a leader of the Adivasis. This man had been educated in England and was a staunch reactionary. In the presence of Netaji, he delivered a speech, which was anti-Congress, anti-worker and even anti-Netaji. Netaji, however, could not follow the speech as he did not know the Adivasi language. Some of the people who had attended this meeting rushed to me and exclaimed, 'This Netaji, whom you have brought all the way from Calcutta, is a strange man. The speaker was criticizing him openly, while he continued to sit quietly on the stage.'

After the main rally was over, we called a workers' meeting to which Netaji was also invited. We criticized him for violating the conditions placed on him by the workers. I complained, 'It was known to us that Sri Ram was your friend. Yet, you should not have accepted his invitation, for the workers are agitating against him. Doubts have been created in their minds by your visit to the house of our enemy. Your indiscretion has placed us, the organizers of the rally, in a embarrassing position. Second, you have visited the Bengali Club, which is a body of reactionary elements. You did not agree with us and undermined the cause of the working class. Third, you failed to excuse yourself from Jaipal Singh's function. If you ask our workers, they will enlighten you about the anti-Congress, anti-worker and anti-Forward Bloc tenor of his speech delivered in your presence. Only then you will realize that we gave you sound advice. But what has caused us the greatest pain is your failure to pay tribute to Comrade Hazara Singh, the most popular leader in Jamshedpur, who laid down his life for the cause of the workers. We strongly feel that when a new society is established after the revolution, Jamshedpur should be renamed Hazara Nagar. It is a matter of deep regret that you focused on the class of exploiters, while you did not utter a word in favour of the workers or their leaders.'[22]

At this juncture, the members of the Forward Bloc felt constrained to declare that whatever I had said was correct and that Netaji's conduct in Jamshedpur did not further their cause. I openly said, 'Subhas Sahib! You must understand that we stand for the unity of the working class. This unity is a matter of fundamental importance of us, for it is only through unity that the workers' movement can be strengthened. Whenever we find that this unity is being threatened by the action of an individual, we do not support him. If it is your intention to form a separate unit of workers at Jamshedpur so as to assume their leadership, we will not support this move. Our aim is to work in a single union in order to solve the problems of the workers. As such, your proposal of creating a distinct organization of workers is not acceptable to us. We have unanimously rejected the move at our meeting.' After listening to what I had to say, Netaji became disappointed and demoralized. However, credit should be given to him for admitting that he had erred. The basic reason for his humility was that he had been deeply impressed by the warm and enthusiastic welcome that had been extended to him. We made him realize that he had failed in his attempts to convene a meeting in the past because of the power of goondas, who had forced him to flee from the field. The communists had successfully fought the goondas and prepared the ground for his visit. Everyone in Jamshedpur was talking about the role of the communists in the organization of the rally, in counter-attacking goondaism and in preparing the banners and mottos, etc. Even the members of the Forward Bloc admitted that all this could not have been possible without the support of the communists.

As a result of this development, the influence of the communists in Jamshedpur increased manifold. Their superiority over the other political groups was fully established. The socialists had left the field during the strike of the wire products factory. By providing appropriate guidance to the workers, we proved that it was not Jayaprakash Narayan (who considered himself to be a great leader), but the communists who were really committed to fight for the workers' cause. Moreover, we had effectively broken the back of goondaism. Even when we entered the bazaars after 6.00 p.m., no goonda dared to confront us. Apart from guiding the workers in their day-to-day struggles and exposing the ineffectiveness of the pseudo-leadership of various reformist groups – Abdul Bari (Congress), Jayaprakash Narayan (Congress Socialist Party) and Manick Homi, the imperialist agent – I also attended to the organizational aspect of the workers' movement. During the course of the recent struggle, as many as fifty young men were enrolled as members of the CPI. We invited Muzaffar Ahmad from Calcutta and Sunil Mukherji, secretary of the Community Party of Bihar, to lay the formal foundation of the Jamshedpur unit of the party. They readily accepted the invitation. We held a meeting of the workers on the occasion and informed the visiting leaders that workers had not only been instructed in Marxism but also in political and organizational issues and they could even test them by asking questions. A visibly pleased Muzaffar Ahmad founded the Jamshedpur unit of the CPI and appointed someone by the name of Sen as its secretary.

Around this time, a group of workers arrived from the coal mines of Jharia and requested us to visit their mines, 'You have done a lot of good work in Jamshedpur. We are deeply impressed. We invite you to visit Jharia and organize the miners on similar lines and strengthen their unity. We feel that we need the kind of leadership which you have provided here.' In response to this request, five of us decided to leave for Jharia by train early next morning. But before we could go, there was a police raid and seven of us were externed from Bihar. These included Sunil Mukherji, Dijan Babu and Parmathu Ghosh from Bengal and myself. We went to Calcutta, but the circumstances were not favourable for any political work. It seemed likely that I would be externed from Bengal as well. I analysed the situation along with other associates, who were of the opinion that I should proceed to Kanpur. I accepted the advice and left for Kanpur.

In Kanpur, I joined hands with R.D. Bhardwaj, who was a member of the Central Committee of our party, being its representative in UP. I stayed either at the party office or with Bhardwaj. Though I was not the secretary, I performed routine work of the office simply because I was staying there. I attended to the calls of workers and participated in their political activities. I organized study circles for the members of the trade union, which was headed by Santa Singh Yusuf. I availed of the opportunity to work with such prominent activists as Arjun Arora, Santosh Chand Kapoor and Shiv Singh; Shiv Singh had returned from Moscow after studying Marxism-Leninism. After spending a few months in Kanpur, I returned to Punjab.

NOTES AND REFERENCES

1. Originally a penal settlement had been established at Port Blair to segregate the so-called mutineers, who were sentenced to transportation for life. The construction of the infamous Cellular Jail with 663 cells was completed in 1910. Freedom fighters engaged in revolutionary terrorism, including the Ghadar activists and convicts of the Lahore Conspiracy Case, were imprisoned here. Though the settlement was abolished in 1921, it was revived after a decade to punish the convicts of the Chittagong Armoury Raid (1930), the Kakori Conspiracy Case (1924), the Lahore Conspiracy Case (1928) and Babbar Akalis (1925), L.P. Mathur, *History of the Andamans and Nicobar Islands*, pp. 157, 196-209.
2. For a detailed study of the growth and expansion of the Tata Iron and Steel Company from 1912 to 1946, with reference to the role of the colonial government as well as national and international forces, see Vinay Bahl, *The Making of the Indian Working Class: The Case of the Tata Iron and Steel Company*, pp. 150-99.
3. In the early 1930s, the labour movement in Jamshedpur became placid, as the Bose-led Jamshedpur Labour Association and Homi-led Jamshedpur Labour Federation had been virtually paralysed. Mangal Singh, a communist, made strenuous efforts to revive the movement with the help of Calcutta-based activists and the Kirtis. His externment from Jamshedpur in 1934 indicated that the Bihar government sought to prevent the communists from establishing a base in the city. Sunil Kumar Sen, *Working Class Movements in India*, p. 100.
4. Baldev Singh (1902-61) was born in a family of Chokar Jat Sikhs in Dumna village, Ropar district. His father Inder Singh, who began his career as a government official in the Central Provinces,

became a contractor and rose to be a steel magnate in Jamshedpur. After receiving his education in Ambala and Amritsar, Baldev Singh joined his father's firm as a director. Returning to Punjab in the mid-1930s, he made his debut in politics. Banking on the family's philanthropic reputation in the field of education, he was elected to the state assembly in early 1937 as a candidate of the Panthic (Akali) Party. On 26 June 1942, he joined the ministry of Sikandar Hayat Khan as development minister under the Sikandar-Baldev Pact. He appeared before the Cabinet Mission and presented the Sikh case. On 2 September 1946, he joined Nehru's cabinet as defence minister. Harbans Singh, ed., *The Encyclopaedia of Sikhism,* vol. I, pp. 266-7.

5. The communist weekly carried a front page story (with two photographs) of the circumstances leading to the death of Hazara Singh. *Kirti Lehar,* 23 July 1939. Also see a special number in memory of the deceased, *Kirti Lehar,* 30 July 1939.
6. On 21-22 October 1934, some radical Congressmen led by Jayaprakash Narayan, Sampurnanand, Acharya Narendra Dev, M.R. Masani, Rammanohar Lohia and Mohan Lal Gautam formed the Congress Socialist Party, as they were dischanted with the suspension of the civil disobedience movement and the futility of revolutionary terrorism. A blend of Vedanta and Bolshevism, its socialism was to be independent of the Comintern and consistent with the country's genius and class collaboration. B.B. Misra, *The Indian Political Parties: An Historical Analysis of Political Behaviour up to 1947,* pp. 282-8.
7. According to offical sources, the dispute could have been settled but for the death of Hazara Singh. Mercifully, the deceased has been described as an ex-revolutionary and communist who had been convicted in the Ooty Bank Robbery Case. Home Department (Political), File No. 18.7.39.
8. Jayaprakash Narayan (1902-79) belonged to a middle-class Kayastha family of government servants, based in Saran district of Bihar. After completing his schooling at Patna Collegiate School and I.Sc. from Bihar Vidyapeeth, he won a scholarship from a Calcutta association in 1922 and went to the USA for higher studies and completed his post-graduation from Ohio University. Inspired by the writings of M.N. Roy, he studied Marxist literature. Returning to India in 1929, he joined the Benares Hindu University as Professor of Sociology. He joined the labour portfolio of the Congress at Nehru's advice. A prolific writer on socialist themes, he advocated the abolition of zamindari, peasant proprietorship of

land and nationalization of heavy industries. S.P. Sen, ed., *Dictionary of National Biography*, vol. III, pp. 224-5.

9. On 11 July 1939, a gang of the relatives of Baldev Singh, armed with swords and lathis, tried to force their entry into the factory. When they were stopped at the gate, they attacked the picketing strikers. In this attack, Hari Singh received serious injuries. Acting on a complaint of the workers, the goondas were arrested. *Kirti Lehar*, Meerut, 23 July 1939.
10. On 3 August 1939, a delegation led by Jayaprakash Narayan and Baba Gurdit Singh and consisting of Desa Singh, Abani Sen, Naina Singh Dhoot, Basawan Singh, Imamuddin, Sohan Singh and Sarfraz Ali submitted a memorandum to Rajendra Prasad and Nehru, giving in detail the development of the strike from the beginning to the end. *Kirti Lehar*, Meerut, 13 August 1939.
11. Carrying two photographs on its front page, the communist weekly reported the incidents of 10 August 1939 under the following headlines – Atrocities of capitalist owners of the wire company, police lathi charge and arrest of striking workers, many women receive injuries and Comrade Naina Singh Dhoot arrested despite serious injuries. *Kirti Lehar*, Meerut, 20 August 1939.
12. Born in a Bhumihar family of Muzaffarpur district, Yogendra Shukla (1896-1966) ranked in the category of Bhagat Singh and Batukeshwar Datta. Inspired by the Anushilan Party of Bengal, he adopted revolutionary nationalism as his creed. He was involved in numerous sensational cases of looting trains and treasuries, thus becoming a legendary figure. He was imprisoned for over 16 year. He was a member of the CSP. S.P. Sen, ed., *Dictionary of National Biography*, vol. IV, pp. 194-5.
13. The fortnightly offical report, which was dispatched from Ranchi, grossly underplayed the magnitude and seriousness of the 10 August 1939 incident and failed to record the brutal assault by the police on the striking workers. Home Department (Political), File No. 18.8.39.
14. A nationalist Muslim with earlier socialist leanings, Abdul Bari was a trusted lieutenant of Rajendra Prasad and deputy speaker of the Bihar legislative assembly. In 1937, the Congress and TISCO conspired to send him to Jamshedpur, with a view to contain Manick Homi. In speech, he used intemperate and even sexist language. Outwardly he identified himself with the workers by criticizing both the TISCO management and the Congress ministry of Bihar. His real aim in Jamshedpur, however, was similar to that of the Congress, i.e. to steer the working class on the path of

collective bargaining and negotiation, with a view to check their growing militancy. Vinay Bahl, op. cit., pp. 348-50.

15. During the course of the strike, the workers passed resolutions of no-confidence against Bari on 1 and 20 July 1939 for (*a*) hob-nobbing with the owners of the wire products company with a view to break the strike, (*b*) refusing to give reasons for his opposition to the strike to a delegation comprising Yogendra Shukla, Harminder Singh Sodhi and Abani Sen, (*c*) making false claims of destroying the owner Inder Singh and sending him to Punjab with a pot (*lota*) in hand, (*d*) describing the pro-strike communist and socialist leaders as plunderers (*luteras*) and bullies (*badmash*), and (*e*) declaring the death of Hazara Singh as the result of differences between the Sikh and Muslim workers. *Kirti Lehar*, Meerut, 23 July and 6 August 1939.
16. A Parsi, Manick Homi had studied law in the USA before joining TISCO. When he criticized the company as a witness before the Indian Tariff Board, he was dismissed from his job and his father was forced to resign. He became a ardent enemy of the Tata management. In 1928, he led a strike against TISCO as leader of the newly formed Jamshedpur Labour Federation. A fiery orator, he influenced all sections of workers, except Bengalis who held clerical jobs. From 1930 to 1935, he was embroiled in cases, which were slapped on him by TISCO, with the help of colonial bureaucracy and the police. In 1937, he won the assembly election by defeating the TISCO-supported Congress candidate by a huge margin. As TISCO tried to win him over, he lost the confidence of the workers. His leadership having come to an end, the Congress sought to fill the vacuum through Bari. Vinay Bahl, op. cit., pp. 335, 388-9.
17. For a positive judgement on the role of Bari in this strike, see Sunil Kumar Sen, *Working Class Movements in India*, pp. 103-4; Nirban Basu, 'National Upsurge and the Working Class Movement: A Study of the 1942 Movement in the TISCO, Jamshedpur', *Proceedings of the Indian History Congress*, Calcutta, 1990, p. 612.
18. Since the right wing in the Congress stood for reaction and the left parties had failed to support the formation of the Left Bloc, a Forward Bloc was established with the help of fresh elements from the left. It was the result of an inner urge within the Congress and also the product of historical necessity. Subhas Chandra Bose, 'Why Forward Bloc', signed editorial, *Forward Bloc*, 5 August 1939, Netaji Researh Bureau, *Crossroads: Being the Works of Subhas Chandra Bose 1938-1940*, pp. 174-7.

19. The Calcutta Anushilan Samiti was founded in 1902 to promote physical, mental and moral culture among students of Calcutta. Its organizers, P. Mitra and Jatindranath Banerjee and Aurobindo Ghose, viewed these activities as a means of promoting pro-nationalist attitudes among young Bengalis. Anushilan and similar other samitis were viewed as the training ground for men who would take part in a future military uprising against the British. Peter Heehs, *Nationalism, Terrorism, Communalism: Essays in Modern Indian History*, p.18. Also see, Sumit Sarkar, *The Swadeshi Movement in Bengal*, pp. 483-92.
20. Born in 1901 in Nabha, Niranjan Singh Talib discontinued his studies at Khalsa College, Amritsar in 1921 and joined the non-cooperation movement. He worked as private secretary to the ruler of Nabha, who had been interned at Kodaikanal. After three years, he moved to Calcutta and launched a Punjabi paper, the *Desh Darpan*, which continued to be published till the end of the Second World War. He was imprisoned many times for his anti-British writings. A lifelong Congressman, he was closely associated with Subhas Chandra Bose. He was detained for five years on the charge of assisting Bose to escape. From 1957 to 1967, he served as a legislator and minister of Punjab. Fauja Singh, op. cit., pp. 175-6.
21. A native of Pakhtun village Ghalla Dher near Mardan, Bhagat Ram Talwar was a devoted activist of the Kirti Kisan Party. He remained in constant touch with Teja Singh Swatantra and travelled frequently to Lahore, Delhi, Bombay and Calcutta to confer with the leadership of the CPI. He served as the guide and companion of Subhas Chandra Bose, when the latter travelled from Peshawar to Kabul. He worked tirelessly, using contacts with the Russian and German embassies as well as with the local people, to secure a passage for Bose up to Moscow. For a detailed account of the enterprise, see Bhagat Ram Talwar, *The Talwars of Pathan Land and Subhas Chandra's Great Escape*, pp. 41-121.
22. A number of national leaders visited Jamshedpur to pay homage to Hazara Singh. Swami Sahjanand, the famous kisan leader, addressed a mammoth meeting of workers on 5 July 1939 and demanded a suitable memorial for the martyr, while condemning the silence of the Congress leadership on the gruesome incident. *Kirti Lehar*, Meerut, 16 July 1939.

CHAPTER 7

Deoli, Okara and Amritsar

After returning to Dhoot Kalan, I began to work in the Hoshiarpur district along with other comrades. I revived my contact with Master Hari Singh, who was associated partly with the Congress and partly with the Akalis. He had been a member of the legislative assembly when Sikandar Hayat Khan's ministry was in power in the province of Punjab.[1] I had met him earlier and wanted to meet him again. For the venue of the meeting, I selected Garna Sahib gurdwara in Bodlan village, which lay somewhere between Tanda and Dasuya. A big fair (*mela*) was held here on Baisakhi every year. At that time, Giani Zail Singh was serving as an attendant (*sewadar*) at the gurdwara. When I reached the gurdwara, I met Amar Singh Almast, who was a staunch communist, and asked him to bring Master Hari Singh there. I had about thirty meetings with Master Hari Singh in a small room within the compound of the gurdwara. Deeply influenced by my talk, he admitted that I was an intelligent person with a deep understanding of Marxism-Leninism. Later, he organized a camp for Congress workers at Bajwara. As many as twenty-five delegates, who had been working for the party in the Hoshiarpur district, attended the ten-day camp. On an invitation from Master Hari Singh, I delivered two lectures on communism.[2] I believed that if Ram Singh Dutt, who was a very learned man, could be invited to speak to the delegates, they would benefit immensely. Master Hari Singh agreed to my suggestion. I left for Jalandhar where Ram Singh Dutt was underground at that time. Dutt accompanied me to Bajwara and delivered a lecture.

The next day (June 1940) a general round up of the

communists was launched in Punjab.[3] The police swooped on Bajwara and encircled the camp. In this dramatically tense situation, my first and foremost priority was to ensure that Dutt escaped. I gathered a few communist youths and devised a plan. A man pretending to be Dutt was asked to run in one direction and when the attention of the police was diverted to pursue him, Dutt made his escape. The police came in and asked a number of us to step aside. These included Master Hari Singh, Pandit Ram Krishan of Bharolian village, Una tahsil, Balwant Singh Dukhiya of Bainsan village, Hoshiarpur tahsil, Thakur Waryam Singh of Amb village, Una tahsil, Harjap Singh (who had returned from Moscow in 1928) of Mahilpur and me.[4] All of us were brought to Hoshiarpur. The next day we were sent to different places. I was sent to Rajanpura (a kutcha jail of feudal times in Baluchistan), Pandit Ram Krishan to Montgomery, Master Hari Singh, Balwant Singh Dukhiya and Thakur Waryam Singh to Muzaffargarh. When I was being taken to Rajanpura, I reached a place from where a boat was to cover the remaining distance in one and a half hours. At this point, I met Master Mota Singh, the famous Babbar Akali leader.[5] He asked me who I was. When I told him that I was Naina Singh Dhoot, he was overjoyed and exclaimed that he had heard a lot about me. It is worth mentioning here that the current drive of the imperialist government to stamp out the communist movement was launched under the draconian provisions of the Defence of India Act, 1939.[6]

At Rajanpura jail, I met a large number of renowned patriots including Baba Sohan Singh Bhakna, Baba Wasakha Singh, Baba Kesar Singh, Baba Karam Singh Cheema, Baba Bujha Singh, Dr. Bhag Singh, Jaswant Singh Kairon (the younger brother of Partap Singh Kairon, who had received his education in the USA and had returned from Moscow), Bachan Singh Mehatpur and many others. Most of our time was spent in political discussions. As Lenin had stated that jails were universities for the communists, we availed ourselves of the opportunity to exchange views on important political issues, including Marxism. A memorable feature of our two months' stay was that the local people regularly brought fruit and other foods for the prisioners.[7] This extraordinary gesture could be explained in terms of their own feelings of patriotism and their appreciation of our sacrifices.

After about two months, political detenus all over the country were transferred to Deoli, which lay to the south of Ajmer in Rajasthan. Deoli was originally the headquarters of the 42nd Deoli Regiment and later of the Mina Corps. The number of arrested persons totalled nearly 250.[8] Apart from those who had been transferred from Rajanpura, others included B.T. Ranadive, S.A. Dange, S.V. Ghate, Rahul Sankrityayan, Santa Singh Gandiwind (a Moscow-trained communist), Sohan Singh Josh, Sunil Mukherji (secretary of the communist party of Bihar), Jayaprakash Narayan, Dhanwantri and Harnam Singh Chamak (secretary of the CPI, Sangrur district, Punjab). Kulbir Singh and Kultar Singh, the two brothers of Shahid Bhagat Singh, were also in Deoli.[9]

Our life at the so-called Deoli Detention Camp was organized in a systematic manner. We were divided into two camps, A and B, each consisting of six barracks. Sub-commmittes were formed to organize various activities like boarding, education, social functions and sports. Every morning, the mess committee consulted the detenus and drew up a list of food requirements. The list was subsequently handed over to the contractor, who procured the various commodities. Cooking, serving and cleaning tasks were performed by prisoners who had been convicted of moral crimes. Our school started after breakfast and continued till noon. Subjects included Marxism-Leninsim, political economy, history, anti-imperialist movements, trade union activities, etc. B.T. Ranadive and Feroz Din Mansur delivered lectures on political economy, Mohan Lal Gautam on the problems of farmers, Dhanwnatri on the Communist Manifesto and S.A. Dange on state and revolution.[10] At noon, there was a two-hour break. This was followed by sports in the evening. We also spent much time in private study. For example, we rewrote the notes, which we had already taken in the class. We had regular access to newspapers and one of the teachers was assigned the task of discussing the happenings of the past one week. We also discussed international affairs like the rise of fascism and the People's War. The emerging consensus was written down and sent to the central committee of the party which, in turn, despatched it to the Communist Party of the Soviet Union.

We were confined at Deoli for about two years. Though this was a fairly long period, yet we did not feel bored even for a moment because we were engaged in extraordinarily interesting pursuits. In fact, we did not know how weeks, months and years passed by. The detenus were not permitted to establish contact with any outsider, without the permission of the administrative committee. In spite of this restriction, the CPI smuggled the latest literature into the prision so as to keep us abreast of all the developments which were taking place in colonial India and abroad. Since the paucity of progressive literature continued to be a major drawback, the task of translating important works into the regional languages was undertaken in earnest. The underlying reason for this was that we would not face any difficulty in propagating progressive ideas, once we returned to our homes.[11] These works included the Communist Manifesto, Liontieff's treatise on political economy and the programme of the Comintern. These books were translated into Punjabi (as also into Hindi) because the majority of detenus at Deoli were Punjabis.

As a matter of policy, the Comintern wanted the various communist groups operating in India to come under a single central leadership. We had been trying in Punjab to unite the Kirti Kisan Party with the CPI, but our efforts had failed. The crowning achievement of Deoli was that the merger between the CPI and the Kirti Kisan Party became a reality. To achieve this, a three-member committee comprising Comrade Dhanwantri, Santa Singh Gandiwind and myself was formed. On the one hand, the committee established contact with the Kirtis and on the other, remained in touch with the central committee of the CPI, which was represented by S.V. Ghate and Sunil Mukherji. Without going into the details, suffice it to say that the merger was successful and the Kirtis were enrolled as members of the CPI.[12]

The socialists too were present at Deoli. They included Jayaprakash Narayan and the two brothers of Shahid Bhagat Singh, viz., Kulbir Singh and Kultar Singh. But they were unable to exercise any influence on the political prisoners.[13] In fact, some of the socialists such as Mubarak Sagar and Teeka Ram Sukhan were so impressed by the scientific nature of Marxism, as highlighted in the programme of education, that they joined the CPI. However, it was not an easy task to enlist these people, who were gradually attracted to Marxism, as full-fledged members of the CPI. The reason for this was that the changing fortunes in the Second World War played an important role in determining the attitude of these enthusiastic aspirants. When the fascist powers were treading the path of victory during the early phases of the conflict, these aspirants had doubts about joining the CPI and withdrew their applications. They feared that in the case of a fascist victory and their triumphant entry into India, the communists would be the first to be liquidated. We also received letters from outside the prison, asking, 'You were telling us that the Red Army is invincible, but Hitler has reached Moscow. How do you explain this?' In response to one such letter, I wrote, 'Please wait. Only time will answer your question.'

In this context, it is worthwhile recalling the story of Gulzara Singh Kandeghat, a native of Ambala district. He was a Moscow-trained communist yet he was a simpleton. As already mentioned, political prisoners who had applied for the membership of the CPI, began to have second thoughts when the Nazi troops rolled into Moscow. These people would chide Gulzara Singh, 'You were claiming that the Red Army cannot be defeated. What do you have to say now ?' Gulzara Singh tried his best to refute these objections. But the doubters had deliberately chosen him for their attacks on the communists and the Red Army, because of his simplicity. Every night, he, after being harassed by the doubters, would approach me to unburden his mind and seek fresh enlightenment. I would arm him with fresh arguments against fascism and strengthen his faith in communism. Thus armed, he would defend communism against all criticism from well-known quarters. When the Red Army turned the tables on Hitler, the doubters renewed their requests for membership of the CPI. I told them that they would be enrolled only if Gulzara Singh recommended their case. They were surprised to learn that a simple-minded rustic commanded such importance in the cadre of the CPI. On his part, Gulzara Singh reprimanded them severely for their wavering attitude and refused to recommend their enrolment, 'This is not a college examination that you can appear again and again even after repeated failures.' Ultimately, these people were not admitted into the party.

Our seventeen-day hunger strike (23 October to 8 November 1941) was an important event in Deoli. We adopted this extreme measure to press our demand for being transferred to our respective provinces, so that we could meet our kith and kin. We also demanded the abolition of division on class lines, payment of family and personal allowance, increase of dietary allowance to Rs. 1.6. annas, abolition of solitary confinement, lifting of censorship on letters and restrictions on interviews, besides ending the segregation of Ranadive, Dange and Batliwala.[14] The authorities adopted an indifferent attitude towards our demands, while we remained firm in our resolve. Ultimately, the authorities resorted to force-feeding and hired some men for this task. Our committee decided that all communists should resist the attempt to be force-fed while lying on their beds. When they began the exercise, my cot was the first one in their way. As the two hired men approached, I (being physically quite strong) caught hold of them and pushed them under the cot.[15] I said to Inspector Banta Singh (who had met me during my imprisonment at the Lahore Fort), 'Banta Singh! You know me well enough. Take these people away from me.' The hired men, thoroughly demoralized, expressed their inability to perform the task and left. Thereafter, the authorities requisitioned the services of Gurkhas of the Indian Army. Around a dozen of them arrived to perform the operation under the supervision of a senior officer. Some of them gripped the arms of the prisoners, others pinned down their legs and yet others passed a tube through the nose. In this manner, we were forced to take glucose or milk. Whenever any prisoner was carried away to the camp hospital for force-feeding, we raised revolutionary slogans calling for the downfall of British imperialism.

Finally, our demand was accepted and the hunger strike was called off. N.M. Joshi, a representative of the working class in the Central Legislative Assembly, came from Delhi to convey the decision of the government to us and pave the way for the formal termination of the seventeen days old agitation.[16] A doctor by the name of Moti Singh, who was extremely sympathetic towards us, was summoned to assess the medical needs of the strikers and to prescribe a new diet for us so that we could lead normal lives. Dr Moti Singh examined each one of us and prescribed suitable medicines. He also delivered lectures on health care and physical ailments. The hunger strike had an adverse effect on my health. I suffered from bouts of pain in the entire body and I had to lie prostrate on the floor. Even Dr Moti Singh's medicines did not alleviate my suffering. I continued to take medicines when I was imprisoned in the Gujarat jail, but to no avail. It was only when I returned to my village that a local physician (*hakim*) cured me with indigenous medicines.

It must be pointed out that the colonial government was forced by the changing international situation to alter its policy towards the detenus. So long as Hitler did not attack the USSR, the military conflict had a imperialist character. Once the Nazi army entered the USSR, the imperialist war transformed itself into a people's war. The USSR was the only country where capitalism had been destroyed and a socialist revolution had been successful. Power had come into the hands of the proletariat. It was imperative for the working classes of all countries of the world to fight for the cause of the Soviet Union and protect the fruits of revolution by defeating the fascist forces.[17] Britain and the USA, which had earlier assisted Hitler in establishing his hegemony in Europe, joined hands with the Soviet Union. In these circumstances, the government adopted a somewhat lenient attitude towards political prisoners. Our demand for being shifted to our respective provinces was accepted. And we were transferred from Deoli to Gujarat, a district in colonial Punjab.

Political prisoners in the Gujarat jail included a large number communists. The most prominent among them was Harkishan Singh Surjeet. Free of other worries, we revived the programme of political education, which had been formulated and implemented at Deoli. There was no interruption in the learning programme. Besides other subjects, Surjeet lectured the prisoners on party organization. We remained in the Gujarat jail for a few months. In keeping with the changes on the war front, the government further modified its policy towards the communists. Slowly, we were released. But this was done in such a manner that we were interned (*nazrband*) in our native villages. Those who were released included Harkishan Singh Surjeet, Comrade Dhanwantri, Master Hari Singh, Teja Singh Swatantra, Achhar Singh Chhina and Bhagat Singh Bilgha. Apart from the prisoners at Deoli, activists who had been confined in various other jails like Campbellpur, were also released.

I returned to my village. Though I was *nazrband*, I began to work secretly and established contact with the communists of the area. The position of the party was quite strong in Punjab. Its headquarters were at Lahore with Sohan Singh Josh as its secretary. Subsequently, Teja Singh Swatantra held this office. Ajoy Kumar Ghosh was the representative of the CPI in Punjab and guided the entire movement in the province. The party controlled the Kisan Sabhas, which were gaining strength in such places as Multan, Montgomery, Lyallpur, Patiala, Hoshiarpur, Mukerian and Una. The position of the party in the trade union movement was equally strong. Besides the railway workshop at Lahore, it had full-fledged units at Putlighar, Chheharta, Lyallpur, Okara and Ludhiana. The party had constituted a sub-committee, which guided the activities of the trade unions, patriculary in the case of a strike at any of the industrial centres. Among students, too, the party enjoyed increasing popularity.

During my *nazrbandi* in the village (1945), my associates and I organized the first ever conference of landless agricultural labourers, who were popularly known as *adharmis*, at Dhoot Kalan.[18] We invited all the reformist (*sudharwadi*) leaders of the *adharmis*, viz., Mangu Ram, Mula Singh, Master Sadhu Ram and Charan Das Nidharhak. The people of the village, particularly the *adharmis*, collected a substantial sum of money to make the conference a success. The reception committee, which included Master Hari Singh and myself, drafted various resolutions. When the issue of social inequality and untouchability came up for consideration, we argued that these evils could be eliminated only in a socialist society, and not under the prevailing system because capitalism itself was interested in perpetuating all types of inequlities for its own survival. However, Mangu Ram said that they would not support this resolution for it reeked of revolution. Mula Singh also spoke in a similar vein. Master Sadhu Ram thought it prudent to keep silent on the matter. Master Hari Singh urged me to explain the issue in detail to these men. I did it to the best of my capacity. My explanation had such a spontaneous impact on the members of the reception committee that all of them unanimously supported me, declaring that their salvation lay only in a socialist society. The conference was a great success, because there had never been such a large gathering in these areas in the past.

In 1946, I received a letter from the party's Lahore office, intimating that restrictions imposed on me would be withdrawn on a particular date and that I should reach Lahore because a strike was under way in Okara where I had been assigned duty. When I reached Lahore, I learnt that as many as seventy active workers, including those comrades who had been specially sent from the city, had been arrested during the course of the struggle in Okara. In these circumstances, I was directed to leave for Okara and assume the charge of guiding the agitation. After reaching Okara, I studied the prevailing situation and established contact with the workers. I found that about 2,000 workers of a textile mill had been on strike for the last fifteen days. Their demands included an increase in wages, provision of additional allowances to offset the price rise, release of arrested workers and an improvement in the management of the industrial unit. I guided the struggle in a systematic manner and set-up a committee of workers who could be activated in the prevailing circumstances. Among them was Beni Bhushan, a young Bengali, who was a good orator. I trained him in the practical aspects of trade unionism and frequently sent him to address gate meetings as well as open rallies.

As a result of these efforts, the capitalists were unnerved. It appeared that they were inclined towards accepting the demands and that the workers were likely to emerge victorious in the struggle. But Kartar Singh Dhamija, the local Congress leader, did not approve of this as he was clearly anti-labour and pro-capitalist. While campaigning against a settlement, he advised the mill owners to stick to their position and not to bow to pressure from the workers. His propaganda was based on the argument that the resistance was bound to collapse as the prominent leaders had been put behind bars. My experience of working in the trade union movement had convinced me that whenever we were locked in a conflict, it was important to have a source which kept us abreast of the position and moves of the adversary. Since we had succeeded in establishing such a contact, we learnt the Kartar Singh Dhamija had prevented the capitalists from reaching an agreement with the striking workers.

Around this time, a delegation of workers complained to me that Beni Bhushan had delivered a highly objectionable speech. On probing, they revealed that he had unnecessarily criticized the working of the police. I was surprised to hear this, for I had not instructed him to talk about this issue among various others, which I had singled out for him to explain and elaborate. When I assured the agitated workers that I would take Beni Bhushan to task for his indiscretion, they were pacified. As soon as he appeared, I asked him why he had trespassed the boundaries which had been set for him. Beni Bhushan admitted that he had gone beyond the instructions given to him, because he had been swept away by his passion and zeal. I made it clear to him that he should discuss only those issues which had been decided by us before the rally and that emotional outbursts led only to adverse consequences, which did more harm than good to our cause.

At another meeting of workers a decision was taken to organize a massive demonstration at the factory gate and they were expected to devote all their resources to make it a success. They were asked to come prepared with banners and to rent the sky with slogans like 'Inquilab Zindabad', without being intimidated by police action. The next day, as planned by us, a massive demonstration was held. The participants displayed unprecedented courage and enthusiasm. The police resorted to lathi charge, but failed to frighten the workers. At this juncture, I must point out that I was personally never present on such occasions, because I was still working underground. I lived among the workers after selecting a centre in their midst. Only active workers had access to this centre, from where I maintained contact with the others.

That day I had instructed Beni Bhushan to speak only on one issue, i.e. the police. He was asked to make a frontal attack on the police, while ignoring all other issues. In accordance with this directive, Beni Bhushan delivered a sharply anti-police speech. In the evening, a group of workers informed me that Beni Bhushan had delivered an excellent speech, the kind of which he had never delivered earlier. In fact, they were at a loss for words to praise him. Why did they reverse their stance? In the first instance, they had raised a strong objection when Beni Bhushan had condemned the police, but now they were praising him to the sky for having done the same thing again. To answer this question, it was important to understand that in the entire phase of their struggle, the workers hoped that the government would sympathize with their cause and they did not want to alienate the government. Further, they had no reason to be unhappy about the role of the police. Therefore, they had disapproved of Beni Bhushan's criticism of the police. After the lathi charge, however, the attitude of the workers underwent a sea change and they were convinced that the government had no sympathy for them. In the changed circumstances, they accepted Beni Bhushan's angry tirade against the police. To them, the theme of the speech appeared to be in perfect harmony with the changed situation. The moral of this story was clear. An agitation of workers had to be guided with great tact and intelligence. While delivering a speech, a leader had to have his hand on the pulse of the workers. He must understand workers' psychology, feelings and mental state. In the presence of this factor, a leader could lead the agitation to a successful conclusion, while the workers could also contribute their best in the struggle. In the absence of this factor, on the other hand, an agitation was not expected to make much headway.

As a result of the powerful demonstration and mounting pressure from workers, Kartar Singh Dhamija's tactics ended in failure. Realizing that the position of the striking workers was visibly strong, the capitalists were compelled to reach a compromise with them. Accordingly, we received an invitation from the mill owners for negotiations. Acting on my directions, workers insisted that they would not send any delegation for negotiating a settlement, rather the capitalists should send a responsible representative for the purpose. The condition was accepted. A representative of the capitalists began to confer with me. Before the real issues could be taken up for discussion, I placed another condition: all our comrades who had been arrested during the course of the agitation and who had been confined in Montgomery jail should be released forthwith. This condition was also accepted. The authorities passed an order for the immediate release of the arrested persons. I sent two workers armed with flags and banners to Montgomery jail to escort our men to Okara. The released comrades were brought in a procession to the railway station, where they boarded a train for Okara. When the train steamed in, they were seen waving red flags of the CPI. Meanwhile, a large number of workers and sympathizers converged on the platform and accorded a hero's welcome to their colleagues. After this grand reception, a meeting of workers was convened to decide the policy to be adopted at the negotiating table. During the course of the talks almost all the demands concerning increase in wages, full payment of salaries for the days of the strike and improvement in the management of the factory were accepted. The triumphant workers, carrying banners of the party entered the factory in a jubilant mood and resumed production.

The positive outcome of the strike had important implications for the furture. The trade union movement received a new lease of life. The base of the CPI was enlarged with the recruitment of fresh cadre. Those actively involved in the agitation were enrolled as members of the party. In this manner, the trade union movement was politicized. I stayed at Okara for a while and visited the town on many subsequent occasions. My purpose was to maintain contact with the new cadre and consolidate the party's recent gains.

One of the important consequences of workers' victory was that the session of the Provincial Trade Union Conference was held at Okara. The party's sub-committee for trade unions asked me whether the session could be held at Okara as it had only a small unit of the party. I assured the sub-committee that the conference could be held as we would both provide money and make the necessary arrangements. Since I had worked in the Nili Bar on an earlier occasion, I hoped to collect funds from muzaras in the villages and industrial workers in the towns. I was in contact with those comrades who were engaged in political work among the peasantry. Moreover, we had become immensely popular among urban workers because of the success of the strike. On the basis of our encouraging track record, I sent a favourable report to the sub-committee. It not only appreciated my positive attitude, but also included me as a member. Soon after Ram Singh Dutt was also enrolled a member. The conference, which continued for three days, was a great success. Delegates poured in from various industrial centres of Punjab – Lahore, Lyallpur, Amritsar, Ludhiana and other towns – where the trade unions existed. They availed of the opportunity to learn the theory and practice of the trade union movement. The party's provincial committee formulated the policy and methods to be adopted by the various trade unions. Moreover it lauded the manner in which the local unit had made arrangements for the conference.

After the conference, I stayed in Lahore. Since I had become a full-time worker of the party, I travelled to wherever the party directed me to go. At the time, there was a strike at two places in Amritsar – Putlighar and Chheharta. Karam Singh Maan, a barrister educated in England, approached our Lahore office with a request that an experienced person be deputed to guide the strike. Ajoy Kumar Ghosh,[19] the representative of the central committee of the party in Punjab, proposed my name. But Karam Singh Maan, like most literate people who attached greater importance to degree-based formal education than to practical experience in working class struggles, had reservations. He preferred a wiser person. Ghosh assured him that there was no one wiser than me. Dissatisfied with his reply, Maan returned to Amritsar. When the local leaders lost control over the strike, he visited our office again. Ghosh proposed my name again and Maan had no choice but to accept the suggestion. Ghosh summoned me and informed me that I had been assigned the task of guiding the strike at Amritsar. I said, 'In ordinary circumstances, I would have taken up the assignment without any condition. But in view of Comrade Maan's initial reluctance, please give me in writing that I have been authorized by the provincial committee to guide the strike at Amritsar.' Ghosh accepted my request and gave me the kind of letter I had asked for.

After reaching Amritsar I convened a meeting of the distirict committee of the party. I placed Ghosh's letter before the members. Some of them had reservations about accepting me as the organizer of the strike. Sensing their reluctance, I asked them to discuss the issue of leadership in the light of ground realities and to convey their decision to me. Besides, I expressed my willingness to assume full responsibility for guiding the agitation. At the moment, the district committee was feeling helpless because of the growing pressure of the strike on its leaders. It had no alternative but to accept me as the organizer. Having crossed the first hurdle, I studied the prevailing situation with regard to the strike. In Putlighar, over 2,000 workers, a large number of whom were Muslims, had struck work in several industrial units which were engaged in the production of textiles, hosiery and machine parts. Things were different in Chheharta. Here, about 2,000 workers of a large blanket factory had adopted the path of agitation. At both places, however, the strike had been under way for over a week. Workers of different industrial units had almost similar demands such as increase in wages, provision of bonus and reinstatement of those workers who had been dismissed from service. There were, however, some minor differences in the nature of issues involved.[20] I encamped at Putlighar and visited Chheharta regularly, thus maintaining control over the movement at both places.

At the outset, I called a meeting of the general body of all workers. This was followed by several meetings with activists, who had evinced a keen interest in the agitation. I lectured them on the theoretical and practical aspects of trade unionism. Since they were in the midst of a struggle, they were fairly receptive to the new ideas and tactics. My mission proceeded smoothly because politicians of various hues were absent, unlike the scenario I had encountered in Jamshedpur and Okara. I was fortunate in receiving active support from a young man named Jaswant Rai (who was the son of Dhani Ram Chatrik, the famous Punjabi poet).[21] I established contact with the Kisan Sabhas which were working in the hinterland of the city. People living in the neighbouring villages sent grain rations, which were passed on to the striking workers who found it difficult to make both ends meet. To ensure that none of the workers, either in Putlighar or Chheharta, were reduced to starvation, a community kitchen (*langar*) was set up.

As the strike continued in an organized manner, two different types of situations developed in Putlighar and Chheharta. The capitalists in Putlighar were ready for a compromise, while workers in Chheharta were demoralized. We noted that the capitalists of the two industrial centres were in regular contact with each other. The mill owners of Chheharta sent a message to their counterparts in Putlighar, advising them not to enter into any agreement with their workers because the strike in their plant was rapidly heading towards failure. As I was pondering over this information which had been given to me by activists of Chheharta, I realized the gravity of the situation and the need to take action to strengthen the resistance at Chheharta. I asked these activists to organize a general meeting of the striking workers and promised to attend it so as to place the movement on a firm footing once again.

The next day I went to Chheharta. During the course of the meeting, I promised to lead the strike to victory, provided the strikers held out for another two days. The workers implored, 'Please win the strike for us. We are willing to resist even for seven days.' I gave this assurance on the basis of a minute analysis of the situation. I was conviced that the information passed on by the mill owners of Chheharta to their counterparts in Putlighar was incorrect. I directed the workers to hold forceful rallies at the factory gate over the next two days, putting every ounce of their energy in this crucial phase of their agitation. With a view to add a touch of militancy to this decisive effort, I sent specially trained speakers from Putlighar to Chheharta.

The new strategy produced the desired results. The owners in Putlighar realized that the position of workers of Chheharta continued to be strong and that they had been misinformed.

They invited us for negotiations. The same sequence was repeated at Chheharta. I despatched a message to the district committee to send Karam Singh Maan, so that we could work out the policy to be adopted at the negotiations. The factory owners were willing to accept a number of demands relating to wages, allowances and internal management of the industrial units. In fact, they had already accepted such demands of a minor nature. But the composition of the negotiating committee, which was expected to sort out important matters, became a bone of contention between the two sides. This committee was to have three members – one representative each of workers, capitalists and the government. There was no difficulty regarding the choice of the first two. The third member could not be easily agreed upon. Since I was an outsider in Amritsar, I was not in a position to take a decision about the government's representative. The local comrades suggested three or four names. We unanimously agreed on an expert on woollens, who had been educated in England and was a friend of Karam Singh Maan.

Ultimately the remaining demands of the workers were also met. The strike was called off at both places, Putlighar and Chheharta. We escorted the workers to their factories (*karkhanas*) in a procession, carrying the party's banners and raising revolutionary slogans. The influence of the CPI among the working class of Amritsar increased manifold. My mission, in which I had been ably supported by Jaswant Rai and a full-time party worker from Una, came to a successful end. The local comrades informed Ajoy Kumar Ghosh about my valuable contribution to the victory of the workers. Thereafter, I returned to Lahore.

It must be pointed out that our party was leading the trade union movement at many centres, other than Okara and Amritsar. Lyallpur was one such centre where a strike was led by Ram Singh Dutt, Pandit Kishori Lal and Jagjit Singh Lyallpuri. Unfortunately, the strike did not lead to any favourable outcome for the workers. At least, this was the information which I had received.

Around this period (September 1946), a large kisan conference was held in Jangpur. This place was situated on the

Ludhiana-Ferozepur rail route via Jagraon and Moga. Groups of peasants and workers arrived from various parts of Punjab to participate in the conference.[22] I led a large contingent of workers from Okara. As pointed out earlier, unity had been achieved in the state committee of the CPI. Yet, things were not satisfactory, because three kinds of unity – unity of word, unity of action and unity of discipline – which formed the basis of a political organization, continued to be elusive. It was unfortunate that the state committee lacked these three principles. I was deeply concerned about this weakness in the party. I availed of the opportunity provided by the conference to make another effort in the direction of unity. In the first instance, I spoke to Teja Singh Swatantra, 'We have the chance. Ajoy Kumar Ghosh is present here. If you agree with me, I can arrange a meeting between the two of you, so that differences in the party organization can be resolved.' I also talked to Ghosh with whom I enjoyed good relations. I pleaded with him that since he was the organizer of the party in Punjab, it was his responsibility to repair the breach in the organizational structure through mutual consultations. Ghosh accepted my suggestions and a meeting was arranged between Ghosh and Swatantra.[23] The two remained closeted for one and a half hours, during which they exchanged views on a number of issues. In the end, Ghosh said to Swatantra, 'If the central committee of the CPI nurtures any doubt about you, I take the responsibility to remove it.' After the meeting, I asked Swatantra about the outcome of the discussion. Swatantra, who was in a happy mood, declared, 'The meeting was fruitful. Ghosh was positive and constructive in his approach. I congratulate you for taking the initiative for this meeting.' When I put the same question to Ghosh, he too expressed his happiness at the development, but said, 'It remains to be seen if practical action is taken on the issues, which have been sorted out.'

At this point it is important to digress and discuss the circumstances which led to my marriage in 1945. I had returned to India in 1936 and ever since my family had made consistent efforts to get me married. Yet I had succeeded in resisting all such attempts. My reason, which I put forward to justify my rigid attitude, was that the life of a revolutionary passed through extremely difficult times and that I did not want anyone married to me to suffer for no fault of hers. However, there was one factor which broke down my resistance. My mother had given birth to four sons, but I was the only one who had survived. She was growing old and becoming weak with every passing year. As for myself, the government often made me *nazrband* in the village. Whenever this happened, a numhber of comrades and friends came to me in connection with political consultations. Owing to my mother's declining health, it was becoming increasingly difficult for me to be a good host to the visitors. The household, in short, could not be managed in a satisfactory manner. Meanwhile my relatives continued to pressurize me with increasing vigour, so that I was made to relent. Ultimately I bowed before these circumstances and expressed my willingness to enter into matrimony. When the question of marriage came up for discussion, my relatives wanted to know the kind of girl I would have in mind. I made it amply clear that she should come from a poor family and should be willing to shoulder the responsibility of running the entire household.

I did get a life partner (Swaran Kaur), who made a significant contribution to the success of my political missions. In fact, she assisted me in all activities in every possible way. She was quick to realize that whatever I did was for a good cause. She also understood that the nature of my work was such that I had to remain underground for long periods, when the police issued warrants for my arrest. During such times, I moved from place to place and stayed with comrades, who looked after me. My wife was aware that when these people sought shelter in our house under similar circumstances, it was her moral duty to provide them with all the available facilities. Only then her honour was vindicated. Whether I was at home or not, she gladly served them. All the comrades, who had the opportunity to come to our house, acknowledged her hospitable and hardworking nature, which did not regard them as a unwelcome burden.

Due to my influence and the impact of her new environment,

my wife slowly became politically enlightened. Though this transformation was slow and gradual, yet it did become a concrete reality. For example, when warrants for my arrest were issued and the government was actively considering attaching our ancestral property, she did not panic. This stoic indifference stood in complete contrast to the attitude of her tradition-bound parents. Engaged in conventional agricultural pursuits and absolutely unaware of the changes taking place in society, they were politically ignorant and extremely religious. They failed to understand the significance of my political acitivities. They began to worry about the fate and future of their daughter. My mother-in-law pleaded with her husband, 'Our son-in-law has already wasted a lot of time in wandering. You should advise him to settle down peacefully and take adequate interest in running the household.' The old man replied, 'I have failed to understand him. People, whom we consider to be intelligent and wise, have the greatest regard for him. Whenever he comes here and sits in the orchard, these people gather around him and listen to him in rapt attention. I am illiterate and ignorant. I am not in a position to give any kind of advice to him. I am not equal to the task.' In a state of helplessness, they asked their daughter to convey their feelings to me. My wife explained my position to them, 'Have I complained, ever since I got married, that I am not happy? Have I ever said that I am facing any problem? Have I ever demanded anything from you? Not even once. Therefore, you should not expect me to convey your advice to my husband. If your feelings reach his ears, I am sure that he will sever all connections with you and will never talk to you again. He has chosen his path after having lived in various countries of the world, after acquiring proper education and training, and having understood all aspects of his mission including its innumerable hazards. As such, there is none who can make him change his course.' In short, the old couple gave up their idea of influencing me through their daughter, who remained firm in her resolve to cooperate with me in my hazardous political pursuits.

NOTES AND REFERENCES

1. In the wake of a landslide victory of the Unionist Party in the 1937 assembly elections, Sikandar Hayat Khan became the premier of Punjab and held this office till his death (26 December 1942). He introduced agrarian legislation to undo the ruinous impact of rural indebtedness and launched an ambitious programme of rural uplift. He extended unconditional support to the British war effort by raising troops and food supplies. His political base began to erode following a shortage of consumer goods, inflation, rationing and requisitioning of food grains. For details see, Ian Talbot, *Punjab and the Raj*, pp. 117-18, 142-6; Raghuvendra Tanwar, *Politics of Sharing Power: The Punjab Unionst Party*, pp. 112-23.
2. Born in 1902 in Dhoot Kalan, Master Hari Singh graduated as a teacher and served as the headmaster of the Khalsa High School, Baddon, Hoshiarpur district. He was one of the founders of the Punjab Riyasti Praja Mandal and a prominent organizer of the All India States Peoples Conference held at Lahore and Ludhiana in 1929 and 1938 respectively. During 1934-5 he led an anti-feudal struggle in the princely state of Kapurthala. In 1937, he was elected to the Punjab legislative assembly from Hoshiarpur on a Congress ticket. In the same year, he was elected president of the Punjab Riyasti Praja Mandal and became one of the chief organizers of the All India States Peoples Conference held at Ludhiana in 1938. He was imprisoned for his participation in the Lahore kisan morcha. After release from Deoli, he plunged into peasant struggles, becoming general secretary of the Punjab Kisan Sabha in 1946. After partition, he became a member of the executive of the Punjab unit of the CPI. Fauja Singh, *Eminent Freedom Fighters of Punjab*, pp. 115-16.
3. The official reports were quick to observe the dominant communist influence on the satyagraha training camps which were organized by the Congress in villages and towns during the summer of 1940. Sohan Singh Josh, *My Tryst with Secularism: An Autobiography*, p. 237.
4. The government action was prompted by the CPI's attempt to make a revolutionary use of the war crisis, i.e. armed insurrection and general strike in major industries coupled with a countrywide no-rent and no-tax campaign, which was manifested in a wave of strikes in Bombay, Kanpur, Calcutta, Jamshedpur, Dhanbad and Jharia. B.T. Ranadive, *The Independence Struggle and After*,

pp. 86-7; Bhagwan Josh, *Struggle for Hegemony in India*, vol. II, pp. 296-303.

5. A native of Patara village in Jalandhar district, he was the headmaster of the Anglo-Vernacular Khalsa Middle School, Mahilpur. Resigning from his job, he emerged as a effective leader of the Babbar Akali movement. A fiery orator, he addressed huge gatherings at night with a sword in hand, after which he disappeared. In 1922, he was sentenced for five years and deported to Mandalay, Burma. After his release from jail, he began to associate with the communists and became an active member of the Punjab Kisan Committee. David Petrie, *Communism in India*, pp. 227-28; Master Hari Singh, *Punjab Peasant in Freedom Struggle,* vol. II, p. 138.
6. Rules framed under the Defence of India Act, 1939 authorized the government to detain a person without trial, with the purpose of preventing him from acting in a manner prejudicial to the defence of British India, public safety, maintenance of public order or the efficient prosecution of war. Ujjwal Kumar Singh, *Political Prisoners in India*, p. 159.
7. For a detailed account of the experience of political prisoners in Rajanpur jail, which was based on interviews with participants, compare with Bikram Singh Ghuman, *Ghadari Baba Wasakha Singh*, pp. 165-8.
8. At the Deoli Detention Camp, there were 255 security prisoners, 111 in Class I and 144 in Class II. The province-wise break up in the two classes respectively was – UP: 78 and 27, Punjab: 17 and 94, Bihar: 0 and 10, NWFP: 3 and 6, Central Provinces and Delhi: 13 and 7. N.M. Joshi's Adjournment Motion in the Legislative Assembly, Home Department, Political (Internal), File No. 24/14/41, pp. 83-97.
9. Naina Singh Dhoot was placed in Category II of security prisoners. His name figured at serial No. 33 in a list of 103 detenus from Punjab. Home Department, Political (Internal), File No. 43/65/41, p.139.
10. The imperialist bureaucracy perceived the detenus as belonging to two distinct classes. On the one hand, there were intellectuals with university degrees and well educated professionals, including lawyers. On the other hand, there were professional agitators of a definitely lower order of intelligence and with little education beyond their narrow political field. The latter included the Sikh Kirti agitators from Punjab who were of the lowest status, without any landed property and who took to political agitation as a mode

of earning their living. The mixing of the two was considered undesirable both on account of the pronounced differences in family and breeding and on account of the possibility of the intellectuals availing of the opportunity of furthering the political education of these less sophisticated yokels. Note of the Additional Secretary, Papers for N.M. Joshi's Adjournment Motion in the Legislative Assembley, Appended in Home Department, Political (Internal), File No. 24/14/41.

11. The editor of this volume has examined Naina Singh Dhoot's collection of books and pamphlets preserved in a room in the upper storey of his ancestral house at Dhoot Kalan. He came across more than half a dozen notebooks in which NSD has elaborated Marxist principles in Punjabi and that, too, in his own handwriting. The title page of each notebook bears the seal of the Deoli Jail Superintendent, who has certified the number of pages in each case.
12. Bilgha attributed the unity to the collective efforts of three elements, viz., detenus of Campbellpur jail including the role of Teja Singh Swatantra, the detenus of Deoli detention camp and political activists working outside the jails. Josh gives credit for unity to S.V. Ghate, whose persuasive powers induced the Kirtis to forgo their separate identity. Bhagat Singh Bilgha, op. cit., p. 289; Sohan Singh Josh, op. cit., p. 240.
13. Jayaprakash Narayan tried to smuggle a letter out of Deoli jail through his wife, but it was intercepted by the police. In this letter, he had expressed deep concern about the unity between the CPI and the Kirtis. He had also condemned the attitude of the communists towards socialists as extremely hostile and childish. Home Department, Political (Internal), File No. 24/14/41, p. 54.
14. The demands were contained in several identical petitions, which were collectively signed by the security prisoners. Refer to the petition sent on 10 October 1941 by Harsh Deo Malviya to the Home Secretary, Government of India. Home Department, Political (Internal), File No. 43/65/41, pp. 90-4.
15. In a letter to the Commissioner of Ajmer Merwara, Lieutenant Colonel R.F. Craster, the superintendent of the Deoli Detention Camp, reported a case of violent resistance to force-feeding by a security prisoner. Home Department, Political (Internal), File No. 24/14/41, p. 135.
16. N.M. Joshi (1879-1955) graduated from Deccan College, Pune, and taught at various schools in Maharashtra. Because of his keen interest in labour problems, he set-up night schools, medical

clinics and industrial training centres. In 1921, he founded the AITUC and served as its general secretary from 1925 to 1929 and from 1940 to 1948. From 1919 to 1948 he was invariably nominated to respresent Indian labour at the ILO conferences in Geneva. For twenty-six years (1921-47) he was the sole nominated member of the Central Legislative Assembly to represent labour. He was responsible for the enactment of several labour laws. Parshotam Mehra, *A Dictionary of Modern Indian History*, pp. 368-9.

17. For a comprehensive statement by Indian communists on their characterization of Britain's military involvement in the People's War and the justification for their support to the war effort, see 'A Note from Jail Comrades (Popularly Known as the Jail Document), Task of the Communists: The People's War Against Hitler's Fascism', in Subodh Roy, ed., *Communism in India: Unpublished Documents 1935-1945*, pp. 278-325.
18. During the mid-1920s, Mangoo Ram and his associates launched the Ad Dharm movement in the central districts of Punjab. It endeavoured to mobilize the untouchable castes for social uplift and political action, by claiming a religious indentity distinct from Hindus, Muslims and Sikhs. For details regarding its ideology and objectives, see 'The Report of Ad Dharm Mandal 1926-1931', in Mark Juergensmeyer, *Religious Rebels in the Punjab: The Social Vision of Untouchables*, pp. 290-307.
19. Born in 1909, Ajoy Kumar Ghosh graduated in science from Allahabad University. He began his political career as an extremist in Punjab and helped organize the Hindustan Socialist Republican Association. He was one of the defendants along with Bhagat Singh in the Second Lahore Conspiracy Case. In the early 1930s, he began trade union work in Kanpur and embraced Marxism under the influence of S.G. Sardesai. In 1931-3 he was imprisoned and soon after became a member of the central committee of the CPI. In 1951, he rose to be the general secretary of the party and edited the party's theoretical journal, the *New Age*. Pyotr Kutsobin, *Ajoy Kumar Ghosh and Communist Movement in India*, pp. 14-27; Overstreet and Windmiller, op. cit., p. 562.
20. The absence of foreign competition and increase in demand, which had been caused by the Second World War, created favourable conditions for the industrialists of Amritsar. However, the industry found it difficult to adjust to peacetime conditions. Manufactured goods lay in godowns, industrialists' money was blocked, some factories had closed down permanently and their workers were rendered jobless. However, some industries were

unaffected by the post-war slump. Anand Gauba, *Amritsar: A Study in Urban History*, pp. 144-5.

21. During the years just before independence, Jaswant Rai served as secretary of the district committee of the CPI for Amritsar (Urban). Jagjit Singh Anand, *Chete Di Changer Chon*, p. 132.
22. Presided over by Baba Gurmukh Singh, the session decided to intensify tenant struggles in Patiala, Ferozepur, Una, Kangra and the Nili Bar. The participation of industrial workers and the striking soldiers of Patiala, besides the presence of Ajoy Kumar Ghosh and Baba Prithvi Singh Azad, were the distinctive features of the session. Master Hari Singh, op. cit., p. 323.
23. From April 1946 to November 1946, Ajoy Kumar Ghosh served as the provincial organizer for Punjab and adopted several measures to bring a defiant Swatantra-led provincial organizing committee in line with the official policies of the CPI, besides forging unity between the Ghadar Kirtis and the Lahore-based official group. However, these efforts did not produce any positive results. Gurharpal Singh, *Communism in Punjab: A Study of the Movement up to 1967*, pp. 97-101.

CHAPTER 8

Partition and its Aftermath

Since the beginning Indian communists had opposed the idea of partition of the subcontinent along communal lines and had consistently argued for a united India.[1] But the British policy of divide and rule, the rising tide of communal forces and the opportunistic stance of the Congress led to the partition of the country.[2] In fact, it was divided into three parts, viz., India, Pakistan and the princely states. The British policy was aimed at advancing their imperialistic interests in the entire world by continuing their presence in the princely states. The CPI raised its voice against these dubious moves, but it was not strong enough to change the course of events. The party's organization was weak. It was not properly centralized, i.e. various leftist groups working in different parts of the country were not connected with the central leadership. Its mass organizations had failed to bring a large number of people to their fold. Moveover, its growth and development had been uneven; strong in some states, not so strong in others and weak in still others. In these circumstances, the political line evolved by the party could not be implemented effectively and uniformly. The Congress was anxious to seize power once the colonial rulers left. Even during the course of the national movement, the Congress had played a dual role. On the one hand, it launched and intensified anti-British agitations and, on the other, it tried to extract concessions on the basis of the pressure of the movement and to compromise with the British through negotiations.[3] In this situation, the creation of Pakistan could not be prevented.

Such was the impact of partition that it caused tremors even within the CPI. The differences, which had been resolved in the past, erupted once again. Teja Singh Swatantra, Ram Singh Dutt, Bujha Singh, Chhaju Ram and Dr. Bhag Singh – most of whom belonged to the Kirti Kisan Party – held a meeting in Ludhiana and discussed the idea of forming a separate communist party. They believed that Pakistan, which had become a sovereign state, ought to have a communist party of its own and that it should work to bring about a socialist revolution in that country. Against this background, they held another meeting in a village in Jalandhar district and announced the formation of the Pakistan Communist Party on 16 July 1947.[4] Some communist parties, based in different parts of the world, recognized it. When the CPI read about the founding of the new party in the newspapers, it made a careful analysis of the development and reached the conclusion that this step was not warranted by the concrete situation obtaining at that time. For, the social composition of the CPI was such that its mass organizations were largely dominated by Sikhs and Hindus, while the presence of Muslims was neligible. It was true that political consciousness was gradually increasing among the Muslims – particularly among muzaras, factory workers and educated classess – yet they continued to be politically backward in a relative sense. The new party, therefore, could not hope to gain sufficient numerical strength. When the CPI made its views public, communist parties abroad retraced their steps and withdrew their hasty statements recognizing the breakaway group.

As a result, the Pakistan Communist Party began to wither away. This was bound to happen as it had neither a programme or a constitution, nor was it based on the principles of Marxism. It was established on fallacious foundations, erroneous policies and wrong methods. It died on its own within one month of its birth. No effort was needed to destroy it. The leaders of the new party returned to the parent fold. Their temporary withdrawal did create much confusion among the working class. The base of the party, which had been eroded by the partition of the country, was further weakened by this division in leadership. Had the leaders of the breakaway group remained within the party, we could have revived early. The ultimate reunification was a good sign for the future of the party. All of us welcomed the happy development. It was another matter that differences surfaced again, leading to the formation of the Lal Communist Party on 8 January 1948.[5]

In the wake of the partition, Muslims of Indian Punjab left for Pakistan, while Hindus and Sikhs migrated from Pakistan to Indian Punjab.[6] Our party observed that big landlords, rich industrialists and flourishing businessmen crossed over to India well in time and did not suffer any losses. On the other hand, small farmers, agricultural labourers and other poor sections, who migrated at a much later stage, suffered heavy economic losses.[7] Moreover, the rich lay claim to goods which had been looted from the fleeing Muslims. These people filled their stores (*kothis*) with the booty and buried the valuables in their fields. The passion to plunder became so overpowering that Jats rushed into the lands which had been left behind by the Muslims. They demarcated boundary lines on their own, 'Land up to this line has become mine.' In the prevailing confusion and turmoil, every zamindar believed that wherever he had carved out a furrow with his plough, the entire chunk of land up to that point would automatically come under his ownership.

In these circumstances, the CPI adopted the line that since partition could not be averted, nothing could be done to reverse it. But something could be surely done about the loot. People who belonged to India had no right to the booty which ought to be distributed among those who had lost everyting while fleeing from Pakistan with bare lives. The party demanded that the government should recover the booty from unlawful possessors. The government launched such a campaign, but the concerned officers, who were in league with the plunderers,[8] recovered such useless items as dilapidated furniture, broken cots, torn mattresses, tattered rags, diseased donkeys, discarded cattle and buffaloes. What was even worse, these goods were recovered during raids conducted in the residential quarters (*bastis*) of the toiling classes, i.e. landless labourers in rural areas and poor workers in urban centres. The officers did not make any effort to recover valuables as they were in the possession of the rich and influential groups.

Recognizing the need of the hour, the CPI decided to

cooperate with the government in the campaign for the recovery of goods. For this purpose, the Hoshiarpur unit of the CPI set up a voluntary corps, which was divided into four sections to cover the different areas of the district. Since the party had established its roots among the people, it was able to acquire information – the identity of looters, the methods employed for plunder, the nature of the booty and the place where the stolen goods had been hidden – which none else could claim to possess. The voluntary corps for Dasuya area coordinated its efforts with an official group led by an army major. While evolving a joint strategy, we asked the major to tell us if he had any complaint against our volunteers and we promised to do likewise in the case of his men. A decision was taken to prepare detailed lists of the goods recovered, so that even a needle did not go unaccounted. These goods were to be distributed equitably among the indigent refugees. We began to conduct raids in accordance with these principles. Special mention must be made of the raids carried out at Zahura, Johlan and a few other villages, where our targets were the big plunderers who had buried their loot in the ground. From Zahura alone, we recovered three truckloads of goods. Fortunately, the major was scrupulously honest. Once he learnt that a toy had been seen in the possession of his orderly. He summoned the orderly and inquired, 'From where did you acquire this toy?' The man replied shamefacedly, 'I picked it up from the goods that were recovered from Zahura.' The major reprimanded him, 'Why do you want me to be humiliated and defamed? Do you know the stuff of which these comrades are made? They will not spare me even if an insignificant irregularity is committed by my staff.' The next morning, the major apologized for this lapse on the part of his orderly and saw to it that the toy was duly returned, to be included in the list of goods recovered.

Thereafter we went to a place in Mukerian. We had received specific information that chests, containing gold and silver ornaments, had been buried under the newly constructed portion of a house. We asked the major to order the demolition of the room (*kotha*) to unearth the valuables. The major was confused because he did not imagine that he would be called upon to go to that extent. He decided not to demolish the building. But we were adamant and a meeting was held to resolve the stalemate. We argued, 'You know quite well that our efforts have not been futile wherever we have conducted raids. We have recovered a considerable quantity of goods from each of these places. Our efforts have always been well rewarded. We assure you that our information is absolutely correct. We urge you to go ahead without any hesitation.' At last, the major relented. As soon as the walls were demolished and the floor was dug, chests containing gold and silver jewellery were found. The news of this incident spread in all directions.

Some avaricious people, having lost the opportunity of acquiring ill-gotten wealth, became hostile to us and said, 'You do not know what the Muslims are doing to our brethren in west Punjab. If you learn about their atrocities, you will not oppose us.' Our response to these irrational arguments was, 'What you have heard may be rumours. Even if your information is correct, this does not justify your looting of these unfortunate Muslims, who have been trapped here and who have done you no harm.' The Congressmen did not take kindly to the communist-led campaign. Their party included the rich and privileged and this precisely was the class to which the plunderers belonged. Even more shocking was that many of the plunderers were actually Congressmen. Therefore it was not surprising that they had amassed a lot of wealth during the recent weeks and months. These Congressmen went to Hoshiarpur to meet the Deputy Commissioner and poisoned his ears against our social work. Following this, the government disbanded our voluntary corps and sent the major back to his unit. During these troubled times, the CPI launched a relentless campaign to ensure that the refugees were provided with houses to live, land and cattle to till the soil, and household essentials to start life afresh. The party played an effective role throughout the state of Punjab and left a favourable impression on the minds of people, particularly the underprivileged.

Then arose the issue of rehabilitation. The CPI was convinced that the privileged among the refugees, being in league with the officers of the rehabilitation department, had cornered the best possible lands. We took up this matter with the concerned department with a view to ensure that land was allotted on an equitable basis and that influential people were not permitted to reap undue gains at the cost of those who were not influential.[9] After being uprooted from Lahore, a group of farmers sought our assistance in allotment of agricultural plots in the neighbouring village of Jallowal, where land was famous all over the district of Hoshiarpur for its fertility. But the powerful landowners (*sardars*) of Machhiyan, who had access to the higher authorities, had their eye on this piece of land. We put pressure in favour of the refugees and secured the allotment for them. The sardars were deeply offended by our move, 'Comrades! You have not done the right thing. You have been our neighbours, but you have supported unknown outsiders.' We told them, 'We have helped those who needed our help. You already have plenty of land and you have links at the top. But the refugees have no support.' We cautioned the refugees to be vigilant against the machinations of their rivals, who could go to any extent to oust them from their land. We promised to help them in case the sardars brought in hired goondas to put their nefarious designs into practice. The farmers said, 'Do not worry about our safety. We are a strong group and we have got weapons as well.' It was a different story that these refugees were able to secure an equally good plot of land in another place and the land in Jallowal was acquired by the sardars of Machhiyan. What I want to emphasize is that we left no stone unturned to ensure that the process of rehabilitation was carried out on the principles of justice and fair play and that the powerful were not allowed to trample on the rights of the underprivileged.[10]

We also focused on the immediate needs of the refugees. In many cases, we provided shelter, food and other essentials to the more vulnerable among them. The government also set-up camps for the migrants at various places like Hariana and Mukerian in Hoshiarpur district.[11] I made sure that the people of my village did not take to loot and plunder. At one time, Dhoot Kalan was a stronghold of notorious dacoits who were feared in the region. Since it was one of the twenty-four villages of the Bhunga pocket in Kapurthala state, criminals of

British Punjab often took shelter here, while criminals of the village easily crossed over to British Punjab in order to evade detection and arrest. When people with criminal proclivities in Dhoot Kalan saw plunderers bringing in cartloads of goods which had been looted from Muslims, they were tempted to do the same. Since we prevented them from indulging in such madness, they felt cheated and complained about us, 'These comrades have prevented us from becoming rich like others, who have been making hay while the sun shines.' But communal feelings ran high. Muslims and non-Muslims – who once had great affection for each other, shared food and participated in each other's family functions – not only became complete strangers, but also turned into bitter enemies, thirsting for each other's blood. The cadre of the CPI, however, was not swayed by these communal feelings. On humanitarian grounds, the party extended aid to all – without any discrimination – who had suffered in different ways as a result of the mass transfer of population, particularly those who belonged to the economically weaker sections and who could expect no support from any other quarter.

Before partition, when communalism had raised its ugly head, the party played a vigorous role in fighting the communal forces. We organized rallies and processions in order to spread the message of communal amity among the masses. The task proved to be extremely difficult because the environment was charged with hatred and fear. Comrade Gehal Singh Chajjalwadi laid down his life fighting for the cause of secularism.[12] Some of the comrades, who had been fighting for the same cause in Pakistan, also sacrificed their lives. We adopted all conceivable methods to prevent communal riots. But the die had been cast by the British, the Muslim League and the Congress. The riots became inevitable.

As rioting spread, tensions mounted. In some villages Muslims were in a majority, in others Hindus and Sikhs were preponderant. This was the situation in India as well as in the newly created state of Pakistan.[13] I have already referred to Rarha, also known as Rarha Tahli, where my sister lived. Since the area had a large Muslim population, I feared that in the case of a riot her family would be butchered. When sectarian violence raised its head in this area, I decided to go to Rarha and bring my sister's family to Dhoot Kalan. On my way, somewhere between Ahyapur and Tanda Urmar, I met Jathedar Karam Singh. He exclaimed, 'Comradeji! I am fortunate to have met you. We have organized a meeting of the people of this area. Kindly come along with me to address it.' I agreed to accompany him to Ahyapur. When we reached the venue of the meeting, I took a close look at the gathering and saw that the heads of religious establishments (*mahants*) of the neighbouring villages – Khuda, Bhagautipur, Dadiala and Bodlan – were present. I quickly realized that these people had gathered here with the intention of planning a riot. Later, I learnt that their aim was to attack the small *qasba* of Miyani, which was dominated by Muslims.[14]

The organizers of the Ahyapur meeting asked me to address the gathering. I expressed my reluctance on the grounds that I did not know the agenda. They insisted, 'You are well aware of the prevailing circumstances. You should have no difficulty in deciding what to speak.' Since they continued to press me, I stood up to speak. I said, 'In these difficult times, our foremost duty is to protect the people from both genocide and plunder. On the other side of the border, Hindus and Sikhs are being massacred and looted, while their sisters and daughters are being dishonoured. The same thing is happening to Muslims on this side of the border. We must put an end to what we are doing here. Whatever happens here has a direct repercussion across the border. All our actions on this side are retaliated with equal ferocity on the other side. Thus, the vicious circle of action and reaction continues endlessly. You should make every effort to ensure that Hindus and Sikhs, who have been trapped in Pakistan, are brought here along with their families and belongings. You should pressurize the government to send special trains and buses to Pakistan for this purpose. Special care has to be taken in the case of the old and infirm, women and children.' While I was speaking to them, I realized that they were extremely disappointed as my suggestions could never form a part of their agenda and that they had assembled for some other purpose.

At that place was present a delegation of Hindus and Sikhs,

which had arrived from Lyallpur. They were asked by the local organizers to present their views before the gathering. They said, 'We have got nothing to say, except what the comrade has already stated. We demand that the Indian government should send army and police along with its trains and buses to Pakistan. Similarly, the authorities in Pakistan should undertake the same task in this country, so that further loss of life and property is stopped, or even minimized.'

After I had left, the meeting continued and they decided to attack the Muslim dominated *qasba* of Miyani the next day, after making full preparations. During the monsoon, there was excessive rainfall in the region, particularly in the Siwaliks, so that both the Beas and the Bein had merged with each other after having overflowed their banks.[15] Unfortunately, the cream of youth of a number of villages, extending from Garhdiwala to Dasuya and from Hariana to Bulhowal, were mobilized for the assault. Besides arming themselves with crude weapons, they collected tools of every description, viz., hammers, wedges, wrenches, tongs, rods and whatever else they could lay their hands on, so as to break open boxes, almirahs and chests. When the attackers reached Miyani, the residents challenged them. As they turned back, they were caught in the rising waters of the Bein. Not only were they unfamiliar with the deceptive nature of the terrain concealed under the muddy waves, they did not know how to swim. In their anxiety to escape, over 600 people were drowned in the floods of the Bein.

Who was responsible for this tragedy? It was the *mahants*, *jathedars* and ringleaders of the plunderers who had led innocent and promising young men to their death. Unfortunately, they accused Gian Singh, a communist of Moonak village, for having forewarned the Muslims of Miyani about the impending attack. The party made independent inquiries and concluded that Gian Singh had nothing to do with the incident. The tragedy was, in fact, nature's retribution for the evil intentions of a gang of riot-mongers. I was myself present among them, by sheer coincidence, when they took the unfortunate decision, which ended in the annihilation of the youth of the region. Such were the circumstances that prevailed during the post-partition riots.

The CPI organized many peace meetings to put an end to violence and plunder. At one such meeting in Jalalpur, a village near Rarha, which was situated at a distnce of six kilometers from Tanda, people from Jalalpur, Bhogpur, Salimpur and other neighbouring villages were present. Master Hari Singh, some other communists and I also attended it. We emphasized the need to foster communal brotherhood among Hindus, Muslims and Sikhs. While the speeches were being delivered, a man of Jalalpur suggested that we should invite the Maulvi of Talwandi Daddiyan, who was known to be a gifted orator. The man argued that all the speakers so far had been either Hindu or Sikh, but the presence of a Muslim speaker would have an extremely favourable impact on the peple. I readily agreed to the proposal and immediately sent someone to fetch the Maulvi. As soon as he arrived, I said to him, 'Maulvi Sahib, you have done well to accede to our request. You are aware of the purpose of this meeting. We are strong advocates of unity among Hindus, Mulsims and Sikhs, for these people have lived for centuries in close social harmony. We must see to it that these centuries old ties are not broken. Kindly say a few words to the gathering in this connection.' The Maulvi was initially reluctant because he felt that everything had already been said and he had nothing more to say. When we insisted, he delivered a powerful speech in Urdu. He quoted extensively from the Quran, the Guru Granth Sahib, the Bible and other religious scriptures. On the basis of these texts, he clarified the moral duties which were binding on each and every person in that hour of trial and tribulation. He asserted that the killing of human beings belonging to another creed was not permitted in any religion. He declared that plundering the property of others and molestation of women were irreligious acts. In fact, he touched upon each and every aspect of the prevailing situation. Needless to say, the Maulvi's appeal had a tremendous impact on the villagers, who were spellbound by the power and beauty of his oration.

The workers of our party were moving about everywhere, as if they were on a sacred mission. Driven by the idea of putting an end to the sectarian strife, they did not hesitate to risk their own lives. Two of our comrades, Hukam Chand Gulshan and

Pritam Singh, organized a public meeting (*jalsa*) at Zahura, where the Maulvi's maternal grandparents lived.[16] During the speeches, the Maulvi's maternal grandfather declared, 'Look here, comrades. The mission of my grandson is the same as yours, i.e. to foster feelings of brotherhood, amity and peace.' Thereafter the Maulvi invited Hukam Chand Gulshan and Pritam Singh to his ancestral village, Talwandi Daddiyan, and called the people to listen to them. But the fanatics of the area had other ideas. They did not want to miss this golden opportunity of killing a Hindu and a Sikh, both of whom were defenceless. Fortunately, the organizers got wind of the murderous intentions of the fanatics. They not only extended a warm welcome to the visitors, but also activated every source to protect their lives. They felt that since they had invited the speakers who had reposed implicit faith in them, it was their moral duty to ensure that no harm was done to them because if the two visitors were murdered by their fellow villagers, then they would earn universal condemnation. These right thinking people informed the Maulvi about the impending threat. The Maulvi took the matter in his own hands. He summoned all his supporters and gave them requisite instructions to ward off any attack, declaring that he was morally responsible to send the two visitors back unharmed.

The potential murderers had already made their plans. They knew that the Maulvi would definitely go to the local mosque on Friday to lead the congregational prayers. In his absence, they hoped to make short work of the two communists. On his part, the Maulvi saw through the game plan of his adversaries. At the time of the prayer (*namaz*), he decided against going to the mosque even though he had been summoned. When he received another message to lead the prayers, he said, 'If we listen to the sacred words of the two men of piety, this would be a proper equivalent of observing the Friday (*jumma*) prayers.' He sent a message to the villagers to assemble at a particular place to listen to the views of the visitors. In response to the Maulvi's appeal, a large number of people flocked to hear the speeches. As a result, the nefarious designs of the fanatics came to naught. The Maulvi's courage and wisdom saved the lives of Hukam Chand Gulshan and Pritam Singh. In the end, he put his arms around the waists of the two communist activists and accompanied them to Zahura. On reaching this village, he confessed that it was a mistake on his part to have taken the two comrades to his village at a time when communal hatred was at its peak. He expressed much satisfaction at having succeeded in bringing them back to safety.

The Muslim fanatics of Miyani condemned the Maulvi for his role in thwarting their plans. They roused communal passions by their propaganda and succeeded in mobilizing a large mob with the intention of attacking the non-Muslims of Zahura. They forced the Maulvi to join them and urged him to carry his rifle and gun. Gauging the mood of the angry mob, the Maulvi realized that if he did not submit to their wishes, they would not hesitate to kill him. However, he firmly refused to carry any weapons as he declared that he did not need them, not even for self-defence. Much against his wishes, he marched along with the mob, which ignited the flames of a riot on reaching Zahura. Small groups of the two rival communities roamed the countryside and fell upon their opponents in a state of utter frenzy. As blood flowed, the Maulvi made valiant attempts to extinguish the flames of madness and establish peace between the warring groups. Unfortunately, his efforts did not produce any positive result and, in one of the petty clashes, he lost his life.[17] The people of the area, particularly the Hindus and Sikhs, plunged in grief on hearing about the murder of the Maulvi, who had risen above all narrow considerations and had stood up bravely for the cause of universal brotherhood and communal amity. And in the process, he did not hesitate to alienate the fanatics among his own community. He had sacrified his life for the ideals which he had preached and practised all his life. For a long time, the people of the area remembered, with a deep sense of loss, the Maulvi's commitment to high ideals which had culminated in his supreme sacrifice.

Before the declaration of independence, the CPI had opposed the division of the country along communal lines. When it failed to prevent the partition, it made vigorous efforts to minimize the loss of life and property, while the population of one part was being transferred to the other. The next task of the party related to the rehabilitation of those who had migrated from Pakistan in extremely difficult circumstances. The party held that these unfortunate people had the priority of claims over the property, which had been left behind by or looted from Muslims who had migrated to Pakistan. The party played a significant role in the campaign for the recovery of booty, which had been unlawfully cornered by the leading Congressites, influential jagirdars and even high ranking police officers. If I start relating the massive work done by the members of our party during the partition and its aftermath, my story will never come to an end. The manner in which our comrades followed the party directives and came to the rescue of the vulnerable sections of society, created an extremely favourable impression on the minds of those who had suffered owing to the partition in one way or the other. In this manner, we succeeded in widening the base of the party among the masses.

It must be admitted that communal riots delivered a severe blow to the progressive forces, which were engaged in a class struggle to bring about a socialist revolution. During those troubled times, farmer was ranged against farmer, worker against worker and employee against employee. The communal divide was evident in all walks of life and among all classes. The phenomenon of communalism undermined the unity of our mass organizations, viz., kisan sabhas, trade unions and student bodies which had been fighting under the banner of the CPI. In the wake of this big blow, the party took a long time to recover its strength and come into its own. In Pakistan, the progressive forces could not recover at all. The main centres of our movement in Punjab had been present among the railway employees who were spread all over the province, besides the industrial workers of Lahore, Okara, Sialkot, Batala, Goraya, Putlighar and Chheharta in Amritsar. Our party guided the agitations of workers at these industrial centres. Similarly the party organized morchas articulating the demands of the muzaras in the Nili Bar, Patiala, Kishangarh, Una, Mukerian etc. The partition, undoubtedly, disrupted the progress of our movement towards our cherished goal i.e. the socialist revolution.

Four decades have passed since the tragedy of partition, it is possible to make an estimate of our achievements. It was quite satisfying to note that the above damage did not remain a permanent feature of our movement, which was back securely on its rails. Our party was once again playing a significant role in mass organizations of peasants, workers, youth, students and women. It came to power and formed governments in three states of India. Recently, the Congress deprived us of victory in Tripura elections by taking recourse to betrayal, fraud and violence. The Congress declared Tripura a disturbed area, called in the army, resorted to mass intimidation and managed to succeed in its nefarious designs. In spite of this reverse, the people of Tripura showed their determination, while fighting under the leadership of the CPM against undemocratic tendencies. The party has become quite strong, as indicated by the massive response to the call for a recent nationwide bandh. The party has actively supported the international peace movement so as to protect mankind from the horrors of another war. It is working in close cooperation with such international bodies as the Trade Union Federation which represent the working class of various countries. Thus, we have gradually overcome the setback inflicted on us by the partition and we are moving with confident steps towards the people's democratic revolution.

NOTES AND REFERENCES

1. During the Second World War, the CPI identified the slogan of self-determination of nationalites with that of Pakistan, in order to enlist the support of the Muslim League for the anti-fascist struggle. Early in 1946, the CPI proposed the setting up of seventeen sovereign national constituent assemblies, which would constitute an independent India as a willing union of antonomous sovereign bodies or two sovereign federations or an union of autonomous but not sovereign provinces. In its memorandum to the cabinet mission, the CPI dropped support for Pakistan and substituted it for the demand for self-determination of linguistically demarcated provinces. Shri Prakash, 'CPI and the Pakistan Movement', in Bipan Chandra, ed., *The Indian Left: Critical Appraisals*, pp. 253-5.
2. There has been a contentious debate on the factors leading to partition. According to a recent study, apart from the separatism of the Muslim League and the future needs of the British

commonwealth diplomacy, the failure of the Congress to integrate the strategy to combat communalism with the strategy of anti-imperialism led to the tragic outcome. Sucheta Mahajan, *Independence and Partition: The Erosion of Colonial Power in India*, pp. 386-8; also see, Anita Inder Singh, *The Origin of the Partition of India*, p. 237.

3. The basic strategic perspective of the Congress was to wage a long-drawn-out hegemonic struggle which alternated between phases of extra-legal mass struggles and phases of truce functioning within law or in Gramscian terms between phases of war of manoeuvre and war of position. Bipan Chandra, 'The Long Term Dynamics of the Indian National Congress', Presidential Address, *Proceedings of the Indian History Congress*, 46th Session, Amritsar, 1985, p. 21.
4. Teja Singh Swatantra's strong criticism of the official line of the CPI on British imperialism widened the rift between the Ghadar Kirtis and the official group of the party in Punjab. From April to November 1946, in his capacity as the Provincial Organizer, Ajoy Kumar Ghosh made last ditch efforts to unite the two factions. However, his attempt to reorganize district committees by marginalizing the Gadhar Kirtis produced the opposite results on 16 July 1947. Swatantra-led Ghadar Kirtis announced the formation of the Pakistan Communist Party to forty communist parties abroad. Gurharpal Singh, *Communism in Punjab*, pp. 96-101.
5. The Kirtis disagreed with Adhikari's thesis on Pakistan and rights of national minorities, characterizing the demand as pan-Islamism and religious fanaticism. After their release from jail, they moved among the people and explained the concept of People's War. But the politically inactive provincial secretariat, manned by Sohan Singh Josh and Iqbal Singh Hundal, weeded out prominent Kirtis in a arbitrary manner. As the patience of the Kirtis wore out, their dissatisfaction was manifested in the formation of the Lal Communist Party, which was just another name for the Kirti Kisan Party. Bhagat Singh Bilgha, op. cit., pp. 294-301.
6. It was estimated that 21 lakh Muslim refugees had migrated to west Punjab since 1 August 1947 and 20 lakh non-Muslims had migrated to east Punjab during the same period. Another 32 lakh Muslims and 18 lakh non-Muslims had still to be moved across the new border. Satya M. Rai, *Punjab Since Partition*, p. 109.
7. It is clear from several accounts that for most of the displaced rural population the traumatic period of uncertainty of whether to go or to stay was relatively short and the ultimate decision was

often made abruptly. Tai Yong Tan and Gyanesh Kudaisya, *The Aftermath of Partition in South Asia*, p. 126.

8. The official circular issued to district magistrates to indentify the plunderers and recover the looted property was violated by various government officers. A member alleged in the legislative assembly that two truckloads of goods worth Rs. 58,000 were recovered from a sub-inspector of police and an inspection of seven thanas revealed the involvement of all men, from constable to the Deputy Superintendent of Police, in retaining the booty. Rai, op. cit., p. 128.
9. In the first phase, 2.5 lakh migrant families were sustained for two and a half years by temporary allotment of plough unit (10 acres each) irrespective of their holdings in Pakistan. In the second phase, they were given quasi permanent allotments in proportion to the land abandoned in Pakistan, after determining a standard acre on the basis of productivity and applying the rule of graded cuts to meet a shortfall of 20 lakh acres in available land. For this purpose, an elaborate exercise involving verification of claims and exchange of revenue records from Pakistan was undertaken. M.S. Randhawa, *Out of the Ashes*, p. 67; Tai Yong Tan and Gyanesh Kudaisya, op. cit., pp. 130-3.
10. The Rehabilitation Commissioner claimed that special police and intelligence staff in plain clothes was appointed to keep a watch over the officers of the Rehabilitation Department, which was manned by 7,000 persons during the peak of operations, a large number of whom lived in tents around the Rehabilitation Secretariat in Jalandhar. Randhawa, op. cit., p. 89.
11. There were more than 160 refugees camps all over the country, providing shelter to 12,50,000 refugees. In east Punjab there were 85 camps which, accommodated 7,21,396 refugees by the end of December 1947. Rai, op. cit., p. 144.
12. Gehal Singh Chhajjalwadi, Megh Singh and Ujagar Singh (the later two were natives of Kot Dharam Rai village, Amritsar district) fought for the cause of communal peace and were martyred by Sikh fanatics. Master Hari Singh, *Punjab Peasant in the Freedom Struggle*, vol. II, p. 338.
13. According to one estimate, between 200,000 and 250,000 non-Muslims lost their lives during the riots. It was believed that an equal number of Muslims also perished. Gopal Das Khosla, *Stern Reckoning*, p. 299.
14. Miyani was a small town near the Beas, 25 miles from Hoshiarpur and 4 miles from Tanda. The proprietors comprised a few families

of Mohmand Pathans, but a greater part of land was cultivated by Arain and Jat tenants holding tenancy rights. A number of butchers resided here and carried on a trade in cattle with the neighbouring villages. Other trade consisted principally of wheat, sugar and hides. *District Gazetteer, Hoshiarpur,* 1904, p. 225.

15. After debouching from the Himalayas, the Beas entered Hoshiarpur district at Talwara and turned northwards after reaching the Siwaliks. Turning south-west at Motla, it formed a boundary between Hoshiarpur and Gurdaspur. The western or Black Bein commenced in the Terkiana swamp near Dasuya and flowed into Kapurthala. Though only a few feet in width, it was difficult to cross the river because of its depth and soft bottom. *District Gazetteer, Hoshiarpur,* 1904, pp. 6-7.
16. Hukam Chand Gulshan was born in 1910 in a priestly Brahmin family of Bahla village in Hoshiarpur district. After completing his matriculation, he studied traditional medicine under the tutelage of Maulvi Ghulam Qadir. He used his knowledge and expertise for the welfare of the poor, instead of amassing wealth. Having come into close contact with Chanan Singh Dhoot, he embraced Marxism-Leninism. He was involved in numerous struggles against the British, the princely state of Kapurthala and the feudal-capitalist classes of free India. He spent ten years in jail, besides remaining underground or being confined to the village for long periods. An efficient organizer at the grass-roots level, he enjoyed much popularity as a progressive poet. A close associate of Chanan Singh Dhoot, he served as a member of the district committee of the CPM in Hoshiarpur for many years. On 20 Februrary 1987, he was slayed by Khalistani terrorists. CPI(M), *Pranam Shahidan Noon* (Salute to Martyrs), pp. 26-8.
17. In large parts of East Punjab, Sikh mobs attacked every Muslim village and harried the columns of Muslim refugees. At places like Dasuya in Hoshiarpur district, where Muslims formed a majority, they accommodated a large number of Muslim refugees and armed themselves with firearms and other weapons. There were open fights between the warring mobs. Kirpal Singh, *The Partition of the Punjab*, p. 121.

CHAPTER 9

Underground in Independent India

After partition, the office of the CPI was set-up in Jalandhar. It was from here that the party guided progressive and militant movements in the new state of Punjab. The party also organized a provincial conference around this time. The organizational structure of the party consisted of a politburo, a central committee and a secretariate. Similarly, it had a control commission whose function, among other things, was to look into the complaints against members, specially those relating to charges of indiscipline.[1] I was nominated a member of the control commission, an office I held for two terms of three years each. Kishori Lal, Des Raj Chadha and Mohan Singh Mahawa were the other members of this body. The state committee of the party collected complaints against members and passed them on to us. We examined all aspects of every case and recommended the course of action to the state committee, which was authorized to take the final decision in the matter. As members of the control commission, we worked with honesty and sincerity. We made certain that no injustice was done to any member, while we gave the most appropriate recommendation to the state committee. Even in complex cases, we exerted and strained ourselves so as to reach the most objective conclusions, free from any element of subjectivity.

Besides serving in the control commission, I began to work among peasants and workers of Hoshiarpur in an attempt to organize the party in the district. We created a cell in every village, which had three or more members and one of them served as secretary. We convened frequent meetings of each cell, in which the policies and decisions of the central committee and state committee were communicated and explained. We also interpreted the principles of Marxism, the constitution of the party and its political programme. We selected intelligent, committed and militant members from the cells and called them to special meetings in which we surveyed the entire political scenario. Following the activization of cells, the influence and prestige of the party among the people began to increase. They were convinced that not only were we well informed and understood matters of national and international import, but also that we possessed a sympathetic understanding of the problems confronting them. Though our aim was to create a cell in every village, yet we were not able to expand to this extent. Our growth was not uniform: our presence was strong in some pockets, not so strong in others and entirely absent in still others. For example, we were quite strong in the villages of Garhshankar and Mahilpur, besides those areas of Mukerian where the muzara movement had been active. The same was the case with the villages of Tanda, Garhdiwala, Sham Churasi, Nasrala and Chabbewal. Where we set up cells, we also established kisan committees, dehati mazdoor sabhas and youth wings. Admittedly, our cells did not exist in many villages of the district, but we were making active efforts in the direction.

There was one problem however: we were not able to adequately mobilize the landless agricultural labourers. We were able to get support from small and middle farmers, besides the salaried employees. Those who were themselves not so well off, but had prosperous relatives, were also able to help us. But things were different in the case of landless labourers who were entirely dependent on their wages, which were barely sufficient to meet the needs of their families. They contributed to the party funds with much difficulty. Our district committee, therefore, was always in debt to the state committee. In these conditions, we could not alter the internal social composition of our cadre. That is to say, we could not mobilize the labour class in a manner that it could play a leading role in our movement. The significance of this class lay in the fact that it did not easily deviate from its course, while the middle class tended to vacillate. Marx had rightly asserted that the proletariat (*mazdoor jamaat*) was the most revolutionary class of contemporary times. Therefore, it was our aim to de-class all those people, belonging to different strata of society, who were desirous of joining our cadre. In other words, we made constant efforts to cut off their tail signifying any past associations, which they brought along with them and to implant into them the thinking of a mazdoor, the actions of a mazdoor and the discipline of a mazdoor. Only then could they play a meaningful role in the progress of our movement in accordance with the principles of Marxism. If this process of de-classing people became weak, a number of deviations crept into the party. Lenin had stated that the struggle against capitalism and jagirdari was easy, but the ideological struggle within the party was far more difficult, as it entailed bringing the opponent round to one's point of view with the help of logical argumentation.

I always believed that the most important source of strength of the party was its cadre. If the cadre was strong, the cells would be strong and so would be our mass organizations of peasants, workers, youth and students. Therefore, I attached considerable importance to the education and training of the cadre in the theoretical and practical aspects of mass movements. In this connection, we visited a large number of villages where the people welcomed us with great enthusiasm, because they anticipated a lively debate on important political matters. Generally, they would assemble at the venue of the meeting on their own. Sometimes, we would make a formal public announcement (*munadi*) about a meeting (*jalsa*). This was how we functioned in the district of Hoshiarpur.[2]

In those days, we organized the kisan conference for the entire province at Chabbewal. Our biggest hurdle was the lack of financial resources, as the people were not in a position to donate generously and our own resources were limited. Even in these difficult circumstances, we collected a sum of Rs. 15,000 which, considering the purchasing power of money in those days, was no mean achievement of the district committee. A monthly wage of Rs. 5 was fixed for full-time activists of the party. None of our comrades, however, claimed their wages. It went to their credit that all of them donated it to the party. Rather, they exerted themselves to the best of their capacity to collect as much funds as possible. Hoshiarpur district, one of the most backward areas of Punjab, was divided into three distinct geographical regions, viz., the hills, the kandi and the plains. It was spread over a large area, touching the Beas on one side and the Satluj on the other. But since the land holdings were small, the people were poor. This handicap was neutralized to some extent by the district committee which was intelligent and active, making its presence felt even in the affairs of the state committee. Men who played an important role in the district committee included Chanan Singh Dhoot, Babu Gubux Singh, Pandit Ram Krishan, Jarnail Singh Bhungarni and Thakur Waryam Singh. I was not associated with the district committee before partition. But after partition, my association with the body began in the earnest. All of us worked tirelessly to give a practical shape to the decisions of the district committee.

The conference at Chabbewal was held in 1947 when the party office was set-up in Jalandhar. A lot of preparation was made for the big occasion. Prominent among those who participated in the conference were Sohan Singh Josh, Teja Singh Swatantra and Dr Bhag Singh. The resolutions pertained largely to the muzara movements in Patiala and Una, besides the general demands of farmers like the prices of agricultural produce. Political resolutions on national and international issues were also passed. The leadership gave effective expression to the problems and demands of the people. I was in charge of the voluntary corps, which was entrusted with the task of making all arrangements for the conference. The delegates were deeply impressed by the manner in which we organized the conference and ensured its success.

At this time, the Congress was in power and there were a number of other lesser known parties as well. However, there was no basic difference between the Congress and the other parties, because their common objective was to deprive all others of political power. They did not have any programme or ideology or policy. The capitalist class was aware of this and was not scared of any of these political outfits. It was only scared of the Communist Party because it had an ideology, a programme and a policy, besides making steady progress towards its goal of socialism. Before independence, the CPI's basic aim was to fight against imperialism, princely states and feudal lords. Without eliminating them, it would not have been possible for the party to make progress. As a result of the compromising attitude of the Congress, our movement retained neither its national character nor the character of a bourgeois democratic revolution. Rather, it was placed at a intermediate stage between the two, viz., people's democratic revolution.

At this juncture, the socialists, too, were creating a lot of confusion in the minds of the people. All political parties in India (including the socialists led by Jayaprakash Narayan, Rammanohar Lohia and Achyut Patwardhan) were not only hostile to the communists, but were also opposed to the Soviet Union and Marxism-Leninism. When Shahid Bhagat Singh was sentenced to death, two words from Gandhi would have prevented the British from carrying out the sentence. In reaction, the students threw rotten eggs at Gandhi in Karachi, where the next session of the Congress was held.[3] Having been disillusioned with the Congress, the youth increasingly turned towards the CPI. A Congress Socialist Party was formed, with Jayaprakash Narayan as its leader, with the sole purpose of ensuring that the youth remained within the fold of the Congress. It must be pointed out that this was my personal opinion. I was not in a position to identify the party's analysis of the situation, immediately after partition. We had been consistently fighting against the Congress and the socialists, whose dubious attitude towards the working class had been repeatedly exposed. In Punjab, such socialist leaders as Munshi Ahmad Din, Mubarak Sagar, Kulbir Singh and Kultar Singh had gradually disappeared from the political stage. The demarcation between the non-communists and communists was becoming increasingly pronounced. We constantly explained these trends to the party members at the meetings of the cells.

Soon after, the second congress of the CPI was held (28 Februray to 6 March 1948) at Calcutta. Along with other party members I attended it.[4] When the delegates were returning after the end of the congress, Baba Gurmukh Singh, treasurer of the party, said to me, 'Comrade, we are terribly short of funds. We need money to pay rent for the party office, publication of literature and the nominal wages of the full-time party workers. Since you have travelled widely and have lived in many states and you know a number of people living in these places, you are in a position to collect donations for the party. You must make some efforts in this regard.' In response to this demand, I promised to do something. While the other delegates returned to Punjab, I went to Lakhimpur Kheri, a district situated on the border of Nepal.[5] Here, a number of people belonging to Hoshiarpur district, particularly the Tanda region, had settled as big landlords even before the creation of Pakistan. They had acquired large tracts of land at low prices. My wife's uncle (*chacha*) was one of them, though I knew many others. I met my wife's uncle who was known to everybody as Thekedar Teja Singh. He was initially delighted to see me. But when I disclosed the purpose of my visit, his enthusiasm waned. I did not lose hope and I contacted several other people – Jagat Singh of Goraya village, Buta Singh and Kesar Singh of Baichan village – and explained to them the weak financial position of the party and dwelt on the need to collect funds so as to fight for the farmers, workers and other oppressed sections. They agreed to help me to the best of their ability. In fact, those who were present made a good beginning themselves and contributed a few hundred rupees at the very moment. Displaying a considerable zeal, they accompanied me to many other farms and assisted me in collecting donations. Encouraged by the favourable response of these people, we went to the town of Bheera, where a good number of Punjabis had settled. I still remember Ajit Singh of Khudda Kurala village and another man of Baichan village, both belonging to the Hoshiarpur district. Here, too, the Punjabis donated generously. By the end I had collected nearly Rs. 5,000, which was, by no means, an insignficant amount in those days.

During the course of my travels in Lakhimpur Kheri, I did not get a chance to read the newspapers and was therefore unaware that the government had ordered a crackdown on the communists all over the country.[6] When I reached Jalandhar, I found to my surprise that the state committee had shut down its office and Des Raj Chadha had packed his bags and was about to leave. Aware that I had been sent on a mission to collect funds for the party, he said to me, 'Give me the money you have brought and disappear quietly. Do not go to your village or to any of your relatives. A general round-up has been ordered in Punjab. Police is desperately searching and has already arrested many of our activists.' I handed him the money which I had collected. Thereafter, I went underground and sought asylum with my political contacts. I learnt that the police had conducted raids at Dhoot Kalan, Jhawan (my wife's parental village) and Digana (her maternal grandparents' native place) in an attempt to arrest me. From then onwards, I remained underground for five years.

I was convinced that the party could advance towards its goal if it formulated such a policy as could give a befitting reply to the assault of the capitalist class, which was out to destroy its base in every state. Our party, which had been engaged legally in political mobilization, was forced to change its strategy and go underground. However, this did not mean the termination of our political activities as we had effective methods through which we could continue to function. For example, a number of our mass organizations like Kisan Sabhas, trade unions, employees' associations and members of certain societies had not gone underground and they were activated by us in the changed circumstances. During this critical period, the entire state committee of the CPI went underground in Hoshiarpur district. It was a matter of pride for us that all the prominent leaders of our party were provided with safe shelter in our own and the neighbouring villages. For example, Avtar Singh Malhotra stayed for a long time in a upper storey room (*chaubara*) opposite my ancestral house in Dhoot Kalan. Besides meeting the needs of the activists, we helped the state committee to create a new apparatus, including a communication system, so that the party office could function even while remaining underground. The members of the state committee, who had been assigned different districts, began to organize meetings of the respective district committees. Harkishan Singh Surjeet often visited the area in connection with underground political work. On our part, we acted with great caution and vigilance. The task of providing a safe shelter to the state committee was performed with such dexterity that not even a single activist could be apprehended by the police.

Nothing could be more creditable for the district committee of our party for Hoshiarpur.

Before I discuss my activities in Bhakra and Una, it would be appropriate to recall the incident of Mallewal firing and the response of the local units of the CPI. When the party was underground, Chandu Lal Trivedi, the governor of Punjab, paid a visit to Hoshiarpur on 11 October 1949. The district committee of the party met in secrecy and decided to organize a black flag demonstration against the governor, so as to pressurize the government to accept the demands of our comrades who were on a hunger strike in various jails. I came out of my hiding place in the hills, got in touch with our local units and issued guidelines for mobilizing the maximum number of people. I instructed them to avoid using public transport, lest they should fall into the police trap. Therefore some people started a day before and walked through the villages to reach Hoshiarpur. Others cycled their way to their destination. Police kept a strict vigil on the various roads leading to Hoshiarpur from Garhdiwala, Tanda and Mahilpur. The district administration had imposed Section 144 in the city. An important aspect of our mobilization was the presence of a large number of women including the wife of Master Hari Singh, Joginder Singh Saggal's mother and my own wife. Though the workers succeeded in reaching Hoshiarpur without being detected, they could not converge at the starting point of the march.

I had also sneaked into the city and, after making an assessment of the situation, I decided on a new course of action. I asked the leading CPI activists to come out of the city and reach a guava orchard in the outskirts. We had a short meeting at this place and arrived at a decision regarding our next move. Baba Randhir Singh and Amar Singh Almast were chosen to lead the demonstrators, who had assembled on a road which came from the Kotwali and forked – one leading towards the old bus stand of Hoshiarpur and the other leading to Jalandhar. The demonstrators congregated within the premises of a girls school, which stood next to the Gurdwara Singh Sabha. Forming themselves into a procession, they started marching towards the Kotwali. When they reached the Ghanta Ghar, the police pounced upon them.[7] The leading activists, including

Baba Randhir Singh and Amar Singh Almast, were arrested and bundled into a truck. Those who tried to march ahead, carrying aloft the banners of the CPI, were pushed back violently. The police did not permit anyone to reach the Kotwali. A large number of our workers were driven away in vehicles and left at remote places in the wilderness. Those who had been taken into custody were released only after six months. The anti-governemt demonstration had been held, despite the strict police bandobast. The press gave a considerable coverage to the communist-led campaign. It may be added that our volunteers had covered the city walls with slogans, condemning the government policy of banning our political activities.

It was expected that the police would apprehend those who had come to participate in the demonstration. Our party issued instructions to these people to return to their villages, avoiding the main roads. Consequently, they walked all night through unfrequented side-routes and by-lanes, reaching their village homes in the early morning. In accordance with the new directions issued by the party, they began to make preparations to organize meetings (*jalsas*) in their respective villages. The aim was to win the sympathy of the masses regarding the demands of our comrades on hunger strike in the various jails of the state. One such *jalsa* was scheduled to be held at Mallewal, the native village of Comrade Beant Singh Mallewal, on 13 October 1948. The police had been misinformed that Master Hari Singh and I would arrive on the scene to address the gathering and that anything was possible as the CPI had adopted a strident posture. A large contingent of police, including constables of the Punjab Armed Police on horse back, descended on the village and apprehended Beant Singh Mallewal, who was asleep at a safe distance from his house. In a bid to scare away the villagers, who were expected to put up a resistance, the police fired in the air. One of the bullets accidently hit a thanedar, who died on the spot. In panic, the police opened fire again and Beant Singh Mallewal was hit by five bullets, three in one leg and two in the other. He was taken to the hospital under arrest and a murder case under Section 302 was registered against him.[8]

As the news of the incident spread, a number of communists

(including some who were underground) held a meeting in an orchard in Data village where Beant Singh Mallewal's parents-in-law lived. They deliberated on the various ways in which the innocent accused could be saved from capital punishment. It was considered necessary to counteract the state terror, which had been created recently in the villages around Garhdiwala, so that no one was forced to appear as a witness against the accused under police pressure. A team of twenty strong volunteers, including Gian Singh Moonak and Takht Singh Chanauta, was selected. Five mares were procured and a drummer was hired. An itinerary was carefully drawn up.

As soon as it was dark, the riders and their supporters (all of whom were carrying flags of the CPI) began to march through the streets of the villages. Amidst slogan shouting and the beating of the drum, a stern warning was issued to anyone who had decided to appear as a witness against the accused. At Bagha village two policemen on horse back joined the marchers for a short while and then left. It was feared that they had gone to bring a large contingent of police and that there could be a violent encounter. On reaching Gondpur village, the leading activists drew a line on the ground, and said, 'Those who wish to save their lives may turn back from this line. But those who are willing to sacrifice themselves for a just cause may stay.' No one stepped back with any cowardly intention. The campaign ended just before dawn at Mallewal, the site of the incident. Later on, it was learnt that the move of the communists had given such a fright to the local police that it had fortified itself in the police station (*thana*), closing it from all sides and took up defensive positions, fearing an armed attack by the people. Because of an extraordinary action, no one came forward to appear as a witness for the prosecution and Beant Singh Mallewal was acquitted.[9] It is another matter that the police issued warrants for the arrest of all those (including Harbhajan Singh Ramdaspur) who had participated in the night-long demonstration.

Our party received information that with the arrest of Pandit Ram Krishan and Thakur Waryam Singh, the muzara movement in Una had come to a standstill in the jagirdar-dominated areas. Around this time, the Bhakra Dam was under construction and the state committee directed me to visit the site of construction and work among the large number of labourers who were employed there. I was selected to take the place of Comrade Kishori Lal who had been transferred to the plains. Harbhajan Singh Ramdaspur accompanied me. This young lad had just completed matriculation. Since his sister was married to Chanan Singh Dhoot, he regularly visited Dhoot Kalan and would drop in on me. On the other hand, I also met him whenever I was required to go to Ramdaspur, especially when I was underground. In this manner, he had become familiar with the nature of my political activities. Now, this same lad was to be my constant companion. Simultaneously, Pritam Singh Littar and Gian Singh Moonak were assigned the task of working among the muzaras of Una.

These comrades, to begin with, were reluctant to go to the hills. But I encouraged and persuaded them to come along with me. Introducing ourselves as building contractors, we rented a small house in Dukli, a village near Bhakra.[10] We started our activities at a number of places in and around Bhakra, including Ganguwal. We got in touch with our existing contacts and established several new ones. Since Harbhajan Singh was unknown in these areas, he went out during the day and fixed meetings with workers. As I had to be more cautious, I went out at night to address the same. At the end of every week or fortnight, Pritam Singh Littar and Gian Singh Moonak also joined us and, sitting together, we made a critical evaluation of our political inputs. Sometimes, Harkishan Singh Surjeet dropped in on us and participated in our deliberations. We regularly sent reports of our activities to the party office and received weekly and monthly literature, which enabled us to carry out political work in the new circumstances. Gradually, we evolved our own network to send important papers from one side to the other, without rousing the suspicion of the police. Young comrades like Partap Chand Dhoot acquired intimate knowledge of the local routes and this helped immensely during the ongoing underground phase.

The labourers working at Bhakra faced a number of problems.[11] The most serious related to the blasting of rocks. A hole was made in the mountainside and filled with dynamite.

The labourers were warned to maintain a safe distance. As the sticks were ignited, huge boulders were thrown up into the air and fell down at different places. Many innocent and poor labourers lost their lives during the process. Another hazard was landslides. Labourers lost their lives due to the gross negligence of contractors and the lack of requisite offical controls. The dead bodies of the victims were tied to heavy stones and thrown into the river, to be swept away out of sight. Such was the extent of cruelty that sometimes the accident victims, who cried in pain and gasped for breath and who could be easily revived after a little medical attention, were thrown into the river. The contractors were so obsessed with their own profits that they would not spend a single paisa on the health of the poor workers. They were not even slightly conscious of their responsibility towards paying compensation in the case of a mishap.

The cruel treatment of workers was matched by widespread corruption involving lakhs of rupees, which was prevalent in the construction department. For example, an overseer and a Sub Divisional Officer hatched a plan to lay a road connecting Nangal with Bhakra. Their estimate showed the blasting of a hillock at a cost of one lakh rupees, the levelling and removal of earth costing another one lakh and the final construction of the road costing still another one lakh. Thus they claimed almost three lakh rupees for the whole project. But in reality, the hillock did not exist at all. No blasting was done and no soil was removed. It was only on paper that these tasks were shown to have been completed. Forged bills for the entire project were submitted and the money was duly sanctioned. The case of a canal passing by Ganguwal and Anandpur also needs to be mentioned.[12] The canal had to pass through the seasonal torrent (*choe*) near Naina Devi. Since the *choe* itself was deep, there was no need for any digging. Soil was carried from the neighbouring mounds and deposited on both sides of the *choe*. This was done along the entire stretch of the canal, till it reached Anandpur. However, they claimed the cost of digging also, by manipulating records and bills. Such examples could be easily multiplied, in which a large number of engineers, officers and accountants were involved.

In the initial phase, construction work on a massive scale was undertaken to meet the housing needs of officers and workers. A large number of masons, carpenters, mechanics, smiths, semi-skilled and unskilled workers were employed on a massive scale in order to build residential quarters. We took up the problems of these workers and tried to settle the disputes in their favour. The most common problem facing workers was the oppressive practices of the contractors, who made them toil for twelve hours a day and paid them paltry wages. Payment of wages was often delayed or sometimes refused outright on extremely flimsy grounds. Since there were no labour laws, workers were dismissed without any prior notice or compensation. In order to solve disputes revolving around these problems, we had to contact the SDOs and overseers. Through our hard work, we were able to create a favourable impression on these lower rung officers. In fact, they were so impressed by my conduct that they requested me to give up my rented accommodation in the village and invited me to live with them. While appreciating their gesture, I told them that the present living arrangements suited us because we could easily meet them as and when the need arose. These officers frequently contributed funds for the party and we were able to send money regularly to our underground office. Though we were fighting for the cause of the workers, yet we rarely had a conflict with this class of officers. Our cordial relations with them could be attributed to the fact that these people were young, having joined their profession not long back. Whenever we tried to make them understand anything, we found that they were willing to listen and accept our point of view. In this manner, we were able to make them adopt a sympathetic attitude towards the workers. We would often argue jokingly, 'You people get a lot of opportunity of making extra money. You can easily spare the poor toilers.'

We succeeded in setting up a union of the workers, besides enrolling the deserving among them as members of the party. The Bhakra unit of the party was established around that time. There was no strike because the workers belonged to different categories and worked for various contractors. Our most significant contribution was politicization of a large number of artisans with diverse skills, petty contractors and semi-skilled labourers. We believed that once these people became politically educated, they could play a meaningful role in political struggles in the future wherever they went after completing their jobs at Bhakra.

A sizeable number of workers originally belonged to the agriculturally backward area of Una. Whenever they visited their villages, they disseminated the new political ideas to which they were exposed at Bhakra and associated themselves with the emerging muzara movement. In the same way, we drew much benefit from the tenant struggle of Una, while we were working at Bhakra. Therefore, our political work served a dual purpose because the two movements – among the workers of Bhakra and the muzaras of Una – not only grew at the same time, but also strengthened each other.[13]

Let us now turn to the scenario, which prevailed in Una after partition.[14] The local population consisted of Jats, Rajputs, Brahmins, Gujars and many other communities. Though the farmers raised a number of crops, cattle rearing constituted an important part of their economic activities. They brought newborn calves from Malwa, raised them and made large profit by selling them. Many of them were also engaged in the trade of clarified butter (*ghee*). The region had a special characteristic, i.e. crops like sugar cane were not adversely affected by frost (*kora*) in winters. According to folklore, this was because of a warm wind which blew from the Siwaliks at 3.00 a.m. in the morning. This warm wind, locally referred to as *dhadoo*, neutralized the harmful effects of *kora* on sugar cane. Whenever the sugar cane crop was ruined because of frost in the Doaba, farmers came to this area to purchase seed for the next sowing. The impact of *dhadoo* was exhausted at a point, which was about four miles from our village. The poor people of this area also worked as porters (*pandis*) in the grain markets in the plains. During the paddy harvesting season, they arrived with their bullock carts and transported grain to the godowns.

Of the various problems facing these people, the most serious related to the lack of drinking water. They drew water from the same dirty ponds in which clothes as well as cattle were washed. When the CPI revived its political activities in the area, the demand for clean drinking water was the first to be taken up. The local people wholeheartedly cooperated with us. In this context, I am reminded of the vigour shown by Comrade Hardyal of Beniwal, an extensive village. As a result of our campaign, a tubewell was installed, pipes were laid all over the plain (*beet*) and distribution centres were set up to provide clean and hygienic drinking water to the people.

Another problem in Una was related to the exploitation of the muzaras (locally known as *bahtis*) at the hands of the jagirdars. Most of the jagirdars were either Rajputs or Brahmins.[15] A large part of the population comprised the muzaras who tilled the land of the jagirdars as tenants. When the crop was harvested, the jagirdars managed to corner 75 per cent of the produce. They affixed their wooden seal (*thappa*) on the heap of grain and chaff (*bohl*) formed on the threshing floor. The jagirdars extracted unpaid forced labour (*begar*) of various kinds from the muzaras, who were not even treated as human beings. The muzaras had to seek the jagirdar's permission if they wished to raise a crop of chillies. They were not permitted to cut fodder for their cattle. If they produced jaggery (*gur*), they had to give half of it as share (known as *bhabi di patt*) of the jagirdar's wife. They were humiliated in numerous other ways. A muzara bridegroom was forbidden from riding on a horse and had to go to the bride's house on foot. The jagirdar travelled from one place to the other in a palanquin (*palki*) and whenever he looked out of its window, the muzaras had to make a deep bow as a mark of submission. The muzaras lived in abject poverty and faced social degradation.[16] For them, even a bicycle was an object of curiosity; they referred to it as 'the iron horse'.

Being strangers to the area, we tried to win the confidence of the local people. We helped the muzaras in whatever task they were engaged. In course of time, we moved freely in the three large villages of Dhandarhi, Biswal and Padoga. The muzaras did not feel the need to lock their doors when we were present. We organized small meetings of muzaras with the help of Shiv Dutt, our most reliable local contact. We investigated and analysed their major problems and helped them organize themselves against their oppressors. We quoted the case of Telengana as a source of inspiration. Once they became aware of their rights and conscious of their strength, their collective efforts enabled them to secure a better deal from the jagirdars. In pockets where the muzaras remained steadfast in their resolve, they were able to obtain two-thirds of the grain as their share of the harvest and, what was even more important, the division was done at the threshing pit itself. Further, the jagirdars were forced to allot a separate plot of land where the muzaras could raise fodder of their choice. In pockets where the muzaras were not sufficiently organized, they had to remain content with the traditional one-half of the produce as their share and continued to face age-old social disadvantages.

As the struggle between the muzaras and jagirdars sharpened, the changed relations were manifested in violent incidents. Once when the goondas of jagirdars besieged some muzaras in their houses, their women came out with bamboo sticks and, led by a woman named Bhago, clashed with the assailants and forced them to flee. On another occasion, an agent of the jagirdars, who acted as a spy, was paraded in the streets with his face painted black. On yet another occasion, one of our comrades, who had been nicknamed Bande Matram, received serious head injuries in a clash.

The main stronghold of our political activity was located at Dhandarhi, a large village. There were two wide tributaries (*soans*), one flowing into the Beas and the other merging with the Satluj. Once we held a meeting in this village, which was to be presided over by Harkishan Singh Surjeet. The organizing committee, consisting of the local muzaras and party activists, decided to include fish as a part of the meals to be served on the occasion. Since fish was available there in plenty, there was no difficulty in catching a few. When it was served along with the meals to Surjeet, he said, 'Comrades! How is it that you have prepared such a lavish feast.' We said, 'You are our honoured guest. You have come from a long distance to meet us. We are bound to give you a warm welcome, besides offering to you the best we have.' Later on, Surjeet addressed a meeting of muzaras and activists. We availed ourselves of the opportunity to place before him our report of the ongoing peasant movement. In this manner, Surjeet continued to pay frequent visits to Una. In fact, he had become quite popular among the muzaras. Ram Krishan Bharholiyan exercised much influence among the locals, so that he was elected a member of the state assembly from that constituency. There was a *babti* comrade (whose name I cannot remember) who was a veteran of many a struggle and had carved out a special place for himself in the hearts of the muzaras. The same position had been earned by Gian Singh Moonak, who worked under the assumed name of Pratap. Similarly, Rakha Singh of village Dasgrayeen also played a vigorous role in the movement.

Though we faced numerous risks and problems, yet the element of adventure often relieved us of perpetual difficulties. One of our hideouts was located at Bela Dhiyani, where a local associate by the name of Prabh Singh owned a patch of land. It was in fact an island formed at a point where a stream bifurcated. There were numerous such islands in the area and were known as *belas* in local parlance. The inhabitants used a *sarnai* – an air filled leather bag whose mouth was held tightly by the hand – to cross the stream and reach a *bela*, especially during monsoons. The local population found the device so convenient that even womenfolk and young girls used to cross over, while carrying food for men working in the fields. We also learnt the use of *sarnai* to reach Bela Dhiyani and what appeared to be a hazardous exercise became a source of enjoyment and every such visit to Prabh Singh's place became a picnic.

When the water receded in winters, people crossed the stream by simply walking over the *gahn* or a path constructed by placing stones on raised earth. The water level was shallow on the *gahn*, but was deep on both sides. Though it was easy to walk over the *gahn* in winters, it was a hazardous exercise when there was an unexpected inflow of water due to the melting of snow or rainfall in the upper reaches. The locals always remained aware about the condition of the *gahn* at any given point of time. For us, it was not so easy. Once four of us – Gian Singh Moonak, Pritam Singh Littar, Harbhajan Singh Ramdaspur and I – tried to cross a *gahn*, only to get caught in deep waters. As the pressure of angry waves threatened to sweep us off our feet, we held each other's hands tightly. Even if we had made a slight mistake we could have been drowned in the swollen stream. It was a nightmarish experience indeed.[17]

Underground political activity brought about a radical change in our lifestyles. We, perforce, had to adopt flexible attitudes to cope with adverse circumstances. We learnt to suppress our personal preferences in such basic requirements as food and shelter. In this connection, I must put on record one of our many experiences. A group of five persons – Gian Singh Moonak, Pritam Singh Littar, Iqbal Singh, Partap Chand Dhoot and I – was passing through a hitherto unknown pocket of Una. We had been on the move continuously for two days and had not eaten a morsel. As we pushed on relentlessly, some of us began to show signs of despair. Fortunately, we came across a grinding mill (*gharat*) turned by a running stream in a little hamlet. We purchased maize flour for Re. 1. In a state of bewilderment, someone asked, 'Who will cook?' I remarked spontaneously, 'Today, the bangle-wearing new bride (*choorey wali*) will cook.' Everyone burst into laughter. The sagging spirits were revived. I borrowed a flat dish (*thali*) from the owner of the *gharat* and kneaded the dough and made chapatis on a borrowed griddle (*tawa*) and an improvised hearth (*chulah*), but there was nothing to eat with the chapatis. We looked around and saw a bed of radish. We expected that our problem had been solved. However when we pulled out a stalk, we found that the root had not been formed. We plucked a few leaves, chopped them and sprinkled some salt. We ate the chapatis with this unusual preparation. Unmindful of the humble fare, we felt elated at our success in putting something in our empty stomachs. Unable to control his joy, Iqbal Singh said, 'The food was wonderful. I have never enjoyed anything tastier than this.' Gian Singh Moonak remarked, 'If you stay in our company, you will continue to enjoy like this.' We burst into laughter and resumed our march.

Here I must mention an important fact. Though the muzaras of Una were extremely poor, they were quite aware of the legal aspects of their problems, because they had been oppressed for decades by the jagirdars and had been embroiled in a long-standing conflict. In fact, their legal insight often took us by surprise. This quality of the muzaras enabled us to put up a tough fight on such issues as control over land, evictions, *begar* and the moral misdeeds of the jagirdars. One of our important achievements was securing the right of ownership of land for a number of *marusis*. These people tilled their plots of land, but paid taxes to the jagirdars. This ancient custom was perhaps prevalent since feudal times. The erstwhile rulers of the petty hill states drew their power from the support of the jagirdars. After we had succeeded in eliminating the jagirdars, a direct relationship was established between the *marusis* and the government. That is to say, the *marusis* paid their revenues directly to the government. As soon as they had the right of ownership, their position underwent a qualitative change. The struggle between the muzaras (or *marusis*) and jagirdars transformed itself into a struggle between the landowners and the government.[18]

It was during this period that the tehsil of Una and the *beet* of Garhshankar became the nucleus of a larger region, which was undergoing a perceptible economic change. A large number of unemployed people were able to find work at the construction sites at Bhakra and other places. Many of them brought milch cattle from Malwa and sold milk on large scale. The opening of the canal and the construction of Ganguwal also contributed to their material growth. This process of economic development was matched by the emergence of a new political consciousness, which was largely due to the sustained efforts of our comrades and which transformed the very complexion of the social scenario. Whereas it must be admitted that the material conditions of life began to improve, it has also to be recognized that the prevailing social system did not permit a more radical transformation. Nevertheless, our pressure on the jagirdars continued to increase with every passing day. So much so that they began to fear us. Our comrades moved freely in three large villages, viz., Dhandarhi, Biswal and Padoga. Whenever they entered the residential streets (*muhallas*) of the muzaras, they knew that none could dare to cross their way or to arrest them. We succeeded in setting up a unit of the CPI in the tehsil of Una.

Parallel to the muzara movement of Una, a struggle was launched in more than twenty villages including Shibo Chak,

Sariana and Hajipur, which extended from Mukerian to Talwara. In these villages, the jagirdars subjected their muzaras to various forms of exploitation. The former enlisted the help of agents or *muhassils* to obtain their share of grain. These agents not only received a fixed quantity of grain from their masters, but also forced the muzaras to part with some of their share. However, the unreasonable and oppressive practice of *thappa* was the most potent instrument of exploitation. Under this practice, the jagirdars spread finely powdered earth on one side of the heap of grain and chaff (*bohl*) and affixed a wooden seal (*thappa*) on it, which was inscribed with their name or a distinctive mark. Then the jagirdars disappeared for days and thus delayed the division of grain. When they reappeared, they allowed the division only if they were satisfied that the *thappa* was intact. The seal safeguarded the freshly threshed heaps of grain. If the mark got even slightly disfigured, the jagirdar accused the muzaras of theft and imposed a arbitrary reduction in his share. The *thappa* had to be protected against damage by wind and rain, besides tampering by useen hands.

Our campaign to organize the muzaras of this region was manned by Pritam Singh Littar, Gian Singh Moonak, Pandit Kishori Lal, Gurbax Singh Bodal, Pratap Chand Dhoot, Sant Chanan Singh and a local comrade named Bawa. I often came from Bhakra and Una, stayed here with secret contacts and attended important meetings. The struggle of the muzaras was successful as they acquired the right to take two-thirds of the produce and that, too, at the threshing pit. The practice of *thappa* was abolished and became a thing of the past. Finally, the muzaras ceased to be *marusis* of the jagirdars and instead became proprietors (*maliks*) themselves. It must be mentioned that our task was never easy. The jagirdars and their agents were always on our trail, trying to locate our hideouts and report to the police. They also filed a number of legal suits against us. We had to struggle hard and squeeze our meagre resources to fight these cases. Ultimately, we were acquitted.[19]

At a time when most of us were underground, Chanan Singh Dhoot was arrested and imprisioned at the Yol Camp.[20] When the assembly elections became due, we put him up as a candidate from our constituency. Though the prominent leaders of our party were either underground or behind bars, yet we conducted our campaign in a manner that our candidate came out with flying colours. The local comrades – Pritam Singh Littar, Hukam Chand Gulshan, Beant Singh Mallewal, Harbhajan Singh Ramdaspur and I – were actively involved in the election campaign and our candidate won by a comfortable margin.[21] It was only then that Chanan Singh Dhoot was released from prison. His election had a tremendous impact on the politics of Punjab. For, the manner in which the communist legislator conducted himself was worthy of praise. This fact was acknowledged both by the ruling party and the opposition groups. His greatest quality was his ability to grasp the instructions, which were issued by the state committee after in-depth deliberations and were communicated to him in writing or otherwise. These guidelines were the basis of his effective interventions in the political debates of the legislative assembly. Besides the party guidelines, Chanan Singh Dhoot was naturally endowed with the qualities of a doughty fighter. He was clear-headed and courageous. When provoked, he did not hesitate to engage in a physical combat with his opponents. His membership of the legislative assembly enhanced the prominence of the district committee of Hoshiarpur.[22]

When I was pursuing my underground activities at Bhakra and Una, I often came down to attend party meetings because some form of political work did continue, in spite of the ban imposed on us. Once I received a message that I should visit my parents-in-law as and when I came from Bhakra. This opportunity came when I had to attend a meeting at Bodal village. After participating in the meeting, I went to Digana (the ancestral village of my wife's parents). I did not go to the house as I did not want anyone to know about my visit. Instead, as soon as it became dark I went to their well, which was situated at a point where the outer boundaries of three or four villages met. It stood in the midst of a pear orchard – the first to have been laid in the area – which was owned by my in-laws. Several thanedars had been posted, one after the other, to arrest me. At this time, thanedar Darshan Singh, who belonged to Halerh village near Dasuya, was assigned the task of arresting me. I was lying inside on a cot, drawing lines on the ground and lost in thought. The thanedar passed by and saw my arm through the window. He immediately stopped and asked my brother-in-law as to who was lying inside. The young lad replied spontaneously, 'It is our son-in-law (*prauhna*).' Responding to another question, he said that the son-in-law was married in Digana village. When the same questions were put to my father-in-law, he did not respond.

Lest he should make any mistake in facing the thandedar, my father-in-law informed me that some people had come to see me. I came out in the clothes I was wearing – a *chadar*, *kurta* and turban – but without putting on my shoes. Though it was dark, I recognized that the two persons in plain clothes, who were standing under the huge mango tree, were none other than the thanedar and a policeman. I went forward and greeted the thanedar. We exchanged pleasantries and I realized that they had already talked about me to my brother-in-law. Therefore, I made it a point to see that our statements did not contradict each other. When my brother-in-law joined us, the thanedar asked me whether I knew anyone in Digana. I replied, 'What do you mean. This is my own village. There is none who is not known to me. Malkiat Singh is our *zaildar*.' I mentioned a number of names which were common among villagers. The confidence with which I conducted myself befuddled the thanedar. Taking advantage of the situation, I said, 'Let us be frank. Why should we beat about the bush. Come to the point. I know that you are policemen and I am the person you have come to arrest.' The two did not dare to move, as they knew that I had earlier thrashed a policeman who had come to arrest me. They stepped back and began to confer with each other.

Meanwhile I got an opportunity to finalize my strategy to meet the exigency. I directed my brother-in-law, 'Do not fear. Just make two bamboo sticks (*dangs*) ready and place them in the verandah. I am going to break their limbs, make them sit on their own camel and throw them into the gorge (*khad*) of Dholbaha. They will remember for a long time that they were confronted by somebody.' The lad regained his confidence and did as he was told. The policemen anticipated that we had prepared ourselves for a fight, in which they were sure to be at the receiving end. The thanedar decided to stay there in order to keep an eye on me and sent his subordinate to bring more police force from Jhawan. I began to plan my escape, keeping in mind that all the neighbouring villages – Jhawan, Masiti, Chhauniwala, Kandhali and Kandhala – were strongholds of the communists. Since I was one of the rebels and the police was after me, they would be able to catch me sooner or later. It seemed that such an opportunity had come in the way of the police. But it had come to them at a place which was extremely unfavourable to me. I felt that if I was arrested from that place, the family of my parents-in-law would also be implicated for having given shelter to a rebel. These simple folk, who knew nothing about the ways of the world, would not know how to handle the legal consequences. My first priority was to ensure that my parents-in-law were not involved in the matter.

With this in mind, I planned my escape. In a loud voice I said to my brother-in-law, 'Oh Gurbux! Put a cot for thanedar sahib. Make some tea for him. I am just coming after answering the call of nature.' After having said this, I disappeared in the fields of maize crop, which had grown as tall as a man. I unwrapped the *chadar* from my waist and threw it on my shoulder and ran as fast as I could. After covering a long distance, I reached the road connecting Tanda with Dhoot Kalan. When I did not return from the fields, the thanedar said to my brother-in-law, 'So you have helped your sister's husband (*behnoi*) to escape.' The boy replied, 'Yes. He is my behnoi, all right. But he had become your son-in-law before he slipped away.' The thanedar set out on my trail but I had taken a long lead. On reaching Khiala (adjoining Dhoot Kalan), I contacted a sympathizer and sent him on a bicycle to meet my brother-in-law. This man conveyed the message that I was safely out of the police net and they should not worry about me. The man brought along my bag and shoes which had been lying at the well, where my encounter with the police had taken place in such dramatic circumstances. The news of my escape spread in all directions. The police felt humiliated. In order to cover up their own inefficiency, they began to say, 'He was coming on a bicycle at tremendous speed. It is only when he had gone past us that we realized that it was him. We could do nothing to overtake him.'

Such incidents often took place when I was underground. On one occasion, Harnam Singh Chamak of Sangrur and Chaudhury Basawa Singh of Dhariwal came to Dhoot Kalan to discuss some political matters. They asked me whether I had a radio set, because they wanted to listen to the news. I told them that I did not own any radio set, but we could go to the house of my father's younger brother (*chacha*) who had one. They accepted my suggestion. We went to the neighbouring house which belonged to my uncle. As we were sitting inside, I saw that a CID man was standing outside in a corner. I sent someone with a message for him that he should leave immediately. But he continued to hang around. I suspected that he may be followed by a police party and if they succeeded in apprehending the two comrades from my place, it would be a great insult to me. To circumvent this, I asked them to forget about listening to the news and to leave immediately. We stepped out of my uncle's house and went towards my cattle pen (*haveli*). The CID man followed us. I lost my temper and asked him angrily, 'Who are you? What are you doing here?' He said that he was merely passing through the village. As he stepped towards me, I caught hold of his neck and pinned him to the wall. I delivered a number of powerful blows on his face. I asked a cousin of mine, who had come out of his house, to get a *dang*. I threatened to kill the man there and then. My cousin and some other people intervened and prevailed upon me to let him go. The poor fellow went to the police station of Bhunga. The thanedar, who had already been informed about the incident, wanted to know why his face was swollen. The man did not speak the truth for fear of being laughed at. He lied that he had been stung by a swarm of bees. Instead of being sympathetic, the thanedar severely reprimanded him, 'Do you think that you could have arrested him on your own. Perhaps, you wanted to take all the credit yourself. We also know that the wanted man comes here sometimes. But we do not act with indiscretion. We do not want to get the kind of treatment which you have received.'

In this context, I am reminded of another incident. The

village of Dhootan was located at a distance of about four miles from Dhoot Kalan. Initially members of our clan had settled at Dhootan, but later they moved to Dhoot Kalan which was a settlement of Muslims. When I was underground, a small police contingent of ten horsemen patrolled the area to nab us. Once I was coming from Dhootan on a bicycle and I saw that mounted policemen had blocked the road with their horses. I was in a fix. If I turned back, their suspicions would have been aroused. Therefore, I decided to continue regardless of the consequences. It was quite possible that they would not stop me, because they did not recognize me. With these thoughts in mind, I continued to go straight. I acted as though I was unconcerned about the presence of the police. When I reached near the group, I deliberately passed by their commander and saluted him. He reciprocated my gesture in a equally spontaneous action. As soon as I approached a kutcha pathway, I left the main road and sped on my bicycle. In this manner, I gave another slip to the police and did not fall into their trap.

My purpose in narrating these incidents is merely to emphasize that the life of an underground political activist was extremely hazardous. He had to be on his guard all the time as anything could happen at any moment. He had to be equipped, mentally and physically, to cope with all types of situations. He was not to panic in critical circumstances or succumb under pressure in adverse conditions. He had to develop the faculties of intelligence, tact and presence of mind. One golden rule, which ought to be followed scrupulously, was that nobody should ever know the place where he was to sleep on a particular night. It was for this reason that we slept even in cremation grounds, if the need arose.

Having repeatedly failed to entrap me, the police became increasingly desperate both in its intentions and actions. This was evident from the words of Gurbax Singh, a thanedar. Once Pratap Chand Dhoot, some other comrades and I were returning to our village, after attending a secret meeting at Sikri village. When we saw a police party coming from the opposite direction, we quickly hid our bicycles in the standing maize crop and prostrated ourselves along a raised bed of the field, so that we were within hearing distance. As the police party crossed us, we heard the thanedar saying, 'We keep on hearing that Naina Singh Dhoot is moving about in these parts. If I catch him, many coloured strips will be affixed on my uniform.' His companions began to laugh and remarked, 'But your desire will be fulfilled only if you are able to arrest him.' Little did they know that I was present so close to them. When they had reached a safe distance, we retrieved our bicycles and sped away.

In its desperation, the police often raided my house in Dhoot Kalan. On these occasions, the police confiscated whatever was at hand and threatened to auction the goods, if I was not produced. My wife had learnt to deal with such pressure tactics. She would tell them to appropriate whatever they wished, but never dithered in her commitment to our cause. Whenever a police raid was anticipated, she would send the household goods to the houses of our sympathizers, where they would remain for months. In most cases, the goods were either lost or damaged due to lack of care. It became a habit with illiterate villagers to take my books from the place where they were hidden and sell them to a dealer in junk and second hand goods (*raddiwala*). That was how I lost a large number of valuable books on various aspects of Marxism from my personal collection. A police party, which raided the house of Gian Singh Moonak, impounded his cattle and carts. Another team descended on the house of Ram Krishan Bharoli. When they failed to extort information about his whereabouts and also failed to lay their hands on anything worthwhile, they took away the dolls with which his daughter was playing.

The second important principle in clandestine political work was punctuality. Whenever a secret meeting was fixed at a particular time, an underground activist had to reach the appointed place on time, regardless of all obstacles. Even the slightest delay became intolerable, as it led to much misunderstanding and inconvenience. Whenever a comrade failed to reach on time, the others perforce believed that either he had been caught by the police or he had become weak in his commitment to our cause. In such cases, the venue of the meeting had to be changed at the last moment. It was another matter that most fears entertained temporarily by the group turned out to be unfounded.

In 1952, our warrants were cancelled, as the restrictions on the CPI were withdrawn.[23] We came out from our hiding places. A number of us, including Pandit Kishori Lal and I, were given rousing public receptions at Hoshiarpur. We were placed at the head of a procession, which passed through the streets and bazaars of the town.

NOTES AND REFERENCES

1. Up to 1958, the organizational structure of the CPI was hierarchical, highly centralized and compact. The provincial committee stood at the apex of the structure and the cell at the bottom. In between were placed the area, tahsil, city and district committees. Elected by delegates to the provincial conference, the provincial committee supervised the work of all lower organs, including the provincial control commission. J.S. Brar, *The Communist Party in Punjab,* pp. 44-5.
2. Compare with the methods employed by peasant activists, who worked at the grass-roots level in different pockets of Punjab during the 1930s. Mridula Mukherjee, 'Peasant Protest in Punjab: Forms of Struggle and Mobilisation', *Proceedings of the Indian History Congress*, 59th Session, Patiala, 1998, pp. 812-23.
3. Gandhi refused to make the commutation of death sentences of Bhagat Singh and his comrades a condition for signing the Gandhi–Irwin pact. The pact itself was seen as proof of the vacillating nature of the Indian bourgeoisie and Gandhi succumbing to bourgeois pressure. All along the route to Karachi, Gandhi was greeted with black flag demonstrations. At the session (beginning 29 March 1931, i.e. six days after the execution of Bhagat Singh and his comrades), the Congress passed a resolution drafted by Gandhi which expressed admiration for the bravery and sacrifice of the three martyrs, while disassociating itself from and disapproving of political violence in any shape or form. Bipan Chandra et al., *India's Struggle for Independence*, pp. 281, 284.
4. By this time, P.C. Joshi had been replaced by B.T. Ranadive as general secretary of the CPI. The latter's supporters had acquired a dominant position in the central committee and the party's

policy of supporting the Nehru government had been discarded. Attended by 632 delegates, the congress reversed its earlier position with regard to the Nehru government and gave a call for mobilizing the working class, peasantry and petty bourgeoisie in a final assault on imperialism and capitalism. For a detailed exposition of the strategy, see M.B. Rao, ed., *Documents of the History of the Communist Party of India*, vol. VII, 1948-50, pp. 75-8.

5. Lakhimpur was the central tahsil of Kheri district in the United Provinces. It comprised the parganas of Bhur, Srinagar, Kukera, Mailani, Paila and Kheri. Covering an area of 1,075 square miles, it included 666 villages and two towns, viz., Lakhimpur and Kheri. The low lying north-eastern area was prone to inundations, while the south-western was agriculturally stable owing to a loam rich soil. The area exported grain and sugar. *The Imperial Gazetteer of India,* vol. XVI, pp. 128-9.
6. The crackdown was prompted by Ranadive's application of people's democratic revolution, involving an armed struggle by the peasantry coupled with a general strike by the industrial proletariat. Two adventurist actions – continuation of the armed peasant struggle in Telengana and the call for a nationwide strike in the railways – as well as some isolated incidents of violence appeared to confirm the Nehru government's perception. Overstreet and Windmiller, op. cit., pp. 276-80.
7. Sir Chandu Lal Trivedi, the governor of East Punjab, arrived in Hoshiarpur at 9.30 a.m. by a special train. He was scheduled to lay the foundation stone of the biological laboratory at the Government College. Elaborate arrangements had been made by the police, in view of the expected demonstration by the communists. A group of communists which entered the city from Hariana was cordoned at Adda Hariana. *The Tribune*, 12 October 1949.
8. This incident was corroborated by Beant Singh Mallewal in an interview conducted on 2 April 1997 at Dhoot Kalan.
9. This episode was confirmed by Harbhajan Singh Ramdaspur in an interview conducted on 2 April 1997 at Dhoot Kalan.
10. The Bhakra-Nangal hydroelectric project involved the construction of a 680 ft. high straight gravity dam, which was the second highest in the world. It created a huge reservoir, the Gobind Sagar, spreading over an area of 168 sq. km. and having a gross storage of 7.4 million acre ft. Operated in conjunction with the powerhouses at Ganguwal and Kotla, it has an installed capacity of generating

1,204 MW of electricity. The project comprised a network of canals, designed to irrigate 3.6 million acres of land. On completion in 1963, the project cost Rs. 2,385 million. K.C. Ghosh, *Economic Resources of India and Pakistan,* p. 253 ; Bhakra Beas Management Board, *History of Bhakra Nangal Project,* pp. 38-44 ; Tai Yong Tan and Gyanesh Kudaisya, op. cit., pp. 135-6.

11. The size of manpower employed at the project varied considerably during the different phases of construction. Estimated at over 11,000 in 1948, it rose to 34,000 in 1951 and further to 1,22,000 in 1954. The unskilled labour required largely for canal construction was recruited by private contractors, while the labour working with mechanized methods was recruited directly on a departmental basis. The daily wages of unskilled labour varied from Rs. 1.88 to Rs. 2.25 and that of skilled workers from Rs. 4.00 to Rs. 5.50. As a rule, all workers were paid in accordance with the input of labour and amount of work done. K.N. Raj, *Some Economic Aspects of the Bhakra Nangal Project,* pp. 70, 76-7.
12. The entire project envisaged the construction of the 40 mile long Nangal Hydel Canal so as to bring water from the Nangal reservoir, the Bhakra Main Line Canal with its three main and smaller branches, the remodelling of the Sirhind Canal and the construction of a new Bist Doab Canal. These works involved an expenditure of Rs. 48.78 crore, which worked out to be 30 per cent of the total cost of the project. Raj, op. cit., pp. 36-7.
13. Activities regarding the mobilization and education of workers at Bhakra were corroborated in an interview with Harbhajan Singh Ramdaspur on 2 April 1997 at Dhoot Kalan.
14. Agrarian relations in Una were not uniform. In 84 villages, occupancy tenants paid 40 per cent of produce to the landlords. There were 24 taluqdari villages, where the customary rent was 2 sers per maund. In 200 villages, superior owners received cash rents from inferior ones ranging from 4 annas to Re. 1 for every rupee of the land revenue payable to the government. The rent was paid in cash in the case of commercial crops like sugar cane, cotton and oilseeds. Master Hari Singh, *Punjab Peasant in Freedom Struggle,* vol. II, p. 263.
15. Landlords possessed extraordinarily large holdings in Una and Garhshankar. The Rai of Bangarh exercised superior rights over 52 villages, the Rai of Chandian over 26 villages and the Rai of Garhi Manswal over 22 villages, each receiving 5 per cent of produce from inferior owners. Among big landlords, Parmeshwari Das of Takrala owned 4,000 acres, Zaildar Narain Chand of Khud

2,000 acres and Rai Sahib Gajinder Singh of Panjwar 1,000 acres. In the like manner, Zaildar Sidhu Ram Basal, Zaildar Tulsi Ram Padoga and Rai Bikram Chand Lalpur owned 500 acres each. Master Hari Singh, op. cit., p. 264.

16. The forms of oppression suffered by the muzaras of Una was confirmed by Gian Singh Moonak in an interview on 23 September 1995 in Moonak village, Hoshiarpur district.
17. The description of the local conditions, with reference to the traditional modes of transport, was corroborated by Harbhajan Singh Ramdaspur in an interview conducted on 2 April 1997 at Dhoot Kalan.
18. Some recent studies have made note of the forceful mobilizations involved in the tenant struggles of Una and Pathankot during the early years of free India. Partha Nath Mukherji, 'The Farmers' Movement in Punjab: Politics of Pressure Groups and Pressure of Party Politics', *Economic and Political Weekly*, 2 May 1998, pp. 1045-6 ; Sucha Singh Gill and Ranjit Singh Ghuman, 'Land Reforms in Punjab and Haryana: Trends and Issues', Sucha Singh Gill, ed., *Land Reforms in India,* vol. 6: *Intervention for Agrarian Capitalist Transformation in Punjab and Haryana,* p. 41.
19. This account of the muzara movement in Una as well as in a pocket of nearly twenty villages including Shibo Chak, Sariana and Hajipur was corroborated by Pratap Chand Dhoot in an interview on 1 April 1997 at Dhoot Kalan.
20. From the point of view of its structure, the Yol Camp jail had three rows with ten cells each on the slope of a hill. For the personal experience of a 87-day hunger strike, see Jagjit Singh Anand, *Chete Di Changer Chon*, pp. 41, 129.
21. The Punjab unit of the CPI participated in the election campaign of 1952 under a semi-legal status and deliberately limited an electoral understanding with small democratic parties like the Lal Communist Party and the Forward Bloc. Out of the 24 seats contested by it, the CPI won only 4 while the LCP contested 9 seats and won 2. Gurharpal Singh, op. cit., pp. 144, 176.
22. Born in 1910 in village Dhoot Kalan, Chanan Singh Dhoot was the nephew of Karam Singh Dhoot, the famous Ghadar Kirti who rose to be the president of the Punjab Riyasti Praja Mandal. After graduating from Khalsa College, Amritsar, he took an oath (1935) along with five others, in the presence of Harkishan Singh Surjeet, to devote his life to communism. He played an active role in the Praja Mandal movement in Kapurthala state, the Lahore Kisan Morcha, the muzara movement of Una and the anti-betterment

levy agitation. In 1934, he was released from Kapurthala jail after serving a sentence of 27 months. During the Second World War, he was imprisoned in Montgomery and Gujarat jails. In 1948, he was detained in Ambala jail, where he undertook a hunger strike for 60 days. After being elected to the Punjab legislative assembly in 1952, he emerged as a prominent leader of the opposition. A lifelong student of Marxism-Leninism, he fought resolutely against left deviation, which appeared in the form of the Naxalite movement. He served as a member of the state committee of the CPM and as secretary of the district committee of Hoshiarpur. On 15 February 1987, he fell to the bullets of Khalistani terrorists. CPI(M) Publication, *Pranam Shahidan Noon* (Salute to Martyrs), Jalandhar, 1988, pp. 12-17.

23. With the appointment of the Ajoy Kumar Ghosh as general secretary in 1951, the CPI adopted a new programme and tactical line. While adhering to its earlier understanding of the Indian state and the ruling bourgeoisie, it withdrew the armed struggle in Telengana and rejected both the Russian and Chinese paths. It postponed the task of overthrowing the Indian state as the people, owing to their illusions about Nehru and the Congress, were perceived to be unprepared for it. The party also became willing to participate in the first general elections. In these circumstances, Nehru saw no objection in legalizing the CPI. Bipan Chandra, Aditya Mukerjee and Mridula Mukherjee, *India After Independence*, p. 204.

CHAPTER 10

The Onward March

As soon as my warrants were revoked (1952), I began to work openly. The state committee of the CPI appointed me a member of the control commission, which functioned in the following manner. At times, disciplinary action was taken against a comrade by the cell, branch or district. If he felt that injustice had been done to him, he appealed to the cell, branch or district. If his appeal was rejected and he was convinced that he had not been given a proper hearing, he appealed to the state committee. The state committee, in turn, referred such cases to the control commission which examined these cases in detail and placed its report before the state committee. The basic function of the control commission was to maintain discipline within the party, keeping in view the provisions of its constitution. It also served as a guard against such tendencies in the party whereby members, out of sheer prejudice, took action against a comrade. It was our endeavour to provide justice to an aggrieved comrade and protect his democratic rights within the party. Thus, the control commission played a significant role in building the party organization, by constantly weeding out weaknesses which raised their head from time to time.

Normally, the control commission met before every meeting of the state committee and prepared its report on various cases. It was invited to place and discuss this report at the meeting of the state committee. The commission also reported on those cases in which its inquiries were incomplete. At times, the members of the control commission invited the district representative to collect detailed information on a particular case. I was often assigned this task if the case pertained to Hoshiarpur district. If the case was related to Amritsar district, Mohan Singh Mahawa was assigned this task. The cases which were referred to the control commission were diverse in nature, e.g. political adventurism, creating indiscipline within the ranks, acting as a police informer or moral turpitude.[1] Our purpose was to ensure that the party members remained strong, steadfast and upright in every respect, so that the people did not get an opportunity to point an accusing finger at them.

In this context, it is worthwhile to recapitulate the government offensive against the party in 1948. As mentioned earlier, the entire state committee went underground in Hoshiarpur district. Prominent party leaders were given shelter by the common folk of Dhoot Kalan and the neighbouring villages. These people, particularly women, recalled the simple living and high moral character of the comrades. The householders took pride in remembering that these unkown outsiders never looked at a fair face with raised eyebrows. The old generation of Dhoot Kalan often spoke highly of Avtar Singh Malhotra in this connection. This was true of Harkishan Singh Surjeet who easily mingled with the members of a family – old and young, children and grandchilden, brothers and sisters, uncles and aunts – in such a manner that he appeared to be one of them. The character of a communist has to be implecable. Only then he could become popular with the masses, who could have faith in him. Only then he could provide leadership to them. It was quite easy to bring up a son, but it was extremely difficult to groom a communist and ensure that he remained committed to the principles of Marxism.

The members of the control commission, were assigned other duties as well. For instance, Des Raj Chadha served as secretary of the party office at Jalandhar. He maintained the records of the state committee, supervised its political activities and also acted as the treasurer. I was engaged in strengthening the party in Hoshiarpur district. Since there was hardly any large industry, the trade union movement among industrial workers was weak. It was only at the Bhakra and Pong Dams that the units of the party were functioning. However, the party exercized considerable influence on the peasantry and its strength was uniform right from the Beas to the Satluj. The area of Garhshankar, the higher *beet*, Mahilpur and Chabbewal was covered by Gurbux Singh Bodal, Jarnail Singh Bhungarni and Avtar Singh Chabbewal. Dharam Singh was active in Hoshiarpur, while Sewa Singh worked in Soosan Wala and Nanda Chaur. Tanda had been assigned to Pritam Singh Littar. Beant Singh Mallewal, Hukam Chand Gulshan and Harbhajan Singh Ramdaspur worked in Garhdiwala. Those who served the party in Dasuya and Mukerian included Gurbux Singh Bodal, Gurcharan Singh Randhawa, Basant Singh Kalyanpur and Baldev Singh. These comrades performed various functions in accordance with the directions of the district committee. They distributed the party newspaper, collected funds and organized study circles. I was primarily interested in bringing more young men into the fold of the party and, for this purpose, schools and colleges were included within the purview of my activities. We strongly believed that the pivot of our movement lay in contemporary agrarian problems. Therefore, we expended much of our energy and resources in politicizing the peasantry and communicating their outstanding demands to government officials. In this direction, major contributions were made by Chanan Singh Dhoot, Jarnail Singh Bhungarni, Babu Gurbux Singh, Pandit Ram Krishan Bharoliyan, Thakur Waryam Singh, Pritam Singh Littar and Bhag Singh Sajjan. We paid special attention to the muzaras of Una and Mukerian, where we had made substantial gains during the course of our underground activities.

The nature of the party's relative strength in the various pockets of the district was best revealed by the results of an assembly election, which was fought by Chanan Singh Dhoot. His main opponent was the Congress candidate, Principal Ralla Ram, whose prominent stronghold was in the higher areas of Rakdi-Karadi. Downwards from Hajipur and Datarpur to Mukerian, we gave a neck and neck fight. In some polling segments the party was ahead. This success could be attributed to the fact that the party had struck roots among the muzaras, who had been politicized and who believed that, by supporting the CPI, they would be able to secure the value of their votes in the fullest measure. The popular belief was that our performance would be relatively better in the Garhdiwala tract, which was inhabited by the educated and petty bourgeoisie. But contrary to the popular belief, the party did not get an adequate number of votes in this region. The reason was not far to seek. The party had not politicized these classes to any significant extent.[2] Though the party had considerable general influence there, it was not enough. General influence being deceptive and unreliable, could be swayed in any direction, depending on the political winds at a given point of time. Influence, in the real sense, meant the existence of strong cells and powerful kisan committees, which were politicized vigorously by intelligent comrades through study circles and involvement in their struggles.

In view of this, the party admitted at the national level that it had not been able to consolidate its position among the labour class to the extent possible. Therefore, special efforts were made to rectify this particular drawback by creating strong units in every section of society. It was true that kisan sabhas, trade unions, student bodies and women's wings were important, but it was the duty of the party to politicize these mass organizations by providing leadership to them in their economic struggles. We, in the district committee of Hoshiarpur, constantly endeavoured to put these principles into practice. In this context, it is important to mention a huge conference which was organized at Dhoot Kalan, some time after our warrants were revoked. Veteran communists like Teja Singh Swatantra and Sohan Singh Josh attended the proceedings. The arrangements were adequate, the gathering was large and the speeches were meaningful.

Membership of the district committee entailed considerable responsibility. The district committee set-up a secretariat comprising senior members. This secretariat managed the day-to-day functioning of the party, whereas the district committee met only after a month or two. One of the members of the secretariat was appointed as its secretary. The secretary implemented the decisions of the state committee in the district.[3] He also noted the new issues that emerged in the district and placed them for discussion before the secretariat. If these problems were important, they were discussed at the meeting of the district committee. The secretariat also received reports from mass organizations and guided them in their struggles. The district committee constituted a number of sub-committees, each of which was responsible for a particular area, e.g. agriculture, industry, labour and education. In this manner, the party distributed political work among its members.

Our political activities assumed various forms in response to the changing needs of the times. Once there was a severe shortage of foodgrains. We demanded that the people should be provided minimum rations by the government. When the authorities failed to take any concrete step in this direction, the people took the matter in their own hands and carried away foodgrains from the government depots and stores. The party took the stand that if the government did not act quickly, lawlessness would escalate into violence. A potentially violent situation was thus brought under control. Second, we continued the campaign, which we had launched in the wake of partition. We highlighted the problems of the refugees and assisted them in settling their claims of rehabilitation. Third, we were deeply involved in local matters and communicated the local demands to the authorities, by leading deputations to the Deputy Commissioner of the district.

The all-India congress of the CPI was held (6-13 April 1958) at Amritsar. The state committee constituted a three-member body, comprising Fauja Singh Bhullar, Captain Nahar Singh (formerly of the INA) and myself, to make all arrangements for the conference. The state committee decided to utilize my services because I had considerable experience of organizing various types of conferences at different levels in Hoshiarpur district. It was confident that if the task of a similar nature were assigned to me, I would be able to fulfil it with the fullest sense of responsibility. The sub-committee, assisted by numerous volunteers, made arrangements for the pandal, stage, security, food, etc. And while doing so, we followed the plans drawn up by the state committee and came equal to the task.[4] Delegates from various parts of the country – Bengal, UP, Maharashtra, Madras and Kerala – attended the congress, which turned out to be a big event.

Besides other things, the congress decided to participate in the assembly elections to be held at Mehna constituency in Ferozepur district. Chanan Singh Dhoot was given the overall charge of the party's election campaign. I was assigned duty in the two Kokaris, an important segment of the constituency. Accordingly, I went to these villages and plunged wholeheartedly into my assignment. As I came into contact with the various classes of people, they learnt that I had come to canvass for the CPI candidate. When I met the young farmers, they warned me against one Ujagar who was a big local bully (*badmash*) and was actively canvassing for the Congress candidate. When I visited the quarters (*muhallas*) of Balmikis, they not only expressed much sympathy for the party, but also warned me against Ujagar. I met the local people at every conceivable place, viz., farms, stables and shops. I had discussions with educated people as well. At this stage, some of the villagers advised me to talk to the local women. I was hesitant because, being an outsider, I did not know how to establish the necessary rapport. By now, I had identified our staunch supporters and I visited their households and talked to their womenfolk. These women said plainly, 'Baiji! We will vote for your candidate. But Ujagar is a dangerous man and his hegemony (*tarhi*) is fully established in the two Kokaris. You must see that he is not able to harm you.' I assured them, 'You do not have to worry. Ours is a political fight and not a personal clash. The two contending parties are engaged in their respective propaganda. There can be no possibility of a confrontation between them. But if Ujagar comes in my way, I will tell him to mind his own business, just like I am doing.'

As the election campaign drew to a close, the CPI's position progressively strengthened. Its influence among the people continued to deepen and expand. A number of misconceptions – like defining the communists as destroyers of their community (*kaum nasht*) – that had been spread by our uncharitable opponents, were removed. In this context, it is worthwhile to relate an anecdote. During the course of my door-to-door contact programme, I met an old woman. She lived all alone, but maintained a buffaloe in her yard. She said to me, 'I will vote for your party. But tell me, where do you eat?' I replied, 'There is no fixed place for me to eat. I am busy meeting people at different places. I eat wherever food is available or wherever someone offers me food. At other times, I go without food as I am not very particular about my meals.' She called me son and insisted, 'You may go wherever you have to for your work. But you must come here to take your meals. You have come here from a long distance and you do not have any relatives in this village. Your party, too, has not made any arrangements for you. Who knows you may have to go to bed without any food. You must have your meals here from now onwards. In fact, I would say that after work you should come here and sleep in my house at night. You should do this till you are staying in this village.' Deeply touched by the old woman's sentiments, I said, 'Mataji! I am extremely grateful to you for your kind words. If I face any difficulty, I shall definitely come here.' As things turned out, I got the opportunity to eat at her house only once or twice. By that time, I had a solid team of sympatizers and, in accordance with their wishes, I ate at the house of one of them, depending on the time and place of my activities.

Soon it was time for polling. The polling station for the two Kokaris was set up at Ajitwal, a village on the Ludhiana – Moga – Ferozepur road. The respective polling booths of the CPI and the Congress were set up not far from each other. I had a discussion with our symathizers and formulated a strategy to ward off any threat from our adversaries. We decided that our hard core supporters would lead the voters, who were expected to report at our polling camp to obtain their serial numbers in the voters' list. Of course, the voters were a mixed lot: some approached our camp while the others went to the Congress booth. In view of the fear psychosis created by Ujagar, a number of people had assured us, 'Though we will go to the Congress camp to receive our serial numbers, yet we will definitely vote for your candidate.' When polling was at its peak, a group of about fifteen voters came to our camp. Ujagar, who believed that these voters were staunch supporters of the Congress, could not tolerate this. As soon as another voter turned towards our camp, Ujagar held him by the arm and said, 'Where are you going ?' Objecting to this high-handed behaviour I said, 'Look here, Ujagar. If you have to say something, use your tongue. Let no one hold the voter by force. Neither you nor me.' Ujagar did not agree with me and declared, 'How can we allow our voters to join your side.' I tried to persuade him to see reason and argued, 'If he is your voter, he will never cast his vote for us, whether you use your tongue or you use your hands. But if you forcibly pull him towards your camp, he will vote for us when he goes inside the polling booth. Why should you hold anyone physically, when we are not doing anything of that sort ?'

I must confess that our inner circle of supporters had taken a decision to pick up a quarrel with Ujagar, if the myth of his *goonda-gardi* had to be shattered. With this in mind, I moved slowly towards him, while saying that we should allow the voters to exercise their right freely. As soon as I was within striking distance, I punched him on his waist in perfect European style. When he fell flat on the metalled road, I delivered a few kicks on the different parts of his body. A thanedar, who was standing at some distance, came running towards me and asked, 'What has happened ?' I complained that the man was forcibly leading away our voters. The thanedar also delivered a few blows of his stick on the fallen adversary. Ujagar picked up his turban and roared at me, 'It seems that you do not know me.' I said to the thanedar, 'Sardar Sahib! Kindly get aside. Let me introduce myself to him more closely.' The thanedar, however, did not let me have my way. He hit Ujagar with his stick and led him away. Immediately, I was surrounded by our jubilant supporters, who declared, 'Comrade! We had been hoping for a trial of strength. This has actually happened. You need not do anything more.' The incident had a dramatic impact. Ujagar's terror dissipated. A sizeable section of his supporters voted for our candidate.

If I thought that peace had been restored at the polling booth, I was mistaken. For, Ujagar's wife stormed into the place and began to pull two women by their arms. I said to her, 'Bibi! You cannot say or do anything to the voters, once they have entered the polling booth. We will not allow the use of force. You could have called them outside and talked to them.' She was as big a bully as her husband. She declared, 'You cannot stop me. These are our voters.' Since I had been confronted by a woman, I kept my cool and said, 'Bibi! In this place, certain rules and regulations are in operation. It is wrong on your part to interfere in the process of polling.' While we were arguing in this manner, a policeman was watching, but he did not make any move. Realizing that my arguments had failed to have any impact on her, I caught hold of her arm and tried to pull her out. She shouted, 'Vey Bhai! Who are you to hold me by the arm?' Now, this was too much on her part. I lost my temper and retaliated, 'Bibi! Listen to me. You should not say such silly things. You must understand that this is a political fight. Do you think that I have fallen for you at this polling booth.' At this juncture the policeman, who had been a silent spectator, came towards us to find out the cause of the quarrel. I told him that she was Ujagar's wife and was forcibly pulling the voters. The policeman raised his baton to hit her, but I stopped him from doing so. Anyhow, he forced her to leave the polling booth.

The pattern of voting was tilted in our favour because we were able to get even those votes which would not have come to us had this incident not occurred.[5] While we were waiting in our camp at the end of the polling, a number of inquistive persons came to see the man who had taught a lesson to the infamous local goonda. Even long after this election, the people of the area did not forget to invite me to their place. In this manner, I tried to perform, like a true communist, all those duties which were assigned to me from time to time by the party.

During the tenure of Pratap Singh Kairon as Chief Minister of Punjab, over Rs. 32 crore was imposed as tax on the peasantry of Punjab. This was known as the betterment levy (*khush haisiyati* tax). The rationale behind this move was that the productivity of agricultural land and the economic condition of the peasantry had improved following the use of canal water, which had became available in the wake of the completion of the Bhakra-Nangal project.[6] The move was seen as a major challenge by the peasantry of the state, which saw no justification in its imposition. The CPI opposed the measures by launching a massive and sustained struggle against it. In fact, it was the biggest mass agitation of the post-independence period, when the peasantry was mobilized on an unprecedented scale.

A.K. Gopalan, a member of Parliament, and N. Prasada Rao, general secretary of the All India Kisan Sabha, came to Punjab and provided active leadership.

It was true that the levy could not have any impact on Hoshiarpur district, except some areas of Garhshankar tahsil. The district unit of the CPI made a significant contribution in building up the movement: we visited each and every village and explained the implications of the levy.[7] Day after day, we organized a contingent (*jatha*) from a particular village and escorted it to Hoshiarpur in a procession. The contingent was invariably accompanied by drummers and *gatka* parties. People of the villages, which lay on the way, came out in large number and joined the procession. Amidst shouting of revolutionary slogans, these *jathas* boarded buses bound for Chandigarh, where they courted arrest. The district committee also organized a hunger strike at Dasuya in connection with the agitation (*morcha*) where Pratap Chand Dhoot, Charan Das, Banta Ram and others played a prominent role.[8]

The movement gathered momentum during February and March 1959, as an endless stream of *jathas* (from different villages by turn) poured into the state capital. A power-drunk Kairon adopted an aggressive posture and refused to see the writing on the wall. He took recourse to state repression in order to suppress the movement.[9] Police opened fire at Narur Panchta (near Phagwara) and Atiyana (in Ludhiana district) where eleven persons were killed. Some of our comrades, who were trying to reach Narur via Bhungarni, were forcibly prevented by the police from proceeding further. The firing failed to demoralize the peasantry, even as a shock wave swept the country. A militant upsurge began to be felt in every village and hamlet of Punjab. The state government was brought to its knees. It announced the withdrawal of the hated levy, but caused a considerable amount of confusion which was designed to salvage its battered image.[10] This victory of the peasantry should be attributed to the tireless efforts made by the CPI's workers in the countryside and that, too, in the face of growing police repression. It should be noted here that the morcha was led by the communists, while the leadership of other political parties remained aloof. But the political boundaries crumbled at the level of the masses. Since the issue affected almost the entire peasantry of the state, it participated in the morcha with great enthusiasm and remained indifferent to the official attitude of the political parties with which they were otherwise affiliated.

In 1962, elections for the Panchayat Samiti were held. Four of us – Chanan Singh Dhoot, Harbhajan Singh Ramdaspur, Beant Singh Mallewall and myself – were elected to this body from the Bhunga block. The elected members were required to co-opt two members, a woman and a Harijan.[11] The ground situation was such that if the four of us appeared together, we could dominate the situation and secure the co-option of members of our choice. Since this did not suit the interests of the government, it began to sabotage the democratic process. It evolved a game plan by which the four of us were prevented from taking part in the co-option. It issued warrants for our arrest. What could be done to meet the challenge? The party decided that Chanan Singh Dhoot and I should not attend this particular meeting of the Panchayat Samiti. However, Harbhajan Singh Ramdaspur and Beant Singh Mallewal were directed to go ahead and participate in this meeting. The question was how to enable these two members to perform their duty. In order to find an answer to this question, the four of us met a day before the meeting and deliberated over the prevailing situation and examined various ways to outsmart the authorities. The co-option was to be held at the Government Rest House at Bhunga and it was to be presided over by a magistrate. Since the government had its own axe to grind, it had deployed a large number of policemen at the building, which had been transformed into a fortress. Undeterred by this information, we finalized a plan of action.

Harbajan Singh Ramdaspur and Beant Singh Mallewal had to wade through a flowing torrent (*choe*) to reach Bhunga as this was the only route to approach the place. The Government Rest House stood in the midst of a garden, which was surrounded by a fence of barbed wire. Inside the garden, there was a grove of trees, which led right up to the building. The two elected members of the Panchayat Samiti were directed to enter the garden through the barbed wire fence, to approach the building quickly by using the trees as a cover and to rush into the building in a sudden burst of speed. The next morning, the two comrades reached Bhunga and saw that the police had laid a tight cordon around the Government Rest House. Constables were posted all around the roof to keep a watch on the visitors from a long distance. A large number of common people had gathered in full strength, in anticipation of our showdown against the authorities. In accordance with our plan, the two comrades entered the garden through the barbed wire fence and reached the grove of trees. From this point, Harbhajan Singh Ramdaspur ran across the verandah and reached the durbar of the presiding officer, where our candidates were already present. Beant Singh Mallewal could not run fast because of his physical disability and was arrested. Harbhajan Singh Ramdaspur was also taken into custody. The police action provoked the crowd which, unable to control its passion, raised anti-government slogans. The police also arrested those who seemed to be leading the crowd. The arrested persons, including Harbhajan Singh Ramdaspur and Beant Singh Mallewal, were taken to Nabha jail where they were incarcerated for a month.[12] In this manner, the elected representatives of the people were deprived of their democratic rights. The oft-repeated claims made by the government regarding the revival of basic democratic institutions turned out to be a farce.[13]

During the assembly elections of 1962, Pratap Chand Dhoot was chosen by the CPI as its candidate from Sham Chaurasi.[14] It was an extraordinarily large constituency which included the villages of Sikri, Boorey, Nariayi, Mallewal, Zail Dhaddar, Janauri, Dholbaha, Nangal Bihala and Budhewal. Extending from Dasuya, it covered the entire hilly area up to Tangar Mahora, near Kangra. I was appointed as the campaign in-charge. A core group of activists was formed which included Harbhajan Singh Ramdaspur, Beant Singh Mallewal, Bhulla Singh, Puran Singh and Sampooran Singh, besides the new workers of Nangal Bihala. Organizing an election campaign in such a large constituency was indeed a challenging task because of limited financial resources. We had a mini bus which could accommodate about twenty-five workers. We also hired a fleet of twelve bicycles from the neighbouring town of Hoshiarpur. I planned the entire schedule of engagements for each day. At least ten meetings were organized everyday. Every morning, we started from Dhoot Kalan at 7.00 a.m. and returned late in the evening at 11.00 p.m. Sometimes we convened a single meeting for two or three villages, so as to contact the maximum number of people. We did not hesitate to hold a meeting even if the gathering consisted of twenty or thirty persons.[14]

Each meeting (*jalsa*) began with my introductory remarks. I was followed by the main speaker, Master Hari Singh, who spoke for about ten to fifteen minutes. At the end, the candidate delivered a short speech for about five minutes. Thereafter we drove in our bus to the next village. We explained the policies and programmes of the CPI, besides exposing the Congress for having failed to fulfil its promises of the pre-independene period and for pursuing an anti-poor agenda of economic growth. The influence of the CPI continued to increase because majority of the people in the constituency, being the poorest in Punjab, were able to identify themselves with us. However, scarcity of resources was a major problem. Our humble collections were just enough to meet the expenses of fuel for our bus, but not enough for the wear and tear of our bicycles. We were forced to approach our relatives and friends in every village to provide for our workers. In spite of these difficulties, our candidate secured over 11,000 votes against 13,000 of the winner.[15] Nevertheless, the election campaign went a long way in consolidating the base of the party in the area.

The sixth congress of the CPI was held (7-16 April 1961) at Vijayawada. A Soviet delegation had been invited to take part in the proceedings. It included Prof. Kajloff, who was my teacher when I was studying in Moscow about three decades ago. He met Chanan Singh Dhoot, who was attending the congress as a delegate from Hoshiarpur district, and inquired about me. When he learnt that I was unable to attend because of an illness, he said, 'We are supposed to stay for another eighteen days in New Delhi. We would be extremely happy to see him. If possible, let him come to our embassy.' On his return from the south, Chanan Singh Dhoot conveyed the message to me. I recalled my days in Moscow and had a strong desire to meet my former teacher. Prof. Kajloff had not only lectured us on political economy and history, but had also cultivated affectionate social relations with us. A wise and intelligent person, he would explain various subjects in Punjabi. (Of course, Prof. Dyakov was more proficient than him in Punjabi, as he had also mastered the ability to write in this language.) Prof. Kajloff would accompany us whenever we visited factories and clubs, as part of our curriculum. On these occasions, he acted as a very efficient interpreter between us and the Russians. There was no doubt that he was an unforgettable character. I did not want to miss the opportunity to meet him and pay my respects.

I travelled to New Delhi and reported at the office of Tass, the Soviet news agency, which was located on the Barakhamba Road. The officers were informed about my visit. I was driven to the residential street, where a large number of Russians were staying. Since it was extremely hot, the delegates had taken off their clothes and were resting. They were looking forward to my visit, as they had been informed about my association with the Soviet Union. When they saw me, they guessed my identity. At that moment, Prof. Kajloff was not present, as he had gone to a neighbouring building. When I appeared on the scene, I greeted the delegates in Russian, 'Darastey'. They were delighted hearing this and extended a warm welcome to me. A message was sent to Prof. Kajloff and a feast was arranged. When Prof. Kajloff arrived, we embraced and inquired about each other's well-being. The delegates asked me whether I still knew the Russian language. I told them that I could understand it to some extent, but could not express myself in it as I had not used it for a very long time. Prof. Kajloff said to me that he had been receiving regular reports about my political activities in Calcutta, Jamshedpur and other places. He informed the other delegates about my education in Moscow, the one-year advanced training given to me at the instance of the Comintern, the struggles in which I had been involved and the hardships I had faced in various jails. He added, 'Other teachers and I often recalled your sincerity and attachment to your studies. We had nurtured a high opinion about your commitment to Marxism. We took pride in the fact that you have risen more than equal to the expectations which we had formed about you.'

After the delegates had been given complete details about my political activities in India, a brief ceremony was organized to confer a number of medals on me. I thanked them profusely for their gesture of goodwill. At this moment, Ajoy Kumar Ghosh's wife came to escort some of the delegates who wanted to go shopping. I rose to take my leave, but the delegates insisted that I spend more time with them. Some of the visitors left for shopping and others stayed back to continue their discussion with me. Fortunately, one of the delegates knew a smattering of English. We continued to exchange views on a variety of subjects, using an instant mixture of Russian and English. Finally, I bade farewell to the Soviet comrades and prepared to leave. As a parting gift, they gave me tinned food which I carried back to Dhoot Kalan.

There had been a long-standing dispute within the CPI on the issue of its programme. It had been argued that the programme should be based on the concrete conditions prevailing in the country. It was true that a few programmes had been formulated – one around 1934 and another later – but they had failed to make an accurate scientific analysis of the Indian society.[16] A struggle was launched within the party to resolve this issue, and evolve an appropriate and viable political programme. We understood that sailors were guided on the high seas by the needle of the magnetic compass. Similarly, revolutionaries marched towards their cherished goal by following the path chalked out by the programme.

There were two approaches to such a programme. The first approach adhered to those principles on which the earlier programme was structured and which had been rejected by us as flawed. In spite of our rejection, these old tendencies persisted. Two different viewpoints emerged both in the central committee and the various state committees (including that of Punjab) whenever any resolution, thesis or blueprint came up for discussion. This kind of conflict had persisted for ten to twelve years in the party forums. In spite of this, the party managed to pull along by accomodating the two contradictory approaches.[17] Such a situation, however, could not continue indefinitely because of the fundamental differences in the political thinking of the two sides. A stage was reached in the ongoing tussle, when the possibilities of compromise were exhausted. To put it more appropriately, there was no scope for compromise in Marxism. If the true scientific principles of Marxism were permitted to make any compromise with any other approach, then its real substance was likely to be diluted. There was a powerful trend against right wing thinking, while the latter described us as ***markabad***. As the common ground between the two approaches continued to shrink and the differences refused to be reconciled,[18] a formal split in the party took place in 1964.

Here, we were confronted by an important question. According to the principles of Marxism and the guidelines laid down for party organization by the first, second and third Comintern, only one communist party could exist in a country. But in India, two communist parties – CPM and CPI – emerged, the members of each calling themselves communists. What was the position on the international front? After the death of Stalin, Khrushchev came to power and led the CPSU towards the right wing.[19] The decisions of the twentieth congress of the party were loaded heavily with reformist content. While advocating parliamentary means to achieve a socialist revolution, it laid much emphasis on peaceful competition, peaceful coexistence and peaceful transformation.[20] On the other hand, we firmly believed that a socialist revolution could be brought about only by a revolution of the proletariat, for history had clearly shown that capitalism could never be eliminated through peaceful or parliamentary means. Second, there were fundamental differences between us and the right wing on the role of various classes in the Indian society. The right wing believed that a section of Indian capitalism could play a revolutionary role in society. But we did not accept this position.

At the other extreme were the Naxalites (who were fairly similar to the Nirodniks of Russia) who had adopted the path of terrorism.[21] Instead of having faith in the strength of the working class, they relied on acts of individual heroism. They received strong support from the Communist Party of China, which believed that the objective and subjective conditions for bringing about a revolution were ripe in India, that the path chosen by the Naxalites to achieve their goal was correct and that the Congress-led Indian government was a mere tool in the hands of US imperialism and comprador bourgeoisie and, therefore, these forces had to be fought against with all their might.[22] Historical experience has shown that the approach of the Naxalites, too, was seriously flawed. Thus, the situation was exacerbated by more than one theoretical complications.

The phenomenon of differences within the ranks of the communists was not confined to India. In Russia also, two opposing trends had emerged in the Social Democratic Party during the early part of the twentieth century. The one represented by Lenin adhered strictly to Marxism and developed serious differences with the right wing reformists on the issues of party programme and the role of various classes in the Russian society. Whereas it was important to analyse the underlying logic of the two trends, it was equally essential to examine their respective consequences. Historical experience has clearly indicated that only Lenin's approach ultimately assumed a practical shape. When the revolution of 1905 took place, the Mensheviks did not support it. During the First World War (1917), Lenin made an incisive analysis of the international situation at Brussels and other places, where the communists of various countries had gathered. Unfortunately, the supporters of the right wing approach did not support Lenin's viewpoint, but joined hands with the capitalist forces in their respective countries. After the February Revolution, the Mensheviks and social revolutionaries collaborated with the Cadet Party which represented the interests of the Russian capitalist class.[23] They fought tooth and nail against the Bolshevik Party which was led by Lenin. These groups acquired a majority in the Soviets, which were formed after the collapse of the Czarist regime, and enabled the formation of the Kerensky-led government comprising pro-capitalist political outfits.

Kerensky's government failed to fulfil any of the promises which were made during the February Revolution, e.g. withdrawal from the war, abolition of the feudal system and autonomy for the nationalities. It was little wonder that within eight months it was reduced to a minority.[24] On the other hand, the Bolsheviks, under the leadership of Lenin and Stalin, adopted an appropriate programme and effective policy so that they succeeded in acquiring a majority in the Soviets. They took up the unfinished tasks of the previous regime and completed them with the support of the masses and on the basis of a correct application of Marxist principles. Thus, within a period of eight months, they brought about the October Revolution. Thereafter, the Mensheviks and social revolutionaries aligned themselves with counter-revolutionaries, feudal lords and Czarist stooges. They supported the fourteen monarchies, which invaded the Soviet Union to suppress the revolution. Having emerged clearly as counter-revolutionaries, they fought along with the White Guards, became agents of the invading imperialist powers and even conspired to kill Lenin. To begin with, the Mensheviks and other similar groups described themselves as communists. But the outcome of the struggle, during the three revolutions, proved that the Lenin-led Bolshevik Party was the true representative of Marxism.

Some people alleged that our differences with the right wing were not based on principles or ideology and that they reflected merely a clash over leadership. But this was far from true. We did not join the party to capture offices and posts. We were adherents of Marxism-Leninism, which we have always kept in the centre of our vision. We have been fighting to ensure the success of this principle. We were engaged in organizing that force which was supposed to show the path leading to the revolution, by placing all its fighting contingents on the front, as it were, so as to inflict a crushing defeat on the capitalist enemy. Our detractors often highlighted our inadequate numerical strength. These people should bear in mind that when Marx and Engles propounded the Communist Manifesto in 1848, very few people were attracted to the idea. The position of communists was extremely weak. The common masses could not understand Marx when he stated that capitalism had given birth to its own grave diggers. It was now easy to comprehend the significance of his words because over two arab people (out of a total of five arab) were engaged in constructing communism in different parts of the world. The ideology developed by Marx and Engels showed the right direction to the toiling millions of the world. Marx had predicted that those nations, which had enslaved others, could never remain free. This proved to be true, for a large number of colonies have succeeded in throwing off the yoke of imperialism. Imperialists and social democrats of various powerful European countries did not express any interest in improving the lot of the people living in their colonies. On the other hand, Marxism has assumed a practical shape in many parts of the globe.

After the split, the CPM formulated its programme at the Calcutta congress, while the CPI did so at Bombay. More than two decades have passed since then but our party, the CPM, has never been called upon to amend its programme, as it has proved to be correct in practice. On the other hand, the reformists who also claimed to be communists and who were supported by the Khrushchevites, failed to develop an appropriate programme. When we separated from them, our position (both at the national level and in the various states) was quite weak.[25] More than two decades later, all political parties – including the ruling Congress and the various opposition groups – had no hesitation in admitting that the CPM had emerged as a strong cadre-based party and that it was continuously growing in strength. The party succeeded in forming ministries in Bengal, Tripura and Kerala. In the coming elections, it was hoped that it would not only win in Bengal and Tripura, but it would also come back to power in Kerala. The party has strengthened its position in the entire country.[26]

During the course of my visit to England in 1986, some former comrades expressed the view that the CPM existed only in name. Strongly refuting this observation I argued, 'On what basis can you hold that our party has a nominal existence? You people left India long time ago. You do not have first-hand knowledge of the present situation. The only thing you can do is to criticize the party. Do you know the means to measure the strength of the party? In the first instance, the number of our cadres has gone up tremendously. We have become strong enough to establish our own trade union, though we were nowhere to begin with. Similar is the case with the kisan sabhas, student bodies and women's organizations. Look at the number of our newspapers which are being published at the national level as well as in the regional languages. Look at the circulation of these journals and the number of their subscribers. All these factors, taken together, indicate the growing strength of the party. The decisions taken by the party at the twelfth congress, which was held in Calcutta, is another pointer in the same direction. It has consolidated its position on every front. That is why it succeeded in implementing its constitutional and organizational principles. Look at the developments in Kerala. The party learnt that some prominent comrades of that state were going on the wrong track. It sent a delegation of senior members to Kerala to persuade these people to correct themselves. However, when the comrades of Kerala refused to listen to sane advice, they were expelled from the party. Such a stringent action can only be taken by that party which is exceptionally strong. Similar action was taken against Jagjit Singh Lyallpuri, an important communist leader of Punjab. As opposed to this, there is no discipline and co-ordination among the right wing communists. As a consequence, their party is becoming progressively weak, with no steps having been taken to stop the downward slide.'[27]

After the split, some people asked the question, 'Which party is supporting you at the international level?' Our answer was that we did not need the support of any party belonging to another country. Our only support lay in Marxism. We were marching forward in accorandance with the ideological direction given by Marxism. What do we see in recent times? The Communist Party of China violated the organizational principles of Marxism while determining its attitude towards us. If it had observed any shortcoming in a sister party, it ought to have conveyed its objection in writing, or better still, it could have sought clarifications in a specially convened meeting. Instead, it took open recourse to its radio and international media to broadcast its criticism of our party. In fact, it went to the extent of launching personal attacks on our leaders. These highly objectionable tactics were the same as those adopted by certain countries to damn their enemies in the eyes of the world. Things have, however, changed for the better. The Chinese not only thoroughly reviewed their earlier policy, but also realized that they were wrong. On their invitation, an Indian delegation (which included Harkishan Singh Surjeet) visited China. During the course of detailed discussions, almost every outstanding issue was sorted out and the misunderstandings were resolved. It was true that a few differences continued a persist, but it was hoped that these, too, would be resolved soon. Cordial relations were established between the two parties because of our party's correct approach, which was based on the Marxist principles of party organization.

On the other hand, the right wing communists have described the Communist Party of China as their main enemy. They have indiscriminately condemned our Chinese counterparts and, in doing so, they have discarded all restraint and caution. On many occasions, we have refuted their false propaganda and have come out in defence of the Chinese. We followed the same policy when the Russians made unfair ciriticism of the Chinese. But we have taken care to be impartial in these matters.[28] In line with this, we were bold enough to differ from the Chinese whenever they adopted an unreasonable attitude towards the Soviet Union. At the international level, too, we have followed the correct Marxist approach.

A delegation of the party visited North Korea, where communism has been established. Their experiences were reported to us by Harkishan Singh Surjeet. It was good to hear that the country had witnessed spectacular economic growth in a short span of time. During the course of mutual discussions, the Indian delegates wanted to know which factors had contributed to the dramatic improvements. The Koreans attributed their economic progress to a scientific and judicious use of their natural resources, which they had in abundance. During its stay, the Indian delegation was asked by the hosts to praise the son of Kim-il-Sung, who had played an active role in the Communist Party of Korea.[29] The delegation, however, refused to oblige the hosts, 'We are quite familiar with the great contribution of Kim-il-Sung to the spread of the communist movement in the world. His political thinking and sacrifices have already become a part of history. His shining example will always serve as a source of inspiration for communists all over the world. But, at the moment, we are not in a position to say anything in favour of his son.' My purpose in mentioning this is to emphasize that delegations of our party – wherever they have gone – have never resorted to sycophancy or cheap politicking to secure temporary gains. Instead, we have always been fair and impartial in our approach. We have established our position at the international level only by following the path of Marxism.

The attitude of the Communist Party of the Soviet Union towards us was different. The CPSU and the CPI had supported each other since the beginning, because both of them were guided by the decisions of the twentieth congress, which had taken a sharp turn towards the right. Therefore, the CPSU had attacked our standpoint. The leadership of our party met this criticism with courage and equanimity. In fact, we did not succumb to the pressure of either China or the Soviet Union. We continued to follow an independent policy. When I went to England in 1987, an old comrade by the name of Sarwan Singh (who worked at the London airport) informed me that a delegation of our party, including Harkishan Singh Surjeet, had been invited to attend the twenty-seventh congress of the CPSU. The news filled me with so much joy that I could not sleep that night owing to sheer excitement. I remained awake, reflecting on the evolution of our party's policy, which had been vindicated in the long run.

NOTES AND REFERENCES

1. Since the CPI endeavoured to shape the total life of its members, its discipline embraced their public as well as private lives. Apart from political errors, disciplinary action was taken if a member was found guilty of being a strike breaker, a habitual drunkard or a betraryer of party confidence. J.S. Brar, *The Communist Party in Punjab,* pp. 70-1.
2. Membership of the provincial unit of the CPI increased from 1,527 in 1948 to 10,587 in 1961. The 1958 analysis of social and occupational background indicated that peasants formed 70.5 per cent of the membership, agricultutral labourers 13.1, industrial workers 9.5 and non-manual workers 6.7. The majority of recruits were from the same familiar social background, i.e. Jat Sikh middle peasantry which formed nearly 80 per cent of the membership. Gurharpal Singh, *Communism in Punjab,* pp. 209-11.
3. Prior to 1958 the provincial unit was headed by a secretariat,

consiting of the state secretary and two or three leading members, which performed routine operational duties. The premier provincial body was the Provincial Committee comprising thirteen to seventeen members. In 1958, it was bifurcated into the State Council and the State Executive Committee with seventy-five and twenty-four members respectively. Functions of the provincial unit were clearly demarcated and decentralized, while the size of executive units was increased. The District Committees, organized geographically and functionally, emulated the divison of responsibilities in the higher bodies and supervised the work of lower units like branches and cells. Gurharpal Singh, op. cit., pp. 207-8.

4. An extraordinary congress of the CPI was held at Amritsar (6-13 April 1958) against the backdrop of the recommendations of the twentieth congress of the CPSU and the formation of the first ever democratically elected communist government in Kerala. Adopting a new constitution, the CPI committed itself to achieving full democracy and socialism by peaceful means, i.e. by winning a majority in Parliament which was backed by mass sanctions. For details, see Victor M. Fic, *Peaceful Transition to Communism in India: Strategy of the Communist Party,* pp. 333-67.
5. The percentage of votes secured by the CPI in the 1957 Vidhan Sabha election was substantially more than that secured in subsequent elections. In Ludhiana, the figure was 14.6 per cent. For a tabular representation of electoral support, see Brar, op. cit., p. 217.
6. The Punjab Betterment Charges and Acreage Rates Act (1952) allowed the government to charge a betterment levy on capital gains (from rising land values) on irrigated lands to recover the uproductive cost of the Bhakra-Nangal project. On 5 January 1959, the Kairon government promulgated an ordinance to collect advance payments, ranging from Rs. 80-225 per acre. Gurharpal Singh, op. cit., p. 196.
7. To understand the case against the betterment levy built up by the left faction within the Punjab unit of the CPI, which was leading the agitation, see Gurharpal Singh, op. cit., p. 197.
8. The nature of political mobilization was confirmed in an interview with Pratap Chand Dhoot on 1 April 1997 at Dhoot Kalan.
9. The Kairon government adopted repressive measures to demoralize the agitating peasantry. A fine of Rs. 200 or two months' imprisonment was ruthlessly imposed on farmers who failed to pay the levy. The properties of leading communists and kisan activitsts were attached. By March 1959, 7,000 agitators had

been arrested and 11 persons had lost their lives. The agitation, which continued for over six weeks, was finally withdrawn on 22 March 1959. Gurharpal Singh, op. cit., p. 198.

10. Taking Advantage of the ideological rift between the left faction in Punjab and the national leadership of the CPI, Kairon opened direct negotiations with Ajoy Kumar Ghosh, general secretary of the CPI, and N. Prasada Rao, general secretary of the AIKS. Acting on the vague assurance of the Kairon government, Ghosh authorized withdrawal of the 48-day long agitation, without consulting the Action Committee. Since the basic demand had not been met, the embarrassed left faction in the Punjab CPI turned its ire against Ghosh and Rao. Gurharpal Singh, op. cit., p. 200.
11. The local government in rural areas had a three-tier structure, viz., village panchayats, panchayat samitis and zila parishads. In Punjab, these bodies included eight to twelve primary members who were elected by panches and sarpanches, legislators of state assemblies who were treated as associate members and the subdivisonal officer or block development officer who was regarded as an ex-officio member. Another category of members was included by co-option, viz., three members from cooperative institutions, two from scheduled castes and scheduled tribes and four women. Shriram Maheshwari, *Local Government in India,* p. 103.
12. The entire episode was confirmed by Beant Singh Mallewal and Harbhajan Singh Ramdaspur, the two persons directly involved, in their interviews on 2 April 1997 at Dhoot Kalan.
13. This experience has been corroborated by recent studies on Punjab, which noted that the panchayati raj institutions failed to function in a satisfactory manner. The Administrative Reforms Commission identified several factors contributing to this situation. These included, among others, the government's lack of faith in these bodies, political interference, police hostility and faulty methods of election. G. Ram Reddy, ed., *Patterns of Panchayati Raj in India,* p. 239.
14. The facts regarding this election campaign were corroborated by the candidate, Partap Chand Dhoot, in an interview on 1 April 1997 at Dhoot Kalan.
15. During the 1962 Vidhan Sabha elections in Punjab, the CPI won 7 out of 47 seats contested by it, securing 7.10 per cent of votes. Brar, op. cit., p. 208.
16. After frequent shifting of positions on outstanding political issues during nearly three decades of its existence, the CPI adopted in 1951 its first ever programme and tactical line. However, it had

three major flaws. For details, see Javeed Alam, 'Communist Politics in Search of Hegemony', in Partha Chatterjee, ed., *Wages of Freedom: Fifty Years of the Nation State,* p. 192.

17. The intra-party dissensions over some fundamental issues – characterization of the Indian bourgeoisie, nature of the Indian state, the configuration of diverse social classes and the stage of the Indian revolution – divided Indian communism into Right, Left and Centre. However, formal separation was avoided by compromises between the various factions. Differences were intensified by the Sino-Soviet ideological dispute and the Indo-China war, leading to the historic split of 1964.
18. The two parties presented two distinct communist models which differed sharply on the nature of the Indian state, the character of the Indian bourgeoisie, the course of Indian capitalist growth, tactics during a trasitional stage on the road to socialism, relative utility of parliamentary and extra-parliamentary forms of struggle, the role of violence in the quest for socialism, the attitude towards the Congress, particularly the so-called progressive measures of Indira Gandhi. For details, see Bhabani Sen Gupta, *CPI-M: Promises, Prospects, Problems,* pp. 31-52.
19. Nikita Khrushchev (1953-64) introduced wide ranging reforms, which transformed all aspects of Soviet life. Emphasis was laid on the production of consumer goods. Prices were reduced and wages of the lower paid were raised. A seven-hour day was introduced for workers, while factory trade unions were given more responsibilities. Modern industries like chemicals and plastics were encouraged. Multinational corporations like Pirelli, Shell and Fiat entered into 49 per cent partnership with the government. In the agricultural sector, the authority of the central ministry was reduced, while supervisory functions were delegated to the local party organizations. The number of collectives was reduced owing to mergers, while that of state farms increased. Procurement price was raised, but procurement quotas were reduced. In the drive for de-Stalinization, political terror was abolished. J.N. Westwood, *Endurance and Endeavour: Russian History,* pp. 387-95.
20. Formulations of the twentieth congress (February 1956) of the CPSU constituted a significant departure from the existing Marxist-Leninist understanding of socialist construction. First, it advocated peaceful existence of countries, with different social systems, failing which there could be devastating wars. Second, it visualized the real possibility of averting wars of aggression, owing to the existence of socialist and peace loving states. Third, it recognized

diverse forms of transition to socialism, including conquest of parliamentary institutions by the proletariat. Fourth, it denounced the Stalinist personality cult for introducing several distortions in the Soviet socialist system. Andrew Rothstein and Clemens Dutt, eds., *History of the Communist Party of the Soviet Union,* pp. 643-51.

21. The word was derived from narodnichestvo, a form of socialist thought peculiar to Russia. Developed largely during the second half of the nineteenth century, it was promoted through the writings of Herzen, Chernyshevsky, Pisarev, Bukanin, Tkachev and Lavrov. It envisioned a mass peasant uprising in which the critically thinking individuals had a crucial role to play. These ideas were propagated by hundreds of men and women who flocked to the villages and took up jobs as teachers, doctors, nurses and clerks. Realizing the difficulty of mobilizing people from below, they resorted to terrorist actions. On 1 March 1881, they succeeded in killing Czar Alexander II. These terrorist outfits were ruthlessly crushed by an autocratic state. Jesse D. Clarkson, *A History of Russia: From the Ninth Century*, pp. 370-83.
22. In 1969, the Naxalites accused the CPM of being revisionist, discarded parliamentarianism and advocated the liberation of rural masses from the clutches of landlords through an armed agrarian revolution, following in the footsteps of Mao Tse Tung. Apart from Bengal, the movement spread to Andhra Pradesh, Tamil Nadu, Kerala and Punjab. For an exhaustive evaluation of the revolt, its fragmentation and defeat in 1972, besides its recent resurrection, see Sumanta Banerjee, *India's Simmering Revolution: The Naxalite Uprising*, New Delhi, 1984.
23. The Constitutional Democratic Party, known as the Cadets, emerged at the beginning of the twentieth century and was a liberal-bourgeois organization, which included the representatives of the middle classes as well as commercial and industrial groups. Its programme, like the English liberals, envisaged a constitutional monarchy curbed by a parliamentary body. Led by the historian Miliukov, it had some brilliant intellectuals and businessmen in its ranks. A.G. Majour, *Russia: Past and Present*, p. 366.
24. During the tumultous period of July-October 1917, Alexander F. Kerensky served as the prime minister of a provisional government, which was composed of diverse political elements. He made frequent changes in his cabinet, convened several political conferences, aimed at victory in the war and announced ill-defined reforms. As the army threatened to disintegrate, the

peasants took to violence on a large scale and workers demanded seizure of factories and mines. The Kornilov affair, the continuous advance of the Germans and the Bolshevik victory in the Petrograd Soviet led to the fall of Kerensky. For details, see E.H. Carr, *The Bolshevik Revolution: 1917-1923*, vol. I, pp. 102-11.

25. The factual position appears to be quite different. Even two decades after the split, the CPI was the larger of the two communist parties in terms of membership. In 1986, the CPI had 4,78,905 members, a decline from 5,46,732 in 1978. In 1985, the total membership of the CPM was close to 3,70,000. Achin Vanaik, *The Painful Transition,* p. 228, n. 12.
26. In 1981, the total membership of the CPM was 2,78,247 which rose to 3,67,828 in 1985 – an increase of nearly 90,000. During the same period, Bengal registered an increase of 54,480 and Kerala 17,986. Over 2.4 lakh members, i.e. nearly two-thirds joined the party after 1977. Membership of mass organizations crossed 14 million. According to the 1984 statistics, the membership included kisan front 6.7 million, labour front 1.8 million, youth front 2.5 million, agricultural labour front 8.9 million, women front 1.2 million and student front 1.05 million. *Political Organisation Report of the Twelfth Congress of the Communist Party of India (Marxist),* Calcutta, 25-30 December 1985, p. 59.
27. Statistics enable us to compare the political space occupied by the two main communist parties in parliamentary politics.

	Results of Lok Sabha Elections				
	1967	1971	1977	1980	1984
CPI	23 (5.1)	23 (4.7)	7 (2.8)	11 (2.6)	6 (2.7)
CPM	19 (4.4)	25 (5.1)	22 (4.3)	36 (6.1)	22 (5.8)

Adapted from T.J. Nossiter, 'Communism in Rajiv Gandhi's India', *Third World Quarterly,* October 1985, in Achin Vanaik, op. cit., p. 228, Table 12. [Figures in brackets show percentage of votes.]

28. At its ninth congress (1968), the CPM decided to adopt equidistance from the Soviet and Chinese communist parties. At the tenth congress (Jalandhar, 1978), it defined equidistance as the right to cultivate friendship of the two giant communist parties on its own terms and criticize the domestic and foreign policies of both. Unlike most communist parties of the world, the CPM favoured expanding friendship between the developing countries and communist giants, but opposed the interference of Moscow

and China in their domestic affairs, particularly linkages with revolutionary movements. Both have been accused of subordinating the development of revolutionary forces in underdeveloped countries to the opportunistic needs of their foreign policies. Bhabani Sen Gupta, op. cit., p. 20.

29. Born in 1912, Kim-il-Sung joined the Korean Communist Party in 1931. He led an armed resistance against the Japanese occupation of Korea in the 1930s. During the Second World War, be joined the Soviet army at the head of a Korean contingent. In 1948, he assumed the chairmanship of the Korean workers party and established a communist government in the Democratic Republic of Korea (North Korea), with the support of the Soviet Union. In 1950, he made an unsuccessful attempt to bring South Korea under his sway. With Chinese support, he repelled the invasion of North Korea by the UNO-led American forces. Since then he concentrated on building a socialist state in North Korea.

APPENDIX

From the Split to the Emergency

[Owing to a technical snag in the recording system, we were not able to preserve the record of NSD's personal experiences, pertaining to the post-split phase. However, we succeeded in obtaining considerable information on the subject from several CPM activists, who were intimately associated with him during the course of numerous struggles and agitations. These associates included Pratap Chand Dhoot, Harbhajan Singh Ramdaspur, Beant Singh Mallewal, Mohinder Singh Sangha, Dalbir Singh Dhoot (the younger son of NSD), Kewal Kaloti and Nirmal Singh Ashant. The information obtained from these activists/participants has been consolidated in the following chapter, which refers to NSD in the third person.]

The twin villages of Khiala-Bulanda lay adjacent to Dhoot Kalan. Here, the Bedis had been granted 500 acres of land. Of this, they had sold 55 acres to the government which developed it into a seed farm for wheat and other crops. The government managed the farm for a few years. In 1966, it decided to sell the 55-acre farm through public auction, because the enterprise was no longer financially viable. In order to attract the highest bidders, it made a public announcement (*munadi*) in the area. The Hoshiarpur district committee of the CPM decided to oppose the move on account of a number of reasons. First, the farm provided employment to hundreds of workers, who had no other means of livelihood. Second, they were able to procure fodder for their cattle from the farm. Third, the farm could be allotted to a number of landless peasants, as per the government policy of providing 5 acre of land to the poorest stratum of society, instead of handing it over to the urban rich. Fourth, the land could be distributed among these people for building small houses for themselves as they did not have even this necessity.

NSD played a leading role in the movement to save the farm. He visited the neighbouring villages – Khiala, Bairampur and Sotra – and addressed the landless peasants in small meetings. Volunteers were selected, duties were assigned and an action plan was drawn up with a view to frustrate the move for auction. Two days before the auction, the CPM activists launched a vigorous campaign in the villages surrounding Khiala-Bulanda and succeeded in mobilizing the landless peasants.

On the day of the auction, a large number of people, including activists and sympathizers, arrived in Dhoot Kalan to participate in the demonstration. They gathered near the village gurdwara and marched in a procession towards the farm, raising slogans in support of their demands. Meanwhile, the authorities had made extensive arrangements for the auction. The Deputy Commissioner mounted the specially erected stage and explained the official policy on the farm. He highlighted the financial losses incurred by the management and the inability to pay wages to the workers, forcing the government to undertake the auction. The processionists raised slogans and approached the venue. The police intervened and stopped the 1,200 strong gathering from moving ahead. The agitators became restive and raised angry slogans. The Deputy Commissioner sensed the popular mood and asked the police to withdraw. He also permitted the processionists to approach the stage and asked one of their leaders to have his say.

Pratap Chand Dhoot, who had been trained and guided by NSD, went on to the stage and began to speak. He complained, 'Our government has been repeatedly declaring its policy of giving land to the landless. We are poor. We have no land to till, no grain to eat and no fodder for our cattle. You talk of distributing five acre to each one of us, who are spread over these five villages. But you have invited these rich outsiders and urban moneybags to deprive us of our due. We will never tolerate this injustice. We will fight till we achieve our aim.' These words had an electrifying effect, as new slogans were raised – 'Down with the gang of traders' (*veopari tola murdabad*). Seeing their determination and enthusiasm, the Deputy Commissioner felt constrained to cancel the auction. Not only this, he acceded to the request of the demonstrators and visited the interior of Dhoot Kalan. Escorted by Pratap Chand Dhoot and some other prominent activists, he inspected the dwelling places of the poor. He saw that the landless villagers, due to their poverty, lived and cooked in the same place where their cattle were kept. Moved by the appalling living conditions of the poor, the Deputy Commissioner assured that he would not recommend the auction of the farm. Impressed by the manner in which Pratap Chand Dhoot had presented the case of the landless, he inquired, 'How much education have you acquired? When did you join the CPM?' Pratap Chand Dhoot replied, 'I have acquired all my education only in jail. I have been in this party ever since I became a political activist.' The officer took his leave of the villagers and went away.

People of the area thought that the matter had been settled for all times. But they were wrong, for the government revived its policy of auctioning the Khiala-Bulanda farm. Two weeks after this incident, Syal, a Sub-Divisional Magistrate (SDM), arrived with the aim of accomplishing what his predecessor had failed to do. He was accompanied by the usual official entourage, including a sizeable police contingent. Once again a stage was constructed and security arrangements were made. On this occasion, too, people of several villages congregated in full strength and staged an angry demonstration against the government's decision. In fact, they were more determined than ever before. While anti-government slogans were being raised, the front liners pushed aside the police and jumped on to the stage. They snatched the microphone and did not allow the SDM to speak. Though some landlords of Khiala village had come out in support of the government, the latter failed to hold the auction. It was later decided to give the farm on lease. A nursery of various plants was established, which has been operating since then.

In this movement, a major role was played by activists belonging to the landless classes. They included Pratap Chand

Dhoot, Nasib Chand, Ragh Mal, Tulsi Ram and Bakhshish Singh, a Jat of village Sotra. The participation of women on a considerable scale was a noteworthy feature of the movement. They had formed a contingent (*jatha*) of their own and jumped into the fray whenever the police threatened to attack their men. Prominent women participants included Rattan Kaur, Lachhmi, Raj Kaur and Rajjo. Apart from the CPM flag, they carried bamboo sticks (*dangs*), which they did not hesitate to wield.

Government employees, including school teachers, constituted an important segment of society. Their number was large and they were spread all over the state. Being more educated than the peasants and workers, they were politically more conscious and, therefore, played a larger role than was warranted by their numbers. However, it was not easy for them to acquire the capacity of exercising their influence. It was essential for the activists to be adequately conversant with the theory of Marxism-Leninism, the day-to-day tactics of trade union movement and the rules governing the service of employees. They had to be alert and vigilant, for any slackness on this front could be disastrous. Unfortunately, the federation of government employees had been weakened owing to two splits. The first split occurred in 1968, when the federation was divided into two groups – one led by Ranbir Singh Dhillon and the other by Tarlochan Singh Rana. The former was affiliated to the CPI and the latter to the CPM. To begin with, the former was more powerful of the two.

Some government employees, who were posted in Hoshiarpur district and who were affiliated to the CPM, formed an unofficial five-member steering committee comprising Harkanwal Singh, Gurbachan Singh, Jodh Singh, Shavinder Singh and Narinder Singh Ashant. It is worth recalling that a united front of three unions, representing three different categories of teachers, had organized a strike from 2 August 1970. Three leaders, viz., Tarlocan Singh Rana, Bahadur Singh Mangat and Satpal Sharma went on a fast unto death. However, the movement split, as the strike was withdrawn and over thrity activists languished in jail for six to seven months. Though an agreement was reached with the Punjab government through the mediation of Sohan Singh Bassi, it was never implemented. It was in these circumstances that the above-mentioned five-member steering committee decided to launch a united movement for the acceptance of the outstanding demands of government employees. A school of this committee was held (towards the close of 1970) at Hoshiarpur in the district office of the CPM. NSD had been specially invited to this meeting. The committee explained its position, 'We wish to build a united movement of the government employees. We are sincerely committed to our cause. But our problem is numbers. We are not numerically strong.' NSD advised, 'You should enter the movement without any precondition, even if the leadership is not in your hands. Those who are able to establish themselves firmly at the base are bound to emerge at the top. In order to build a movement, it is not necessary for you to be a part of the leadership.' Following this advice, the committee joined the movement with great enthusiasm. It ensured the participation of a large number of employees in the strike of 16 December 1970, the call for which had been given by the Ranbir Singh Dhillon group. The strike turned out to be a huge success.

Encouraged by the overwhelming response, the leadership gave a call for another strike in January 1971. Since the government had decided to suppress the movement, it issued warrants for the arrest of prominent activists who were engaged in mobilizing support for the strike. The police conducted raids to apprehend them but failed in its efforts as a number of them, including Narinder Singh Ashant who was a member of the working committee, went underground. Instead of being a deterrent, the government action proved to be a catalyst. Working underground, activists went from town to town and from village to village, using various modes of transport. Sometimes they covered long distances on bicycles. During the day they contacted their colleagues in schools and offices. In the evening, they converged at Dhoot Kalan which had become a common meeting centre. They held extensive meetings with NSD to assess their progress and prepare press notes. They evolved new tactics to meet the ever changing situation, while chalking out their future course of action. They derived immense benefit from these meetings. On the one hand, they were able to sharpen their understanding of the practical aspects of trade union movement and, on the other, they had a rare opportunity to learn the various methods and devices of underground political work. One golden rule, which they learnt from NSD, was that they should never remain at one place and should always be in the midst of the masses. Besides guiding the movement of government employees, NSD also arranged pre-arrest bail for as many as twenty activists. When Ranbir Singh Dhillon withdrew the agitation, he was isolated. In contrast, the CPM-led group was firmly established, a fact that was increasingly recognized by the people. The movement brought fresh cadre into the ranks of the CPM, thus strengthening it further. The government of Prakash Singh Badal, on its part, adopted a vindictive attitude towards the strikers and began to transfer them to far off places. This gave rise to much resentment among the employees, a fact that was reflected in the next assembly elections (March 1972), when the Akalis were decisively defeated.

A positive outcome of the strike was that it built up unity among school teachers. They met at a conference in Phillaur and decided to hold the first ever election of a teachers union on the principle of 'one teacher, one vote'. The process was to begin at the block level and, passing through the district level, it was to reach the state level. Presidents of the district unions were to form a presidium which, in turn, was to elect office-bearers for the entire state, viz., president, general secretary and treasurer. On the basis of this consititution, the first election was held on 23 January 1972. The CPM activists of Hoshiarpur district evolved their tactics in consulation with NSD, because his involvement in the cadre-building activity was the sole guarantee for their success. Their opponents belonged to the CPI-led group of Ranbir Singh Dhillon, which was supported by the Congress. However, the CPM candidates won at all levels – the blocks, the districts and the state. In Tanda block, Udham Singh won by a large margin and so did Harkanwal Singh in Hoshiarpur district. In seven out of twelve districts, the leadership passed into the hands of the CPM. Tarlochan Singh Rana was elected president, while Harkanwal Singh became the general secretary. If the CPM continued to dominate the teachers union in Hoshiarpur district during the subsequent period, a large part of the credit went to NSD. The leadership, which emerged at the top in the wake of the 1972 elections, drew up its charter of demands and called a one-day strike on 23 January 1973 to attract attention to it.

In the early 1970s serious efforts were made to organize unemployed school teachers. On the one hand, their number was quite large and, on the other, their problems were many. There were numerous vacancies in government schools and no effort was made to fill them, even as trained and qualified men and women continued to swell the ranks of the unemployed. Of course, some of them were able to get employment on a temporary basis. Rules regarding the service of temporary teachers were such that they led to avoidable harrassment. In the case of such teachers, a break of one day in service was imposed after every six months. To be able to join again they had to secure a fresh order from the office of the District Education Officer, which was not easy, given the rampant inefficiency, red tape and corruption in government offices. Moreover, a temporary teacher was revlieved from service as soon as the permanent incumbent resumed duty. Such a teacher had to be in regular contact with the employment exchange till he or she was called for an interview and secured a fresh selection. In Hoshiarpur district, the outstanding demands of unemployed teachers were taken up by numerous CPM activists including Narinder Singh Ashant. They began to build the movement from the block level and carried it upwards. During the summer vacation of 1974, they organized special camps for unemployed teachers. This was followed up by a series of demonstrations, the biggest of which was held at the Desh Bhagat Yadgar Hall, Jalandhar. At that time, the union of umemployed teachers was led by Ajit Singh Kang of the CPI. As many as six participants of the movement died in a major accident at Chaheru, an accident prone area on the Phagwara-Jalandhar stretch of the G.T. Road. A large rally was held near Rampura Phul (Bathinda) to pay homage to the deceased. The tragic incident left a deep impact on the minds of the common people. Bowing to the public opinion, the Punjab government redressed some of the grievances of this particular category of employees such as the practice of imposing a one-day break in the service of temporary teachers.

At that time, the CPM made vigorous attempts to penetrate the union of paramedical staff. Initially, this union was controlled by the pro-Congress group of Ranbir Singh Dhillon, which had considerable influence in the entire district of Hoshiarpur, extending from Talwara to Balachaur. The district unit of the CPM chose Narinder Singh Ashant, an active trade unionist, as the political advisor of the union. He and his associates toured all parts of the district and formed unions of paramedical staff at the primary level. This was followed by delegate sessions at the block and district levels. As a result of these efforts, the CPM candidates secured two-thirds majority in the union of Hoshiarpur district. This victory was won on the CPM plank, according to which relations between the staff and government were akin to those between employee and employer, there was no scope for any collaboration between the two and the demands of the staff could be secured only by fighting against the government. The CPM group of Tarlochan Singh Rana succeeded in establishing its control over the union in Hoshiarpur district. The CPM activists sent the selected cadre of the union to attend NSD's school, where they took advanced lessons in theoretical and practical aspects of trade unionism. The product of these activities – Mohan Singh Roshi, Bhajan Singh and Randhir Singh – became active members of the CPM.

The early 1970s witnessed a severe international economic crisis. In the past, a crisis of this nature had emerged after a long gap. Now this gap had been reduced because of the intensification of the crisis in the entire capitalist world. It was reflected in massive strikes in the advanced capitalist countries – France, Germany, England and Japan – which were staged by farmers, workers, employees and students. India could not remain impervious to its impact, as economic stagnation led to price rise, closure of factories and unemployment. In order to suppress any movement of protest, the Congress government, assumed dictatorial powers in the form of MISA. At that time, NSD was busy building popular movements in every front, viz., peasants, workers, employees, unemployed teachers, students and youth. The purpose was to create mass awareness among various classes, to enable them to fight against the fresh assaults on their economic status and political rights. All classes experienced a sense of growing frustration, as the central and state governments began to shift the economic burden on the people. Railway employees went on strike throughout the country. In Punjab, the government increased bus fares by 40 per cent. However, greater injustice was done to the employees as they were deprived of a few instalments of the dearness allowance (DA).

It is important to describe the conditions in the late 1960s in order to understand this problem in its true perspective. In response to a call for a strike (15 December 1967), the ministry of Lachhman Singh Gill agreed to grant DA to employees on the pattern of the central government. This continued to be paid for many years. From April 1972, the ministry of Zail Singh added interim relief to the pay packet of employees, in addition to DA. However, the Finance Minister Hans Raj Sharma withheld three or four instalments of DA on the grounds that the government had already paid more than was due to the employees. His contention was that interim relief consisted of two parts, viz., the pay portion and the DA portion and since the latter had been merged with the pay, the government would adjust it in the salaries of the employees.

In protest against the unjust attitude of the Punjab government, a massive general strike was held on 9 January 1974. The CPM activists, who toured all over Hoshiarpur district with the purpose of mobilizing the maximum number of people for the strike, admitted that they had succeeded in their aim because of the scientific training, which they had received regularly from NSD in his study circles and group meetings. As a result, the strike turned out to be the biggest of its kind in the history of post-independence Punjab. All establishments – offices, colleges, schools, banks and public transport – were closed in an unprecedented act of solidarity. Even the chauffeur and stenographer of the chief minister abstained from work. The state secretariat at Chandigarh wore a deserted look, as only a few IAS and PCS officers reported to work. Undoubtedly, the strike was unparalleled both in its strength and magnitude. One of the important consequences of the strike was that the acceptability of the CPM among the employees increased substantially.

It is evident from the preceding discussion that the CPM played a major role in the struggles of all classes – peasants, workers, students, youth and government employees of different descriptions – in Hoshiarpur district. The party, too, benefited from its increasing participation on various fronts. The above-mentioned sruggles brought fresh cadre to the forefront which was absorbed in the party. For example, the trade union movement produced such people as Harkanwal Singh, Gurbachan Singh, Gurmesh Singh, Charan Singh Virdi and Jodh Singh. All of them eventually held important positions in the party structure of the CPM.

The Students Federation of India (SFI), the student wing of the CPM, made significant strides in Punjab during the early 1970s. It launched a powerful agitation, under the presidentship of Lehmbar Singh Taggar, to secure concessional bus passes for students. Earlier this issue had been raised for discussion at the successive delegate sessions. At the third delegate session held in December 1970 at the Desh Bhagat Yadgar Hall (Jalandhar) the proposal was included in the charter of demands. A majority of delegates, however, were not sure if it could be adopted as a major demand of the students or if a mass agitation could be built around it. It was true that concessional passes were being issued by the railways, but no one was sure about the viability or genuineness of the proposal in the case of road transport. Moreover, this concession was not available to students in any other state.

In 1973, the SFI organized a signature campaign to highlight the economic, educational and democratic demands of the students. As a result of this exercise, the demand for concessional bus passes became extremely popular with the students. At the beginning of the 1974-5 academic session, a vigorous movement was launched to press for the acceptance of this demand. On 5 August 1974, the SFI organized rallies in the colleges of Punjab. On 7 August 1974, the students went on a one-day strike in response to a call given by the SFI in connection with its All India Demands Day. Since these actions failed to move the government, the SFI made some concrete efforts to step up the agitation. It organized a protest week from 24 to 30 August 1974, when rallies and demonstrations were held all over the state. Demands were scribbled on the walls in order to draw the attention of the publilc. On 28 August 1974, the SFI organized dharnas at the district headquarters – Hoshiarpur, Jalandhar, Amritsar, Ludhiana and Patiala – and presented memorandums to the Deputy Commissioners of these areas. On 30 August 1974 a complete strike was observed in colleges all over the state. It may be noted that the SFI took the initiative, at every step, to secure the cooperation of such student organizations as the Randhawa-led PSU and the AISF, which was affiliated to the CPI. However, the former distanced itself and the latter played a negative role throughout. As a result, the SFI had to go it alone.

On 7 November 1974, the SFI organized a state level demonstration at Jalandhar which culminated in a massive rally. The SFI warned that it would stop buses in the state, if the government failed to accept its outstanding demands. The government made some positive but vague announcements. Acting on its ultimatum, the SFI decided to gherao buses on 21 and 22 November 1974 for an hour everyday. The government retaliated by unleashing a reign of terror against the agitating student. During the gherao, the police resorted to lathi charge at many places and several students were arrested at Kapurthala, Ajnala, Sangrur and Rajpura. Mangal Singh and Harbans Singh, two student leaders of Kapurthala, were tortured in the police station after being arrested. Sampuran Singh Gujjapir was tortured for three days by the Ajnala police. Mit Singh, a student leader of Sangrur, was given inhuman treatment in police custody.

Throught out this movement, Lehmbar Singh Taggar and other leaders of the SFI remained in regular contact with NSD and drew up their plans in consultation with him. They also sought his advice on numerous day-to-day matters connected with the movement at various levels. In fact, he remained encamped at Tanda during the decisive phase of the agitation. The town (*qasba*) of Tanda, which lay on the Jalandhar–Pathankot highway, boasted of a Government College which became an important centre for the activities of the SFI, as

Lehmbar Singh Taggar addressed several rallies of students. The Jalandhar-Pathankot road was a extremely busy road and all types of vehicles moved in both directions throughout the day. To stop the buses at this point was a major challenge. But owing to the guidance of NSD, the task was accomplished easily. While finalizing the plans for the demonstration, he explained to the local leaders of the SFI, 'When you stop the buses, you must ensure that you are not causing any harassment or inconvenience to the passengers. You have to win their sympathy by your conduct. You have to convince them by sober logic and reasonable arguments about the genuineness of your demands.'

On the appointed day, students of the Government College turned out in large numbers on the Tanda bypass. Mohinder Singh Sangha, a science student, who had been trained in Marxism by NSD, led a group of boys and girls. As soon as they stopped a bus, Mohinder entered the bus and spoke to the passengers in the manner of a hawker selling indigenous medicines, 'We are like your own sons and daughters. We do not want to put you into any inconvenience. Nor do we want to make you suffer in any way. If any one of you wishes to get down to fetch water for your child, you may do so. But you must give us a patient hearing. Our demand for concessional bus passes is a genuine one. When we try to talk to the government, it lets loose its police on us and beats us with lathis. But you must decide, after listening to us, if our demands are genuine or not. If your verdict goes against us, we will stop this blockade and allow you to go.' The passengers and the driver invariably declared their support for our cause by raising their hands. This process was repeated every time a bus was stopped during the two-day demonstration.

The blockade at Tanda turned out to be both effective and peaceful. The credit for this went to NSD, who had worked hard to ensure that there was no untoward incident. If the students had gone out of control, there would have been violence and the police would have resorted to lathi charge or firing. The students of Tanda were not only unharmed, but also succeeded in their objective. The blockade at Phagwara surpassed every other place in its sheer magnitude. At Kapurthala, however, the police resorted to lathi charge and the local president of the SFI received several injuries. The SFI sponsored two-day protest succeeded in its larger aim. Gurmail Singh, the Education Minister of Punjab, declared that the government had accepted the major demands of the students. However, a number of points remained ambiguous in the declaration. Compelled to intensify the struggle, the SFI announced that it would observe a total strike on 5 December 1974 and buses would be stopped for two hours. Eventually, the government stopped playing tricks and adopted a reasonable attitude. On 3 December 1974, it made a formal announcement that monthly bus passes would cost Rs. 12.45 for a journey of 60 km. The concession was calculated on the pattern of a similar provision made by the Indian Railways. In addition to bus passes, the government agreed to supply notebooks at concessional rates: 35 paisa for a 88-page notebook and 70 paisa for a 176-page notebook. These notebooks were available even more than two decades after the introduction of the scheme, but only at the depots run by the village societies. Further, the Punjab government also agreed to provide representation to the students on the senates of the universities and to supply rations at subsidized rates to hostel messes.

The acceptance of the demand for concessional bus passes led to important consequences. It was a great boon for the poor rural youth, both boys and girls, who did not have the means to pay the normal bus fares and could not afford to stay in college hostels. They could now travel to the nearest town or city, wherever their college was located, without being burdened with a heavy expenditure on transportation. They could return to their villages before sunset, so that they had sufficient time to study as well as to help in agricultural activities and household chores. Further, they could pursue a course of their choice – science, commerce, management, postgraduation in various disciplines, Bachelor of Education and Industrial Training Institute. Since these courses were not available in the small rural colleges, the youth of these areas had been suffering from a great disadvantage in the past. Now they could go every day from their respective villages to the nearest urban centre, so as to study a course which could improve their employment prospects.

After acquiring suitable educational qualifications, they began to compete for jobs in various sectors. This concession enabled a good number of rural young men and women to become doctors, engineers, architects, lawyers, teachers and managers. Those who succeeded in getting jobs began to work hard in order to raise the socio-economic status of their poor households.

The acceptance of this demand led to a significant change in the political situation, particularly on the student front. Since the movement had been spearheaded by the SFI, the student wing of the CPM, its superiority was established beyond doubt and its influence continued to increase in the colleges of Punjab. The struggle, which had been fought along scientific lines, produced positive results. In contrast, the PSU led by Prithipal Singh Randhawa began to lose its hold and was eventually confined only to the Punjab Agricultural University, Ludhiana. This was hardly surprising because this organization believed in staging violent demonstrations and inviting equally violent police action. At the same time, the NSUI (the student wing of the Congress) and the AISF (the student wing of the CPI) stood exposed in the eyes of the student community on account of their dubious role during the agitation.

During the late 1960s and early 1970s, the Naxalite movement emerged in Punjab. A number of college students, who were based in the rural areas, were attracted to the cult of violence and heroism. Ajit Singh of Sikri, Dharam Pal of Dasuya and Piara Singh of Jandaur joined their ranks. They rejected the programme and policies of the CPM and described its leaders as cowards. They incited the youth to attack police stations, snatch guns and eliminate their class enemies. In Hoshiarpur district, a number of innocent people became the target of their misplaced anger. They killed Master Prem because, in their distorted view, he was a hated moneylender (*sud khor*). Similarly, they murdered Sadhu Singh who was the president of the managing committee of Khalsa College, Garhdiwala, as well as a member of the block samiti.

NSD was deeply concerned about the growth of the Naxalite movement. He made tireless efforts to wean away youth from the CPI(M-L). Whenever he heard that a particular young man had joined the ranks of the Naxalites, he would travel all the way to his village to meet him. While doing so, he did not hesitate to cycle 20 or 30 kilometres on unmetalled kutcha tracks. He held long discussions with such a person and tried a convince him about the weaknesses, contradictions and dangers inherent in the path of violence. He used every possible device – logic, reason, wit and common sense – to bring him back to the CPM fold. He often argued, 'Your ideology is basically flawed. You have no base among the masses. How can you do anything for those who are not with you? You will be killed by the police rather easily.' In this manner, NSD succeeded in bringing many young men, who had joined the ranks of the Naxalites, back into the fold of the CPM. Prominent among such persons was Baldev Singh, who belonged to a village in Mukerian and who has, since then, remained steadfast in his loyalty to the CPM. Jagdish Singh of Chohkan also belonged to this category as also Gurmesh Singh, who has risen to become the office secretary of the Hoshiarpur unit of the CPM. NSD was instrumental in saving the lives of several promising young men, who otherwise would have been eliminated by the police in false encounters. During these days, he would say, 'If it were within my means, I would have brought each and every one of these boys back to our path.'

In this context, the most important case was that of Baldev Singh Pota of Pota village, near Mukerian in Hoshiarpur district. Though he was not involved in any violent incident, he was quite active in the Naxalite movement. The police managed to arrest him and brought him to the Dasuya police station, from where he was shifted to Tanda. The CPM learnt through its secret sources that the police intended to kill him in the Bet near Rarha village and throw his body into the Beas. Chanan Singh Dhoot instructed Pratap Chand Dhoot to bring NSD (whose arrest warrants had been issued) to Tanda in complete secrecy. Accordingly a meeting was held at Tanda. It was attended by NSD, Chanan Singh Dhoot, Pratap Chand Dhoot and Dr Khushal Singh of village Masiti. An emergency plan was evolved to rescue Baldev from the clutches of the police. While NSD stayed back, the others went to the local police station. At first, the police denied having detained Baldev in the lock-up. Chanan Singh Dhoot, in his characteristic and inimitable style, threatened to expose the police in public if it failed to release Baldev forthwith. Ultimately, the police registered a minor case against him and released him. Baldev returned to the fold of the CPM and, through commitment and hard work, rose to be a member of the state commitee.

That the attitude of NSD aroused the hostility of Naxalites was proved by the following incident. Once three members of the CPM – NSD, Chanan Singh Dhoot and Pratap Chand Dhoot – were sitting at Pratap Chand Dhoot's poultry farm. They were having tea, while discussing some matter of common interest. Ajit Singh of Sikri, who was a well-known Naxalite of the area, appeared on the scene. The CPM leaders offered him a seat as well as a cup of tea. Ajit Singh refused to accept their hospitality, declaring that he had come only to speak to them. Since he was already overflowing with anger, he adopted a threatening tone and asked, 'Did you go to village Nadiali?' Getting an affirmative response, he roared, 'I have learnt that you have been uttering all possible nonsense against us.' NSD mustered his courage and declared, 'We own whatever we had stated. Our statements were based on our logic. We have no reason to retreat from our known position.' Taken aback, Ajit Singh threatened in desperation, 'I will see you.' Since this was a naked threat, NSD and Chanan Singh Dhoot rose to their feet, rolled up their sleeves and challenged him, 'Come. We will see you now and here.' Ajit Singh became nervous and sped away. The news of this encounter spread like wild fire in the area.

Whenever a Naxalite died at the hands of the police, NSD was deeply distressed. On such occasions, he would say,

> I am sad because the deceased, after all, was a revolutionary. Our ultimate aim is to bring about a socialist revolution. We require this revolutionary element in our youth. Since the deceased did possess this element, his removal from our midst is a definite loss to us. Such deaths make me very sad. I cannot reconcile myself to the wastage of human life in this manner. I see a clear distinction between an ordinary young man and a Naxalite. The former is like

a stationary bus. We do not know whether it will move or not. In fact, we do not even know if its engine will start or not. Who knows whether it will need a new battery or it will have to be pushed from behind by the passengers. On the other hand, a Naxalite is comparable to a bus whose engine has started and it has begun covering the distance also. The only problem is that it is going in the wrong direction. From Adampur it was to go towards Jalandhar, but it has taken the road to Hoshiarpur. Even then it is a better bus than the one which is still parked at the bus stand and we are absolutely uncertain about the condition of its engine. In the former case, we have only to turn the bus in the right direction. The same rule applies to the Naxalites. If we are able to give them proper guidance and put them on the right course, we will have contributed much to the cause of our revolution.

In the early 1970s, pro-Naxalite student unions (affiliated to Prithipal Singh Randhawa's Punjab Students Union) were formed in the colleges of Punjab. This phenomenon was also witnessed in Khalsa College of Garhdiwala, a town near Dhoot Kalan on the Hoshiarpur-Pathankot road. In 1974, this union led a procession of students through the main bazar. A few processionists plundered the roadside mobile stalls (*rebris*) and grabbed some eatables. This unruly behaviour of the students left a bad impression on the people, particularly the shop-keepers. There was a strong feeling of revulsion against the students. In these circumstances, several important CPM leaders, including NSD and Chanan Singh Dhoot, held a meeting to discuss the fallout of the incident. They decided to activate the CPM cadre among the students and to hold a demonstration in the bazaar, so as to neutralize the negative impression, which had been created in the minds of the urban population. Two days later, a large number of students were mobilized. They marched in a procession through the bazaar. Several CPM activists walked alongside to ensure discipline and prevent any untoward incident. Some senior leaders of the CPM were also present for the same purpose, though they were not visible to the processionists.

The CPM activists realized that some mischievous elements had infiltrated among the students and were determined to create trouble and wanted the peaceful procession to assume a violent form. These undesirable elements were identified and their actions were neutralized. In this manner, the procession continued to proceed without any disturbance. A Congress flag was seen fluttering on the shop of a local leader of this party. In a sudden action, which took everyone by surprise, one of the undesirable elements pulled down the flag and put it on fire in the middle of the road and even pushed it towards a police inspector. The police swung into action and fired gunshots in the air, threw tear gas shells and resorted to lathi charge. The vanguard of the procession, including Amarjit (the son of Chanan Singh Dhoot), received serious injuries, inflicted by the lathi blows. When Amarjit fell on the ground and was being beaten mercilessly by the police, Amar Singh Almast (a CPM activist) threw himself on top of the former in a bid to block the lathis and was injured in the process. Incensed by this, the students picked up bamboo sticks from the roadside shops and attacked their assailants. Finding themselves at the receiving end, the policemen started fleeing away. The students ran after them in hot pursuit and reached the bus stand, where a heap of stones lay in a corner. The students pelted the policemen with stones. The CPM acivists, who did not want the situation to take an ugly turn, intervened and stopped the students from attacking the policemen. In spite of their best efforts, some policemen received injuries in the stone throwing. By the time reinforcement arrived from the police station, the students had been persuaded to disperse. Thus, further confrontation was averted.

It was anticipated that the police would retaliate. The alert CPM workers went underground and were able to evade arrest. Those who were not alive to the danger fell into the police trap. In cases where the police failed to apprehend the wanted person, it began to harass their households. For example, the police impounded cattle from the houses of NSD, Chanan Singh Dhoot and Harbhajan Singh Ramdaspur. In this connection, NSD and Charan Singh Dhoot became involved in a long-drawn battle with the police. They made many trips to the district headquarters (Hoshiarpur) and complained to the higher authorities about the indefensible actions of the police. The police, in turn, filed a case under Section 307 against eleven persons, including some members of the CPM and a few students. The case dragged on for two years at the Dasuya court. Police inspector Kirpal Singh did not give any evidence against those implicated. Even the local Congressmen followed suit. Ultimately, the charges could not be proved and all the accused were acquitted.

The economic crisis of the early 1970s shook the college teachers out of their slumber. There were nearly a hundred privately run colleges in Punjab. The managing committees, which were composed of local politicians, enjoyed unlimited powers and exploited the teachers in every conceivable manner. They were given a basic salary of Rs. 450 per month. However, this amount remained inscribed only on paper, as the managing committees invariably withheld a certain percentage of salaries. Further, teachers could be easily dismissed as there was no job security. Since the teachers were at the mercy of managing committees, their status was no better than ordinary school-masters. In 1972, the teachers organized one of the biggest strikes to secure redressal of their long-standing grievances. At that time, Umrao Singh was the education minister of Punjab. The government adopted a negative attitude towards college teachers and the strike continued for over two months. Prohibitory orders were imposed all over the state to interdict the holding of demonstrations. The teachers, on their part, formed contingents (*jathas*) and courted arrest, so that thousands were confined in jails. Ultimately, the strike was withdrawn unconditionally, leading to a split in the college teachers union and widespread anger against the existing leadership.

An interesting feature of the strike was that whereas the government released the arrested teachers after a short period, the *jatha* of teachers from Khalsa College, Garhdiwala, was not released. The government was aware of the fact that the teachers of this college, including such popular professors as Bansal and Sharma, held NSD in high esteem and sought his advice on all matters relating to the struggle. Similarly, the teaching staff of the newly established college at Bulhowal, including a CPM activist named Kewal Kaloti, sought the expert opinion of NSD as and when it was faced with a difficult situation.

Another significant feature of the strike was the emergence of a solid group of pro-CPM members in the teachers' union of Punjab. This group was spearheaded by Kaloti, Miloo, Maan and a few teachers of Phagwara and Amritsar. Though small and informal, it was vocal enough to have its views accepted by the union leadership. Encouraged by this development, NSD and Chanan Singh Dhoot made earnest efforts to set-up an exclusive cell of college teachers, like various other categories of employees, in the CPM at the state level. However, Satwant Singh and Gurcharan Singh Randhawa, who held the post of state secretary in succession, could not be persuaded to support the move. Instead, they appointed Rajinder Singh Shrinh as incharge to oversee all matters pertaining to college teachers. Later, Dalip Singh Johal revived the move to create a cell for college teachers at the state level, while admitting that failure to do so in the past was a mistake. The move, however, did not succeed.

It would be appropriate to acknowledge the role played by college students of Bulhowal in numerous struggles involving different sections of the society. A beginning in this direction was made by Kewal Kaloti, who had been trained in Marxism-Leninsim by NSD. He joined the newly established college at Bulhowal as a lecturer and initiated many of his students into the leftist ideology. Due to his enthusiastic and vigorous efforts, this number increased to nearly a hundred students. This group played a militant role in a number of agitations, which were organized in the villages around Bulhowal. Whenever a complaint or information was received about any act of injustice – eviction of a tenant, oppression of a peasant, dismissal of a teacher or the sacking of a headmaster – two truck loads of students, led by Kewal Kaloti, arrived on the scene. This intervention was made when any particular agitation had reached a deadlock. On such occasions, the students rushed to the spot and held such powerful demonstrations that the oppressors were compelled to submit and the issue was invariably decided in favour of the oppressed. In such actions, Narinder Singh Ashant and Master Joginder Singh (a teacher aligned with the CPI) provided much support and cooperation. As a result, the college at Bulhowal emerged as a strong bastion of the CPM and those who garrisoned the citadel always acted in accordance with the advice of NSD, lest they should make any mistake.

The following examples illustrate the kind of activity undertaken by the Bulhowal group on the advice of NSD. In the first case, a headmaster of Kandhala Jattan village (Hoshiarpur district) had been removed from his post in an unjust and arbitrary manner. The Bulhowal group launched an agitation with the active participation of students. The management of the school was forced to appoint a five-member committee, other than itself, to hold an enquiry into the dispute and give a verdict. The committee headed by Pritam Singh Littar, a well-known local leader of the CPM, gave a judgement in favour of the headmaster, who was reinstated.

In the second case, a few school teachers of Miyani village (Hoshiarpur district) were dismissed by the management. The latter body was dominated by Lakhi Singh, whose word carried the force of a royal edict. The agitation to secure the reinstatement of these teachers continued for six or seven years. All political groups, except the CPM, distanced themselves from the agitation. The Bulhowal group, supported by its hundred odd students, remained steadfast and continued to fight till the bitter end. During the last phase of the agitation, an extreme step had to be taken. When the court reinstated the teachers of Miyani, the managing committee employed every conceivable trick to prevent them from joining their duty. Not only were the gates closed, but also all entry points were sealed with barbed wire. In these circumstances, the students of the Bulhowal group jumped over the walls and entered the school compound. The two groups clashed with each other and there were casualties on both sides. Ultimately, the matter was settled in favour of the teachers who resumed their duty. It may also be mentioned that the students of the Bulhowal group spearheaded militant agitations to free lands from illegal possession and to secure justice for a poor tenant from his oppressive landlord.

While maintaining thematic continuity with the agitations of college lecturers, we will skip the chronological sequence to highlight the CPM-led battle for the reinstatement of eighteen teachers of DAV institutions of Hoshiarpur. This campaign was launched during the regime (March 1977–July 1979) of the Janata-led coalition at the centre. The central managing committee of DAV educational institutions based in Delhi assumed control of two colleges, the DAV College and the DAV College of Education. In the process, Chaudhary Balbir Singh a powerful politician who headed the local managing body, was removed from his position. His dismissal came at a time when he was lodged in jail in the wake of the emergency. When general elections were held in March 1977, Chaudhary Balbir Singh was elected from Hoshiarpur parliamentary constituency. Soon after, he dismissed eighteen teachers from the two colleges which were under his control.

This action constituted a major assault on the rights of college teachers. The teachers union failed to take any action, as the district leadership had resigned and the state leadership did not intervene. The CPI decided not to interfere because of certain internal reasons. NSD raised the issue before the district committee of the CPM which found itself in a dilemma because the party had just extended electoral support to Chaudhary Balbir Singh, while the dismissed teachers also had to be supported. Finally, it was decided that the party should take up the cause of the teachers in the right earnest. Kewal Kaloti, who had been dismissed from Bulhowal college during the emergency, was nominated president of an action committee. He selected some people as membes of the committee which began to coordinate with the state committee of the CPM. In fact, the latter was eager to take up the issue because it had been provided with a readymade base to act upon. Within two weeks, a powerful agitation was built up, whereas nothing had moved in the previous nine months. The agitation continued for three months during which six huge demonstrations were held. The struggle was the biggest of its kind after the emergency.

Efforts were made to secure political support for the agitation, with a view to increase pressure on Chaudhary Balbir Singh. A delegation of agitators met Prakash Singh Badal, the Chief Minsiter of Punjab, but he expressed his helplessness in the matter. Another delegation, which incuded some workers of the Janata Party, was sent to Delhi to seek the assistance of senior leaders of the then ruling party. Yet another delegation met the senior CPM leader Harkishan Singh Surjeet at Jandiala near Amritsar. Since the CPM was one of the supporting parties of the central government, Surjeet exercised his influence in the concerned quarters, but nothing was known about the exact outcome of the attempt.

Ultimately, Chaudhary Balbir Singh was brought to the negotiating table, through the mediation of Jeewan Tiwari, a long-standing senator of the Punjab University, Chandigarh. A settlement in favour of the dismissed teachers could not be reached easily because Chaudhary was adamant. He expressed his willingness to reinstate the concerned teachers only if they first submitted their resignations. Apparently the precondition was meant to satisfy the ego of Chaudhary Balbir Singh, who was known widely for his arrogance and high-handedness. The teachers were persuaded to submit their resignations, after which they were honourably reinstated in their posts. The victory proved that the CPM was the only political organization which could fight for the rights of college teachers, who had been suffering at the hands of their oppressive employers. The manner in which the whole agitation was guided by NSD was an exemplar for those who were engaged in similar struggles.

Towards the end of June 1975, a provincial level kisan conference was held at Dhoot Kalan. NSD, who had earned a tremendous reputation as an efficient organizer, played a major role in the success of the conference. At the beginning, meetings were held at the village level to chalk out the programme, indentify the tasks, enrol volunteers and assign duties. The entire population of the village was involved in the conference. People rose above their differences – political and personal – and willingly offered assistance. NSD, Chanan Singh Dhoot and Pratap Chand Dhoot toured the neighbouring villages, spoke to the people in small groups and made appeals for funds. They received assistance both in cash and kind. The most challenging task, however, was arranging accommodation for nearly 600 delegates. The villagers placed their own houses at the disposal of the organizers. For the purpose of convenience, the delegates of a particular district were placed together in a particular set of houses. Each group was provided with its own volunteers, who looked after all the needs of the delegates including beddings, toilet, bath, soap, etc. On the other hand, venues were fixed for the general house as well as small committee meetings. A large and impressive platform was constructed for staging revolutionary plays, which attracted people from the surrounding twenty-five villages.

All the front ranking leaders of the Punjab unit of the CPM including Harkishan Singh Surjeet, Sarwan Singh Cheema, Harnam Singh Chamak, Pandit Kishori Lal, Gurcharan Singh Randhawa, Chand Singh Chopra, Dalip Singh Johal and Satwant Singh reached Dhoot Kalan for the conference. The delegates were conscious of the fact that they had come to Dhoot Kalan, which was famous for being the native place of NSD who was universally respected for his intelligence, commitment and sacrifices. They were aware of the fact that the village had produced several internationally renowned communists and for this very reason, it was acclaimed as the 'Moscow of Punjab' both within and outside the state. They expected the ordinary villagers to be far more progressive and enlightened than their counterparts in other parts of the state. Therefore they had prepared themselves for the occasion, having read all the relevant literature. They were also equipped with notebooks in which they had made notes as might be useful during discussions and deliberations. They could not afford to cut a sorry figure among the people of a village which had acquired an awesome reputation in the political life of the country. If they did not measure up to the expectations of these politically advanced locals, the latter may question the organizers, 'Where was the need to invite such a large number of people, who know so little about the subject under discussion ?'

Since NSD overflowed with the spirit of hospitality, he paid special attention to food. He sat in one corner and supervised with watchful eye when the delegates sat over their meals. He had assigned the responsibility of serving food to five young volunteers – Ranbir, Dalbir, Mohinder, Baldev and Jagir – who had played an important role in the agitation for concessional bus passes. He directed each of them to serve only one item –

dal, sabzi, chapati, piyaz and *gur* – and to concentrate only on his own work. He generated a sense of healthy competition among the volunteers, with a view to extract the best out of them. He summoned them at the end of every meal and made a critical assessment of their performance. Absolutely impartial in his judgement, he did not show any favour to his own sons, Ranbir and Dalbir. On one occasion, he declared, 'The work of Mohinder was efficient and praiseworthy, but that of Baldev was somewhat slow.' Baldev, who possessed a exceptionally strong physique, explained, 'Mohinder's duty of distributing *chapatis* was easy. My task was difficult, because the *sabzi* kept on sticking to the ladle and consumed much time in being placed on the delegate's plate (*thali*).' NSD responded by saying, 'If this be the case, then the two of you should exchange your duties.' At the end of the next meal, the volunteers collected around NSD and waited for his verdict, with suspense in their minds. NSD declared, 'Mohinder's work was difficult, but he has still carried the day. Baldev's task was easier, but he has continued to be his usual self.' Everyone present burst into laughter.

On one occasion, NSD and Harkishan Singh Surjeet were sitting on a cot while the delegates were having their meals. Summoning Mohinder Singh Sangha, NSD said to Surjeet, 'Let me introduce you to a promising young communist, who has played a vigorous role in the recent SFI-sponsored agitation for concessional bus passes. He comes from your area and belongs to village Jandhu Singha.' Surjeet remarked spontaneously, 'How have you raised grass in saline soil ?' (*Eh tusin kallar wich ghah kiven paida kar ditta*?). The remark was made with reference to the fact that no communist had emerged from this village, ever since on old communist had migrated to England. The unassuming NSD replied, 'I have done nothing in this case. As he is studying with my son, he often comes here to get answers to his questions and to satisfy his curiosity.' This apparently trivial incident throws light on the encouragement and motivation NSD gave to youth and students so as to train new cadre for the party.

By the time the news of the declaration of the emergency (26 June 1975) spread, some delegates had left Dhoot Kalan, but a majority of them were still present. The latter category included Harnam Singh Chamak, Chand Singh Chopra and Doda Ram who had arrived from the neighbouring hills. In accordance with NSD's directions, the delegates were led into hiding in grape orchards and other safe places. When the police raided Dhoot Kalan, it failed to detain any CPM leader. NSD had made sure that none of the delegates fell into the police trap. Later, the local volunteers escorted each delegate, through unfrequented kutcha routes, to the safest bus stop or railway station.

During the emergency, the Congress government imposed severe restrictions on the democratic rights of the people. Political activities were not only curtailed, but were also ruthlessly suppressed. The police, assisted by intelligence agencies and informers, worked overtime to apprehend political activists. In these circumstances, the CPM workers were not able to evolve their political response. A.K. Gopalan, the leader of the CPM in Parliament, delivered an address, which did not reach the common people because of censorship on the press. However, a cyclostyled copy of Gopalan's address fell into the hands of Narinder Singh Ashant, a CPM activist whose name has been mentioned earlier in connection with the agitations of employees. He made more copies and distributed them among like-minded friends. As a result, the text of Gopalan's address began to be discussed and debated, though in limited circles only. The gist of this document was that the CPM had failed to anticipate the transformation of the world economic crisis into a major political crisis, that the Congress government had abandoned the democratic path in favour of an authoritarian dispensation and that it was incumbent on true revolutionaries to begin work at the grass-roots level.

Inspired by Gopalan's understanding of the situation, Narinder Singh Ashant and Kewal Kaloti were convinced that there was no certainty about the duration of the emergency and they should not sit idle, but should begin productive work immediately. During the day, they revived contact with activists and sympathizers, who were spread over several villages around Garhdiwala and Dasuya. With their assistance, they decided the venue and time of meetings, besides indentifying the participants. At these meetings, which were invariably held at night and in complete secrecy, they educated small groups on the prevailing political and economic conditions. In the morning, the two resumed their normal routines. They made every effort to ensure that such meetings appeared social visits so as not to arouse the suspicion of political opponents or government agencies.

In this manner, political activities were revived even when the draconian laws of the emergency were in operation. These study circles were held in villages like Zahura, Miyani, Jajja, Masiti, Ambala Jattan, Maddakalla, Khudda, Kandhala Jattan, Ramdaspur and Keshopur. Sometimes exclusive study circles were held for students, sometimes for peasants and at other times for workers. The number of people attending these was ten to twelve. Some of the members of each of these groups were selected to attend the study circles of NSD. This was how NSD became associated with this particular form of political activity, which continued throughout the duration of the emergency. NSD spoke on theoretical issues, political economy and the current situation. However, it was on the united front tactics that he possessed absolute mastery. According to this thesis, originally propounded by Georgi Dimitrov to fight against fascism, small political groups should join the larger forces without any preconditions when they were pitted against a powerful common enemy. It was under the guidance of NSD that this principle was successfully applied in Masiti village: the non-Congress groups were brought on a single platform, leading to a complete isolatation of the Congress. Interestingly, this success was achieved during the dark days of the emergency.

On most occasions, NSD's study circles began on Saturday evening and continued till noon Sunday. The venue was either the house of Kewal Kaloti in Masiti village or the house of Narinder Singh Ashant. The most important rendezvous was the 'Well of Parrots' (*Toteyan Wala Khooh*), which was located in the ancestral farm of NSD's parents-in-law. The place enjoyed a number of advantages. Technically located within the confines of Jhawan village, it lay on the boundary of five or six villages. It was protected by a huge orchard of pears (*nashpatis*), the first of its kind in the locality. There was no house or settlement in the vicinity. Any visitor approaching the place could be seen from a long distance. During the pre-independence period, it enjoyed a unique political and administrative status. It lay in the territory of British Punjab, while many of the neighbouring villages (including Dhoot Kalan) were part of the princely state of Kapurthala. Political activists and other offenders, when chased by the police of their own territory, took shelter within the jurisdiction of the other administration where they could not be arrested. Since then, the place had been the venue of innumerable secret meetings of communist organizations, both provincial and national. Over time the place has acquired some degree of romance. It would be no exaggeration to designate *Toteyan Wala Khooh* as the pivot of the communist movement in the area. This position continued to exist during the emergency and later.

Bibliography

PRIMARY SOURCES

A. Unpublished Official Records

Files of the Home Department (Political), National Archives of India, New Delhi.

B. Official Reports and Publications

Administration Report of the Punjab and Its Dependencies, 1907-8.

Board of Economics Enquiry (Punjab), The Size and Distribution of Cultivators Holdings in Punjab, 1928.

Imperial Gazetteer of India, Provincial Series, Punjab, vols. I & II, Calcutta, 1908.

Punjab District Gazetteer, Hoshiarpur District, 1904, Lahore, 1908.

Report on the Progress of Education in Punjab, 1901-2.

Major Norman F. White, *Twenty Years of the Plague in India, with Special Reference to the Outbreak of 1917-18.*

C. Communist Documents

CPI (M), *Pranam Shahidan Noon (Salute to Martyrs)*, Jalandhar, 1988.

Political Organistaion Report of the Twelfth Congress of the Communist Party of India (Marxist), Calcutta, 25-30 December 1985.

M.B. Rao, ed., *Documents of the History of the Communist Party of India*, vol. VII, *1948-1950*, New Delhi, 1976.

Subodh Roy, ed., *Communism in India: Unpublished Documents 1935-1945*, Calcutta, 1976.

Mohit Sen, ed., *Documents of the History of the Communist Party of India*, vol. VIII, *1951-1956*, New Delhi, 1977.

D. Newspapers

Kirti Lehar

The Pioneer

The Tribune

E. Interviews

Bachan Singh Mehatpur, Jalandhar City, 18.3.1995.
Beant Singh Mallewal, village Dhoot Kalan, district Hoshiarpur, 2.4.1997.
Beant Singh, village Dhoot Kalan, district Hoshiarpur, 29.3.1997.
Dalbir Singh Dhoot, village Dhoot Kalan, district Hoshiarpur, 3.4.1997.
Darshan Singh, village Hussainpur, district Hoshiarpur, 30.3.1997.
Gian Singh Moonak, village Moonak, district Hoshiarpur, 23.9.1995.
Gurbachan Singh, village Sikri, district Hoshiarpur, 30.3.1997.
Harbhajan Singh Ramdaspur, village Dhoot Kalan, district Hoshiarpur, 2.4.1997.
Ishar Singh Sodhi, State Secretariat, CPI(M), Chandigarh, 11.3.1997.
Kewal Kaloti, Tanda, district Hoshiarpur, 31.3.1997.
Mohinder Singh Sangha, village Dhoot Kalan, district Hoshiarpur, 3.4.1997.
Narinder Singh Ashant, Tanda, district Hoshiarpur, 31.3.1997.
Pratap Chand Dhoot, village Dhoot Kalan, district Hoshiarpur, 1.4.1997.

SECONDARY SOURCES

A. Books

Muzaffar Ahmad, *Myself and the Communist Party of India, 1920-1929,* Calcutta, 1970.
Imran Ali, *The Punjab Under Imperialism, 1885-1947*, Delhi, 1989.
Anju Arora, *The Princely States, British Paramountcy and Internal Administration, 1858-1948 (A Case Study of the Kapurthala State),* New Delhi, 2001.
Vinay Bahl, *The Making of the Indian Working Class: The Case of the Tata Iron and Steel Company 1880-1946*, New Delhi, 1995.
Himadri Banerjee, *Agrarian Society of the Punjab (1849-1901),* New Delhi, 1982.
Sumanta Banerjee, *India's Simmering Revolution: The Naxalite Uprising*, New Delhi, 1984.
Kelly Boyd, ed., *Encyclopaedia of Historians and Historical Writing,* vol. II, London, 1999.
J.S. Brar, *The Communist Party in Punjab,* New Delhi, 1989.
Allan Bullock, *Hitler: A Study in Tyranny,* London, 1973.
Fred A. Carlson, *Geography of Latin America,* New Jersey, 1959.
E.H. Carr, *The Bolshevik Revolution, 1917-23,* vol. I, rpt, Harmondsworth, 1984.

E.H. Carr, *Twilight of the Comintern 1930-1935*, New York, 1982.
Bipan Chandra, *The Rise and Growth of Economic Nationalism in India*, rpt, New Delhi, 1984.
Bipan Chandra et al., *India's Struggle for Independence*, rpt, New Delhi, 1989.
Bipan Chandra, Aditya Mukherjee and Mridula Mukherjee, *India After Independence*, New Delhi, 1999.
Sukanta Chaudhary, ed., *Calcutta, The Living City*, vol. II, *The Present and Future*, Delhi, 1990.
Jesse D. Clarkson, *A History of Russia: From the Ninth Century*, London, 1962.
G.A. Cohen, *Karl Marx's Theory of History: A Defence*, New York, 1978.
Malcolm Darling, *The Punjab Peasant in Prosperity and Debt*, rpt, New Delhi, 1978.
M.N. Das, *A Centenary History of the Indian National Congress*, vol. III, New Delhi, 1985.
James Douie, *The Panjab, North West Frontier Province and Kashmir*, rpt, New Delhi, 1974.
——, *Punjab Settlement Manual*, Lahore, 1930.
Victor M. Fic, *Peaceful Transition to Communism in India: Strategy of the Communist Party*, Bombay, 1969.
Anand Gauba, *Amritsar: A Study in Urban History*, Jalandhar, 1988.
K.C. Ghosh, *Economic Resources of India and Pakistan*, Calcutta, 1956.
Verinder Grover, ed., *J.B. Kriplani: Political Thinkers of Modern India*, Delhi, 1995.
Amit Kumar Gupta, *The Agrarian Drama: The Leftists and the Rural Poor in India, 1934-1951*, New Delhi, 1996.
John Patrick Haithcox, *Communism and Nationalism in India: M.N. Roy and Comintern Policy 1920-1939*, Bombay, 1971.
Peter Heehs, *Nationalism, Terrorism, Communalism: Essays in Modern Indian History*, Delhi, 1998.
Eric Hobsbawm, *Age of Extremes: The Short Twentieth Century, 1914-1991*, London, 1994.
Denzil Ibbetson, *Punjab Castes*, rpt, Patiala, 1970.
M. Mufakharul Islam, *Irrigation, Agriculture and the Raj: Punjab 1887-1947*, New Delhi, 1997.
Ajeet Javed, *Left Politics in Punjab 1935-47*, Delhi, 1988.
Hugh Johnston, *The Voyage of Komagata Maru: The Sikh Challenge to Canada's Colour Bar*, Delhi, 1979.
Bhagwan Josh, *Communist Movement in Punjab 1926-47*, New Delhi, 1979.

Bhagwan Josh, *Struggle for Hegemony in India 1920-47: The Colonial State, the Left and the National Movement*, vol. II, 1934-41, New Delhi, 1992.

Sohan Singh Josh, *My Tryst with Secularism: An Autobiography*, New Delhi, 1991.

Mark Juergensmeyer, *Religious Rebels in the Punjab: The Social Vision of Untouchables,* New Delhi, 1988.

Gopal Das Khosla, *Stern Reckoning: A Survey of the Events Leading up to and Following the Partition of India*, New Delhi, 1952.

Ian Kershaw, *Hitler 1889-1936: Hubris*, London, 1998.

Pytor Kutsobin, *Ajoy Kumar Ghosh and Communist Movement in India*, New Delhi, 1987.

Kenneth Scott Latourette, *A Short History of the Far East*, New York, 1951.

Sucheta Mahajan, *Independence and Partition: The Erosion of Colonial Power in India,* New Delhi, 2000.

Usha Mahajani, *The Role of Indian Minorities in Burma and Malaya*, Bombay, 1960.

Shriram Maheshwari, *Local Government in India*, New Delhi, 1971.

L.P. Mathur, *History of the Andamans and Nicobar Islands*, New Delhi, 1968.

Parshotam Mehra, *A Dictionary of Modern Indian History, 1707-1947*, Delhi, 1985.

B.B. Misra, *The Indian Political Parties: An Historical Analysis of Political Behaviour up to 1947*, New Delhi, 1976.

Kamlesh Mohan, *Militant Nationalism in the Punjab 1919-35*, New Delhi, 1985.

Netaji Research Bureau, *Crossroads: Being the Works of Subhas Chandra Bose, 1938-1940,* Bomby, 1962.

Gene D. Overstreet and Marshall Windmiller, *Communism in India*, Bombay, 1960.

M.A. Persits, *Revolutionaries of India in Soviet Russia,* ed. R.A. Ulyanovsky, Moscow, 1983.

David Pertrie, *Communism in India, 1924-27*, ed. Mahadeva Prasad Saha, Calcutta, 1972.

James Pool, *Hitler and His Secret Partners*, New York, 1997.

A.M. Prokhorov, ed., *Great Soviet Encyclopaedia*, vols. 8 and 12, New York, 1975-7.

Harish K. Puri, *Ghadar Movement: Ideology, Organisation and Strategy*, Amritsar, 1983.

Satya M. Rai, *Punjab Since Partition*, New Delhi, 1986.

B.T. Ranadive, *The Independence Struggle and After*, New Delhi, 1988.

K.N. Raj, *Some Economic Aspects of the Bhakra Nangal Project*, Bombay, 1960.

M.S. Randhawa, *Out of the Ashes: An Account of the Rehabilitation of the Refugees from West Pakistan in Rural Areas of East Punjab*, Bombay, 1954.

M.A. Rasul, *A History of the All India Kisan Sabha*, Calcutta, 1974.

Sibnarayan Ray, ed., *Selected Works of M.N. Roy*, vol. I, Delhi, 1987.

G. Ram Reddy, ed., *Patterns of Panchayati Raj in India*, New Delhi, 1977.

Chaman Lal Revri, *The Indian Trade Union Movement: An Outline History, 1880-1947*, New Delhi, 1972.

H. Robinson, *Latin America*, London, 1961.

H.A. Rose, *A Glossary of the Tribes and Castes of the Punjab and North West Frontier Province,* vol. III, rpt, Patiala, 1970.

Andrew Rothstein and Clemens Dutt, eds., *History of the Communist Party of the Soviet Union,* Moscow, n.d.

Samaren Roy, *M.N. Roy: A Political Biography*, New Delhi, 1997.

T.R. Sareen, *Indian Revolutionary Movement Abroad 1905-1920*, New Delhi, 1979.

Sumit Sarkar,*The Swadeshi Movement in Bengal 1903-1908*, rpt, New Delhi, 1994.

——, *Modern Indian, 1885-1947*, rpt, New Delhi, 1995.

S.P. Sen, ed., *Dictionary of National Biography*, vols. II-IV, Calcutta, 1973.

Sunil Kumar Sen, *Working Class Movements in India, 1885-1975,* Delhi, 1994.

Bhabani Sen Gupta, *CPI (M): Promises, Prospects, Problems,* New Delhi, 1995.

Sanjay Seth, *Marxist Theory and Nationalist Politics: The Case of Colonial India*, New Delhi, 1995.

S. Settar and Indira Baptista Gupta, eds., *Pangs of Partition,* vol. II, *The Human Dimension,* New Delhi, 2002.

A.I. Sobolev et al., *Outline History of the Comintern*, Moscow, 1971.

E.W. Shanahan, *South America: An Economic and Regional Geography (with an Historical Chapter),* London, 1959.

Anita Inder Singh, *The Origin of the Partition of India*, Delhi, 1987.

Fauja Singh, *Eminent Freedom Fighters of Punjab*, Patiala, 1972.

Fauja Singh, ed., *Who's Who: Punjab Freedom Fighters*, vol. I, Patiala, 1972.

Gurharpal Singh, *Communism in Punjab: A Study of the Movement up to 1967*, New Delhi, 1994.

Harbans Singh, ed., *The Encyclopaedia of Sikhism,* vol. I, Punjabi University, Patiala, 1995.

Kirpal Singh, *The Partition of the Punjab,* Patiala, 1971.

Master Hari Singh, *Punjab Peasant in Freedom Struggle*, vol. II, New Delhi, 1984.

Mohinder Singh, *The Akali Movement,* New Delhi, 1997.

Pardaman Singh and Joginder Singh Dhanki, eds., *Buried Alive: Autobiography, Speeches and Writings of an Indian Revolutionary, Sardar Ajit Singh*, New Delhi, 1984.

Ujjwal Kumar Singh, *Political Prisoners in India,* Delhi, 1998.

Ian Talbot, *Punjab and the Raj: 1849-1947,* New Delhi, 1998.

Bhagat Ram Talwar, *The Talwars of Pathan Land and Subhas Chandra's Great Escape,* New Delhi, 1976.

Tai Yong Tan and Gyanesh Kudaisya, *The Aftermath of Partition in South Asia,* London, 2000.

Raghuvendra Tanwar, *Politics of Sharing Power: The Unionist Party, 1923-1947,* New Delhi, 1999.

B.R. Tomlinson, *The Indian National Congress and the Raj, 1929-42,* London, 1976.

Achin Vanaik, *The Painful Transition: Bourgeois Democracy in India,* London, 1990.

Ramesh Walia, *Praja Mandal Movement in East Punjab States,* Patiala, 1972.

J.N. Westwood, *Endurance and Endeavour: Russian History, 1812-1971,* Oxford, 1973.

B. ARTICLES

Javeed Alam, 'Communist Politics in Search of Hegemony', in *Wages of Freedom: Fifty Years of the Nation State,* ed. Partha Chatterjee, New Delhi, 1998.

Nirban Basu, 'National Upsurge and the Working Class Movement in the TISCO, Jamshedpur', *Proceedings of the Indian History Congress,* 51st Session, Calcutta, 1990.

Bipan Chandra, 'The Long Term Dynamics of the Indian National Congress', Presidential Address, *Proceedings of the Indian History Congress,* 46th Session, Amritsar, 1985.

Sucha Singh Gill and Ranjit Singh Ghuman, 'Land Reforms in Punjab and Haryana: Trends and Issues', in *Land Reforms in India,* vol. VI, *Intervention for Agrarian Capitalist Transformation in Punjab and Haryana,* ed. Sucha Singh Gill, New Delhi, 2001.

Paramjit S. Judge, 'The Naxalite Movement in Punjab', in *Social and Political Movements: Readings on Punjab,* ed. Harish K. Puri and Paramjit S. Judge, New Delhi, 1983.

Prakash Karat, 'Naxalism Today: At an Ideological Dead End', *The Marxist*, vol. III, no. 1, January-March 1985.

Aditya Mukherjee, 'The Workers and Peasants Parties 1926-30: An Aspect of Communism in India', in *The Indian Left: Critical Appraisals*, ed. Bipan Chandra, New Delhi, 1983.

Mridula Mukherjee, 'Communists and Peasants in Punjab: A Focus on the Muzara Movement in Patiala 1937-53', in *The Indian Left: Critical Appraisals,* ed. Bipan Chandra, New Delhi, 1983.

——, 'Peasant Protest in Punjab: Forms of Struggle and Mobilisation', *Proceedings of the Indian History Congress*, 59th Session, Patiala, 1998.

Partha Nath Mukherjee, 'The Farmers Movement in Punjab: Politics of Pressure Groups and Pressure of Party Politics', *Economic and Political Weekly*, 2 May 1998.

Shri Prakash, 'CPI and the Pakistan Movement', in *The Indian Left: Critical Appraisals,* ed. Bipan Chandra, New Delhi, 1983.

Mehendra Pratap, 'The Ideological Contradiction of Peasants Movement in UP (1936-7), *Proceedings of the Indian History Congress*, 54th Session, Mysore, 1993.

C. Works in Punjabi

Jagjit Singh Anand, *Chete Di Changer Chon*, New Delhi: Navyug Publishers, 1991.

Bhagat Singh Bilgha, *Ghadar Lehar Dey Anfoley Varkey: Ghadar Party te Kirti Party (1908-1952),* Jalandhar: Desh Bhagat Yadgar Committee, 1989.

Chain Singh Chain, *Kirti Party: Dooji Sansar Jang Samey,* Jalandhar: Desh Bhagat Yadgar Hall, 1990.

Bikram Singh Ghuman, *Ghadari Baba Wisakha Singh*, Amritsar: Guru Nanak Dev University, 1982.

Jaswant Singh Jas, *Baba Wisakha Singh: Jeevani*, Jalandhar: New Book Company, 1979.

Gurcharan Singh Sahnsara, *Ghadar Party Da Itihas,* vol. I, 1912-17, Jalandhar: Desh Bhagat Yadgar Committee, 1969.

——, *Oh Vi Din San,* Jalandhar: K. Lal and Company, 1973.

Piar Singh, *Teja Singh Samundri*, Punjabi Bhasha, Sahit te Sabhyachar Vibhag, Amritsar: Guru Nanak Dev University, 1975.

Index

Abdul Bari 25, 50, 59, 191, 197, 198, 199, 200, 206, 209, 210
Abdul Halim 180, 189
Abdul Majid 45
Adhikari, M. Gangadhar 26, 41, 42
Adhikari thesis 27, 40
Adivasis 198, 200, 204
Afghanistan 43
Africa 106, 189
Ahmed Din, Munshi 159, 257
Ahmed, Z.A. 46, 53
Ahmedabad 23
Ahmednagar 14
AIKS 19, 21, 51, 57, 60, 61, 182, 183, 293, 307
AISF 323, 326
AITUC 14, 23, 139, 146, 181, 234
Ajit Singh 101, 105, 122
Akalis 46, 81, 212, 318
Akali Movement 19, 44, 81
Allahabad 40
Almast, Amar Singh 212, 260, 261, 330
Amritsar 9, 11, 20, 21, 25, 27, 30, 36, 43, 44, 46, 51, 56, 58, 60, 63, 65, 68, 83, 85, 87, 88, 92, 104, 108, 122, 142, 167, 174, 183-5, 208, 211, 224, 225, 227, 234, 235, 248, 282, 285, 287, 306, 323, 332, 335
Andaman Islands 188, 207
Andhra Pradesh 27, 29, 33, 34, 60, 309
Anti Imperialist League 45, 58
Argentina 16, 38, 47, 65, 90-3, 95, 96, 99-104, 106-9, 117, 122, 125, 147, 169, 170, 177
Arifwala 51, 163, 164, 167, 183
Arora, Arjun 24, 157, 207
Ashant, Narinder Singh 12, 313, 316, 317, 319, 320, 332, 338, 339
Asia 106, 121, 189
Attock 36, 185
Australia 65
Ayodhya 8

Babbar Akalis 100, 104, 213, 232
Badal, Prakash Singh 34, 318, 334
Bahl, Vinay 11
Bajwara 212, 213
Balbir Singh, Chaudhary 334, 335
Baldev Singh 189, 207, 208, 209
Balmikis 66, 71, 80, 84
Banta Singh 172-5, 217
Bar 65, 66, 79, 80, 81
Beant Singh 173-5, 185
Bedi B.P.L. 19
Benares 17
Bengal 9, 14, 17, 27, 136, 145, 146, 206, 209, 288, 302, 309, 310
Beni Bhushan 220, 221, 222
Berlin 37, 109
betterment levy 292
Bhag Singh, Dr. 159, 213, 237, 256
Bhagtu 79, 80
Bhagat Singh, landlord 71, 72, 76, 77

Bhagat Singh, Shaheed 15, 36, 39, 44, 101, 209, 214, 215, 234, 257, 279
Bhakna, Sohan Singh 189
Bhakra 260, 262-6, 271, 273, 280, 281, 285, 292
Bhakra Dam 9, 30, 54
Bhakra-Nangal Project 54, 292, 306
bhaoli (crop sharing) 67, 84
Bhardwaj, R.D. 24, 49, 149, 158, 206, 207
Bhargava, Gopi Chand 26, 40, 45, 185
Bhunga 47, 54, 63, 81, 134, 175, 179-81, 241, 276, 294, 295
Bihar 9, 17, 23, 25, 33, 34, 59, 198, 206-9, 214
Bilgha, Bhagat Singh 19, 34, 38-40, 106, 112, 125, 143, 145, 147, 180, 181, 219, 233
Bodal, Gurbax Singh 272, 286
Bolshevik Party 15, 106, 114, 115, 124
Bombay 14, 17, 23, 44, 46, 117, 145, 181, 211, 231, 302
Boorewala 20, 51, 160, 161, 163, 164, 167
Bose, Subhas Chandra 24, 36, 43, 50, 52, 147, 179, 180, 186, 189, 201-5, 207, 210, 211
Brazil 65, 91, 93, 99, 100, 101, 105, 106
Brussels 45, 300
Buenos Aires 91, 92, 94, 97, 98, 102, 103, 108, 118
Bujha Singh 99, 106, 112, 142, 213, 237
Bulhowal 244, 331-4
Burma 38, 65, 232

Cachar 14
Calcutta 9, 24, 29, 30, 43, 49, 52, 56, 86, 117, 121, 127, 129-31, 133, 134, 142, 144-6, 149, 180, 183, 188-90, 202-8, 211, 231, 257, 297, 302
California 16, 147, 183
Campbellpur 36, 37, 40, 42, 104, 147, 233
Canada 65, 96, 103, 106
Canadian, Bhag Singh 45
Canal Colonies 18, 20
capitalism 143, 218, 219, 299, 301
Central America 38, 65, 106
Central Provinces 126, 194, 207
Ceylon 47, 48, 56, 126
Chabbewal 254-6, 286
Chadha, Des Raj 253, 258, 285
Chain, Chain Singh 34, 38, 41-3, 143, 147
Chakravarty, Nripen 137, 139
Chandigarh 12, 321, 335
Chandrika Singh 191, 192, 196
Cheema Kalan 40, 143, 164
Chenab Canal Colony 47, 58, 63, 78, 83, 109
Chhaju Ram 237
Chhattisgarh 194
Chheharta 50, 219, 224-7, 248
Chhimba 66
Chhina, Achhar Singh 37, 40, 106, 112, 142, 147, 167, 185, 203, 219
Chhotanagpur 14, 198
Chichawatni 51, 163, 167
China 38, 103, 106, 121, 123, 125, 183, 299, 303-5, 311
Chirik 20, 22, 43
Chou En-lai 30
CID 45, 52, 117, 121, 126, 127, 131, 133-5, 137-9, 145, 174, 276
Cochin 33
Colombo 90, 120, 125, 145
colonialism 116, 117, 143
Comintern 7, 15-17, 25, 39, 48, 57, 103, 106, 110-12, 115-19, 121, 123, 124, 128, 159, 161, 208, 297, 299
communism 117, 158, 216
communists 15, 24, 110, 129, 146, 158, 181, 186, 198, 200, 201, 203, 205, 213-19, 232, 234, 236,

237, 245, 246, 257, 262, 275, 280, 285, 287, 289, 293, 299, 300-6, 336, 337
Congress 7, 14, 15, 17, 21, 23, 25-7, 30-3, 35, 36, 39, 40, 46, 51, 52, 57, 59, 146, 156, 157, 158, 179, 181-3, 186, 187, 189, 191, 197, 198, 204, 206, 208-12, 220, 231, 236, 242, 249, 256, 257, 279, 283, 286, 289, 290, 296, 300, 302, 308, 318, 320, 330, 338, 339
Congress Socialist Party 21, 24, 27, 46, 50, 57, 181, 184, 191, 206, 208, 209, 257
Control Commission 253, 284, 285
CPGB 46
CPI (pre-1964) 14, 15, 17, 25-7, 29, 31, 37, 39-42, 45, 46, 49, 50, 51, 53, 54, 57, 60, 61, 130, 139, 141, 145, 146, 149, 151, 154-6, 158, 159, 175, 178, 181, 188, 189, 197, 206, 215, 216, 219, 223, 227, 228, 231, 233-40, 242, 245, 247-9, 253, 256, 257, 259-62, 266, 271, 279, 282-4, 286, 288-90, 292, 293, 295, 296, 298, 299, 306, 307
CPI (post-1964) 10, 31, 32, 104, 302, 305, 310, 316, 318-20, 323, 326, 334
CPI (M-L) 33, 327
CPM 10-12, 31-4, 55, 61, 147, 249, 252, 283, 299, 302, 309, 310, 313-22, 326-36, 338
CPSU 121, 124, 215, 299, 305, 306, 308
Cuba 48, 56, 118, 119, 124, 125, 138
Czechoslovakia 48, 117

Dange, S.A. 46, 53, 60, 214, 217
Dasuya 212, 239, 244, 252, 273, 286, 293, 327, 331, 338
Dehra Dun 17
Delhi / New Delhi 17, 41, 92, 139, 175, 181, 211, 217, 296, 297, 334, 335
Deoli Detention Camp 10, 26, 37, 40, 42, 46, 52, 147, 214, 215, 217, 218, 231, 232, 233
Desa Singh 193, 196, 200, 209
Desh Bhagat Parivar Sahayak Committee 21, 36, 108, 142, 174, 184
Dhamija, Kartar Singh 220-2
Dhanwantri 53, 188, 214, 215, 219
Dharam Vir 128, 129, 130
Dhillon, Ranbir Singh 316-18, 320
Dhoot, Chanan Singh 65, 95, 98, 141, 176, 180, 188, 252, 256, 263, 272, 273, 282, 286, 289, 294, 296, 323, 328-30, 332, 335
Dhoot, Jwala Singh 86, 87, 90, 91, 95, 96, 99, 108, 109, 133, 134, 142
Dhoot, Karam Singh 140, 142, 147, 178, 190, 282
Dhoot, Naina Singh 7, 9, 10-12, 16, 19, 23-7, 29, 30, 35, 47-9, 51-6, 109, 185, 186, 209, 213, 232, 233, 278, 313, 314, 317-21, 323, 324, 327-39
Dhoot, Pratap Chand 12, 176, 263, 270, 272, 277, 282, 293, 295, 306, 307, 313-15, 327, 328, 335
Dhoot Kalan 11, 47, 55, 63, 76, 81, 90, 92, 109, 134, 140, 175, 178, 180, 185, 212, 219, 231, 233, 241-3, 259, 263, 275-8, 280, 282, 285, 287, 296, 298, 306, 307, 313-15, 317, 335-8, 340
Dhuleta, Karam Singh 117, 170
Dimitrov, Georgi M. 48, 116, 124, 339
Doaba 43, 64, 65, 88, 108, 266
Dutt-Bradley thesis 15
Dutt, Ram Singh 20, 159, 188, 189, 212, 213, 224, 227, 237
Dyakov, Prof. 114, 124, 297

emergency 334, 337-40

England 320, 337
Europe 96, 101, 103, 105

Faizpur 21, 51, 57
Fascism 116, 214, 216
Fattewal murder case 147, 167, 185
Fazl-ul-Haq 136, 146
Ferozepur 20, 22, 39, 43, 60, 186, 228, 235, 289, 290
First World War 77, 78, 84, 101, 124, 300
Forward Bloc 27, 50, 201, 202, 204, 205, 210, 282
France 47, 48, 56, 90, 95, 99, 119, 125, 170, 320

Gandhi / Gandhian 14, 24, 39, 44, 46, 52, 179, 180, 182, 192, 257, 279
Gandhi, Indira 32, 33, 308
Gandiwind, Santa Singh 214, 215
Garhdiwala 40, 173, 244, 254, 260, 262, 286, 287, 326, 329, 331, 338
Garhshankar 254, 271, 281, 286, 293
Gautam, Mohan Lal 214
Germany 48, 56, 108-10, 122, 125, 320
Ghate, S.V. 46, 53, 57, 60, 214, 215, 233
Gholia, Bachan Singh 107
Ghosh, Ajoy Kumar 26, 31, 50, 60, 139, 219, 224, 225, 227, 228, 234, 235, 283, 298, 307
Ghulam Husain 15
Gill, Kartar Singh 19, 159, 160
Gill, Lachhman Singh 321
Gokul Chand 36, 44
Gopalan, A.K. 293
Gujarat (colonial Punjab) 40, 42, 147, 186, 218, 219, 283
Gujarat state 9, 14
Gulshan, Hukam Chand 245, 246, 252, 273, 286
Gurdaspur 25, 39, 60, 252
Gurharpal Singh 11, 25
Ghadar Di Goonj 16, 47, 48, 89, 96, 100
Ghadarites 17, 26, 36, 38, 39, 48, 51, 105, 106, 147, 184, 189
Ghadar Party 16, 21, 25, 37, 38, 39, 45, 47, 48, 87, 89, 96, 100, 103, 104, 106-8, 122, 140, 147, 159, 183, 186
Golden Laws 23
goondas 20, 50, 73, 74, 163, 165, 166, 184, 185, 189, 193, 199, 200, 201, 204-6, 208, 241, 268, 292
Great Depression 17, 23, 99, 104, 145
Guru Granth Sahib 64, 138
Gurmukh Singh, Baba 45, 188, 235, 257

Harbans Singh 112, 160, 161
Hari Singh, Master 22, 143, 176, 212, 213, 219, 220, 231, 245, 260, 261, 296
Harmandir Sahib 63, 82
Havana 118, 119, 124, 125
Hazara Singh 49, 188, 189, 190, 191, 204, 208, 210, 211
Hazara Singh Akali 130, 136, 137, 180
Hindus 28, 234, 237, 238, 242, 243, 245, 247
Hitler, Adolph 46, 109, 110, 122, 216, 218
Hoshiarpur 11, 16, 25, 53-5, 60, 63, 82, 83, 85, 104, 109, 122, 128, 131, 143, 180, 186, 188, 212, 213, 219, 231, 239-41, 251-3, 255, 258-60, 273, 279, 280, 282, 283, 285-8, 293, 295, 296, 313, 317-23, 326, 327, 329, 330, 333, 334
Homi, Manick 24, 50, 191, 198, 200, 206, 209, 210
Howrah 49, 130, 133, 134
Hundal, Iqbal Singh 40

Inder Singh 128, 129
India 13, 30, 49, 92, 96, 104, 106, 109, 117, 118, 120, 123, 126, 133, 140, 147, 183, 216, 237, 238, 298, 320
Indian Steel & Wire Products Co. 24, 25, 49, 52, 191, 192, 198, 205
Institute of Agrarian Reforms, Ludhiana 21, 22, 184
Islam, M. Mufakharul 11, 18

Jabalpur 52, 179, 180
jagirdars 267, 268, 270-2
Jalandhar 12, 25, 34, 40, 41, 43, 60, 61, 82, 83, 85, 87, 90, 92, 96, 98, 103-5, 109, 117, 122, 133, 135, 142, 147, 148, 160, 164, 172, 212, 232, 237, 251, 253, 256, 258, 260, 285, 310, 319, 322, 323, 324, 329
Jallianwala Bagh 17
Jalwant Singh, Baba 160-3, 183
Jamshedpur 9, 17, 23-5, 37, 49, 50, 52, 56, 147, 185, 188, 189, 190, 191, 193, 195, 197, 200-9, 211, 225, 231, 297
Jamshedpur Labour Federation 24
Jang-i-Azadi 26, 46
Jangpur 228
Japan 123, 320
Jaswant Rai 226, 227, 235
Jauhal, Dalip Singh 46
Jhawan 56
Josh, Bhagwan 11, 19, 22, 41
Josh, Sohan Singh 16, 34, 35, 37, 40, 42, 44, 45, 185, 214, 219, 233, 256, 287
Joshi, N.M. 217, 233
Joshi, P.C. 29, 46, 159, 279
Jwala Singh 90-3, 95, 98
Jwala Singh, Baba 19, 39, 51, 160, 183

Kabul 15, 17, 26, 36, 37, 43, 147
Kairon, Jaswant Singh 213
Kairon, Pratap Singh 54, 213, 292, 293, 307
Kaloti, Kewal 12, 313, 331, 332, 334, 338, 339
Kalsia 20, 22, 39, 43
Kandeghat, Gulzara Singh 216, 217
Kandhala Jattan 63
Kangra 39, 43, 235
Kanpur 9, 14, 15, 17, 23, 24, 49, 51, 56, 145, 149-55, 158, 159, 181, 182, 206, 207, 234
Kapur, Santosh Chand 24, 49, 149, 157, 207
Kapurthala 34, 47, 52, 65, 82, 83, 88, 104, 109, 122, 175, 176, 178, 181, 186, 241, 252, 282, 283, 323, 325, 340
Karnana, Harbans Singh 38, 42
Karachi 17, 279
Kerala 27, 288, 302, 303, 306, 309, 310
Kesar Singh, Baba 19, 159, 189, 213
Khan, Sikandar Hayat 17, 22, 208, 212, 231
Khiala Bulanda 55, 313-15
Khrushchev, Nikita 30, 299, 308
Kirti, the 16, 17, 39, 41, 44, 45, 58, 183
Kirtis 17, 25, 26, 31, 35-7, 40, 42, 43, 45, 46, 58, 188, 207, 215, 232, 233, 235
Kirti Kisan Party / KKP 16, 17, 25, 26, 35, 36, 38-46, 53, 58, 59, 122, 147, 148, 159, 188, 215, 237
Kirti Lehar 12, 17, 20, 21, 39, 43, 50, 184, 192
Kishori Lal, Pandit 227, 253, 263, 272, 279, 336
Kot Saundha 37, 42
Kriplani, Acharya J.B. 155, 182
Kulbir Singh 159, 214, 215, 257
Kultar Singh 159, 214, 215, 257

Lahiri, Somnath 128, 146, 189
Lahore 15, 19, 25, 36, 38, 39, 43,

46, 50, 58, 85, 104, 105, 122, 168, 173, 174, 181, 184, 185, 211, 219, 220, 224, 227, 231, 235, 241, 248
Lahore Fort 52, 147, 168, 169, 170, 171, 173-5, 185, 217
Lajpat Rai, Lala 39, 105
Lakhimpur Kheri 258, 280
Lal Communist Party 26, 29, 31, 40, 53, 104, 147, 148, 238, 282
Lal Jhanda 36, 41, 42
lambardars 19, 86, 101, 178, 179
Lenin, V.I. 213, 255, 300, 301
Leningrad 110, 111, 123
Littar, Pritam Singh 246, 263, 269, 270, 272, 273, 286, 333
London 41
Lucknow 17, 51, 150, 153-5, 158
Ludhiana 21, 22, 60, 178, 183, 219, 224, 228, 231, 237, 290, 293, 306, 323, 326
Lyallpur 16, 20, 44, 58, 65, 66, 83, 85, 184, 219, 224, 227, 244
Lyallpuri, Jagjit Singh 227, 303

Maan, Karam Singh 40, 45, 224, 225, 227
Madhya Pradesh 34
Madras 23, 117, 126, 288
Mahawa, Mohan Singh 253, 285
Mahilpur 40, 213, 232, 254, 260, 286
Majha 71, 140
Majumdar, Charu 33, 34
Malabar 14
Malaysia 38
Malhotra, Avtar Singh 259, 285
Mallewal 260-2
Mallewal, Beant Singh 12, 261, 262, 273, 280, 286, 294, 295, 307, 313
Malwa 88
Mangal Singh 24
Mangoo Ram 219, 220, 234
Mansur, Feroze Din 36, 40, 214
Marx, Karl 114, 123, 254, 301
Marxism 10, 16, 39, 41, 43, 45, 48, 49, 53, 100, 103, 104, 116, 122, 130, 132, 138, 144, 145, 161, 181, 188, 197, 213, 216, 234, 237, 254, 255, 278, 285, 297, 299, 300, 302, 303, 305, 324
Marxism-Leninism 10, 39, 48, 56, 117, 147, 176, 207, 212, 214, 252, 257, 282, 301, 308, 316, 332
Mazdoor Sabha 23, 24, 181
Meerut 15, 17, 21, 25, 43, 45, 140
Meerut Conspiracy Case 45, 145
Mehatpur, Bachan Singh 12, 46, 213
Mehna 54, 289
Mexico 90
Miyani 243, 244, 247, 251, 333, 339
Modi, Narendra 9
Moga 228, 290
Montgomery 20, 38, 42, 44, 58, 65, 159, 184-6, 213, 219, 223, 283
Moonak, Gian Singh 12, 244, 262, 263, 269, 270, 272, 278, 282
Moscow 10, 15, 16, 17, 20, 21, 25, 26, 38, 39, 43, 45, 48, 51, 103, 104, 106-8, 111, 116, 117, 122, 123, 125, 140, 142, 144, 145, 147, 161, 177, 184, 190, 207, 211, 213, 216, 296, 297, 310
Mota Singh, Master 213
Mubarak Sagar 159, 190, 216, 257
muhajirs 15
Mukerian 219, 239, 241, 248, 254, 272, 286, 327
Mukherjee, Mridula 11
Mukherjee, Sunil 53, 206, 214, 215
Multan 44, 58, 65, 159, 184, 185, 219
Muslims 9, 27, 225, 234, 237, 238, 240, 242-5, 248, 252, 277
Muslim League 23, 27, 146, 242, 249
muzara movement 41, 53, 160, 163, 167, 168, 176, 266
muzaras 19, 20, 47, 54, 67, 68, 69, 71, 76, 77, 150, 151, 160-8, 183,

184, 224, 237, 248, 266-8, 270-2, 282, 286
Muzaffar Ahmad 49, 50, 128, 130-2, 136, 139, 145, 146, 180, 189, 190, 206

NALCO 8
Nangal 264
Nagpur 23, 126, 127, 134, 144, 145
Narayan, Jayaprakash 46, 50, 191, 192, 194, 205, 206, 208, 209, 214, 215, 233, 257
National Front 17, 42
National Trade Union Federation 23
Naujawan Bharat Sabha 15, 40, 44, 45, 57, 58, 61
Naxalites 33, 34, 55, 283, 299, 300, 309, 326-9
Nazis 110, 122, 216
Nehru, Jawaharlal 25, 29, 30, 45, 60, 103, 157, 178, 182, 187, 189, 208, 209, 283
Nili Bar 9, 18, 19, 20, 39, 43, 51, 52, 85, 159, 160, 167, 175, 183, 224, 235, 248
New Zealand 106
North Korea 304, 311

October Revolution 14, 15, 113, 123, 301
Okara 27, 50, 51, 159, 219, 220, 223, 227, 228, 248
Orissa 33

Pakistan 27, 236, 237, 238, 242-4, 248, 249, 251, 258
Pakistan Communist Party 26, 237
Panchayat Samiti 54, 294
Pant, Gobind Ballabh 23, 24, 51, 156, 158, 182, 183
Paris 117, 118, 120, 125
Pathankot 63, 282, 323, 324, 329
Patiala 11, 53, 219, 235, 248, 256, 323
Peoples Democratic Revolution 29
Peoples War 26, 40, 214, 218, 234
PEPSU 41
Peshawar 15, 147
Phagwara 324, 332
Philippines 38, 65, 118
Plague 78, 79, 80, 85
Poona 14
Prasad, Rajendra 23, 25, 182, 209
Provincial Trade Union Congress 50, 223
Punjab 9, 11, 15, 17-19, 21-3, 25, 27, 28, 31, 34, 35, 37-41, 43-7, 50, 51, 53, 54, 58, 61, 78, 81-5, 92, 95, 103, 104, 128, 133-6, 139, 140, 147-49, 159, 175, 181, 185, 186, 191, 198, 199, 207, 208, 210, 212-14, 218, 219, 224, 228, 231, 234, 235, 240, 248, 253, 256-8, 260, 273, 279, 292, 293, 298, 303, 306, 307, 309, 316, 319-22, 325, 326, 329, 331, 332, 334
Punjabis 16, 84, 87, 92, 98-100, 107, 111, 130, 135, 136, 138, 139, 146, 193, 194, 215, 258
Punjab Kisan Committee 19-23, 25, 27, 39, 43, 51, 59-61, 104, 183, 184, 231
Punjab Kisan Sabha 55, 147, 159, 160, 164, 167, 176
Punjab Riyasti Praja Mandal 25, 39, 147, 178, 184, 186, 231, 282
Punjab Students Union 34, 323, 326, 329
Punjabi Language 35, 67, 124, 176, 215, 233, 297
Punjabi Suba 31
Putlighar 50, 219, 224-7, 248

Qurban, Fazl Ilahi 40

Radha Singh 90, 141, 172, 173
Rajanpura 213
Ralla 92-7
Ramdaspur, Harbhajan Singh 12, 262, 263, 269, 273, 280-2, 286,

294, 295, 307, 313, 330
Ram Krishan, B.A. National 37, 46, 203
Ram Krishan, Pandit 256, 262, 269, 278, 286
Rana, Tarlochan Singh 316, 318, 320
Ranadive, B.T. 29, 46, 53, 214, 217, 279, 280
Ranchi 14
Rarha 79, 86, 141, 142, 173, 242, 245, 327
Rasifa 94
Rattan Singh 16, 37, 39, 47, 57, 96, 103, 106, 109, 111, 122
Reddy, Nagi 34
Red Trade Union Congress 23
Rome 105
Rosario 48, 95, 98, 103, 107, 122
Roy, M.N. 14, 15, 27, 39, 57, 106, 121, 208
RSS 8
Rur Singh, Baba 19
Rusiyana 71, 75
Rusli 71, 76

Sadhu Singh 66, 71-4, 76, 78
Sahnsara, Gurcharan Singh 34, 35, 37, 38, 42, 43, 46
Saklatvala, Shapurji 45
Samundri 66, 71, 75, 76, 83
Samundri, Teja Singh 66, 67, 71, 75, 77, 83
San Francisco 102, 103, 140
Sangha, Mohinder Singh 12, 313, 324, 336, 337
Sangrur 34, 104
Sankrityayana, Rahul 53, 214
Santokh Singh 16, 188
sardars 20, 66-9, 71, 72, 74-7, 79-81, 163, 165, 166, 241
Sargodha 65
Satyapal 25, 40, 46
Second World War 22, 61, 147, 148, 216, 234, 249, 283
Sen, Abani 193, 196, 209, 210
Sen, Dr. Ranen 130, 145, 146
SGPC 83, 104
Sham Chaurasi 54, 295
Shanghai 65
Sheikhupura 20, 42, 85
Shiromani Akali Dal 9, 31, 83
Shiv Singh 108, 111, 207
Sholapur 23, 145
Shrinh, Kartar Singh 107, 109, 116
Shukla, Yogendra 191, 195, 196, 209, 210
Sialkot 69, 248
Sikandar, Sardara Singh 116
Singapore 38, 47, 86, 90, 96, 101, 141
Sikhism 25, 63, 237, 238
Sikhs 9, 27, 146, 234, 242-5, 247
Singh Sabha Movement 66
Singh, Ujjwal Kumar 53
Siwaliks 63, 65, 82, 244, 252, 266
socialists 15, 40, 158, 191, 192, 194-6, 205, 257
Sodhi, Harminder Singh 17, 38, 43, 190, 210
South America 16, 38, 47, 56, 94, 102, 104, 105
South Asia 7, 35
South-East Asia 56
Soviet Union 30, 36, 37, 43, 45, 46, 56, 100, 108, 110, 111, 117, 121, 128, 130, 132, 138, 140, 170, 177, 218, 301, 304, 305, 311
Sri Ram 198, 204
Stalin, J.V. 121
States People Conference 39, 231
Students Federation of India 55, 322, 323, 325, 326, 337
Sukhan, Tika Ram 159, 216
Sundar Singh 51
Surjeet, Harkishan Singh 31, 61, 218, 219, 259, 263, 268, 282, 285, 303, 304, 335-7
Swarajists 24
Swatantra, Teja Singh 26, 31, 37, 40, 42, 47, 99-101, 104, 106, 111, 112, 122, 125, 211, 219, 228,

233, 235, 236, 256, 287
Switzerland 48, 117

Taggar, Lehmbar Singh 322, 323, 324
Talbot, Ian 22
Talib, Niranjan Singh 202, 203, 211
Talumba 51, 163, 164, 184
Talwar, Bhagat Ram 37, 43, 147, 211
Talwara 272, 320
Tanda 65, 143, 212, 243, 245, 251, 254, 258, 260, 275, 286, 323, 324, 327
Tanwar, Raghuvendra 22
Tashkent 15
Tata Foundry 24
Tatas 189
Tata Workers Union 25
Tarkhanvad, Bachan Singh 143, 144, 177
Telengana 29, 30, 268, 283
The Tribune 20
Tinplate Company 24
TISCO 24, 25, 59, 196, 200, 207, 209, 210
Tripathi, Bishambar Dyal 150-5 157, 158
Tukuman 107

Ujagar 289, 290, 291, 292
Ujagar Singh (Calcutta) 131, 136
Ujagar Singh (Manakrai) 133, 134
Ujagar Singh (Singapore) 87-9
Ujjal Singh, Sardar 164, 165, 167
Una 9, 27, 53, 188, 213, 219, 227, 235, 248, 256, 260, 262, 263, 266, 267, 269-71, 273, 281, 282
Unionist government 20
Unionist Party 22, 231
United Front 15
United Provinces 17, 156, 163, 181, 182, 198, 288
University for the Toilers of the East 10, 16, 39, 48, 104, 106, 111, 147
Unnao 51, 150, 158
Urdu 67, 111
USA 16, 47, 65, 87, 90, 96, 101, 105, 106, 118, 121, 125, 186, 208, 210, 218
Uttar Pradesh 9, 33

Veharhi 51, 163, 167, 176
Vijaywada 30

Waryam Singh, Thakur 213, 256, 262, 286
Well of Parrots 56
women activists 43
World Bank 8
World Trade Organisation 8
WPP 14, 15, 17, 44, 57
wrestling 69, 70

Yusuf, S.S. 24, 49, 149, 157, 181, 207

Zahura 239, 246, 247, 339
Zaheer, Sajjad 19
Zail Singh 321
zaildars 19, 178, 179
zamindari 151
Zhdanov 29